AUTOGRAPHS

AUTOGRAPHS

COLLYHURST & MOSTON BOXING CLUB

100 YEARS

BY JOHN LUDDEN

EMPIRE
PUBLICATIONS

First published in 2018

EMPIRE PUBLICATIONS
1 Newton Street, Manchester M1 1HW
© John Ludden 2018

ISBN: 978-1-909360-51-8

Photography credits
Front Cover: Mike Cleary
Plate section: Mike Cleary, Rachel Jackson, Karin Albisson

ACKNOWLEDGEMENTS

During the writing of this book I have received nothing but goodwill towards me and I hope this is rewarded in the following pages; whether it be an interview, a phone call or simply an act of kindness offering to help. It would be unfair to pick one person, so it is a general thank you to all involved. The generosity of spirit is alive and well at Collyhurst and Moston boxing club. A class act.

Cheers, John

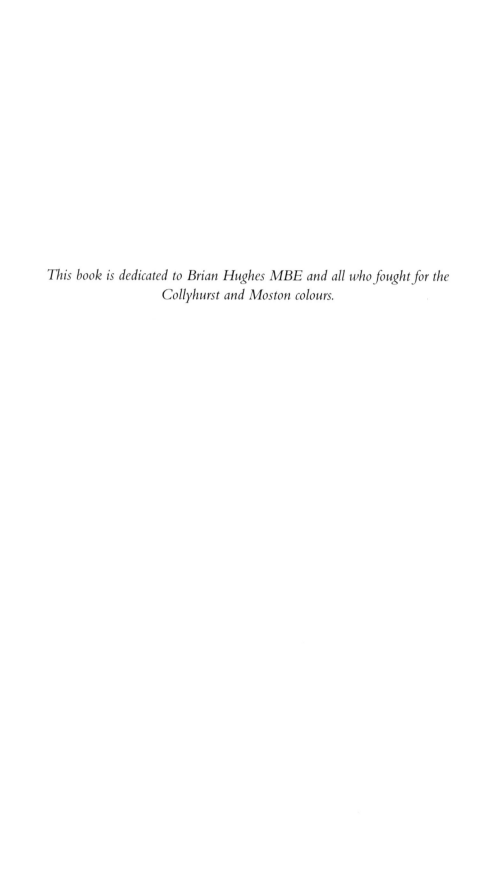

This book is dedicated to Brian Hughes MBE and all who fought for the Collyhurst and Moston colours.

'Up these steps walk future champions.'
BRIAN HUGHES MBE

CONTENTS

FOREWORD

COLLYHURST & MOSTON LADS CLUB epitomises everything that is fabulous about boxing. It is fitting that part of their 100 year anniversary celebrations include John Ludden's wonderful book. It is an honour that I have been asked to write some words about a gym that I will always hold in the highest esteem.

Of course I was familiar with some of the great boxers that had boxed out of Manchester's iconic boxing gym like the legendary Jackie Brown, Jock McAvoy and Johnny King, and later fine fighters such as Kenny Webber, Ensley Bingham and Lance Lewis. But it was not until the early 1990s that I became actively involved in promoting the excellent boxers trained by Brian Hughes. Brian himself is not just a catalyst for all the success drenched years at Collyhurst & Moston Lads Club, but Manchester boxing in general. When I first began working with Brian it was about turning young prospects into champions, and making sure they would retire heads held high. Back in those early days I genuinely believed that Pat Barrett would quickly become a world champion, but it was not to be.

The first major show I staged with the lads from the gym was the night Pat challenged Manning Galloway for the WBO welterweight title in July 1992 at the G-Mex. It was set for Pat to win and become one of the division's superstars, but he failed to perform on the night and went down to a bitterly disappointing points defeat. He will always be known as one of the best British boxer to never win a world title. After the 1992 Barcelona Olympics, I signed bronze medalist Robin Reid believing he would become a world champion. It was a no-brainer to ask Brian to become his trainer. If Pat was expected to win his fight against Galloway, few gave Robin a chance when he travelled to Milan in October 1996 to challenge WBC super-middleweight champion,

Vincenzo Nardiello. Robin was flawless, breaking the Italian's heart and winning in seven rounds. He followed Brian's master plan to the letter. There were so many other excellent fighters based at Collyhurst that I promoted besides Pat and Robin. Top quality operators like David Barnes, Anthony Farnell, Michael Gomez, Michael Jennings, Gary Lockett and of course Thomas McDonagh, who now oversees the gym with Pat, spring to mind instantly.

Even now in 2018, I still enjoy a fantastic working relationship with Pat and Thomas - the men Brian has trusted with the club's future. I am fortunate enough to be promoting Pat's nephew, Zelfa Barrett who I and other good judges consider to be one of the finest prospects in world boxing.

FRANK WARREN

COLLYHURST ROAD

When I was young and lazy, as lazy as can be,
I said farewell to the mother-in-law and off I went to sea.
We sailed with Captain Skipper aboard the Mary Anne
And we all set sail down Collyhurst Road in a Black Maria van.

CHORUS

Oh, Collyhurst Road, I am forsaken,
And it's not that my poor heart is aching.
It's the whisky and the rum that I've been taking
For that charming little girl down Collyhurst Road.

Oh, we got as far as The Vine and the rain turned into snow.
The snow got in the engine and the engine wouldn't go,
So we wrapped ourselves in mainsails and stayed there for a year,
And all we had to bloody-well drink was a barrel of Boddie's beer.

REPEAT CHORUS

Well, the law chased after me and they put me in Number Three.
They said you are a Collyhurst boy and you'll never get away from me.
They said the next time you go sailing, it won't be the Mary Anne;
Be down Collyhurst Road to Collyhurst Nick in a Black Maria van.

REPEAT CHORUS

Oh, they're digging up my granddad's grave to build a sewer (a sewer)
They're digging up his remains
To put down Carsie drains
To satisfy the local residents.
Now all his life my granddad was no quitter,
And I don't suppose he'll be a quitter now.
He's dressed up in white sheets

To warm them toilet seats
And won't there be an awful bloody row!
There is going to be a load of constipation
There is goin' to be an awful bloody fight;
And it serves them Baskets right if they never have a shite
For digging up the British workman's grave.

REPEAT CHORUS PLUS LAST LINE TWICE

INTRODUCTION
IN THE BEGINNING

1917: AS THE WORLD BURNED in the war to end all wars, the Cottingley Fairies were photographed in Yorkshire, England, while, in the Middle East, Arabian troops led by T. E. Lawrence, captured Aqaba from the Ottoman Empire. King George V, of the United Kingdom, issued a proclamation, stating that the male line descendants of the British Royal Family would from now on bear the surname Windsor, dumping their 800-year Germanic bloodline for quite obvious reasons. God forbid there would be another war to end wars.

One of English literature's most important meetings took place when Wilfred Owen introduced himself to Siegfried Sassoon at the Craiglockhart War Hospital, in Edinburgh. In Fátima, Portugal, the 'Miracle of the Sun' occurred, when Our Lady made a guest appearance. In Russia, the October Revolution began and Al Capone, 'Scarface,' inadvertently got his nickname insulting a woman while working the door at a Brooklyn night club, ending with his face being slashed three times.

Meanwhile, back in Manchester, at a murky, smog-ridden part of the city called Collyhurst, the doors were opening to a place that for a hundred years would lend hopes to the dreams of young men aspiring to be champions of the ring. They would fight for their families to put food on the table. Later for honour, belts and glory. This is the story of those who helped, worked, fought and bled for the colours of Collyhurst and Moston gym.

1 - ONCE UPON A TIME IN COLLYHURST

COLLYHURST SITS UNDER MURKY SKIES; a slimy, grimy landscape of industrial chimneys that forever billow smoke into the sky blocking out any rare appearance of a Mancunian sun in this cotton city. A labyrinth of misty alleyways, small courts and endless cobbled streets veering off in every direction, surrounded by squalid, overcrowded and poverty-stricken houses, with spit and sawdust pubs on every corner. Through the area runs the ink-black River Irk, dancing alongside the many warehouses and chemical factories releasing their poison from pipes. Rainbow colours injected into the Irk's dark depths.

"Homes fit for heroes" ran the propaganda at the 1918 General Election. Though, as ever, the politicians who promised better days delivered only dreadful hardships, service medals and few jobs. To a broken *Auld Langsyne*, the Manchester boys came home from the blood-stained trenches of France, Belgium and the sweltering slaughterhouse of Gallipoli.

Returning soldiers were destroyed, if not in body then almost certainly in mind, many still suffering from the then unknown post-traumatic stress disorder (PTSD). Then, shellshock was viewed as cowardice and for many unfortunates resulted in being blindfolded and placed in front of a firing squad. There were seven from the Manchester Regiment alone.

Pte William G. Hunt: (20), Pte Albert Ingham: (24), Pte Alfred Longshaw: (21), Pte Ellis Holt: (22), Pte William Wycherley: (24), Pte Thomas Foulkes: (21) and Pte Thomas Brigham: (22).

Those who survived and came home found that the only way to ease the pain was to drink away fearful memories. They would cry themselves to sleep at night, only to wake up screaming and lash out at loved ones. There was little work in Collyhurst. The world was in the midst of a depression. On every street corner, gangs of young lads with no money would gather to amuse themselves and often cause mischief and boredom inevitably turned to crime. The Victorian Scuttler gangs had long gone; age, prison and war had devoured their numbers, but idle hands remained. Glancing across Rochdale Road residents could see the forbidding presence of Strangeways Prison looming large over Cheetham Hill. It's huge tower a constant reminder of the long arm of the King's constabulary who wouldn't think twice about handing out vicious beatings to mouthy scrotes.

Also, festering, like an eternal running sore, there remained the Sectarian divide that pitted Catholic against Protestant, one that often determined your job prospects. A place was needed for young men to ease their frustration and let fly a few punches. There were already three well established boxing clubs in Manchester. The all-conquering Marchant brothers across the river in Salford, Sammy Hunter's near Heaton Park and Teddy McGuiness's next to Shudehill market, in central Manchester.

One man thought it was time Collyhurst entered into the fray: a handsome, dapper, pipe smoker with slicked black hair, a classy suit and spit-shine shoes, thirty-two year-old Harry Fleming was already running an amateur boxing club. It belonged to Corpus Christi church in Varley Street, off Oldham Road and in this role Fleming was helped enthusiastically by one of the curates, the affable Father McGhie. A man of the cloth, who when he wasn't hearing confessions from his congregation of their previous night's drunken shenanigans in the pubs and back alley of his diocese, liked nothing better than to take up the gloves himself and take a swing at the bag.

It is well known that hard times produce great fighters. Well, something special was brewing amid the murky fog. Harry Fleming quickly recruited former boxer and self-taught trainer Jack Bates to work alongside him. Bates was born and bred in Collyhurst. Together they had a dream. Both possessed a serious eye for talent. Manchester was a hotbed of boxing. Tough young lads stood idle on street corners just desperate for an opportunity to put on the gloves and blast away. Fleming had a handful of decent fighters in his amateur club. He knew that a few of them stood a wonderful chance of holding their own in the brutal professional game. They were all boys born and bred in

Collyhurst. There were the Keogh brothers, 'Boy' Tomlinson, Tommy Armstrong, Jack Curran and the cocky, colourful prodigy Jackie Brown.

Born in a notorious Mancunian slum christened 'Little Ireland' seventeen-year-old Flyweight Jackie, along with Jock McAvoy and another local lad Johnny King, would, in time, be the finest trio of boxing talent in Great Britain.

But for now, these boys needed a home to take their prodigious talents further and one was found just a stone's throw from the legendary Dickie Banks cinema on Paley Street, that in appearance bore more of a likeness to a Wild West saloon. Here was home to the adventures of cowboy Tom Mix, he of the legendary white Stetson fighting the bad guys, who always wore black hats. There was many a Saturday night that ended up like the action on the screen with a bar room brawl and chairs and tables flying through the air. For the princely sum of 5 shillings a week Harry rented a clubroom above a nearby coal yard at the disbanded home of St Malachy's football team and turned it into a gym.

From small acorns...

In this broken-down, decrepit building in Collyhurst's heart, champions would, in time, emerge. Up the creaky, wooden steps, past leaking pipes and soot-covered brick the hopefuls would tread. The equipment in the gym was primitive when compared to their present-day counterparts. Eight-ounce gloves stuffed tightly with horsehair and sticky with sweat, heavy punch bags hung from the damp ceilings filled with wet sand and cement, fighters would hammer these bags, their fists clanging like a ruler being sprung on the edge of a desk. The showers were simplicity themselves - the fighters would stand naked in a damp corner while Jack Bates threw buckets of ice cold water over them. For sparring, a portion of the room was roped off. In this small corner, with Bates constantly pushing, preaching and teaching them, future British and world champions perfected their craft.

The gym accommodation was just as basic; bare-brick whitewashed walls, springy, damp-ridden floorboards with wide gaps that seeped in the fumes from the coal beneath in the yard. As for furniture, a rubbing board and a pair of rickety chairs held together by string and good fortune; a cold water tap against the wall that dripped constantly and an iron fire grate. These hardly seemed like surroundings fit for future kings, but they were paradise to boys who sweated blood daily for the chance to achieve their dream.

The founding members were a formidable sight, hard men, but a fun-loving bunch that were willing to take on anybody, anywhere at a moment's notice. To help achieve this Fleming persuaded promoters, whenever possible, to book at least three or four of his fighters on the same bill. This gave them a sense of *esprit de corps*. They would travel together to venues near and far to defend the colours and cheer on their mates. Fleming would hire a car from a local firm at a discount rate with the promise of future tickets and the boxers would dive in armed only with their kitbags, flasks of tea, sandwiches and biscuits.

On the return journey Fleming would make a habit of getting the lads fish and chips and, as they ate, they would discuss what had gone on that night. Who had impressed? What had they learned? This remains in the genes of Collyhurst and Moston and was continued by Fleming's modern-day successor, Brian Hughes. The boxers trusted inherently in Fleming's match-making skills. A fair scrap against an opponent was all that could be hoped for and their manager never let them down. Fighters could ask for no more. He developed their camaraderie, they were all in it together and had to be there for each other both in and out of the ring, though few dared take on this handy crowd beyond the ropes!

Fleming quoted Alexandre Dumas's epic from *The Three Musketeers*, "All for one, one for all!" Again, this was something Brian would later adopt.

Make no mistake something was stirring down Rochdale Road. A magic in the Mancunian spit and sawdust − from such humble beginnings the club would go on to last a century and beyond.

2 - BRIAN HUGHES

'ALL FOR ONE'

And now, roll back the curtain, ring the bell and enter stage left the man who would go on to be the heart and soul of Collyhurst and Moston Boxing club for close on fifty years.

BRIAN HUGHES WAS BORN at the height of the Second World War in January 1940, in Sand Street, Collyhurst. His birth followed the immediate aftermath of a German made firestorm that ignited the 'Rainy City.' He entered this world just a month after the fearful Christmas Blitz had descended upon Manchester; that terrifying period for Mancunians, when it wasn't snow falling from festive black skies, but the Luftwaffe's deadly cargoes of incendiaries. Illuminated by air raid beams and sound-tracked by that deadly drone, Hitler's bombers took a daily toll. Wave after wave set the city ablaze - from Trafford Park to Piccadilly to the surrounding areas, flames lit up the night, engulfing buildings and in particular a railway yard off Rochdale Road, where Collyhurst met the city. A huge shipment of sugar burnt out of control and caused a sweet, sickly odour that hung around the area for days mixed with the smell of charred wood from wrecked buildings.

Brian was the second of six boys for his mother, Eileen. Brothers, Colin, John, Wilf and Stephen (sadly Wilf's twin, Paul, died in infancy). His early life in Collyhurst is one rich in memories, as happy as it was poor and no more or less than any other poverty-stricken kid could expect in that era. It was a hand-to-mouth existence but even in such dire times Brian always recalled a stranger would recognise that their two-up-two-down dilapidated terraced house was kept spotless.

A pauper's palace.

His mother's constant white-washing (donkey-stoning) of the doorstep was a clear sign that self-respect for an immaculately clean home cost nothing but hard graft and elbow grease. Inside, beneath their feet, the Hughes' had no carpets, just cheap oilcloth and bare floorboards. The walls were not papered, simply distempered. As for the almost unknown luxury of hot water… they would boil a big black iron kettle and fill a bath tub in front of the fire. There was no electricity, with lighting provided only by a little gas-mantle, positioned like an arm coming out of the wall. The toilet was situated in the backyard and come winter time it was extremely uncomfortable with the wind whistling underneath the door! Toilet rolls, an agony beyond screams, was nothing more than old newspapers cut up and hung on a nail. These might seem like almost criminal conditions to allow people to live in nowadays but they were about average for Collyhurst in the 1940s. This was supposedly Great Britain, again jokingly labelled by its uncaring Government 'A land fit for returning heroes.'

However, for Brian, what he remembers most about his younger days was the unique camaraderie and community spirit in Collyhurst. They may have been poor in monetary terms but lottery rich in kindness. There was no such thing as television and very few families could even afford the luxury of a wireless set, so a trip to the cinema was the main source of entertainment for all the family. The early American westerns were a huge favourite among the Collyhurst kids on a Saturday morning, who loved a good cowboys and Indians shootout! For youngsters, there were also the many boys' clubs in the area where they could gather and let off steam.

Abbot Street was a particularly popular venue and Brian would go there after school three or four times a week. You could box, paint or play football in an inside yard. Collyhurst Lads' Club was another good place where young urchins ran happily amok under a watchful eye. Nearby Ancoats and Ardwick had similar clubs, but then again, if you fancied, there was always the option of simply kicking a ball around from morning till night on derelict crofts or wasteland that had been pulverised by German bombs. The labyrinth of rubble and remnants of buildings were a kid's dream playground.

Brian went to Saint Patrick's school on Livesey Street, a legendary north Manchester breeding ground for footballers, boxers, priests and gangsters. Never academically inclined because of an undiagnosed Dyslexic condition and being something of a loner, he joined the Merchant Navy at just fifteen. Two years later Brian returned and worked in nondescript jobs, but it was a love of pugilism where his true calling lay. Brian became fascinated with boxing after watching a grainy black and white newsreel about the great American World Featherweight champion. Guglielmo Papaleo, more commonly known as Willie Pep.

Around Collyhurst, in every pub and café, there were always dozens of former boxers, only too happy over a pint of bitter or a steaming mug of hot tea to regale you with wild and wonderful tales of their career. Brian loved nothing more than to sit and listen. All were natural story-tellers, a talent he would come to inherit himself in later years. Brian would often wander down to the legendary 'Harry the Barber's' (Harry Toft) on Rochdale Road, a favourite haunt for Manchester United players at the time. Next door, in a makeshift gym, the world class trainer Jack Bates, who had trained Jackie Brown, Jock McAvoy and Johnny King, put his lads through their paces and watching through purposely steamed and scratched windows, was eleven-year old Brian Hughes. It was a wonderful moment for Brian when he was finally ushered through and allowed into the inner sanctum.

So began a lifetime love affair.

Fancying having a go himself inside the ropes, Collyhurst neighbour and good friend Andy Lambert took Brian to a famous amateur set up, Lily Lane Youth Club in Moston. There a trainer and true gentleman, Fred Hampston, made a great impression on him. Before he starting training Brian, Mr Hampston visited his mother to ask if she had any objections to her son boxing? Reluctantly she agreed and Brian began to dream of becoming a World Champion! However, it was to be a short-lived dream. After two long years of training he still had not been awarded a fight. Brian all but begged Mr Hampston to let him have a go, but he would always say the same, 'I will let you know when you are ready Brian.'

Terribly frustrated and feeling he was never going to get a chance under Mr Hampston's over-protective management, Brian left Lily Lane and joined another gym, where they weren't so fussy and within three weeks got his first contest. One minute into the bout it was all over, a fighter called Harry Carter was the winner! He had one more try which ended equally painful before Mr Hampston took him back under his wing and they headed back to Lily Lane. There the reality dawned on Brian that maybe he wasn't cut out to be a fighter, but a life in and around the ring could still be had.

In the early sixties Jack Bates moved from his makeshift home on Rochdale Road and settled into the more established Rainbow Gym at the back of the Queen's pub. Brian went with him and this became like a second home. He would sweep up and watch all the top professionals preparing for fights. The formidable British Lightweight champion Frank Johnson and other fine boxers such as Tommy Proffitt and Stan Skinskiss were among the many who trained there. Slowly he was becoming immersed in the art of coaching and Brian would soak up advice like a wet rag. He was learning and by now the sweeping brush was only one of his many jobs around the gym. Suddenly he was knowledgeable and trusted enough to be in the boxer's corner, with Bates' right hand man, Tommy Fynan. A thought began to form that in time, if he watched, listened and learned his trade from the retired fighters who moved around the Collyhurst gyms and boxing clubs like old gurus, then one day he might coach the fighters himself.

These old pros whispered or grunted gems of advice in throw away comments that few heard and most took little notice of... but Brian Hughes did. He remembered everything and would not forget it.

The other great sporting love of Brian's life was Manchester United. Being a son of Collyhurst, this came almost as a birthright. It was a hotbed of United support and from the mid-fifties onwards something truly special was coming together just seven miles down the road at Old Trafford. High amidst the smog, fog and billowing chimney smoke that covered Trafford Park, a dash of red appeared that captured and enthralled all. Reared from the training ground crèche at The Cliff in Salford to pass, move and attack with electric speed, the Busby Babes emerged like flashing red dervishes to light up not only Manchester, but every football ground they appeared in. The names read like a footballing Hollywood A list, capturing not just a flurry of trophies, but the city's heart: Eddie Colman, Roger Byrne, David Pegg, Bobby Charlton, Duncan Edwards, Tommy Taylor... as the Manchester United calypso song blared out at the time, "a bunch of bouncing Busby Babes.

They deserve to be knighted!"

It appeared that this special team, coached, cajoled and drilled to perfection by Matt Busby and his assistant, the passionate Welshman Jimmy Murphy, had the world at their dancing feet. However in 1958, it all came to a heart-breaking, calamitous halt with the dreadful events of the Munich air crash. As Manchester cried a sea of tears, few wept more than Brian Hughes.

As the sixties dawned, Brian was still struggling along. However, one day in the Collyhurst flats, under the arches, he came across two bloodied young lads in the midst of a vicious fist fight. After jumping in and stopping it, he asked them why they didn't go to the local Collyhurst Lads' Club on nearby Willert Street next to the police station, only to be told that it had shut down. The next day, still perturbed by this encounter, he went to meet the warden, a man called Noel Sykes. A former headmaster of Saint James Protestant school in Collyhurst, Sykes was one of the area's real characters. A large, tall man with a booming voice and Jimmy Edwards-style twirling moustache, he somehow persuaded Brian to re-open the club himself. Now approaching his mid-twenties and finding himself drifting, Brian decided to give it a go. So began a journey that would last fifty years and more.

Armed with nothing more than good intentions, enthusiasm and grim determination, he set about his new task. Brian sought out advice from Jack Bates who told him to find an old kitbag and fill it with straw and old clothes to make a punch bag. This Brian did, however someone thought it might be a good idea to add wet cement to keep it solid and steady thus causing many young lads to damage their knuckles, if their fists were not wrapped properly. Come opening night close to sixty eager young rascals turned up. Waiting for them was not just Brian, but the warden Mr Sykes. This rag-tag collection of Collyhurst youth wanted nothing more than to let off steam, but were forced to listen to Sykes' welcome speech. With Brian stood alongside, arms-folded, sensing the worst, Sykes clapped his hands and began.

"Now gather round children, gather round. Come here now! I had my good times as an ex RAF boxing champion." At this Brian stared at him because he knew it wasn't true. As Sykes' speech carried on and on Brian could sense restlessness among the listening mob and attempted to cut him short but to no avail. Sykes stood next to the stuffed kit bag and in a Charlie Chaplin stance prepared to punch it. Brian knew if he did this without wrapping his hands disaster loomed!

"Er, My Sykes don't hit…" too late. Sykes punched the bag and a look of sheer pain cut across his face. As Brian went to end his embarrassment, Sykes was not for turning. Holding the badly bruised and surely broken hand, he carried on, his mood now turning for the worse.

"And you boys, make sure you all wash proper because there is a terrible smell in here."

Suddenly, a voice from the back of the house couldn't help himself, "F--k off!"

"Who said that?" raged a red-faced Sykes, "find me that boy Hughes!" But such was his agony Sykes did not hang around and instead made a hasty exit and retreated down the stairs to an office across the road. From the window Brian and a laughing crowd watched as Sykes ran through his door before falling to the floor and rolling around in agony!

"I did warn him" said Brian, slowly shaking his head before turning to the lads. "Now you lot. Let's get going! Ten press-ups!"

Swiftly the club and Brian's reputation as a decent and fair boxing and football coach grew. With no money, favours and good deeds were called for and they came by the bucketload. Lads whose dads were rag and bone men put the word out about what was needed and they would turn up at the club with the required bits and pieces. Everything from wash basins to skipping ropes. Slowly, with Brian working all the hours God sent, the club began to resemble so much more than its original shell. Encouraged by him, a wonderful atmosphere of camaraderie developed quickly. It was friendly, but also competitive. All were welcome off the street. A great spirit emerged. Brian urged the lads to look after each other, not just inside the club, but on the rough streets of Collyhurst as well. One thing he had adored about his beloved Busby Babes was their team ethic.

"All for one and one for all." It was an echo of the Harry Fleming days.

Word quickly spread and the best of the local footballers and boxers began to drift towards Willert Street. Small acorns had been planted.

Collyhurst was on the march…

At first it was success on the football pitch that caught the eye with cups and leagues being won by the hatful. The hard work being done by Brian did not go unnoticed. The head policeman at Willert Street Station called him in to offer congratulations and to say keep the good work up and that due to the club's increasing popularity, the local crime rate had dropped dramatically!

And yet, although the club swept all before them in local football circles, what was to follow would eclipse everything else.

Maybe it was his own short, torrid experience between the ropes, but although Brian wanted his fighters to show flair and be successful, above all he preached the mantra of defence-first. "Look after yourself" was one of his maxims. The art of counter-punching and side-stepping was a hallmark of Brian's approach to ring craft. For him to see one of his boxers slipping a punch was equally important as seeing them land one. He wanted his boys to be different than anyone else's, to possess a certain style where people could say about a boxer whilst watching him in the ring, "that lad is from Collyhurst." But the main thing, above all else, was that if they were beaten, he did not want them left damaged. Soon it was time to put Brian Hughes' philosophy to the test against outsiders, and in the first boxing tournament put on locally in Manchester since the days of Jack Bates, Collyhurst took to the road.

By mini-bus they travelled the short distance for a show put on by the police at Middleton Baths. Collyhurst had two fighters on the bill, George Kipe and Roger King. On reaching the baths Brian approached the doormen, only to be told they had already arrived!

"What are you talking about?" asked an amazed Brian.

It seems half of Collyhurst were already in the building claiming to be members of the club to avoid paying! It turned out to be a great evening with both Collyhurst fighters winning to set the tone for the future. It wasn't long before the boxing became even more successful than the football. Saturday night trips were organised to Birmingham where tournaments were staged in car factories. Collyhurst would arrive and their fighters, trained in Brian's elusive, safety-first manner, would clean up. Remembering the teachings of Jack Bates and other fine local trainers of old, his lads would go to work. However, it was also dangerous to underestimate the ferocious, attacking qualities of these Collyhurst fighters, for as Brain always stated, "If you can't jab, if you can't hit, then you can't fight and I'm not interested."

Under Brian's leadership the football team continued to sweep all before them and the boxing lads won championships year after year. As the sixties drew to an end and Mancunians began to dream in glorious Technicolor, the seventies arrived and the Collyhurst Boys club trophy cabinet bulged: National Schoolboy titles, National Junior ABA titles, England Schoolboy Internationals, Junior England Internationals, Senior champions and Internationals. What had begun as a dream had turned into a tidal wave of success. On a personal level Brian was the first Manchester coach to gain the ABA Coaching certificate, he had also become great friends with Jimmy Murphy. Over a pint Jimmy would offer tips and even invite Brian to watch United train at the Cliff. He never forgot one particular incident watching the Welshman admonish George Best over a tactical ploy the Irishman had failed to carry out the previous Saturday. Jimmy stayed with George for an hour on the training pitch when everyone had finished, pulling him to one side of the pitch, then to another; pointing, gesticulating, whilst all the time a sheepish George did exactly as his guru told him. Finally, a playful slap around the head, huge smiles and Best was allowed in. However for Brian it was a real eye-opener for this one incident totally dismissed the myths surrounding Best that United just sent him out to do his own thing. The lesson was learned that no matter how special the natural talent, whether a footballer or a boxer, it still required harnessing. It was also no surprise back then to enter the club and see United players such as Nobby Stiles and Brian Kidd working out. Both would also become close with Brian over the years.

Sponsorship was always extremely difficult to find. One-time Brian had one of his boxers, Keith Akanbah, picked by England Amateurs to go and fight in America. It was a tremendous honour but more importantly, and typically, Brian wanted to ensure Keith had some money for decent clothes. He came up with an idea. British Heavyweight champion Henry Cooper was coming to Manchester to speak at the Anglo-American Sporting club at the Piccadilly hotel. It was being organised by his good friend and the night's compere, Nat Basso. Brian rang Nat and asked if there was any chance he could bring Keith down to the hotel the following day and maybe get a photo of them with the championship belt? Nat agreed wholeheartedly.

So now he moved onto phase two and rang the *East Manchester*

Reporter newspaper. Brian explained what was happening. It was a good news story and could they arrange to send one of their cameraman along. The next morning all went to plan and a smiling Henry Cooper, alongside a joyful looking Keith, were photographed holding the belt. Later that same afternoon Brian received a phone call from a reporter charged with putting a story to the photograph. Thinking on his feet Brian came up with the little yarn of Henry Cooper saying that next time he and his boys were in London, they must come to his house near Wembley stadium and Henry's wife would give them all sandwiches and lemonade.

A few weeks passed and Brian was at the Royal Albert Hall with one of his fighters, Kenny Webber. The pair had first met when Kenny arrived from Jamaica in the early sixties. What struck Brian straight away about Kenny was his big beaming, warm-hearted smile, his friendliness, excellent manners and sincerity. The two became great friends and Kenny used to accompany Brian in his other job, making deliveries around the country. He was good at all sports, including football, cricket and athletics, but excelled at boxing. "He was a wonderful stylist and counter and body puncher," according to Brian. As an amateur Kenny had won several trophies and boxed six times in one day to become the Manchester Schoolboy champion. He represented England several times and was the National Association of Boys clubs champion. In 1972, Kenny turned pro and Brian took him to the great Welshman Eddie Thomas, a leading boxing manager at the time. Webber would go on to become one of the finest Welterweights in Great Britain.

However, back to the beginning! Brian was taping up Kenny's hands in the depths of the Albert Hall. A damp, stark looking dressing room lit by only one lightbulb. Suddenly the door opens and three tall men enter, all dressed in trilbies, long black overcoats and wearing dark glasses.

"Can we have a word in the hallway please, Mr Hughes?" came a fearsome Cockney voice from the darkness. Brian immediately thinks it is something to do with the Krays! Once outside, one of the men takes off his hat and removes his glasses. To his great relief it is Henry Cooper, "Henry what's going on?" says Brian, breathing a sigh of relief.

Henry takes a letter from his pocket and shows it to him. "Let me read this to you, Brian. 'Dear Mr Cooper, I read recently in my local paper that you have invited those Collyhurst lads to where you live the next time they are in London. Let me tell you now, you will regret this because they are a load of robbing bastards and will wreck your house! Not only that, they will steal your trophies and wife's jewellery!'"

Henry glared back at Brian who did not know whether to laugh or cry!

In the name of supposed progress, the late sixties, early seventies saw the Lads Club demolished along with most of Collyhurst and the club found temporary accommodation in a scout hut on Lightbowne Road. Funds, as ever, were almost non-existent, but now they were short on space too. Local man Jim Egan, who worked in the timber game back then, remembers sorting the club out with a boxing ring that took up most of the hut! After a while better surroundings were found and in 1976 they moved half a mile up the road to the club's current premises, still on the main road.

Collyhurst became Collyhurst and Moston, but still success came thick and fast. Fighters with class and flair emerged with predictable regularity. Away from the club Brian married his lovely wife Rosemarie in August 1973 at Corpus Christi RC Church, Miles Platting. They would go on to have four children: Anthony, Damian, Christopher and Rachael. In the decades that followed the club went from strength to strength. A quality list of fighters that won titles at British, European and World levels and reads like a who's who of Mancunian boxing: Kenny Webber, Winston Cousins, Delroy Waul, Pat Barrett, Lance Lewis, Michael Jennings, Michael Gomez, Robbie Reid, Matthew Hall, Craig Dermody, Thomas McDonagh and there were so many more who will be mentioned somewhere in this book.

Not that Brian's coaching produced automatons, all were so different in personality and style, but they shared one particular characteristic, they had been taught to box by Brian Hughes and this showed in his loyal disciples too, such as the Ghanaian-born Billy Kotey. A former all-African boxing champion who had moved to Moston; one day, out of curiosity he walked up the gym steps to discover, like so many others, a second home. A warm, humorous character, he was steeped in boxing knowledge and worked closely with Brian for many years.

In time Brian Hughes' name spread across the Atlantic where American boxing coaching greats such as Emanuel Steward sought him out to discuss and share training techniques. Long into the night these students of the game would chat about past legends and modern-day fighters. They became huge friends. Brian stay at Steward's house in Detroit and frequent his infamous Kronk gym. Here Brian made a massive impression and this, allied with Steward's respect and warmth for Brian, meant he eventually asked him to be his assistant coach in the eighties. Sadly, Brian had to refuse his American friend because he had two young children back in England and was reluctant to take them out of school. With typical good grace Steward accepted this, they shook hands and the Kronk's loss remained Collyhurst and Moston's gain.

Amid the countless trophies, belts and accolades, Brian's finest moment as a trainer, and his biggest success, came when, against all the odds, he took Robin Reid to the WBC Super-Middleweight title in 1996 against Vincenzo Nardiello, in his home country of Italy. For the first time since the days of Harry Fleming, the club was home to a world champion.

Come 2000 Brian was awarded an MBE for services to the community in the Millennium Honours list. On first hearing this Brian refused to believe it and thought someone was playing a practical joke! But it was real and nobody had deserved it more. In March of that year Brian and his proud family went down to London to meet Prince Charles and later on Sir Richard Branson, who was receiving his knighthood on the same day. Branson got on famously with Brian and invited the Hughes family to dinner at the Kensington Roof Gardens. It was a truly special day for the Hughes clan and one they would never forget.

For once the good guy had won.

Finally, in March 2011, Brian retired from boxing to concentrate on his family and his writing. Typical of the man, he had not let the dyslexia win and taught himself to read and write. Brian has produced a succession of brilliant books on his two favourite subjects; boxing and Manchester United.

However, this is not the last we will hear of him in this book, it's just the beginning, for you cannot start to tell the amazing story of Collyhurst and Moston without Brian's all-consuming presence in the background, forever shining through.

But now let's go back, way back in the mists of time, down Collyhurst

Road, where the supposed betters; priests, politicians or factory owners would always claim you had to know your place. Whether it to be subservient to God, the law or at your boss's whim. Well Manchester is and always will be a city of poets, fighters and dreamers. We have never been known to lie down for anybody, so what better place than a boxing ring to fight your corner?

Over to you Jackie Brown.

3 - JACKIE BROWN
THE PRINCE OF COLLYHURST

CRUMPSALL HOSPITAL: MANCHESTER, 1971. The old man had been admitted four years earlier. The general consensus among the doctors looking after him had been it was a minor miracle he had survived this long. So many years of abusing his body meant it had finally given up. There had been few visitors. The old man, when conscious, said little, he knew time was short. A life lived to the full shone through in his world-weary face. But there remained a twinkle in the eye; a wicked, cheeky glint that simply refused to dim, even though the old man's light was fading fast. In an agonising manner, he whispered into a nurse's ear that once upon a time he was a real somebody. She smiled and nodded as she wiped his forehead with a wet cloth. Finally, the last bell rang and the name written on the clipboard at the foot of the bed that held his medical notes read - Mr Jackie Brown: Born Collyhurst, 29th November, 1910: Passed away: 5th March, 1971. What the notes didn't say was that here, unknown to all that had looked after him during the dying embers of his life, was one of the greatest fighters not only Manchester, but Britain had ever produced. A world champion, a force of nature who for a while blew away everything in his path, until he himself imploded in maelstrom of wine, women and chaos.

This, then, is the story of Mancunian royalty.

BORN INTO A NOTORIOUS and poverty-stricken area of Catholic Collyhurst, christened 'Little Ireland', Jackie entered this world fighting and kicking, for around those streets there was little choice. As a child he went to Saint Patrick's on Livesey Street. Playtime and outside the school gates was a constant battle for survival. It was a tough and, at times brutal, experience. Only a slight kid compared to others his age, Jackie learnt quickly that you could avoid a beating off the bigger lads if you were good with a smart quip or a joke. But he was also fast with his fists. A ferocious little street fighter, nimble and when the full force of his small frame was behind it, a more than decent puncher. Bullies were never a problem for young Jackie Brown, many were sorted out in straighteners and left with bloody noses, bruised egos and a clear intention to never pick on the cocky little kid from Armour Street again.

It was as a teenager that Jackie Brown first came to the notice of local boxing manager Harry Fleming. For ring experience he had entered a promising young boxer called Farrell from his Corpus Christi club into a semi-professional open-to-all tournament being held in a portable marquee near Collyhurst Road. These contests could be wild with young tearaways from near and far looking to make a name for themselves against better known fighters. As expected, the impressive Farrell did well and reached the final with relative ease, however he then came across a little firebrand who simply overwhelmed him. The crowd roared as their local boy put on a display that stayed with Fleming. This kid showed a natural flair and talent that seemed almost unreal for one so young. All the raw material was there for the making of a superstar, come the end he waved to the crowd and winked over at Fleming.

He would be keeping an eye on Jackie Brown.

Even at the tender age of fifteen Jackie was fighting to put food on the family table, but as the self-realisation grew that he was so much better than his opponents, hopes and dreams for a better life swiftly grew. Jackie wanted so much more than his parents had settled for and possessed the talent and confidence to strive for it. He joined the legendary fighter-turned promoter Len Johnson's extravaganza nicknamed 'The Blood Tubs'. Johnson had been arguably the finest boxer to emerge from Manchester to that date and soon he took Jackie under his wing. Len sensed the greatness denied to him in this small, wiry but truly blessed kid, whose attitude to life was such that he could have a party with a crowd of two or, if the need arose, start a fight with the entire ranks of the Manchester Regiment. Being black, Johnson had been disgracefully blocked from fighting for a Lonsdale belt with the authorities of the time insisting that only white boxers could contest official title fights. It was a scandalous situation that still shames the sport today.

The Blood Tubs were notorious boxing venues across Manchester. By tradition they were usually held in run-down backstreet buildings where anybody willing and able could compete. It was a dangerous business because, although men could earn a little extra money in tough times, the gloves they would be using could easily be of different size and weight to their opponent. It was like a pre-war version of the film Fight Club and it was here in this environment that Jackie Brown cleaned up. He became a sensation, the fight fans adored him and the young boy quickly became a showman. To win was never enough for Jackie, it had to be a performance. Johnson realised his prodigy was heading for the stars, but due to the racial prejudice rampant at the time, he recognised that he could only take Jackie so far before coming up against the colour bar. So, with good grace and a heavy heart, Johnson passed Jackie on to another local promoter with far more push who he felt could take Jackie to where he deserved to be.

Harry 'Kid' Furness was no saint, but was a brilliant matchmaker and a fine promoter. An old-time impresario based in a boxing booth on Rochdale Road, Furness sensed riches in the surrounding area; the ravaging poverty that stretched over this broken-down part of the city making it fertile land for hungry, desperate fighters. He took full advantage of unemployment being rife across the north west and cherry-picked the best of the new flood of boxing talent that appeared almost overnight in a desperate attempt to scrape some kind of a living for their families. Fighters queued, begged and pleaded with Furness for an opportunity. Some weeks he would put up to seven shows on across Manchester, Cheshire and Derbyshire. But although he was a godsend to the sport, Furness was also a hard taskmaster. If a boxer had won, but not performed to a sufficient standard to entertain the crowd, then he would reduce the promised purse. Few could ever argue back for Ted Furness put food on their tables. His word was law. However, that was all before he met Jackie Brown.

The pair had clashed before when Jackie signed with Johnson. He would swagger down to a Furness promotion and cheekily challenge any of his fighters. Furness would angrily turn on Jackie, "Go home lad, you'll get yourself hurt. You're neither big enough, nor good enough to play with the big boys." But that was then…

When Johnson contacted him about Jackie, Furness leapt at the opportunity to manage the young, if troublesome, crowd-pleaser. Under Furness, Jackie swiftly became a sensation and he drew crowds from near and far. Furness and Brown had a love-hate relationship, with Jackie always wary of Furness's ability to 'peel an orange in his pocket' as he once famously said! Money owed and argued over was a constant thorn in their relationship with one never truly trusting the other. Jackie fought many times over a short period and his reputation soared. Still only sixteen, riches appeared sure to follow rags for the boy from Little Ireland, but he was also street smart enough to realise that what was needed now was somebody to teach him the true art of boxing. One who could take him on from the boxing booths and ensure he made the giant leap in fighting for titles. Jackie knew he was good enough and so made the move.

Harry Fleming was only too delighted to welcome Jackie Brown into his stable. Fleming knew the boy was a natural and first impressions only underlined that view. Already in the same gym over the coal yard in Paley Street and training hard was an impressive Flyweight prospect called Dick Manning. Fleming knew immediately that Jackie was a class above Manning. His astonishing speed, ability to slip a punch and hit and move like nobody he had ever seen excited Fleming to the point where he tended to ignore his colourful lifestyle outside the gym. This kid could charm the birds out of the trees and not just the feathered kind.

In no time Jackie made his first professional appearance. On 18th May, 1925, in Collyhurst, he outclassed an opponent from Gorton called Harry Gainey on points. The hapless Gainey failed to lay a glove on him and at the end the crowd roared, Jackie bowed and Fleming smiled wide. What followed was a lightning rise through the rankings as Jackie dealt with all before him with consummate ease. Following a meeting between Fleming and boxing promoter Jack Smith, an opportunity soon arose to fight before boxing aficionados in the splendid Free Trade Hall, Manchester's premier venue at the time. Perform well there and it would be a significant step up the ladder. He was matched against a decent Flyweight from nearby Ardwick, Freddie Webb, easily Jackie's toughest opponent to date. However, a few days before the fight Brown came down with boils, a common ailment in the 20's and 30's, caused mainly through a poor diet. This condition would haunt Jackie throughout his career but despite an insistence from Fleming that he pull out, Jackie refused point blank. "Nobody is calling me a Charlie Howard," (coward) he declared. In the end, suffering the consequences and clearly not his normal, lightning-fast self, Jackie was beaten in three rounds by Webb in a one-way contest. Much to Jackie's chagrin, although he was aware of his ailment, Smith refused him the chance of a return match. Instead Fleming insisted they move on. He explained to Jackie the time had come to move further afield and expand his reputation. The world did not start and end with Collyhurst Road. If Jackie was serious about reaching for the stars a new audience was required.

Together the pair would take flight to a place where boxers like Jackie Brown were lauded like gods. For they themselves were born to fight. With blackened faces they would emerge from deep underground to drink, fight and sing. With a suitcase packed, the boy from 18 Armour Street headed to that ferocious hotbed of boxing - the mining valleys of South Wales.

Jackie was an instant success with the tough, no-nonsense Welsh audiences. There could be no harder boxing crowd anywhere in the world and they loved him. Even today Jackie Brown's name is spoken of in hushed tones in the working men's clubs of former mining communities such as Merthyr Tydfil and Tonypandy. Jackie's photo still adorns their walls.

Convincing victories over tough and hardened local fighters such as 'Boyo' Reece, Phineas John, Jerry O'Neill and Cuthbert Taylor had the crowds on their feet applauding at the finish. This was almost unheard of in the valleys as usually when one of their own was beaten, riots would often occur and the police called. Not for Jackie. A wink to the crowd, a huge smile allied to a fighting style that left the Welsh in awe meant he was taken in as one of their own. However, despite the huge acclaim there was little money earned, for here in South Wales, as the depression kicked in, entire communities lived on the breadline. Word of mouth spread the legend of Jackie's time amongst these ferocious, but fair, boxing fans and it would soon prove to be time well spent. With his reputation considerably enhanced. Jackie Brown was now a contender and Harry Fleming's decision had paid off. A shot at the British title was no longer a pipe dream, it was a reality.

On 12th February 1929, back amid the much-vaunted surroundings of the Free Trade Hall, Jackie fought the experienced Salford-born George Greaves, for the vacant Northern Area Flyweight title. Greaves was a durable fighter, but proved no match for an on-fire Jackie who won a clear points decision over fifteen rounds. As the Free Trade Hall crowd roared their approval it became clear the path to a shot at the British title was drawing near. A succession of further impressive victories in a short span of time, that included three stoppages and a points win, meant there could be no further argument. Jackie had arrived. A date was set for a final eliminator to decide who challenged the formidable and skilful champion, Scotsman Johnny Hill, for the British Flyweight title.

On 13th October, 1929, Jackie came up against Birmingham's Bert Kirby at the Palais De Dence in West Bromwich. Kirby was hugely fancied by the bookies to put paid to this extravagantly talented, but cocky, Collyhurst Manc. Many experts thought that Jackie had been rushed into this fight and the much more experienced and stronger Kirby would have too much power and know-how for the Mancunian. Sadly, for all concerned, tragedy struck when just three weeks before the fight Johnny Hill tragically passed away. He was due to face the Italian New Yorker, Frankie Genaro in a world title fight on 11th October, but fell ill with pneumonia. After a short while Johnny's condition improved, before it sadly deteriorated and four days later a burst blood vessel in his lung was diagnosed. Johnny died the following morning at his home in Strathmiglo, Fife. Suddenly the final eliminator between Jackie and Kirby was declared an official contest by the Board of Control for the British Flyweight title. Both camps held their breath at this much unexpected opportunity. The cruel hand of fate had now given Jackie the opportunity he had dreamed of since he was a child. The kid who had fought to put food on his family's table was set to shock them all.

In Manchester and Birmingham excitement was at fever pitch. This was an era when a British title fight meant everything. Huge crowds travelled to support Jackie and come the night at the Palais De Dence there was an estimated ten thousand people locked out. Those lucky enough to have tickets witnessed a blistering start by both fighters. Jackie came out flying and Kirby was forced to go toe-to-toe. The opening two rounds had the crowd on their feet roaring, it was everything the crowd had hoped for as Jackie fought the fight of his young life. Come the third he continued to go after Kirby and to the utter astonishment of all present, Jackie let fly a left hook that crashed into Kirby's chin and knocked him out flat. He had done it! The referee didn't even wait for the count, instead simply raising Jackie's hand high! Manchester, and more significantly Collyhurst, had a champion. Jackie was £95 richer for his night's work, but this had given him something money could never buy or take away, he was British champion.

Outside the scenes were close to a riot as the visitors celebrated much to the chagrin of the locals. The Mancunians, who were hardly shrinking violets themselves and the Brummies who had backed Kirby, went at it. Unfounded rumours had gone around like wildfire of Jackie head-butting Kirby in the third round and this had led to the knockout. Chaos reigned. There were no gloves, no rules and no final bell. Ultimately law and order was re-established as the West Midlands constabulary laid into all with unrestrained fury. Come the next morning there was many a slashing, black eye and broken nose on both sides. A painful remainder to those suffering of the night Jackie Brown became British Flyweight champion!

Back in Collyhurst Jackie received a homecoming fit for a king. He got back to Manchester in the early hours to find there were already hundreds waiting to greet him. On hearing news of Jackie's victory, the Collyhurst pubs and streets swiftly filled with people celebrating his sensational victory. There were tears of joy that their boy had triumphed to put their much-maligned area on the map. From that night forward when people mentioned Collyhurst they would have to mention Jackie Brown in the same breath. In the following days, Jackie was lauded wherever he went. A visit to his old school of Saint Patrick's turned into a Mancunian fiesta as the four thousand cheering children, nuns and teachers threw a party to celebrate the achievements of a former pupil, who gave hope to the kids that, despite the poverty and hardship filling their everyday lives, nothing was impossible. Miracles, even amid this permanently murky, smog-ridden cobbled labyrinth could occur. Jackie was proof of that.

As expected Bert Kirby was handed the chance of a rematch and five months later on 30th March, 1930, at London's Holborn stadium, the fighters faced off once more. However, all was not right with Jackie, for once more, two days before the fight, he suffered an outbreak of boils and a bout of Tonsillitis. On discovering this, a legendary former boxing world champion from the early 1900's, Salford-born Joe Bowker, pleaded with him to postpone the contest. As with Freddie Webb, Jackie refused to listen and was determined to go ahead. It turned out to be a disaster with a clearly unwell Jackie sleepwalking to defeat in the opening two rounds. As Fleming watched on in horror, the third saw Kirby knock Jackie flat out. As the travelling Brummies' rose to their feet in delight, it appeared the world had ended for the kid from Collyhurst. Whether through being brave, stupid or arrogant it mattered little, the belt he had fought so hard for had been ripped from his hands at the first defence.

Fleming set about immediately looking for a third and deciding fight, but Kirby's management weren't keen. As Jackie fumed and took out his anger on a series of unfortunate fighters over the next year, negotiations continued. Finally, with the Kirby camp still unyielding, the British Board of Control stepped in and insisted the Birmingham man formally defend his title against Jackie. A third venue was called for. In stepped the shrewd promoter John Madden a blood relation to the infamous American gangster, Owney Madden. He offered to stage the decider at Belle Vue, Manchester. Both sides would be nicely rewarded, bad blood was put to one side and they all got down to business. A date was settled on: 2nd February, 1931. The 7000-capacity hall was sold out in record time as boxing fans snapped up the tickets. Jackie trained like a madman: this time determined nothing would go wrong. Come the night, Belle Vue was on fire as it appeared all Collyhurst had made the short journey to ensure their boy did not fail. In what would go down as one of the greatest contests in British ring history, the pair went to war from the first bell. However, Jackie was always on top, his skills at time teasing and torturing the willing, brave, Kirby. Finally, after fifteen rounds, the crowd held their breath, Jackie was declared winner by points and once again his home city and Collyhurst erupted in joy!

As Jackie held the belt high, none present could deny it was truly deserved. Fleming was already thinking of a shot at the European title. He knew they had to strike while the iron was hot because Jackie's life outside the ring was chaotic to put it mildly. The newspaper men dubbed Jackie The 'Manchester Express' and his social life was like a runaway train — by now the women, wine and partying were becoming the stuff of Collyhurst legend. Jackie appeared incapable of escaping the limelight. Dressing like your archetypal Chicago gangster, he was the epitome of sartorial elegance. The Prince of Collyhurst: walking and living life with a swagger. Dark and handsome, Jackie was a magnet for the ladies, whether they were married or not. Trouble inevitably followed: the whiff of scandal and excitement forever in the air. Scrapes and punch ups became the norm, either from the fists of a jealous husband, a boyfriend or a drunk in the pub who fancied his chances against the great Jackie Brown. Jackie was a man who would never back down either inside or outside the ring. Harry Fleming understood only too well that Jackie was a force of nature and a law unto himself. He knew they had to act fast and just three months on from recapturing the British Flyweight crown, Jackie was matched against the tough Romanian Lucian Popescu for the European Boxing Union title.

Again Belle Vue was the venue – it was packed to the rafters on 4th May 1931 as Jackie entered to a tumultuous reception. His opponent, the Bucharest-based champion, was a very technical and dangerous fighter. In what was a gruelling, hard fought contest in which both fighters gave everything, Jackie was deemed by the judges to have just edged it. As the crowd sang his name there was huge respect between Jackie and Popescu, for each knew they could not have tried any more. Now British and European champion and still only twenty-one years old, it appeared a world title shot was inevitable, but first Jackie had a date that he could not miss.

On the 19th October 1931, Jackie Brown tied the knot with local girl Mary Chapman. They married at Saint Patrick's church, both of that parish and amidst joyful, chaotic scenes in which thousands had gathered to catch a glimpse of the happy couple, the churchyard, nearby roads and surrounding buildings were packed: roads were closed and eventually the police were forced to clear a path to ensure the bride and bridegroom actually made it to their own wedding on time! It was as close to a Hollywood wedding as Collyhurst had ever seen. The guests list was a who's who of 'A' list celebs: actors, footballers and boxers such as Johnny King from Jackie's Collyhurst stable filled the pews. Jackie's best man was Harry Fleming, who also gave the bride away as her father was deceased.

The glamorous reception at the Piccadilly café was also an eye-catching affair. Typically, Jackie could not help but steal the show. After listening to speeches lauding him to the heavens regarding his boxing triumphs, he took to the stage and with the audience expecting just a few grateful words of thanks, Jackie instead strolled across to the band and whispered into the bandleader's ear. As the music started up he took to the microphone and performed two popular songs of the time, 'McNamara's Band' and 'Myra my Girl!' Jackie, in typically showmanship style, brought the house down! Whether a boxing crowd, a pub sing-along or a wedding audience, it didn't matter. He simply could not help himself.

Two successful defences of his EBU title followed against Emile Degand and Vincenzo Savo as Jackie seemed to improve in every fight. The next twelve months saw his reputation soar as he fought sixteen times, losing only two. Both these were put down as flukes by Fleming and attributed to his fighter's pre-fight 'bad habits'. A successful defence of his British Flyweight championship belt against Glaswegian Jim Maharg, in September 1932, set up a long-awaited world title shot. Again, Jackie's big night would be at Belle Vue, and against by far the toughest opponent he had faced to date, Tunisian world champion Victor Young Perez.

Manchester held its breath.

Raised in even greater poverty than Jackie, in Dar-El Berdgana, the Jewish quarter of Tunis, Perez had started training as a boxer at fourteen to emulate his idol 'Battling' Siki, an African champion from Senegal. In 1930, Victor won the French Flyweight title in Paris defeating Kid Oliva from Marseille. The following year he won the International Boxing Union and National Boxing Association World Flyweight crowns with a sensational second round knockout of Frankie Genaro in Paris. This astonishing victory made him the youngest world champion in boxing history. He was a tough hombre who, like Jackie, had a chaotic social life outside the ring - his love of life, women and drink was insatiable. After his stunning win over Genaro he began to enjoy his new-found fame. Perez immersed himself in the infamous Parisian nightlife during which he had a scandalous affair with the French-Italian actress Mireille Balin which kept him busy before training resumed for his next fight.

Come the fateful evening of 31st October 1932, Manchester was in meltdown. The 7800-sell-out crowd queued excitedly to enter the

King's Hall, Belle Vue. Across the city, and nowhere more than Collyhurst, prayers were said and candles lit in the hope Jackie could overcome the world champion. An epic encounter was expected and both men went hell for leather in a storming contest for thirteen brutal rounds. The action was spellbinding and it appeared a certainty that the outcome would be settled by the judge's scorecard when, suddenly, from Perez's corner, they threw the towel in and withdrew their shattered fighter. It was all over!

Jackie Brown was king of the world!

The King's Hall and an entire city cried tears of undiluted joy. Their boy, this five-foot-five, twenty-three-year-old from the back alleys of Collyhurst, a teeming hub of humanity that refused to go gently into the night against the stark ravage of poverty and the hardships thrown at them, had produced a world champion. In every house and pub the celebrations began. Bunting and confetti were prepared for the return of their Prince. Parties broke out that would last for days. Rumour had it that even the nuns who taught at Saint Patrick's school broke out in smiles, although many found that hard to believe. When Jackie arrived home in the early hours huge crowds lay in wait. Although exhausted he partied through the night, before finally being allowed some sleep as the sun rose over the dark-chemical wastes of the River Irk. The next morning, as an aching Jackie limped from his bed, his body and face swollen, he went downstairs to find a note tucked in a milk bottle outside his front door.

"Well done Jackie" it proclaimed. "Just champion!"

A sad postscript to this fight was the ultimate fate of the former champion Victor Young Perez. Because of his Jewish heritage, Perez was sent to the German death camp of Auschwitz on 10th October 1943. Whilst there he was forced to participate in boxing matches for the amusement of the German officers and guards. Come 1945, Perez was one of just 31 survivors of the original 1,000 he had originally arrived at the camp with. It was reported Perez was finally murdered by the Germans on 22nd January 1945, a tragic and shocking epitaph to a great champion.

As for Jackie, he had finally reached the top of his mountain. What was required now was self-discipline: the type of dedication that only true champions could. For the rest of the world would now be coming for him. Jackie had to stay hungry and many questioned whether he could adhere to this state of grace when riches and temptation would be close companions.

For a while the 'Manchester Express' thundered on. Away from the ring, Jackie was bigger than any individual Hollywood had to offer at that time. Money and plaudits came his way and he bought a large house in the posh Cheshire suburb of Bramhall. Jackie was box office: his every word and move scrutinised by the newspapers and mobbed wherever he went. Dressed in the sharpest suits, a trilby hat, the shiniest of shoes and, on special occasions, a luxurious fur coat, Jackie was never off stage. Whether he was in the ring, the street or the pub, it mattered little. Jackie had also acquired for himself arguably the flashiest car in Manchester at that time, an American Studebaker. As if this wasn't enough, he also employed a chauffeur! Money to him was like pouring water onto sand. Whereas many boxers of that era feared a return to a previous poverty-stricken existence and spent thriftily, Jackie was generous to a fault. He loved nothing more than returning to Collyhurst and spending hours signing autographs at youth clubs and schools. Or simply stopping in a nearby street and buying ice creams for the kids playing nearby. When word spread that Jackie Brown was around, crowds of kids would flock to his car. Never once did Jackie get annoyed or frustrated, for these were his people. He also thought nothing of helping older residents with money problems.

But there was also a dark side to living the dream. Even though he was now married, the womanising and drinking didn't stop, in fact it got worse. The women proved too hard to ignore - a heady mix of good looks, money and the small fact of him being champion of the world meant that temptation was everywhere and the urge to stray was simply overwhelming. Bar room brawls were also a regular occurrence and it was these incidents in particular that drove Harry Fleming to distraction, for Jackie would never back down. Harry feared for his champion more in the pub than the ring.

And yet for a while all seemed well. On 12th June, 1933, at the Olympia Kensington in London, Jackie delighted boxing fans in the capital with a successful and impressive defence of his world crown against the plucky French opponent, 'Tintin' Valentine Angelmann. As a relieved and smiling Fleming hugged his man at the finish, he had never been prouder. Jackie's performance was that of a true champion and earned him a standing ovation at the end. Full of skill, style and courage, the cockneys took this Mancunian to their hearts. London belonged to Jackie Brown and he was now in real danger of becoming a national treasure. Though, as ever with Jackie, trouble was never far away.

A few months later, on a miserable Sunday evening, 15th October 1933, as the Mancunian rain lashed down, Jackie was driving back to Bramhall from Collyhurst. They had been at their baby daughter Jacqueline's christening. Not surprisingly, it had taken place at Saint Patrick's church. Jackie turned into Bramhall Road, Stockport. Visibility was limited and huge puddles splashed on the tarmac. Suddenly there was a sickening thud as Mrs Margaret Thornley was hit and killed instantly by Jackie's car. Immediately he pulled up and thinking Margaret may still be alive, a distraught Jackie picked up her broken body and drove straight to Stockport Infirmary, sadly to no avail.

An inquest was held and, as expected, passions ran high. The coroner heard two differing versions of what actually occurred. The dead lady's husband, Guy Thornley, testified through tears that Jackie had been driving at a "terrific speed". However, other witnesses gave vastly differing accounts. One said that Jackie's speed was "barely moderate." Others stated that Mrs Thornley carried an umbrella in front of her and this may have contributed in not seeing the car coming towards her. Finally, on hearing the evidence from all parties, the jury took ten minutes to return a verdict. The cause of Mrs Thornley's death was deemed to have been Jackie's "negligent" driving, but that this "negligence" was not enough to constitute manslaughter. Jackie Brown had just got the result of his life.

Although utterly devastated by this event, Jackie tried hard to shrug it off and only fifteen days later was back in the ring at Belle Vue, defending his titles against a dangerous young fighter from Liverpool, Chris 'Ginger' Foran. Fully focused and backed as ever by ferocious Mancunian support and with a fair few from Liverpool there for Foran, Jackie won convincingly on points. This was arguably one of his finest performances considering what he had been through; from the opening bell Jackie was all over the game, if outclassed, scouser and come the final round the result was in little doubt. The crowd roared their approval when Jackie lifted the courageous Foran's arm high to the crowd to signal great respect between the two fighters.

Yet as always in Jackie's rollercoaster life, a shock was just around the next corner. On Friday 3rd August 1934 a sentence of four months imprisonment with hard labour was passed at Manchester Crown Court on twenty-four-year-old Jackie Brown, after a trial lasting three hours ended with him being convicted of bodily harm upon a Louis Tarchman of Choir Street, Lower Broughton. Jackie's address was given as Valley Road, Bramhall. The jury, in returning their verdict, added that in their opinion, "Brown committed the assault under great provocation". In his summing up the judge, Sir Walter Greaves Lord, gave a small statement.

"I think the jury have taken exactly the right view and that there was a considerable amount of taunting, although Brown, of all people, you ought to have refrained from the particular form of violence which has been proved. If it had not been for the jury's opinion that there had been provocation, the sentence would have been more severe. I hope this will be a lesson to you Brown, and that you now keep within the bounds of sportsmanship in the future."

Led from the dock Jackie nodded and smiled over to Fleming, but this time the cockiness and swagger was missing. That was one day by the seaside he would come to deeply regret...

The events in question took place on Sunday 1st July 1934. Jackie had taken himself off to Blackpool for the day and at around 9-30pm was drinking alone in the County Hotel bar. Sometimes even a showman like him needed a break from Manchester's unquenchable interest in his every move. Looking up he noticed a good friend's wife, Vera Sheldon, whose nickname was 'Blondie', enter the along with another woman and two men. All were laughing and joking. They sat down by a window overlooking the vast open beaches across the promenade. Immediately Jackie leapt off his bar stool and was at the table questioning Vera as to what she was doing there, for he knew her husband was away on business in London. Vera gave him short shrift, telling him to mind his own business. This annoyed Jackie, who insisted she return to Manchester with him, mainly because he knew Vera had a baby at home. An altercation swiftly ensued when one of the men, Louis Tarchman, an amateur boxer who Jackie knew from back in the blood tub days, tried to intervene, but was told to "F—k off!"

Tarchman responded, "You maybe a champion, but don't you take liberties with me, Brown." The two were swiftly separated and as Jackie seethed, the four left the hotel bar, got in a car and drove off. Not willing to let this lie he followed the group and told his chauffeur to go after them all the way back to Manchester.

On arriving back and stopping at a traffic light, Tarchman jumped out of the car to confront a livid Jackie. He went up to his car, "Don't be so cocky Jackie. It's only four years ago since you were holding a spit bucket for me." According to onlookers, Brown jumped out and charged at Tarchman. A scuffle broke out in which both men rolled around on the floor before a furious Jackie, ever the streetfighter, took a huge bite out of Tarchman's ear, who screamed in pain. As blood seeped onto the road it was clear Jackie was in big trouble.

The next day he was arrested and come the trial, as Manchester watched on in horror, it took the jury only thirty minutes to reach a guilty verdict. The packed courts were stunned: gasps came from the public gallery. After sentencing Jackie was escorted away in a Black Maria to serve his sentence in Strangeways. The same place he had been warned about since a kid, its tower forever looming high over Collyhurst and Rochdale Road as a warning.

The four month sentence was a sobering experience for Jackie. At the time it was an extremely lenient sentence for the crime. Later it was revealed there was an attempt to bribe Tarchman to drop the charges, but luckily for Jackie this didn't come to light during the court case. From the stars to the gutter is a short journey for so many boxers and even though fellow inmates treated him with sympathy, it was clear the best of times for Jackie Brown had quickly turned into the worst. So, what would happen next? His had been the archetypal rags to riches to rags story. Jackie had lived the dream: the acclaim, the cars, the money, the women, the big house, the adulation and at home a beautiful wife and child. Finally, the candle had burned out on the Prince of Collyhurst and he was sat in a prison cell.

On the day the newspaper placards screamed out the headline: JACKIE BROWN RELEASED! the doors to Strangeways opened and the former champion appeared, rubbing his eyes and clutching a small bag as he walked out into freedom. Swiftly a posse of reporters crowded around. Questions were fired in the boxer's direction.

"Give me a break, lads," Jackie pleaded, "I just want to get home to my wife and kid." His brother Tommy appeared. Similar to his sibling in looks and temper, he pushed the hacks aside and grabbed Jackie, "Piss off you lot. Come on, our kid." Together they walked to a waiting Saloon car and drove off.

By now all wasn't well between Harry Fleming and Jackie. Fleming had brought a boxer into his Collyhurst stable called Mickey McGuire who Jackie couldn't stand, mainly because he had beaten him twice earlier in his career. Jackie let this be known to Fleming from Strangeways, but Harry was not prepared to accept it telling Jackie, "I will sign who I want".

By now, Fleming's option had run out on Jackie's services and it appeared a parting of the ways was inevitable. Gossip spread quickly in boxing circles and the fighter wasn't short of offers. It was here American boxing manager Dave Lumiansky emerged on the scene. The son of Jewish immigrants from Russia, Lumiansky worked in mysterious circles but had an extraordinary talent for match-making. Jackie was aware of this and in his predicament, he needed somebody of Lumiansky's ilk to quickly catapult him back into the limelight. Jackie also signed a contract with the legendary London-based promoter, Harry Levene. As for Fleming, he would continue to handle Jackie's training regime, although the relationship between the pair was never the same. The father/son bond had been broken as Jackie fell for the age old adage that the grass is always greener.

It was a sad parting of the ways. When the pair were returning from South Wales by train, Jackie had urged Fleming to ensure he signed him up whereupon his manager insisted that Jackie's word and handshake were good enough for him. Well, the boxer did nothing more than start to scribble down on a piece of paper: *"This is to say that I Jackie Brown authorise Harry Fleming to be my manager"*, before forcing a reluctant Fleming to accept it.

On 11th February, 1935, a packed Belle Vue held its breath as their favourite son once more made his way into the ring to take on the Italian Orlando Magliozzi in a non-title fight. In the dressing room, only a short time before, Jackie had worried whether the fans would stick with him after the time spent in prison. He needn't have worried as the Mancunians rose as one to cheer their hero through the ropes. As

Jackie appeared in full view, a cacophony of noise echoed around the hall. Chants of 'Jackie, Jackie' deafened ringside journalists. The crowd certainly believed in him, but was that old Brown magic still there after eight months out? Expectations were higher than ever and the Master of Ceremonies could not even begin to make his introduction for fear of being drowned out. They say it's hard to keep a good man down. Well, Jackie Brown was that and more. He was back! Watching at ringside were two of his famous stable mates – Johnny King and Jock McAvoy. Although huge favourites themselves with the Manchester fight fans, neither had experienced a night such as this.

It took Jackie just four rounds to dismantle the unfortunate Magliozzi, who found himself overwhelmed by the 'Manchester Express'. After a nervous start, Jackie quickly found his rhythm as if he'd never being away. In truly emotional scenes Jackie found himself lifted shoulder high by cheering fans and carried all the way back to his dressing room. The fires still burnt bright in Jackie's belly and he would need every last spark of energy for his next fight against the pride of the Gorbals, Benny Lynch less than a month later.

Many felt that Jackie had been badly advised to take on the ferocious Lynch in a non-title fight. He was the up and coming Flyweight sensation and was heavily tipped to take Jackie's crown. The pair came from similar backgrounds; they were both Irish Catholics who had had to fight every step of the way out of poverty. Typically, Jackie would not listen to those who dared to mention avoiding Lynch, and, as he entered the hostile Kelvin Hall, Jackie was determined to put the young pretender in his place. However, he soon realised Lynch was the real deal and after a sluggish start in the opening round, Jackie was put on the canvas with a crashing right hook from the Scot. As the baying crowd screamed, expecting their boy to go on and finish off the Englishman, Jackie roared back and for the remainder of the contest went toe to toe with his formidable opponent. There were times when both had the other in trouble and come the last round there seemed to be nothing between them. A draw was declared by referee Johnny Summers, who raised both arms high. The arena was in uproar as disappointment and anger filled the air, however in the two corners the relief was huge. In Jackie's case, he had come through with honours and no serious damage after that early scare, while Lynch's corner knew there would be an opportunity to take on the Englishman again, this time for his titles.

There was a strange postscript to this fight: rumours were rife that Lynch's corner men had told him to ease off, it is a conspiracy theory that remains to this day. One thing was for certain, Benny Lynch was not going away and he and Jackie were set to meet again in one of the most dramatic British championship fights of all time.

Those closest to Jackie knew that it would be suicidal if he fought the Scot in the same manner a second time and most felt that this had been Jackie's last great hurrah. He had given everything and more to stay with the Scottish firestorm, but still the Mancunian couldn't win. It would be impossible to do so again but then telling Jackie Brown to fight any other way was akin to cutting off his arms. Harry Fleming told him straight on the train back to Manchester. "This fella will stop you inside two rounds if you mix it with him next time."

Never in the history of professional boxing has a fighter fought twice on the same night and on the same bill. Except, that is, for Jackie Brown. In July 1935, the war drums had already started to bang for Jackie to defend his World Flyweight title against Benny Lynch in the coming September. Unspoken around Jackie there was an understanding that now was the time to make hay while he was still champion and a final round of money spinning fights were arranged, as his backers seriously believed his time as title holder was drawing to a close.

Noises were coming out of Ireland that Irish champion, Belfast's Jackie Quinn, was after Jackie's scalp. The fight was made and there was a great deal of Irish money being wagered on Quinn. However, the fighter himself got cold feet and come the day of the fight at Belle Vue, he went missing. The promoter John Madden was beside himself at losing Jackie's opponent at such a late stage. He phoned Quinn's manager and promoter Jim Rice who was disgusted with his man and promised to deliver his fighter on the night. This he did, but the Irishman was clearly overweight and in no mood to take on Jackie. Quinn produced a shambolic performance and fought like a drunkard. He was knocked down twice in round one and with the cat calls of the crowd ringing in his ears. Jackie tore into him from the off, not letting a hapless Quinn, intent only on survival, off the ropes. Finally, the referee stepped in to end the mis-match and there were angry scenes among the Mancunian and Irish fans as police moved to surround the ring. Quinn was hustled away with an escort for his own safety. These were the days when such shows of contempt for paying punters were not accepted.

Luckily, as a fall back, Madden had contacted Preston boxer Syd Rose to step in if Quinn was a no-show. After watching Jackie fight, Rose felt his night was done and had already packed his bags to leave. Back in the dressing room the vitriol and abuse could be heard through the walls. The atmosphere was poisonous. Something was called for to soothe tempers and it was Jackie who came up with the idea of letting him fight Rose as well. Having hardly broken sweat in putting away Quinn he thought, why not? "Give me a few minutes breather and I'll fight the Preston lad" he told Fleming.

A relieved Madden could not thank Jackie enough. Word was sent for Rose to get changed and as the Master of Ceremonies announced the addition to the bill, the mood of the crowd changed from anger to incredulity - their boy was coming back on! Jackie stepped into the ring to a tumultuous reception once more and although a plucky Rose showed great heart, he was put away with ease by the champion in the third round. Rose's brave show and Jackie's historic decision to fight again saw the Belle Vue crowd rise as one to salute both fighters. Only the Prince of Collyhurst could have pulled this off! Sadly, Jackie's only reward for saving the day was to be fined £20 by the Boxing Board whilst Madden was fined £50, as they claimed the contest was against their rules. Small thanks for preventing a full-scale riot and possible lynching…

The time arrived to defend his world title as Benny Lynch and half of Glasgow arrived in Manchester. To prepare, Jackie was whisked off to Blackpool. Surprisingly, his old trainer Jack Bates didn't travel and was deemed surplus to requirements. This really hurt Jack, but Lumiansky's influence over Jackie had by now become total. His promise to deliver big fights had borne fruit and a new brush was slowly sweeping away the old Collyhurst 'All For One' camaraderie. Money corrupts and jealousy and bitterness are contagious. Fleming had already been side-lined and with Bates no longer deemed useful as a trainer, Johnny King no longer sparred with Brown. The pair had once been so close, but grew to share an immense dislike for one another. The animosity was open with Jackie boasting to all who would listen, "I have the beating of Kingie" – it was an opinion he would soon be given the opportunity to back up.

The *Manchester Evening Chronicle* had christened the Lynch fight 'The Fight of the Century': Belle Vue would host it once more after Madden bid a European record £3800 for the rights. Finally, come the night of the contest, a sense of foreboding settled over Jackie's camp. It appeared that the only man who thought he had a chance of beating Lynch was Brown himself, those closest to him felt that Jackie Brown was a condemned man.

And so it turned out - Benny Lynch entered boxing folklore by taking apart Jackie in just two rounds of complete and utter mayhem. It was brutal. Jackie was dropped eight times in all, before the referee Moss Deyong called a halt to the carnage after just one minute and forty-two seconds of the second round. Pandemonium broke out as a staggered and dazed Jackie was led back to his corner. Lynch was carried shoulder high around the ring by his team and the Manchester fans sportingly gave him a standing ovation. They knew history had just been made and those present were lucky enough to witness a changing of the guard. Jackie's three-year reign was well and truly over. His stable mate, Jock McAvoy, climbed through the ropes to offer a consoling arm and a sore but smiling Jackie gave him a gentle pat on the cheek. Amid emotional scenes the Prince of Collyhurst left the ring.

Still refusing to accept that the savage loss to Benny Lynch was a final curtain call, Jackie decided to move up to Bantamweight. Though never using it as an excuse for what happened against the phenomenal Lynch, he had been struggling to keep his weight down for some time. Such was Jackie's urge to show the world once more that he wasn't finished, a mega fight against stable-mate and British Bantamweight champion Johnny King was quickly made. Although it would be a non-title contest, something more was at stake - the pride of being top dog in Manchester and the Cock of Collyhurst. Here Lumiansky came into his own as he managed to fast track the contest and with King equally keen, Jackie, after only two fights at a new weight would be granted his wish. Again, wiser heads urged him not to rush, not everything was about money. Jack Bates, now in Johnny King's corner, urged Jackie to build up his power and speed gradually before taking on the truly formidable King. As ever though, Jackie was not for listening. He was a man in a rush for redemption and in boxing that is always dangerous. One man determined to wash his hands of it all was Harry Fleming. "A bloody mad idea" he raged. It sickened him to see two Collyhurst lads he considered his sons fight. As the two went for each other's throats on the night of 22nd November 1935, Fleming was strolling along Blackpool promenade dressed in a sharp suit, trilby with his hands in his pockets and nursing a broken heart.

Demand for tickets was overwhelming, it appeared everyone in the city, bar Fleming, wanted to be present when these two gladiators went to war. As for Jackie, he was back to his old swaggering self. Even offering to put a side-bet of £100 up that he would win. It was not just bravado, Jackie really believed it. In the end, as the crowd at King's Hall, Belle Vue watched on in stunned awe, a six-round slug fest took place in which Jackie at times threw back the years, before being utterly outclassed by the precision and power of King's punching. Jackie's fighter heart remained, but his stamina and ability to take a blow had waned dramatically and King finished him off in a merciless style that drew gasps from the audience.

Referee Gus Platt jumped in as blood seeped from Jackie's mouth with his eyes closed and jaw hung open. It had been an exhibition of vicious brutality by Johnny King, but as he looked across and saw his stable mate and one-time good mate slumped in the corner, King walked over, clasped Jackie on the shoulder and shook his glove. In Blackpool, on hearing the result, Harry Fleming showed no emotion. When later asked to comment Fleming chose his words carefully, "I'm pleased with the display put up by my two boys". However, that neutrality would soon disappear as Jackie severed all connections with the Collyhurst stable. These two were destined to fight again.

Again, Jackie shrugged off the mauling by King and set about re-establishing his reputation. He joined Ted McGuire's gym on Stockport Road. Lumiansky was constantly telling him that his career was far from over. Such was the American's determination to get King in the ring once more that Jackie fought fifteen times in two years at Bantamweight, losing only once, until the cries from the boxing public proved simply impossible to ignore.

By now Jackie had settled at the weight and many believed this time around he could provide a serious challenge for what would be a clash for King's British title. Sadly, an awful lot of bad blood now existed between the fighters, with Jackie constantly belittling his former friend by mimicking his speech impediment. As the contest drew near the animosity and needle only increased. When asked to pose for the usual pre-fight photo Jackie refused to take part. King, unusually, was in snarling mood when asked what he thought may happen, "I will hammer Brown like last time. Have no fear or doubts. I will catch him and when I do he will go out like a light."

As for Harry Fleming, he came down off the fence and declared himself firmly in Johnny King's corner. Once again, this was Collyhurst against the rest and Brown had nailed his colours elsewhere so Fleming no longer felt a conflict of loyalties.

On 31st May, 1937, again at Belle Vue, but this time outside at the speedway ground, Johnny King finally put paid to the legend of Jackie Brown, however it took thirteen rounds of scintillating action and drama before he ended Jackie's courageous challenge. A record 17,000 crowd watched in jaw-dropping awe as these two men went for each other with unreserved venom. Every punch was laced with bad intentions.

After a promising start Jackie faded and was treated at times like a rag doll as King let fly a never-ending flurry of attacks that had him reeling, but refused to yield. He fought on blind instinct: shouts from the crowd to stop it were ignored by referee Jack Dare, for it simply was not the done thing back then. Punches rained down on Jackie, who beckoned King forward and come he did. Finally, in the thirteenth round, King floored Jackie who, unbelievably, got back up at the count of seven. Though his expression was vacant, King moved in again and this time dropped Jackie to put him out for the count.

It was all over.

A sickening silence initially fell over the mortified crowd as Jackie's body lay still. Finally, as signs of movement were noticed, a thunderous ovation rang out. The audience got to their feet and the applause went on and on. A final accolade to the Prince of Collyhurst. If the Manchester Express had not been derailed before, he surely was now.

Jackie fought on for a while, but was clearly a shadow of his former self. The final bout came against Benny Jones at Belle Vue, on 24th July,

1939. Though no longer top of the bill, a points win was greeted by a still loyal crowd with fantastic cheers. Sadly, these were soon dulled by the shrieking blare of air raid sirens over Manchester as World War Two broke out and one of the first local boxers to volunteer was none other than Jackie Brown. However, Jackie's health was no longer up to scratch, a consequence of him having taken too many punches and he was discharged in early 1940. Even the basics of drilling saw Jackie lose his temper. On medical examination, it was discovered he was suffering from pernicious anaemia and Jackie was sent home. Determined to do his bit, he became an air raid warden working in the city centre. Following the war, life for Jackie grew increasingly worse as he was diagnosed with a perforated brain. Drinking heavily, brawling, yet still whenever seen around town, impeccably dressed, there were times, sadly growing increasingly rare, when flashes of the old Jackie shone through, but he was on a downward path by now.

In 1950 Jackie entered Prestwich Hospital as a voluntary patient in a desperate attempt to get well by shock treatment and severe medication. Sadly, it was to no avail. The bravery shown in the ring, especially in his later years, was returning to haunt him. Jackie was desperately ill. By this time his house in Bramhall had gone and he now lived in a much smaller home at Tudor Avenue, Blackley with wife Mary and their three children. An estimated £25,000 earned through his ring exploits had long since gone.

As the years wore on Jackie's health grew ever worse. Finally, in 1967, he was admitted to Crumpsall Hospital. There Jackie remained until the end of his days. The final bell tolled on 5th March, 1971, but for Jackie Brown his legend will undoubtedly live on.

POSTSCRIPT

COLLYHURST: let the Saint Patrick's bagpipes play as the Whit walks begin. The crowds on the pavements enjoying the wonderful, swirling music, the sights of the children in their best attire and adults in Sunday best. Men with suits freshly pressed, ladies in their prettiest dresses. The floats and the people smiling. A procession through the Mancunian streets. At the back, trailing behind is a small man, middle-aged now. He is wearing a sharp suit with a handkerchief, shoes spit-clean and walks with a swagger, smiling wide and receiving the biggest cheer of the day.

For this man is the Prince of Collyhurst and one-time champion of the world.

Jackie Brown…

4 - JOCK McAVOY
BITING THE HAND THAT FEEDS

MADISON SQUARE GARDEN, New York City, 20th December, 1935. The streets and stores lie bare as a blinding blizzard sweeps 'The Big Apple.' Even with Christmas just a week away, the city that never slept lay dozing, for such was the ferocity of the storm, New Yorkers had decided to stay at home and sit it out. Many are glued to their wirelesses for the big fight live from the 'Garden'. Local hero and Middleweight champion of the world Eddie 'Babe' Risko is fighting an unknown 'Limey' called Jock McAvoy from across the pond. He was expected to be just another successful W on Risko's record. Indeed, so little was known about McAvoy and his fighting credentials that people surrounding the champion did not even bother to give the contest official title status. It was almost as if it was beneath them to let their guy risk his belt by fighting this bum from nowhere. They said he was from some darned place called Collyhurst. Where in the hell was that?

As New Yorkers gathered around their wirelesses the commentator announced the fighters in a staccato tone. "Ladies and gentlemen, welcome to the Garden!" They listen on excitedly, hear the bell ring and imagine the scenes when suddenly the voice on the radio sounds incredulous, "Oh, I don't believe it! What a punch! What a start and the champ is down here at the Garden! It can't be. Just who the hell is this guy?" Outside a storm raged on through New York's streets, playing fitting support to the fury and power inflicted on the city's hero by The 'Rochdale Thunderbolt.'

JOSEPH BAMFORD was born in the Lancashire mill town of Burnley, on 20th November 1907. Though raised in Burnley and Rochdale, he will forever be immortalised as a Collyhurst fighting legend, after becoming the third of the holy trinity after Jackie

Brown and Johnny King to join Harry Fleming's golden boxing stable.

Joseph's mother, Nellie Ginty, had been raised in Salford and like so many others of that time she was forced to move to Burnley to find work as a weaver in one of the town's many mills. There she initially married a local man, George Hardacre, but this relationship was sadly not a happy one and Nellie eventually left to take up with a no-nonsense labourer called Joe Bamford. In tough times the pair worked every hour to scrape, save and borrow enough to buy a small terraced house in Luther Street, where Nellie gave birth to a son, Joseph. In such small communities, this kind of domestic set up was deemed scandalous for the period and circumstances were undoubtedly difficult for the family. They found themselves under constant focus, idle talk and chit chat.

Not much is known about Joseph's early life in Burnley and he rarely spoke publicly of those formative years, but there is little doubt that era contributed to the difficult, bad-tempered man he became. Though never disregarding the fact that here was arguably the finest Middleweight this country has ever produced.

As a young lad he would scrap for every meal - breakfast, dinner and tea. He loved a tear up and was quick to pick a fight in a childhood littered with episodes of violence, many instigated by him. Even at such a tender age Joseph was a spiteful character and a ferocious slugger. He would fight boys twice his size and flatten them, the power in one so young was amazing. As a teenager he was no great lover of boxing, he had an obsession with fighting, but such was his difficulty in being able to hold down a job, this was the only way he could help put food on the table. It also became an outlet to vent his violent temper.

Viewed as the roughest of uncut diamonds, he was taken on by famous Royton promoter and manager Joe Tolley, a man who had been around the boxing circuit for years and thought there was nothing new the sport could spring upon him, but the violence and sheer power that existed in young Joseph both shocked and fascinated him. Astonished at the immense raw talent in one so young, Tolley recognised a Middleweight that punched like a Heavyweight. It was clear to Joe that he had a prodigy on his hands and on 6th November, 1927, age twenty, he put the prodigy in for his first professional fight against another local lad, Billy Longworth. However, before the bell sounded a strange event occurred that would enter boxing folklore. Such was his mother's disapproval of this chosen career that Joseph had decided to box under the name 'Jack McCoy'. However, come the day of the bout at Royton stadium, a confused ring announcer introduced him as 'Jock McAvoy' and the name stuck as he put away the unfortunate Longworthy in two rounds with a ferocious right uppercut, a punch that would become Jock's lethal weapon - poor Billy was the first of many to feel its wrath.

Inside the ropes where dreams are made and nightmares realised, Jock went all out to model himself on his idol, the great Jack Dempsey. The 'Manassa Mauler' had been World Heavyweight champion from 1919 to 1926. Jock would check out every newspaper and magazine to soak up information on the champ. He read and re-read his book on how to box until he knew it by heart. While the vast majority of British fighters fought in the typical English style of a straight up stance and a left jab as stiff as a grenadier guardsman on parade, Jock differed, for he wanted to be an exception.

He became a mirrored version of Dempsey. He built himself a makeshift gym in a wrecked old Rochdale barn that became his second home. Self-trained, he would spend every spare hour training like a madman, always looking to find more power. There Jock perfected Dempsey's stance in front of a cracked mirror. Crouching, bobbing and weaving while throwing short, crucifying punches of devastating strength. His knuckles raw and bloodied as he blasted away at a makeshift punch bag packed with old rubbish, rags, dirt and newspapers. Jock wanted an all-action American style to make him stand out among the hopefuls. It was a style the fans would adore. Soon he turned himself into a formidable and terrifying prospect; brave and laced with a blood curdling mean streak that at times bordered on the frightening, Jock would take on anybody who dared challenge him in or out of the ring. Whether it was in a street, pub or workplace, his short fuse could ignite like the striking of a match and fists would fly. Such was Jock's passion for a fight that some said he would fight a shadow on the wall.

It was only in 1931, on leaving Tolley and joining the Collyhurst gym under Harry Fleming's tutelage, that Jock began to learn the more refined arts of boxing and realise he was still only on the first rung of the ladder. His trainer, Mancunian guru Jack Bates, was a former boxer himself and would teach, or at least attempt to teach, the hot-headed Jock that there was more to this sport than just attempting to punch somebody's lights out.

Fleming had followed McAvoy's career. He had witnessed Jock wreaking mayhem in the various Lancashire tournaments, leaving a long line of battered, bruised, bloodied and unconscious opponents in his brutal wake. Already earning himself a fearful reputation in the ring, he also made a lot of waves out of it. Jock possessed a dreadful paranoia over money owing to him. He was convinced somebody was always ripping him off. There were times when only Fleming, with his calm head and warm persona, appeared able to talk Jock out of his rage, though even he would shake his head in disbelief at some of the tantrums thrown in the gym.

Despite his suspect temperament, Jock was no fool when it came to his career. He needed the right connections and understood signing with Fleming was the best move. His new manager was part of the now legendary 'Belle Vue Syndicate' along with the highly respected newspaperman and doyen of thirties boxing writers, Norman Hurst, and influential promoter John Madden. These three fellows got fights made. Do your stuff in the ring and money would undoubtedly follow. To appear at the top of the bill at the King's Hall, Belle Vue, meant that you were on the road to riches and the easiest way to get to the top of the bill was with these three men in your corner.

Straining at the leash for his first contest, Jock got his wish on 30th August 1931, at the Brunswick Stadium in Leeds against Jack Hyams, a Jewish fighter, who was tough, durable and originally from Stepney, London. It proved an inauspicious start for Jock who, after eight tedious rounds, finally won on a disqualification. Knowing well of his opponent's reputation, Hyams clutched, hit low, grabbed and held before a fed-up referee gave up and raised Jock's hand to end the misery. As Hyams retreated to his corner, an outraged Jock screamed abuse at him. Even the streetwise Collyhurst gym mates who had travelled across the Pennines from Manchester watched in utter disbelief as he vented his anger at Hyams' tactics. Jock cut a despondent figure – he had so wanted to impress his new paymasters, but it was very early days. In time, many opponents would fall before him as he battered them senseless.

Once back home in the gym Fleming and Bates were horrified at the state of their new man's fists. His cave-man tactics of simply blasting out hapless opponent's prize-fighting style rather than boxing, meant so long as the punch was above the belt, Jock cared little where it landed. Such tactics caused untold damage to the hands if it was not remedied and they set out to do so. Fleming asked a friend, a Collyhurst doctor, Doc Graham, to examine his badly mauled knuckles. All kinds of remedies were put forward, but the lasting damage had already been done in Jock's early years. A special method of banding and taping was finally agreed upon, but still the fighter would suffer terribly making Jock's incredible achievements in the years to come even more remarkable.

Gritting his teeth and getting down to business, a swift rise through the rankings followed, with six stoppages inside the distance that were nothing short of carnage. Jock was on fire and impressing enough to finally get his wish to fight at Belle Vue. Johnny King was star billing on 7th September 1931, when McAvoy took apart the unfortunate Welshman Jerry Daley in just two rounds. This bravura showing saw Jock's star rise and his name pushed higher up on the bill.

Topping the bill next time around was the incomparable Jackie Brown, while Jock was in against an experienced French boxer named Alfred Pegazzano. After a tame first round there were a few boos and heckles ringing out from the impatient crowd. They had expected blood, not this nonsense. Fleming watched on, now he would see just what this kid from the Lancashire hills had to offer. It was a true test of character. An incensed Jock heard the calls of derision and charged off his seat for the second. There he stood: impatiently biting on the thumbs of his boxing gloves. This habit would become his trademark. Many thought it was a show of impatience, perhaps temper, but it was in fact down to an accident as a teenager when he broke both thumbs working in a factory. Jock found it almost impossible to fit both hands smoothly into his gloves. Immediately McAvoy tore into a bewildered Pegazzano and was knocking him around like a rag doll. By some miracle and no shortage of guts the Frenchman survived and appeared for the third, although he was now so dazed that he was hardly able to throw a punch before Jock knocked him clean out to delight the audience.

The newspapers went wild and a star was born. The headlines screamed out! The 'Rochdale Thunderbolt' had come roaring into town. Word spread like wildfire as Jock continued in a similar vein to unleash hell on all before him. In no time, such was Jock's rising star,

Fleming managed to negotiate a shot at the British Middleweight title held by the formidable Cornishman, Len Harvey. In style and character the men were chalk and cheese. The champion was an exceptionally skilled fighter, technically sublime: a master of the defensive arts. While the challenger would not think twice of charging an opponent. By this time McAvoy had been refined, to a point, through many hours spent in the gym under Jack Bates' teaching. The long arduous sessions with the wise old dog had taught Jock new tricks of the dark trade: side-stepping, tugging, how to cover up. Despite this, Jock remained at heart a go-forward slugger. Though in no short time, circumstances meant he would have to learn and fast.

In character Jock and Harvey differed wildly. One was a gentleman, the blue-eyed boy of the British boxing scene, who would always say and do the right things. He would shake the hands of stars and the general public with genuine warmth. There was never a bad word about him in the newspapers, he was regarded as a delight to train and a nice guy to be around.

The other man was Jock McAvoy.

Not that Jock cared. Now fully settled in the Collyhurst gym, his worst traits were coming to light. It wasn't just his fearful paranoia over money, but a hypochondriac streak that drove Fleming and Bates to despair. Whether it be bronchial colds, boils, back pain or constipation, Jock reckoned he had them all at one time or another. Fleming would listen patiently as he ranted and raved and then advised him as well as he could. Another problem was McAvoy's refusal to go easy on sparring partners that saw local lads refusing to work with him. This meant Fleming and Bates had to go against the grain and get in outsiders who they paid over the odds for the honour of being badly beaten up by Jock. Prices up to £2 and even sometimes £3 a round were asked for and received. Also, and far worse, there was Jock's bullying nature against other lesser and younger fighters in the gym. He had a cruel tendency to snap, snarl, scream, hit and abuse until he got his way. The only man who was safe from his ill-tempered wrath was Jackie Brown, then at the peak of his powers.

Although by no means kindred spirits, Jock and Jackie hit it off, although Brown's wicked pranks and cruel joking around the gym and legendary reputation as a prankster did not at times appeal to Jock's nature. His wind-ups frequently made the Rochdale man blow his top. Then, with a wink, Jackie would smile and calm would descend once more upon the gym. Until the next time!

However, once outside work, in the pubs and clubs around Collyhurst, whether it be drinking, playing billiards or chasing the ladies in the dance halls, they were a terrible twosome and enjoyed each other's company. Both loved a good time and became notorious for their late night riotous behaviour. Court appearances followed and they got away with an awful lot more than your everyday 'Collyhurst Joe'. Whether it be a drunken brawl with some idiots trying to pick a fight, an irate husband or boyfriend wanting revenge or Jock losing his temper after losing and deciding to smash up a Billiard table, life was rarely dull with this troublesome twosome who always stuck up for one another.

"He's misunderstood is our Jock" Jackie would claim.

Meanwhile Jock always had a kind word for his stablemate, "He's a good bloke is our Jackie."

A frustrated Harry Fleming tore into both on a regular basis, but to no avail, for it appeared the only time they could stay out of trouble was in the ring!

The title shot against Harvey was hugely problematic for Fleming with the champion only agreeing to come and defend his title in Manchester for a staggering four figure sum, unheard of in British boxing circles at the time. With Belle Vue only able to hold a capacity of 7000, and times being so harsh, the notion of hiking up ticket prices was thought of as suicidal by the syndicate. The city, like the rest of the country, was struggling to survive in the depths of a worldwide economic depression. Jobs were like gold dust, money was scarce: to ask people who were already barely surviving to part with more money was unthinkable.

The solution lay in Jock accepting a smaller share of the purse. Fortunately, he was wise enough to realise that this fight would open the door to so much more. Beating Harvey would bring fame, riches and huge fights. So, to Fleming's relief, Jock took the hit on his ego (and his wallet) and agreed to accept a pittance, along with expenses and the fight was confirmed.

On 21st March 1932, a packed and emotionally drained Belle

Vue sighed a collective groan as Jock's attempt to capture the British Middleweight crown ended in gallant, frustrating failure. The fight went as most experts had it called with the challenger constantly on the front foot, pressing forward, bobbing and weaving, looking for that one shot, but denied constantly by Harvey's ability to nullify and smother, whilst firing back vicious combinations on the counter. Little separated the pair as the contest wore on it, but come the end referee Jim Kendrick lifted Harvey's arm high in the Mancunian air and the celebratory roars of a large travelling London contingent were drowned out by the roars from the locals for Jock. It had been a bravura showing by McAvoy who surprisingly took his defeat with good grace.

"It was a great fight. I learned a lot from Len, he is a fine champion. But I'm also sure he learnt a lot from me. A few more fights and we'll try again. I promise you all next time you'll see a different me and a different ending."

It was instead an unusually irate Harry Fleming at the end who complained bitterly to Kendrick about what he claimed was the champion's spoiling tactics. Also, as if to fuel Fleming's anger, he was upset with Jock for not following his pre-fight tactics that included slipping Harvey's left lead, coming inside and punching hard to the body. Instead, as ever with him, it was the proverbial bull in a china shop approach as Jock set out from round one to knock Harvey out. Against a superb tactician who possessed ferocious power in his counter punching, it was naïve. Jock may have previously been involved in seventy professional fights, but title shots like this did not come along easily or often. Though proud, Fleming felt his man, although courageous, had fought the wrong fight. However, there had been moments when Jock had caught and badly hurt Harvey, who like a true champion managed to hold on. It had been a close contest and Fleming thought next time could well be different.

Determined to earn a second chance, Jock set about an exhausting series of 18 fights in 13 months of which he won 17, 14 by knock out. The build up to the re-match was intriguing as Collyhurst's shrewdest boxing brains once more plotted to bring down the champion, only this time there was a difference. Jock was listening and paying full attention to everything his mentors were telling him, for the pain of losing to Harvey still cut deep.

They came up with the idea of bringing a former Belgian Middleweight called Rene Devos over to work with Jock. Devos had fought in the United States and spent a considerable time teaching himself all there was to know about American training techniques. The affable Devos had also fought Harvey, but most importantly he would prove a fine teacher who was able to get his point across to Jock. The two men struck up a close relationship. Devos spoke perfect English and didn't over-complicate his training with Jock and give him too much information. He understood here was a unique character. A fantastic fighter whose style only needed to be polished. The two would spar and chat for hours. Rene had picked up exceptional slipping skills from his time boxing across the Atlantic. Slowly, Fleming and Bates saw a difference in Jock, he was thinking more, the fire and the fury burnt brighter than ever, but the rush to battle had turned into more of a controlled attack. Outside the ring Jock took Rene under his wing and they would become a common sight in local pubs chatting away about not just boxing, but life. The Belgian loved a beer and a singsong and soon became a popular figure in the drinking vaults around Collyhurst. When it came to preparing Jock for Harvey, there was little doubt that he could not be in better hands.

As the fight grew close Devos pulled Jock aside one day and said to him just three words, but one's that made his heart soar.

"You are ready."

On 10th April 1933, the champion Len Harvey, once more came north and a packed King's Hall at Belle Vue sizzled with electricity. The cigarette and cigar smoke drifting over the arena, mixed with the smell of stale beer and the roars of a capacity crowd. When the fighters emerged this Mancunian bear pit erupted! Both men were brought together by referee Arthur Myers for final instructions, they touched gloves and returned to their corners waiting for the first bell. As expected, Harvey remained a keen betting favourite, but he began cautiously and with Jock equally reluctant to attack, Myers was forced to call them both together, demanding more action. From that moment Jock took the initiative and as the fight wore on it was clear all Devos' teaching had been taken on board. Jock was slipping punches and fighting inside, whilst maintaining the same relentless, front-foot fighting the crowd adored. Come the final bell, the King's Hall sensed something special had just occurred and as Myers raised Jock's arm there was an explosion of noise. Jock, Collyhurst's finest boxing minds and their Belgian friend had contrived to bring down one of the greatest champions this country had ever produced. Jock McAvoy, the kid from Burnley, brought up in Rochdale, but now a fully adopted Mancunian and son of Collyhurst had achieved his dream. Fleming hugged Bates: the men were crying with joy. From their small, broken-down gym off Paley Street, they now had three British champions. Jackie Brown, Johnny King and on this tumultuous evening, Jock McAvoy. All three were in the ring as Jock lifted the Lonsdale Belt. It would be one Jock would never lose inside the ropes. That night yet another star shone in the skies above Collyhurst.

To the shock of all who knew him, once he became a British champion, a strange kind of serenity appeared to settle over Jock. The moodiness and rage that were so often evident vanished. In public, he became the very model of good behaviour. It was as if Jock had taken it upon himself to carry on the mantle that Harvey had so successfully worn as an ambassador for boxing. The change was remarkable. Jock would turn up for charity functions and fund raising events with a smile and a kind word for everyone. People watched on open-mouthed and were astonished at the transformation. No one more than Harry Fleming. Jack Bates was a little more dubious. He knew Jock better than most through his endless hours in the gym and was convinced it was all an act.

Jock's laid-back demeanour out of the ring appeared to have drifted worryingly into it, for although successful, his first three title defences were dreary affairs, with the champion only winning on points. The audiences were surprised at the lacklustre showings and there were complaints that they had paid hard earned money to see 'The Rochdale Thunderbolt' unleash hell on their behalf and were not happy with this slow freight train chugging down the tracks. None of the performances had that trademark McAvoy fury, even if, in purely technical terms, they were perfectly adequate victories.

The syndicate of Fleming, Madden and Hurst knew that Belle Vue audiences would not stand for many more insipid showings. Luckily for them, and Jock's fans, normal service was set to resume in a manner that shocked even those who thought they had seen the worst of him.

For his fourth defence Jock would be up against a tough Londoner from Bethnal Green, Archie Sexton (father of future Manchester United manager Dave Sexton). He was coming to Manchester with a more than creditable record of having lost only twelve times in 174 fights, with eighty-four of those wins by knockout. Sexton was a tremendous puncher and a credible opponent for the champion.

Jock recognised the threat and knew something had to change. He set up a training camp at Hollingworth Lake Country Park, a beautiful part of Lancashire, just outside Rochdale, close to the Yorkshire border. Jock stayed at the luxurious Lake Hotel where his every whim was catered for. However, being treated like a country gent only seemed to make his attitude worse to those unlucky enough to be around him. Fleming and Bates watched on with mixed feelings as the old Jock reappeared, but they also knew this was his way of preparing for Sexton. For Jock, it was time to step up and soon the mood swings and loathsome arrogance returned. Training like a madman, Jock hit the bags with renewed venom, ran like a man possessed around the picturesque lush green surroundings of woods, fields and country lanes. He even took to swimming in the icy cold waters of Hollingworth Lake. Hundreds of fans would come and watch him train in a makeshift gymnasium erected in the hotel ballroom. They stared on in awe as Bates put a rampaging, furious Jock through his final paces for the bout and winced as his sparring partners ducked, covered up and ultimately fell in dishevelled bloody lumps. It was clear to all that although Archie Sexton was highly fancied for an upset by the southern press, the Londoner was in trouble.

On 9th October, 1933, an anxious Belle Vue was by no means full for Jock's fourth title defence. His loyal supporters waited to see if their boy had rediscovered his old fire. But sadly, an audience of 6000 watched on again in loud agitation as a slow, turgid contest ground on. The pre-fight hype that Sexton would come and attempt to blast Jock from the opening bell prompting a classic slugging fest failed to materialise. Instead it was obvious the challenger was wary about Jock's punching power and intent on covering up. Tucking his chin down at every opportunity, the crowd soon began to voice their disapproval.

Shouts, boos and catcalls resonated as the bell for the end of round nine sounded and both fighters trudged back to their corners. Sexton had proved a huge disappointment and as hard as Jock tried to put on a show, it simply fizzled out – the old adage of it taking two to make a fight has always been a boxing truth.

As the bell for the tenth rang Jock stood and could clearly hear the abuse being aimed at him from the paying public. They weren't happy. This clearly rattled Jock. Suddenly, he bit once more on the thumb of his gloves and tore across to Sexton. The contest demanded by the King's Hall audience belatedly struck up and Jock ripped into the Londoner. The champion opened up letting fly every shot in the illustrious McAvoy armoury, only to be caught by an unexpected rocket of a right cross smack on his chin by Sexton. The King's Hall held its collective breath. Jock was clearly dazed and hurting. If the boy from Bethnal Green had stepped in and fired another then the Middleweight title would have been heading south, but astonishingly Sexton hesitated. Sensing disaster and fighting only through sheer instinct, Jock roared back and from being almost down and out, he had his opponent on the ropes. Unable to get out Sexton attempted to cover up once more, but this time Jock's wrecking, hurtful shots got through. Body punches took the air from Sexton's lungs and suddenly the King's Hall was on its feet. Their boy was back as Jock, bobbing, weaving and hitting soon unleashed a right uppercut that had Sexton's legs buckling before he collapsed to the floor. As Jock stood over him, desperate to finish it, the referee, Mr CB Thomas, counted the badly hurt Sexton out for the count. Belle Vue erupted, more with relief than any great joy! From somewhere Jock had found a champion's courage and put Archie Sexton away. As the *Manchester Evening Chronicle* reported the next day "McAvoy's enormous punch would have staggered a rhinoceros!"

As a standing ovation greeted the result, a relieved Jock waved to the adoring crowd. His performance in the tenth round proving to any doubters that not only could he deliver when needed, but he had also proved he could take an almighty punch too, ride it and still have enough left to destroy his opponent; the measure of a true champion. It was a tough but memorable night under the King's Hall lights, for the boy from Burnley, who loved a scrap.

The year of 1934 saw Jock seeing off all pretenders to his British title with a ruthlessness that could not be ignored and soon it became clear that a world title shot was only a matter of time. Jock's credentials were confirmed after he demolished the much-lauded Cuban fighter 'Kid' Tunero, in seven brutal rounds at a sold out, rocking Belle Vue on 3rd December. Their boy had arrived on the world scene with a devastating display, Tunero was the real deal. A tall gangly fighter, who was lightning fast around the ring with movie star looks and sublime boxing skills, Tunero was expected to 'school' the ill-disciplined brawler McAvoy. Tunero's own confidence when asked what may happen in the fight showed he had no idea who or what lay in wait for him in Manchester. "I have won forty-eight fights out of fifty-two and never been knocked out. In fact, I have never even taken a count. I am going to destroy your guy McAvoy," he told the assembled press.

In the event Tunero wholly underestimated his opponent and was blown away. He found himself up against a man on a mission as from the first bell and backed with a vociferous Mancunian crowd, Jock set to work. Despite using all his formidable prowess to keep the Englishman at bay, Tunero was finally felled in the seventh with an almighty left uppercut, first practised in a ramshackle Rochdale barn and fine-tuned to perfection in Collyhurst. Showing huge courage Tunero, though glassy-eyed and staggering, got back to his feet to beat the count at eight - only to be dropped once more by Jock, who was so convinced it was over that he returned to his corner and sat on his stool. As the King's Hall crowd roared and readied to hail a stunning victory for their man, the brave Cuban once more made it back to his feet, hauling himself up by the ropes. Tunero's cornerman attempted to throw in the towel but disaster struck when it simply sailed through the ropes and landed outside the ring. Cue another unadulterated slaughter as the referee ordered the men to 'box on!' Jock shook his head, but was left with no choice than to butcher the defiant Tunero into submission. It was a dreadful decision from the referee and the Cuban was a bloodied mess as Jock finally put him through the ropes to end the contest knocking his opponent out cold in the process. It was brutal and beautiful, boxing at its best and worst. The next day, wearing his other hat as a journalist, Norman Hurst wrote in the *Sporting Chronicle* that Jock was 'The world's greatest Middleweight.' The gauntlet had been thrown down to the Yanks.

Drawn to the chance of earning a quick buck, promoter Dave Lumiansky was soon promising Jock that elusive American title shot. Already managing Jackie Brown, Lumiansky acted quickly the moment Jock's contract with Harry Fleming ran down. Once signed, he set about plotting a route for his new man to break America. Lumiansky needed exposure for Jock and there was nowhere better than the cathedral of boxing. Madison Square Garden. It would prove the perfect setting to introduce Jock to American audiences.

Jock arrived in New York in early November 1935. For a kid from the modest hill towns of Lancashire, The Big Apple in the 30s must have been quite a sight. The city's magnificent skyscrapers that reached high into the sky, almost touching the heavens. In comparison Manchester would have looked like a village.

Lumiansky arranged for Jock to train at the notorious Pioneer gym on 42nd Street. Every day it was packed with young gifted fighters. Kids of all creeds and colours would descend on the gym; all were desperate to catch the eye of the trainers and promoters hungry for that one shot that could give them a chance at greatness and change their lives forever. Here Jock kept his own council, never one for mixing business with pleasure, he just trained and concentrated on being ready when called upon to enter one of the gym's four rings. Surrounded by moody faces and cold stares Jock was never the sort to be intimidated, he would simply glare back, refusing to back down. Realising this was not someone to mess with, the gym regulars eventually gave up, smile and shake their heads.

"Just who the hell is this damn Limey?"

Finally, Jock's turn came and curiosity got the better of the denizens of the Pioneer gym as they gathered to watch this mean sonofabitch from across the Atlantic. Dave Lumiansky had spread the word and the fighters were joined by New York's finest boxing writers and newspapermen. Now his man had to deliver. Unlike the Americans, Jock was never one to use headgear and gumshields while sparring. Initially he refused them, but Lumiansky pleaded with him and Jock relented on the headgear, though to the astonishment of all present, refused point blank on the gumshield. His first opponent in the ring was a tough Irish fighter called Ray Finnegan who had a reputation as a decent scrapper. At the call of 'time' both went hell for leather and straight away Jock caught Finnegan with a vicious left hook that floored him. Murmurs went around the gym. Could it have been a one off?

Out went a dazed Finnegan and in came a New Yorker, a no nonsense, tough character named Dan Lyons. Both went tearing into each other but it was Jock landing the better of the punches, utterly outclassing and clearly hurting Lyons. Finally, 'time' was called once more to save the American before he was knocked clean out. The 'Rochdale Thunderbolt' was just warming up!

"Who's next then?" went the shout from Jock! In a tough, almost, impenetrable Lancashire accent that the locals down on 42nd Street struggled to fully understand.

With American pride at stake another local fighter Gordon Donoghue was urged to "Glove up and test this Limey". Donoghue was a Light Heavyweight and within seconds his power showed as he floored an unsuspecting Jock. Cheers went up around the ring.

"He's just like all the rest from over there," shouted out a reporter to huge guffaws.

Fuming with himself, Jock ripped off the headgear and charged his opponent. His foul temper was evident as he spat, raged and snarled insults whilst simultaneously pummelling a ragged, hurting Donoghue into submission. As the right upper cuts and short left hooks flew the big man was soon reeling. 'Time' was called and a sense of disbelief fell over the gym. Jock stood there with every eye upon him. There was no doubt this 'Limey' was the real deal. Dave Lumiansky stood nearby with the newspaper men wearing a huge grin.

"That gentlemen..." he pronounced, "Is Jock McAvoy!"

With part of his masterplan completed, Lumiansky embarked on phase two of the operation which was to get Jock in the ring with New York native Eddie 'Babe' Risko, the reigning Middleweight champion of the world. Later that night Lumiansky invited Jock to dinner, but was a little reluctant to tell him too much about it. Finally, as they stepped out of the cab, the promoter beckoned Jock into Jack Dempsey's joint down on Broadway and a lifetime ambition was achieved when Lumiansky arranged for the former champion to meet an unusually shy Jock!

"I've heard a lot of really good things about you," Dempsey told Jock, "keep it up". The pair shook hands and for once the mask fell from Jock's face and he was a teenager again – stood back in his broken-down barn, posing in front of a mirror as his hero, 'The Manassa Mauler'. With one dream now realised, it was time to work on the next.

Whilst attempting to negotiate his way to the table for Risko, something else quite expectantly fell into Lumiansky's lap – an eliminator for the Light Heavyweight championship of the world with the guarantee of a title shot against the great champion John Henry Lewis the following year. Although only a Middleweight, this was an opportunity Jock simply could not turn down and such was his ego and confidence at the time he would have been confident of knocking out King Kong.

Canadian-born Al McCoy was rightly regarded as one of the best Light-Heavyweights in the world. This was an outstanding opponent with a formidable record that included only one defeat. McCoy was being ducked by every top Light-Heavyweight in the States, but typically, Jock's attitude was simple - "I'll fight anyone, anywhere, anytime."

Few gave Jock a chance, especially with the weight difference, however, after lengthy negotiations with the legendary New York promoter Jimmy Johnson, the fight was scheduled for Madison Square Garden, but the downside was that Jock's problems with his fists had resurfaced again. Now, when training, he could only use his left and had to save his right. Come fight night against McCoy, on 29th November, 1935, Jock's hands were worse than ever. Only a couple of hours before he was set to enter the ring at Madison Square Garden, Lumiansky arranged for an injection to ease his boxer's pain. A well-dressed suited gentleman in a trilby and carrying a briefcase entered Jock's dressing room and introduced himself as a doctor and in a straight forward, typical New York manner told him to place his right hand palm downwards on the rubbing table, before producing a rather disturbing looking hypodermic syringe. At first appearing a little wary Lumiansky nodded toward Jock putting him at ease. Relenting, he did so and before Jock could even flinch, the doctor jabbed the needle into the back of his knuckles and injected him with Novocaine. Suddenly, there was a loud scream and Jock collapsed, unconscious! The syringe had accidentally hit a nerve and floored him. For the first time in his career McAvoy was out cold! Panic ensued: it was an alarming episode before Jock's dream fight at the legendary home of boxing. After being brought back round with the help of smelling salts, he partook in a spot of shadow boxing and within seconds was back to his growling, snarling self. Meanwhile the doctor bid a hasty retreat, Lumiansky crossed himself with relief and Jock McAvoy prepared for the biggest contest of his career!

As referee Arthur Donovan called the fighters together before a packed Garden, Jock realised that this was his audition for an American audience and he didn't disappoint. It was a stunning display in which Jock, in his all action Dempsey style, overwhelmed the much taller Al McCoy, relying on countless devastating left hooks that rocked the Canadian. Bobbing, weaving, hitting inside with killer shots, this was Jock at the peak of his powers. Even when the painkiller eased off and the numbness in the right hand ceased, it made little difference as Jock hunted McCoy down remorselessly. By the finish he had earned a clear point's decision over his battered, bleeding and shell-shocked opponent as the Garden rose to its feet. The American newspapermen christened Jock 'A small Jack Dempsey.' This was the culmination of Jock's boyhood dreams.

There were some in the New York fight fraternity who played down his achievements claiming McCoy had been forced to lose a lot of weight on the day of the fight and was drained. Among these were those in the 'Babe' Risko camp, they feared little in the Limey's showing that would trouble their man. To them it was nothing more than a freak result. Contact was made with Lumiansky, but this was a long way from Collyhurst. Things were done differently in the 'Big Apple'.

Born Paolo Giovanni Carbo on New York's Lower East Side, 'Frankie' Carbo had graduated from being a hitman for the mob to become one of the most important figures in racketeering. An affable guy on the surface, he was once described as 'One of the nicest killers you could ever meet.' Come 1936, Carbo had moved up the ranks and it was an open secret within New York boxing circles that he controlled not just Risko, but a number of top American fighters. On meeting with Lumiansky, Carbo, along with leading mob boss, the cigar smoking Gabe Genovese (one of the heads of the five New York families) made it clear they would allow the fight to be sanctioned on the understanding that the title was not at stake. The three men struck a deal. Initially Jock was infuriated, but Lumiansky made him see that despite there being no belt at stake, this was one time when it didn't matter as everyone would recognise the winner as the true Middleweight champion of the world. Jock took this on board and prepared for the defining fight of his career, for not only would he be up against a superb fighter like Risko and his home town crowd, but he'd also be taking on the Italian mob.

So back to that snowy December night in 1935, just three weeks after the epic dismantling of Al McCoy. As Jock prepared to enter the ring once more at Madison Square Garden, for his date with destiny and Henry Pylkowski, or as he was better known Eddie 'Babe' Risko. This was a fine champion. Born in Syracuse of Polish-Lithuanian parents, Risko was a huge favourite with the bookies, boxing critics and the hordes of mobsters who filled up the front rows at ringside with gorgeous, glamorous 'dames' alongside them. It was the hottest ticket in town, the famous and the infamous mixed openly. Cameras flashed and photographers could not believe their luck; movie stars, singers, politicians, past champions (including Jack Dempsey) chatted openly with New York's own royalty - the mob. The atmosphere was electric. The leading lights of the Cosa Nostra were there to watch their boy take care of business, but little did they realise that as a blizzard swept across the city, heading their way was an equally ferocious storm from the faraway Lancashire hills. Jock would hit New York like a 'Rochdale Thunderbolt'.

As the Garden's spotlights dimmed and the cigar smoke drifted upwards, that sense of heart-in-mouth expectation before any great fight took hold. A roar went up and a cascade of noise rose for Risko. The New York crowd, like the Belle Vue one, would go to war for their man. A sense of excitement hung over the Garden, laced with an unhealthy dose of over-confidence. The referee Charlie Cavanagh called both fighters toward him. If Jock was nervous on this, his biggest stage, he was not showing it. The old ritual of biting his thumbs was mocked by some sections of the crowd. Little did they know. The fighters touched gloves, the bell sounded and one of the most savage and brutal opening rounds in boxing history began.

Almost immediately Jock caught Risko on the jaw with an enormous right that sent him crashing to the canvas with a sickening jolt. Bedlam reigned in the Garden. Gangsters looked at each other with disbelief. Jock's corner screamed at him to finish it, Lumiansky's

58

voice being the loudest! He needed to strike there and then because more chance existed of Jock becoming an opera singer than winning a points decision in The Garden. Jock stood, growling and cursing at Risko. "Get up!" he yelled. Though clearly still hurting, back came the champ to try and take the fight to Jock, only to immediately walk into a deadly hail of body and head shots. Down again! Jock simply had too much strength, movement and class for the New Yorker. He was ruthless. A third time Risko rose to be met by a shower of left hooks and a devastating right that floored him. The Garden was in uproar, their champ was being taken apart. On Risko's fourth effort, he staggered to his feet and tried to grab hold of Jock, who simply brushed him off, before sending him falling to the floor! There were scenes of mayhem at ringside, people screaming and raising their fists at this crazy 'Limey' who simply had not read the script. A fifth knockdown swiftly followed before finally a crashing right hand delivered like a jack hammer put Risko out for the count! He had not been allowed to throw a single punch and it had been nothing short of carnage. Watching on in open-mouthed silence most of the audience were dumbfounded. They simply could not believe what had gone on.

A fuming Genovese and Carbon immediately turned on the Garden's matchmaker Jimmy Johnson. "Are you f----g nuts Jimmy? Where did you find this f----g guy!" Scared and poker-faced, Johnson was at a loss for words and could only mutter, almost to himself, "Some goddamn place called Collyhurst."

As Jock's hand was raised in victory by the referee, a smattering of applause was heard throughout this headquarters of professional boxing. In Jock's dressing room, the machine-gun mouthed Lumiansky was holding court with the doyens of American boxing writers. Scribbling ten to the dozen on their note pads, dressed to kill in smart suits, fancy trilbies, shiny shoes and with the obligatory cigarette hanging from the corner of mouths, the main question on all their lips was "Would Jock now get a return fight with the champ for the world title?" Lumiansky explained that he would be speaking to Risko's people and demand that it was only sporting and proper they give Jock a shot.

That same evening to celebrate the win Jock and Lumiansky went out to celebrate in one of New York's top restaurants. As they settled down to eat Lumiansky noticed a badly bruised Risko sat across the room with Carbon and Genovese. A warm wave and an exchange of smiles followed before Lumiansky informed Jock he was going over to speak about a rematch for the title. Despite Jock telling him it was far too early, explaining that perhaps Risko's wounds were too fresh, Lumiansky headed over. A wary Jock watched on as the conversation suddenly became animated with his manager becoming loud and angry, only for the loudmouth Lumiansky to suddenly go unusually quiet, stand up and walk back toward him. Ashen-faced, shaken and refusing to tell Jock about what had occurred, the pair decided to forget the meal and head off. It was only the next day that Lumiansky admitted that after shouting the odds against Risko, Genovese and Carbon, he felt something poke him beneath the table. On looking down Lumiansky saw Carbo was pointing a pistol!

Boxing folklore has it that at this point Jock and Lumiansky were all but run out of New York by the mob following his stunning victory and told never to mention a rematch again. It appears that night Lumiansky, in typical argumentative style, had simply agitated too far. Word was sent that the chances of Jock fighting Risko for his world crown were zero. Such was their power at the time, the mob would never allow a rematch. Jock was simply too good. So, was Jock robbed out of the ring? Maybe, but at the time all true boxing critics and those inside the sport knew that Jock McAvoy was the world champion in all but name. A king without a crown, but a king nonetheless. That night in New York City, as the blizzard roared, would in many ways come to be Jock's legacy.

However, that was not the end of his adventures in the States, for there remained the promise of a fight against the great champion John Henry Lewis for the World Light Heavyweight Title. The difference in weight was regarded as a mere hindrance to Jock, although the reccurring problem with his damaged fists remained. As ever with Jock, controversy would rage. Determined to keep his man's name in the headlines, Lumiansky was left with little choice but to gamble and put Jock in against two top rated American Heavyweights – Jim Smith and Anson Green in Philadelphia.

Though it was two wins gained, with a knockout and points decision respectively, both were only achieved under extreme pain and the damage caused to Jock's already tortured hands was immeasurable. They were wrecked. With the Green fight taking place only weeks before the showdown against Lewis, there was little time for recuperation. Come the night of the fight at Madison Square Garden, Jock was still in agony. Again, he was injected with novocaine, but it proved to be only a temporary reprieve. Details of Jock's pre-fight chemical assistance was secretly relayed to Lewis's manager John Greenlees, a shrewd old school operator who then deliberately held up the bout for an hour to ensure the pain-killer wore off before the fight.

In reality, John Henry Lewis may not have required such an advantage, for here was an all-time great champion. Fighting as ever with a huge heart, incredible courage and enduring terrible pain, Jock continually took the contest to Lewis. The champion was badly cut and at times rocked by his power, despite every punch being thrown leaving Jock reeling in agony. Lewis was always that little bit faster and slicker, he used the ring to perfection and constantly picked Jock off with stinging counter shots. Ultimately, as the last bell rang, Lewis won a tight fifteen-round contest on points to retain his title. Post-fight, Jock refused to complain about the verdict. "Lewis deserved to win. Good luck to him, he's a great champion, but if my hands had been okay I might have done him."

At ringside, a doctor examined Jock's hands and found there were no broken bones, but was shocked at the severe inflammation. His recommendation was a spell out of the ring for six months. The look given to him by Jock meant such a prescription was likely to be ignored. That night the curtain came down on his American Odyssey, this was to be his last fight in the states, but typically, just six weeks later, Jock was challenging the champion Jack Petersen in London for the British Heavyweight title.

It was the silver-tongued Lumiansky who persuaded Jock to take on the Welshman. Upon his arrival, back in Collyhurst, Harry Fleming examined his former fighter and was appalled at the state of his hands. Fleming begged Jock to take a proper break. He also spoke out against him fighting Peterson, for he was giving away over twenty pounds in weight and several inches in height and reach. This was an enormous disadvantage even against an average fighter, but even more so against such a brilliant opponent as Petersen. Fleming thought it was absolutely crazy. Jock listened to his old mentor, but wouldn't change his mind.

The lucrative sum of £4000 on offer meant he simply had no choice. The American tour, although sending his reputation soaring, saw little return in terms of financial gains. Lumiansky had blamed rip-off merchants and expenses, so when the offer to fight Peterson arrived, Jock jumped at it. It would prove to be an inauspicious return.

On 23rd April, 1936, at Earls Court, Empress Hall, Kensington, the British public saw Jock fail to overcome the much larger Petersen. He laboured throughout, even being dropped for an eight count in the fifteenth round. The champion retained his crown on points, although the crowd booed following a dour contest. It was clear his damaged hands and absurdly busy American schedule had taken a heavy toll. Jock had left something in America that was lost forever. The 'Rochdale Thunderbolt' would never again be the same fighter who once rocked the Big Apple and destroyed Eddie 'Babe' Risko.

There would be other memorable fights, none more dramatic or brutal than a year later on 27th April 1937, at the Empire Pool, Wembley, when Jock added to his British Middleweight title by knocking out the Light Heavyweight champion Eddie Philips in the fourteenth round. It was a remarkable performance that showed despite the problems with his hands, the fire within still burnt brightly enough for Jock to bite down on those thumbs and raise hell. What followed shortly after that fight though almost curtailed his career.

Jock had taken to riding horses at Woodhall's Farm in Cheadle Hulme. One day, whilst out on his thoroughbred steeplechaser, Jock was involved in a horrific accident when the horse stumbled and sent him hurtling through the air. The first diagnosis was a broken back, but it later transpired to be just severely damaged. Jock had landed on his neck causing terrible injury to the muscles. It was said by the doctors treating him that only his superb physical condition and sheer determination to fight again saved him from being permanently paralysed.

Though this was clearly the beginning of the end, just six months later Jock was back in the ring, against all advice to defend his British Middleweight title against old foe Jack Hyams. A capacity King's Hall crowd watched nervously to see what Jock had left. Unsurprisingly, after so long out, it was a sluggish start by the champion, but slowly as the rounds wore on he caught up with Hyams and a ferocious barrage in the eleventh left the London taxi driver battered, down and ultimately

out. Thirty-year-old Jock now had another Lonsdale Belt to go with
the one he had won outright. This, along with the Light Heavyweight
title, was a remarkable haul. Jock ultimately lost this to Len Harvey as
they fought twice more, but would end his career as undefeated British
Middleweight champion. He was simply a class apart but in the end
Jock came up against an unbeatable enemy that in the end brought even
the greats to their knees – Father Time.

Jock's world remained turbulent even in retirement. Three marriages,
countless scrapes with the law and his awkward and abrasive character
meant life was never dull. Jock officially retired from the ring in 1945,
but the magic had waned long before. Like so many boxers, whether
simply journeymen or world champions, once the final bell on their
career sounded, what followed was a drop into the abyss of normal life
few found it easy to deal with. Jock had several run-ins with the law and
narrowly avoided jail following a cheque fraud incident. However, the
biggest blow came when at just thirty-nine years old he contracted polio
and lost the use of his legs. Confined to a wheelchair, yet still a relatively
young man, Jock was unable to work and became bitterly depressed.
After the money earned from his career dwindled to a pittance, he
was reduced to selling postcards of himself in his fighting prime on
Blackpool promenade. Life turned irretrievably for the worse when a
tragic drug overdose killed his youngest son Jackie. This broke Jock's
heart and many thought he lost the will to live. On 20th November,
1971, Jock's 64th birthday, he killed himself just eight months after one
of his closest friends, Jackie Brown, had also passed away.

In 2003, the bible of boxing, *Ring Magazine*, listed Jock as one of the
100 hardest punchers of all time, but there were many who disagreed,
for those who remembered him claimed no one hit harder. Ultimately,
Jock never won the one honour he so desperately craved, but that night
in New York City, as a blizzard raged across the 'Big Apple' and a packed
Madison Square Garden watched on in awe as Jock demolished Eddie
'Babe' Risko, that would always be his world title.

Not all champions need a crown.

5 - JOHNNY KING

LONG LIVE THE KING

The far off South China Sea is perhaps a strange place to begin for a story about a Collyhurst boxer but when that man is Johnny King, it will all soon make sense. Twenty-nine-year-old able-seaman King was on board HMS Prince of Wales on 10th December 1941 when it was sunk off the east coast of Malaya by Japanese torpedoes and bombs. When the call went up to abandon ship and the order "Every man for himself" was given, King jumped overboard and survived in oil-filled, shark-infested waters for ninety minutes before being picked up by another destroyer, The HMS Express. A total of 327 men were lost that horrific day on the Prince of Wales. Johnny was one of the lucky few who managed to survive to tell the tale. One can only imagine the thoughts in his head as he clung on for dear life to a piece of wreckage as sharks circled nearby. No doubt Johnny's mind drifted back home to the place where he was born on Angel Street, in Collyhurst, just off Rochdale Road.

JOHNNY KING came into this world on 12th January, 1912, and he was brought up only a stone's throw away from Jackie Brown. However, their paths may never have crossed if events when Johnny was still in infancy had turned out differently. As World War One broke out in 1914, Johnny's father, Henry, a tall strapping man with a good head for business, decided to make the most out of what was a truly terrible scenario. Knowing it was only a matter of time before he was called up for national service, Henry worked out an idea of moving to Canada. His reasoning was that while British 'Tommies' received only a shilling a day, Canadian soldiers were much better rewarded. Henry's plan was to go first and when settled send for his wife and three children, Johnny, Henry and Edith.

Once word was received they packed a few belongings and set sail, only for the ship to be torpedoed by a German U Boat halfway across the Atlantic. It was an horrific experience for the family, but fortunately they survived and were rescued by a nearby Royal Navy vessel. Finally, the King's reached their destination and settled in Toronto. Henry was soon sent to fight as the children went to a local school. The years passed and as the slaughter of a generation continued in distant far off Europe, Johnny, despite being not just the smallest boy in school, but the neighbourhood, developed an early love of boxing. A constant pleading to his Mother asking when would he grow, was always met with a kind stroking of Johnny's hair and being told, "Don't worry Johnny dear. When you start you won't stop!"

Come 1918, the guns fell silent and those in uniform fortunate enough to have survived the carnage returned home. Henry received his discharge papers but instead of returning to Canada, he went back to England. Before war began Henry had invested in a couple of lodging houses in Rochdale. Once the business was up and running he sent word for his wife and children to join him. Now Henry, as already stated, was a huge bear of a man, over six-foot six. On seeing Johnny again, he was shocked at his size. Also, the boy was an asthmatic and in those times there was little medication for the ailment. Already undersize for his age, to Johnny and Henry's dismay there was no sign of him growing any bigger. Yet Henry could do nothing but admire his son's love of boxing and his adoration, similar to that of a young Jock McAvoy, of 'The Manassa Mauler' Jack Dempsey. Henry took it upon himself to encourage Johnny in the sport. He knew in time his son would have to deal with cruel taunts in regards to his size and health. An unexpected punch in the face was the perfect response to a bully, especially with an audience. Many tried picking on young Johnny King, but they only did it once. The guarantee of a bloodied nose and teary eyes meant he was soon left alone, despite being just knee high to a plant pot.

Johnny soon found his heaven on earth in the form of a gym in Holland Street, Rochdale, run by a man called Mr Platt. By his early teenage years Johnny would make this place a second home. At first Mr Platt refused to entertain him. "You're far too young and too small, lad. Come back when you're older and bigger and I'll make you a member." These words hurt Johnny, but despite being a mere slip of a kid, it occurred to him that if he could afford the membership, then there was no way that a fair-minded soul like Mr Platt would say no again. Johnny came up with a plan that included his grandfather. He would be paid a shilling (5p) a week to clean his hall passage. This covered the gym fee and Johnny King happily handed over the money to a smiling Mr Platt who, admiring the young boy's work ethic and huge determination, finally relented.

"In you come lad. Don't touch owt unless I tell ya!" he told him.

Thin and puny and like a shadow on the wall, Johnny was allowed to practice in a quiet corner and when it was available, allowed use of the speedball or pound gamefully away at the punch bag. In his mind Johnny was becoming the Heavyweight champion of the world, Jack Dempsey; hammering and putting away his opponents in quick order.

It soon became obvious to Mr Platt and others around the gym that Johnny had not just enthusiasm, but real promise. In no time at all he was ushered from his corner to spar with other boxers. There was another local kid at the gym who in style and attitude, both in and out of the ring, was a completely different animal to Johnny, but who was viewed as a real prospect. His name was Joe Bamford and there was already a lot of expectant talk about him in local boxing circles. Here was someone who turned heads and took those of his opponents off their shoulders. He was a ferocious fighter; brutal and terrifying at times. When sparring, Bamford knew only one way to fight. He was forever attempting to land a killer blow. An all-attacking, bobbing and weaving, Dempsey style brawler with punches that, if they connected, would have laid little Johnny King out cold. Wary of this, Johnny learned fast. He developed a lightning ability to move will 'o' the wisp like around the ring in a hit and run style. The bouts between the two became fascinating encounters and the gym would come to a halt to watch whenever the pair came together. Snappy, clever and brave, Johnny was turning heads as he took on the boy who would very shortly become the formidable Jock McAvoy, arguably the finest British Middleweight of all time.

Off his own back Johnny decided it was time to take the next step and at fourteen he had a first professional fight. Not daring to risk his mother and father saying no, Johnny, like he did with Mr Platt, ultimately wore down the famous promoter, Joe Tolley. Being aware of Johnny's father and his fiery temper, Tolley did not fancy upsetting him, so initially refused. However, forever the hard-headed businessman, there were now too many people whose word he trusted telling him that the boy was special and this, allied to Johnny even offering to fight for no purse, was enough to convince him. A bout was arranged against a local lad from Royton, Sid Longworthy. Come the fight, Tolley watched on in disbelief as Johnny with his left jab lead, moved and boxed beautifully to win handsomely on points. A crowd who first jeered at Johnny's small stature and thought this to be a mismatch, were on their feet cheering and applauding him at the finish. A star was born. Word got back to Henry King of his son's exploits and Johnny's worries about him being angry could not have been more wrong, for there was no prouder father in all of Lancashire. So much so that Henry began to train Johnny himself by setting up a makeshift gym in one of his lodging houses. Though lacking in expertise, Henry's head for business was put to good use and in order to find Johnny sparring partners, he offered a free bed for the night, provided they lasted three rounds with his son. If not, they would have to pay. This was still a post-war world of economic depression where homeless men were desperate for work and a roof over their heads, so there were no shortage of takers. Johnny learned fast and hard in those bouts, he perfected his hit and run technique against bakers, butchers and candlestick makers - brawlers all.

There were also regular battles in the bear-pit atmosphere of the travelling blood tubs where, for a penny, fists fights were open to all. Here Johnny, with his father in the corner, boxed many times all over Lancashire against bigger and heavier opponents. It didn't matter who they were, whatever the size or quality, whether the opponent was murderous or meek, a local tear-away or a drunken brute, they were all taken apart and beaten by this frail, skinny looking kid with the waspish jab, frightening speed and barrels of courage. However, Johnny soon needed more, and with his father being not much more than a cheerleader, Johnny knew he could only take him so far. Luckily for young King there was to be an angel on his shoulder, his card had already been marked

In 1927, aged fifteen, he fought at Salford's Adelphi Sporting club against a lad from Collyhurst, Tommy McLeish, a much taller and heavier opponent. In McLeish's corner was none other than Harry

Fleming and after Johnny had beaten his fighter, he decided to act. Harry visited Johnny in the dressing room and invited him to join his Collyhurst stable. It was explained to Henry that interference would not be tolerated and, wanting only the best for his son, Johnny's father had no qualms at handing his son's boxing education into Mr Fleming's care. A delighted Johnny swiftly agreed and he was now in the finest of hands, Collyhurst hands. What he thought once was only make believe, had suddenly become a reality.

In the early days Johnny would make the twelve-mile journey three times a week from the family home in Rochdale by bus, but in time he preferred to cycle. Johnny loved life in the decrepit, broken-down old building that passed itself off as a gym. It was hard to believe that such a hovel would soon produce a host of British and world champions. The friendly atmosphere that existed between those four dilapidated walls was fostered by Fleming and trainer Jack Bates. It was damned hard work, but there would always be time for a laugh and a joke. Bad eggs were not tolerated and if there were suspicions about one of the boxers he was cracked down on fast and warned, "Behave or else!" Quiet, always polite, conscientious and a demon trainer, Johnny soon became a popular figure. He grew close to another boxer, just three years older than him, who had been at the gym for twelve months already. Local and of Irish decent, handsome, cocky and full of life, he would greet you with a wink and smile. This kid walked with a Collyhurst swagger, talented beyond his years and talked of by Fleming and Bates as the boy who was destined for the stars. He went by the name of Jackie Brown.

At that time both King and Brown were Flyweights and often did their roadwork and sparring together. Jackie was not above teasing Johnny, but it was never done in a cruel or mocking way. Despite being very different characters, the pair became inseparable. The streetwise Jackie and Johnny the 'yonner' from the hills of far off Rochdale, made for an unlikely pair, but they were blood brothers. It would only be in later years, when the relationship soured, that a fierce emnity would emerge.

Harry Fleming always suspected that Johnny had decent potential, but it was only after Jack Bates had worked closely with the boy that they realised how good he really was. There were rough edges to polish and Bates spent countless hours teaching Johnny the finer arts of ring craft. Skills that would help him survive in the midst of battle. Only when he considered Johnny ready to represent the Collyhurst colours did Bates pass word to Fleming that the time was right and Johnny King's journey into Mancunian boxing folklore could begin.

In order to perfect his craft Fleming decided that at this stage of Johnny's career, the best classroom was out on the road and in the ring. The fights came thick and fast, as did the plaudits. Johnny was turning heads, a real crowd pleaser. Lightning fast, he could slip a punch and hit and though still very small in stature, in boxing venues such as the Blackpool Tower circus, before 4000 fans, he excelled. The wins mounted, but of course there were also occasional defeats as Fleming matched him with experienced pros who knew their way around the ring over six rounds. Johnny soaked up everything. Each loss hit him hard and would see him return to the gym first thing next morning correcting any defects in his technique. Bates adored him, perhaps because he was not born with natural disadvantages, but made up for what he lacked with hard work. One thing that did come God given was a right cross that Bates recognised as a truly deadly weapon. He taught Johnny that you didn't neccessarily need bulging muscles to knock people over; balance and timing were equally important as power. Although he came alive inside the ring, outside it Johnny remained painfully shy. He could hardly read or write, spoke with a stammer and when interviewed by newspapermen, unlike his charismatic friend Jackie Brown, Johnny struggled to answer questions or get his point across. Yet he was loved around the gym and Johnny was by now making a real name for himself, to the extent that Fleming decided to up the ante and bring in some world class competition from overseas.

On 3rd November 1930, at the King's Hall, Belle Vue, Johnny took on the emerging Algerian, Victor Young Perez. Later Perez, who is already covered in an earlier chapter, would become world champion, only to lose the title to Jackie Brown at this same venue. Here was an opponent who would truly test how far Johnny had come and on the night Perez boxed magnificently, only to many people's surprise see a draw called. His corner was in uproar and Johnny, clearly second best, was deemed lucky not to lose. However, mitigating circumstances made boxing irrelevant for just three days earlier a distraught Johnny had buried his mother. Devastated at the loss, it was only at the insistence of his father, Henry, who maintained she would have wanted her son to fight, that Harry Fleming did not postpone the contest. Having said that, Henry Senior was too upset to attend, it was Johnny's brother Henry, watching at ringside through tears, who was there for him. When the pair spoke afterwards, a sobbing Johnny admitted that throughout, with Perez gunning for him, he couldn't get the image of their beloved mum out of his mind.

Johnny came roaring back and one of his most impressive performances came on 15th March 1931 when he put away the tough and hugely experienced former British Flyweight champion Bert Rigby in just two rounds at the King's Hall. Only three weeks before Rigby had lost his title to Jackie Brown in a memorable fifteen-round scrap. Jackie had warned Johnny in the week leading up to the fight to watch out as this was a man with a point to prove. Jack Bates had instructed Johnny to keep an eye on Rigby's left. "When he throws it, step inside and hit with your right." Such simple but brilliant advice was typical of Bates and Johnny carried out his order to perfection. The first round saw Rigby on top and keeping Johnny at bay quite comfortably, but the second saw King reveal the power that existed in his frail frame. Within seconds of the bell, a crashing left hook followed by a vicious right cross ended Rigby's night to send the King's Hall wild with delight. In Johnny's corner Fleming hugged Bates, whilst Jackie Brown simply smiled, "What do I bloody know?" he said to Johnny afterwards whilst congratulating him!

Collyhurst was on a roll!

With Jackie Brown ruling the roost at Flyweight and Fleming utterly opposed to him ever fighting Johnny King, he instead suggested moving up a division to Bantamweight. Johnny happily agreed and took to the new weight like a duck to water. Within no time he was fighting for the vacant Northern Area Bantamweight title. After working his way through a series of elimination bouts leaving a trail of destruction in his wake, Johnny was back at Belle Vue fighting Durham-born Pat Gorman. Though only nineteen, Johnny was already maturing into something quite unique. Perception, they claim, is everything. At first glance, it would appear a paper bag could trouble him, however within his skeletal frame lurked exceptional skill, balance, speed and energy. Yet the most extraordinary part of the King package was his power. The punches were now so devastating that he was being warned by Harry Fleming to ease up, "Just concentrate on your boxing. Stop trying to blow everyone away." A concoction of fierce self-determination to improve and the promptings of Jack Bates had created a magnificent exponent of the ring who would only get better.

On 10th June 1931, at a rip-roaring, packed King's Hall, Johnny tore into Pat Gorman for six savage rounds, before the carnage was ended by Gorman's seconds throwing in the towel. The Mancunian tortured his opponent from the off, it was a mismatch. Johnny's ability to unleash bombs whilst proving almost impossible to hit was now apparent to all. Seven times Gorman was put down in the fourth, his courage and heart unquestioned. Although bleeding profusely, Gorman simply refused to quit. Soon a staggering, bloodied mess, Johnny finally ended his opponent's gallant resistance in the sixth with a right hook that put Gorman's lights out and ignited the King's Hall. As Johnny celebrated with Harry Fleming in the ring it appeared only a matter of time before a shot at the British title would arrive. The kid from Angel Street was on his way.

On 21st December 1931 Johnny stepped into the same ring once more to challenge the flame haired, blue-eyed, bubbly cockney, Dick Corbett for the vacant British Bantamweight title. It was north versus south – the 'Cotton City' against the 'Big Smoke'. The air was electric: a packed house was ready to roar Johnny to the title. Again the Belle Vue syndicate had outbid all others to ensure one of their own was given the best chance before a partisan crowd. Though not a devastating puncher, Corbett was a class act. A technically superb defensive fighter and fast with a snappy left jab, he impressed on the counter, was ultra-slick and forever on his toes. Ultimately, over fifteen rounds, Corbett outclassed Johnny on the night and was a deserved winner. Constantly slipping his right, making Johnny lose balance and appear clumsy at times, he dominated the contest. A late rally gave the home town crowd some hope but by the end there could be no argument and the Londoner was given a sporting round of applause. Johnny was more embarrassed than disappointed at the finish. Standing in the corner at the end of the fight he was approached by a smiling Ted Broadribb, Corbett's manager who shook his hand, "Don't be too disheartened, son," he said, before adding with a huge grin, "You will win it one day, but not whilst our Dickie is around." As Jack Bates prepared to rip his head off, Johnny put an arm on the trainer to calm him, "We shall see about that Mr Broadribb," he replied with a slight smile. "Have a safe trip back to London and Merry Christmas!"

The next day Harry Fleming met with a downcast Johnny and told him it was time to get back on the road and make some money. He promised that a rematch with Corbett would happen in time, but first he had to maintain his position as Britain's second-best Bantamweight. Over the next months Johnny won ten consecutive bouts before he earned his re-match with Corbett.

The re-match, on 10th October 1932, was again at the King's Hall. The Manchester public again held its collective breath as the boys from Collyhurst and Bethnal Green entered the ring. The Londoners had arrived in Manchester brimming with confidence; they were cocky, arrogant in their belief that victory was certain. Corbett handed over his Lord Lonsdale belt to British boxing officials with a smile and wink, "Keep your eye on that I'll be back for it soon!"

For Johnny the pain and manner of defeat last time around had left him reeling but determined to avenge matters in a rematch. Johnny, Jack Bates and Harry Fleming had retreated to the Paley Street gym and hammered out a strategy to take down Corbett. Newspapermen had complained about a lack of access to the challenger, but their complaints fell on deaf ears. From day one Johnny's concentration was intense. Bates worked endlessly with him on ironing out mistakes made first time out. He based his training on Johnny staying on the front foot and taking the fight constantly to Corbett. Previously he felt Johnny had shown the Londoner far too much respect. It could not be allowed to happen again.

Come the last day of training Johnny was in the shape of his life and knocked a sparring partner clean out. A nod to Fleming from a smiling Bates spoke volumes. He was ready.

In a classic fifteen-round encounter Johnny King overwhelmed Dick Corbett to become British Bantamweight champion. It was a memorable performance from first bell to last that would live long in the memory as Johnny, a study in perpetual motion, didn't allow Corbett a second's respite. A left hook caught him on the chin in round two that left the Londoner staggering but unbowed. A brave champion,

Corbett found himself outfought by the return of the King. Belle Vue roared as the Mancunian air, thick with cigarette and cigar smoke, was gripped with anticipation. The northern storm blew the Londoner away as Johnny boxed skilfully with a huge heart, winning the contest well on points. The decision was greeted with delight by the King's Hall crowd as Manchester saluted their new champion. A tearful Fleming embraced Johnny and amid the cheering and excitement shouted loud into his ear, "This is just the start Johnny. Now we go for a world title!"

The Corbett camp quickly demanded a rematch but despite Johnny willingness, Fleming insisted they wait the statutory six to ten months. He was annoyed at some comments emerging from the London camp saying that Johnny had been lucky. King was too much of a gentleman to bite back but Fleming told them to show some respect and earn their rematch. Instead Harry plotted a course set to reap the rich dividends of Johnny's success which would put the champ on the road and let him make some money.

Because of Johnny's Spartan lifestyle, he very rarely suffered the injuries and illnesses that affected others in the Collyhurst gym. Johnny always managed to steer clear of colds, boils, cut eyes and bad hands and this, allied to his exceptional if under-rated defensive skills, enabled him to become one of the busiest fighters of the era. Johnny would box non-title bouts on average twice a month for purses ranging from £50 to £100 and not once did he duck an opponent. Naturally thrifty, his gym mates often joked light-heartedly that Johnny was tighter than a duck's backside!

When the lads were out socialising, people like Jackie Brown thought nothing of buying a round of drinks and were not averse to being the heart and soul of a Mancunian backstreet pub singalong. He attracted attention, whereas Johnny would slide quietly into a corner with half a mild, content to enjoy the spectacle and let others take the spotlight. His stage was the ring, there the real Johnny King came alive. Now fully established as British Bantamweight champion, little did Johnny know that behind the scenes Harry Fleming was working furiously negotiating a world title shot set to go down in the annals of boxing history.

A familiar figure on the Manchester boxing scene of the 1930s was our old friend, the American promoter Dave Lumiansky. Now he approached Fleming regarding Johnny's contract. Given little encouragement he instead sought the boxer himself out. Lumiansky gave Johnny the full treatment, how the kid would win fame and fortune and fight in Madison Square Garden like his hero Jack Dempsey.

However on this occasion Lumiansky had badly underestimated Johnny's loyalty to Fleming. Theirs' was truly a father-son relationship. Johnny trusted Harry implicitly and Lumiansky's offer was politely, but firmly refused. The American was informed by Johnny he was wasting his time. Lumiansky gave up, the pair shook hands and he never darkened John's door again. Although their paths would cross soon enough for another of Lumiansky's fighters, the phenomenal Bantamweight champion of the world Panama Al Brown, was set to land in the 'Cotton City' as Harry Fleming had negotiated Johnny King the fight of his life.

Based in Paris, Brown was one of the true characters of boxing. A busy champion, he fought anyone who dared challenge him. If the money was right Brown would travel to take them on in their own backyard and usually wreak mayhem. He was fearless and utterly brilliant. Jack Bates referred to him as a 'freak' but not in a derogatory manner, for he had nothing but respect for the man from the coastal city of Colon, in Panama. At over six-foot-tall, Brown was arguably the best Bantamweight the division has ever known, a colossus with a remarkable reach. It was claimed some opponents required a rope ladder to hit his chin. Brown possessed every weapon in the book; he was extraordinarily skilful, with wonderful poise and blistering speed across the ring. His main tools were a long stiff jab that struck like a jack hammer and a stinging right cross that pulverised. Defensively, Brown was again quite phenomenal for he could simply beat opponents by staying out of striking distance and landing painful counter punches when necessary. Reckoned to be thirty-one at the time of the fight, many strong rumours existed amid newspapermen that a few years had been knocked off Brown's true age. Although there was no doubt that as Johnny prepared to face Brown, he was still very much at the peak of his powers.

Nobody outside Manchester gave the boy much hope. This was a step up in class so steep as to be deemed insurmountable. There could be only one result and many seriously feared for Johnny's safety. The fight was arranged for 3rd July 1933 at Belle Vue, but due to public demand the show was moved outdoors to the speedway stadium. It was the hottest ticket in town and spivs could name their price. Admission was three guineas ringside, while the cheapest wooden seats were 2/6d. In no time the bill was a complete sell out with a 25,000-crowd expected. Harry Fleming had delivered for Johnny: outside the ring he could do nothing more, Fleming's worries, like the rest of his fellow Mancunians, now concentrated on what was set to occur inside it.

Come the fateful day Manchester was basking in a heatwave that pushed temperatures well into the eighties. Tarmac melted and the canals filled with kids swimming and playing on the locks. Pre-fight, in Johnny's dressing room, nerves were evident. He was restless and desperate to get going. Training had gone well and Johnny was like a coiled spring. Outside the noise from the huge crowd came crashing through the walls. The echoes of home town expectations were laced with heavy doses of fear for what his daunting opponent would inflict. Jack Bates tried cracking a few jokes, but no one really laughed. Harry Fleming sat down next to Johnny and put a comforting arm around his shoulders, "Fight the man not the legend son and you'll be fine." Johnny nodded, but that was easier said than done. Fleming had spoken to the press detailing the monumental task Johnny faced, though at the same time he insisted that if, God willing, he could land the right punch then anything was possible.

Once in the ring it was clear Panama Al Brown was the coolest customer in Manchester. This was a tenth defence of his title and he appeared supremely relaxed; cocky, calm, collected and ready for business. Brown put on an impressive display of shadow-boxing before smiling, waving and even winking to the crowd. He was an extremely tall, slender figure for this weight and his physique combined with wonderful talent were the source of his longevity as champion. A sporting round of applause was his reward, for although it was felt a privilege to have such a fighter in their midst, Manchester's heart belonged to Johnny King. The referee Jack Dare stood in the centre of the ring and the bell sounded to begin hostilities. Johnny was straight into Brown who swatted him away with stinging left jabs. Every single one jolted Johnny, who was simply unable to avoid them. Round two began in similar vein before Brown, seemingly bored of proceedings, let loose a ferocious right hand that put Johnny down on the canvas with a sickening thud. A gasp of shock went around Belle Vue, their dreams and hopes short lived, the fight already over. Showing great bravery and clearly hurting, Johnny took a count of eight on his knees before standing and urging Brown towards him. As the crowd roared in relief, the champion moved in for the kill, only to be rocked by an unexpected right hander, hit with blind instinct by Johnny, that caught Brown straight on the jaw. The shot Harry Fleming had spoken of had just occurred! Suddenly Panama Al Brown was hurt and Belle Vue exploded with noise!

A dazed Brown lumbered backwards into a corner. His cornermen screamed at him to "cover up!" as bedlam reigned under Mancunian skies. Delirium filled the air. At ringside grown men roared, some prayed: by God they were witnessing a miracle! With eyes glazed, legs tottering and arms down, Brown was all but out on his feet. Fleming and Bates shouted over to Johnny to finish him! Sadly, such had been the thunderous effect of that knock down punch, he simply lacked the power and hard as Johnny tried Brown, by some divine intervention, was able to grab and hold until the bell rang. As the crowd rose to acclaim their boy, the cornermen jumped into the ring. Both fighters staggered back towards them. All eyes were on Brown - the great man appeared to have recovered, his pride hurt, perhaps he'd been a little over confident beforehand, not anymore. Johnny King was the real deal and Panama Al Brown was set for a war.

Within seconds of round three Johnny was down again. Reckless and smelling blood, he had come out looking to land bombs, but Brown's calmly measured left jabs kept him at bay before he let loose a right hook that Johnny never saw coming. Up quickly, maybe too quickly, he attempted to rip into Brown again, but the champion simply glided around the ring, proving almost impossible to hit, and striking back when the mood and necessity took him, like a cobra. As the evening drew on and stars appeared across the sky, the Mancunian kept going forward. It was a strategy laced with danger and in the fifth Johnny was bowled over once more, again he was hurt but unbowed, and up at eight. The spectators gasped, Brown's aim was unnervingly accurate. Still, Johnny went in search of that salvation punch and in the seventh he paid a heavy price again when those lacerating lefts took effect and this time Brown, seemingly becoming frustrated at Johnny's refusal to go away, attempted to hit him as he got back up. In jumped the referee and as Dare dragged Brown away to give him a warning, the angry crowd erupted and hurled abuse. It was bad enough that their boy was getting a fair doing over, they felt little need for the champion to react in such an unsporting manner. Giving Johnny a little breathing space, he survived the round, only to be dropped again in the ninth with a devastating right hook that saw him being forced to take the full count. To all present it felt just a matter of time before the referee stepped in to end the carnage. The Panamanian was simply a class, height and size above Johnny. King was being mercilessly put to the sword. In his corner Harry Fleming gave Johnny the choice. Already downed five times and still fighting on, his courage could never be doubted. Fleming and Bates urged common sense, but Johnny wanted to carry on and as the bell resonated loudly once more, Brown came forward, feinted and fired another right that caught Jonny square on his chin, only this time he stayed up!

The Belle Vue roar grew louder for it appeared Brown's power was on the wane and as a full moon shone in black northern skies, Johnny King went in search of a miracle and set about Panama Al Brown with unbelievable heart and fury. Brown held on and turned to hit and run tactics. Despite being dropped once more, Johnny came off the canvas and launched a last gasp assault forcing Brown to hold on for dear life. The champion clasped him tight in his arms like a flailing octopus. By this time the hysteria amongst the crowd caused some of the wooden seating to collapse and as bedlam continued in the ring, outside it the injured were passed above heads to waiting ambulances. Come the last bell the explosion of noise could be heard loud over the city. At just turned 11-30pm, in still scorching temperatures, referee Jack Dare raised Brown's hand to declare him victorious, but for many present on that long sweltering evening, Johnny King didn't lose, he simply ran out of time.

A weary Panama Al Brown saluted the crowd, hugged Johnny and disappeared from the ring. He had almost been broken amid the fire and furore of this Belle Vue bear pit, Brown had came so close to losing his world title but would never fight in England again. As for Johnny? He was a King without a crown perhaps, but Mancunians always remembered his efforts on that momentous night, for in their eyes,

Johnny was a champion.

After such a savage bout Fleming insisted his fighter take a complete three month break from the ring. Normally Johnny would have kicked up a huge fuss over this for boxing was all he knew, however events in his private life had changed dramatically. A very pretty local girl, Wylma Pickles, captured Johnny's heart and in a whirlwind romance after meeting her on the polished dance floor of the Ritz Ballroom, they were married at St Chad's church in New Moston. However, despite falling madly in love, the urge to fight again never left him.

A third contest to defend his British title against Dick Corbett loomed large and after a series of warm up contests, on 12th February, 1934, the pair met again at the King's Hall, Belle Vue, only this time with disastrous results for Johnny. On a night when he simply never got going, Corbett boxed skilfully on the retreat with a superb game plan to frustrate and eventually put Johnny down in the tenth round. It was a well-deserved victory for the Londoner and the title returned south. Come the end a devastated Johnny was at a loss to explain why he had not performed. Fleming defended him against accusations that his fighter was all washed up. Critics claimed that although only twenty-two, Johnny had been fighting constantly since fourteen years of age and was finished at the top level. This, allied to his brutal encounter with Panama Al Brown, meant that, according to some, we had already seen the best of him.

It was extremely hurtful to Johnny and matters hardly improved when, in his first comeback fight following Corbett, he was knocked out at Blackfriars, London by local boxer Dave Crowley - a decent fighter although nowhere near Johnny's class. Such had been the shattering effect of Crowley's punch, Fleming and Bates had to help him off the canvas and back to the dressing room. At that time a fourth encounter with Corbett to level their rivalry appeared a distant dream, but slowly Johnny recovered. A series of further fights saw a distinct improvement and on 20th August 1934, at the Clapton Greyhound track, this time in front of Dick Corbett's feisty home crowd, Johnny was unlucky not to be given the result, the fight called a draw. The title would remain with Corbett. Both fighters believed they had deserved the decision in an enthralling encounter, however neutrals present claimed Johnny had just done enough to win. Come the end, the pair shook hands and joked. After past gruelling encounters, a great respect had grown between the brash cockney and the quiet Manc.

"You'll never lick me again Johnny," smiled Corbett. "So long as I live" He was right, for although one further fight was arranged at Belle Vue, it turned into a fiasco. A struggling Corbett came to the weigh-in a full five pounds overweight and to the anger and disbelief of all, he was forced to pull out of the contest. With every ticket sold, chaos ensued that would cost Corbett a £100 forfeit and £200 to the Belle Vue syndicate for breach of contract. Considering his fee was £450, he was returning home not just at a huge loss financially and with hurt pride, but most importantly he was forced to forfeit his British title, leaving the way open for Johnny to once again have another crack at bringing the treasured belt home to Manchester.

On 27th May 1935, at a heaving and expectant King's Hall, Belle Vue, Johnny took on a talented and tough young fighter with an explosive punch from across the Pennines, twenty-two-year-old Len Hampston from Batley, for the vacant British Bantamweight title. It was a closely fought fifteen round bout that could have gone either way, however in a brutal 'War of the Roses' battle the Mancunian sneaked home by a whisker. A full house roared their approval for Johnny and the bravery of Hampston. Come the finish, as the new champion held the title belt high, people began to wonder who next for Johnny King? Could Harry Fleming manoeuvre another world shot or maybe someone closer to home? What actually happened would divide Manchester and break the hearts of all involved with the boxing club.

Whilst Jackie Brown was a street-wise Mancunian pied piper; a man who lived for the limelight and soaked up public adulation like an alcoholic squeezing drops of whisky from a rag, Johnny King had the quiet manner of someone who played hide and seek with his own shadow. There was a time when they made an unlikely double act and were quite literally joined at the hip. However by 1935 those days had long passed. Whereas once Jackie's gentle goading over his genial ways would be laughed off or ignored by a shy Johnny, as he grew both in the ring and out, the resentment slowly festered until it became open hostility. One day, after finishing training, the boxers were getting changed and Jackie, as ever immaculate in an expensive, snappy three-piece suit, walked over to Johnny, who was dressed in much plainer attire. He felt the quality of his tie and with every eye in the gym upon him he mockingly declared whilst laughing,

"I wouldn't be seen dead wearing that," before flicking it into Johnny's face. Whilst such acts were frowned upon by Fleming and Bates, Johnny's seemingly lack of offence towards Jackie meant these incidents were usually ignored between the two, however, as Johnny's confidence grew he began to lash back. The pair's success and failures in the ring fuelled the other. It became poisonous. Stablemates in all but name, Jackie told all who would listen and there were many that he had Johnny's card marked, "I could take Kingie any day" he said. Soon the time would arrive for him to back up his idle boast.

Jackie Brown was coming off the beating of his life after losing the British Flyweight title to the ferocious Glaswegian Benny Lynch. Jackie had not just lost on a never-to-be-forgotten night at Belle Vue, he had been taken apart and brutally destroyed by the merciless Scot. It wasn't so much a boxing defeat but an execution. Though never one for excuses, Jackie had been struggling badly beforehand with weight issues and he felt the time was right to move up to Bantamweight. There, in Jackie's mind, lay the road to redemption via beating the then current champion - Johnny King.

For years the war drums had resonated loud in Manchester for a showdown between two of Manchester's finest. With Jackie at Flyweight and Johnny at Bantamweight, it was a contest once deemed impossible to make, not anymore. Determined to drag Johnny into a public slanging match, Jackie was constantly calling for the fight in the press. He was vicious, bombastic and cocky, the newspapermen loved him! Whilst Johnny at first refused to bite back, instead preferring to keep his own counsel, he finally snapped and met with Harry Fleming. Johnny was straight to the point.

"Make the fight!"

With a heavy heart Fleming set the wheels in motion. Though aware of the growing animosity between the two over the years, he never dreamt it would come to this.

Acting fast and knowing such a contest was a license to print money, Jack Madden put in a record bid for Belle Vue to host the ultimate Mancunian grudge fight. A meeting was organised at the venue with all involved; Madden, Belle Vue promoter Henry Isles, Harry Fleming, Jackie's manager, Dave Lumiansky and the two fighters. The atmosphere was strained from the off and there were heated exchanges over who got what and how much. The British Boxing Board had declined to sanction the fight as a title bout due to Jackie having only two fights at the weight. However this contest didn't need a belt to give it legitimacy: it was already the talk of the 'Cotton City.' As ever Lumiansky, with his machine-gun like American patter, was determined to ride roughshod over the negotiations, while Jackie was loud throughout getting over the point that he was the star. The top dog. He had a point because, although Johnny was popular and highly respected, Jackie was adored. The share of the purse, according to Jackie, had to reflect that. All this time, as arguments raged, Johnny sat quietly, he appeared content to listen. Finally Madden pointed towards him, "Come on Johnny," he said. "You've not spoken a word. What do you think?" Jackie glared across and started laughing, "Yeah come on Kingie, what's up somebody stole your tongue?"

A smiling Johnny stared at Madden and then Jackie. "What do I think? I think I'm going to knock you out."

Arrangements were made to keep the fighters as far apart as possible during training in case all hell erupted. Each would use the Paley Street gym at different times. As expected Belle Vue was sold out within hours and the city counted down the days and weeks. When interviewed or with any type of audience, Jackie continued to make Johnny the butt of cruel jokes and mickey-taking, whilst all the time his nemesis drove himself through training with the thought of shutting Jackie up in the ring.

An emotional Fleming was determined once the match was made not to take sides. Jack Bates was assigned to Johnny's corner, whilst Jackie's seconds were Harry Levene and Tom Hurst. Bates loved both fighters, but this was business. Knowing each intimately, he urged Johnny to let Jackie do all the work and be patient. Bates understood Jackie Brown would start like a hurricane. He told Johnny to just ease into the fight, "Let Jackie blow himself out. Tuck up, slip punches, then, when he takes a breather, go after him with your right." However, despite Johnny appearing to take this advice on board, Bates knew that once the bell sounded all bets were off. From the first second Johnny King and Jackie

Brown would be going for each other's throats.

On the evening of 22nd November 1935, with the city drunk on expectation, and Belle Vue bathed in excitement, one man walked alone on Blackpool promenade. As the Wurlitzer music played and the smell of popcorn and fish and chips filled the air, his mind went back to times past when both fighters, whom he considered sons, had given him a father's pride. Not that night. Harry Fleming had washed his hands of the contest, "a bloody mad idea" he called it. Sickened and sad, Fleming looked at his watch and decided in a couple of hours he would make the call to see what had occurred. Fleming sighed. Until then he would be beside the seaside, but his heart, though now broken, could not help but be in Belle Vue.

Amid scenes of unadulterated Mancunian mayhem, the fighters touched gloves. Both their faces were stern, business-like. The pair were now sworn enemies, as if they had come from opposing continents and not the same Collyhurst streets. Respect, however, was clearly evident in the opening two rounds with Johnny fully aware that although Jackie's star may have dipped a little, he remained a truly formidable opponent. The crowd was split: Johnny had decent backing, but it was clear Jackie's support was superior and by the third round they almost raised the roof off the King's Hall as their man threw off the years showing extraordinary speed allied to some rapier-like punches. As the arena rose to its feet cheering both men, Johnny let fly a right hook that dropped Jackie to the canvas. Up quickly, his pride stung, war swiftly broke out again. They went toe-to-toe in the centre of the ring for the title of 'Cock of Collyhurst.' It was if the pair were back in the blood tubs.

Round five saw no let-up: Belle Vue bedlam! Come the sixth, Jackie came out of his corner and was immediately caught off balance with a left hook that sent him back onto the ropes. Momentarily dazed, Johnny hit him with a right cross on the jaw to all but end the fight and Jackie's resistance. Still, though, he tore into him. Punch after punch followed, a volley of left hooks and a bewildered Jackie had gone, with legs wide apart and arms by his side, he stood helpless, sagging in scarecrow mode, being pounded by a one-time best friend. Johnny glanced across to referee Gus Platt who inexplicably waved him on. Suddenly something snapped in Johnny, his eyes glazed over and with unreserved venom he showed no mercy and pummelled Jackie to a pulp. His unprotected chin was wide open for a searing right hand. As Jackie slid ever lower to the canvas, Johnny's punches only increased with venom. This was spiteful and dangerous, the years of taunting suffered at Jackie's hands avenged in a frenzied display of unmitigated violence. Finally the referee grabbed Johnny by the waist and dragged him clear. Jackie lay all but unconscious in a huddle on the floor. Still Johnny pushed people away as he appeared intent on finishing Jackie off. The crowd watched on in shock. What the hell was wrong with him? Jack Madden screamed at Johnny within inches of his face, "Behave yourself son, show some respect, he's bloody unconscious!"

Jack Bates, who secretly feared such a scenario might happen, pulled Johnny into a corner and threw ice water over him. Like a light being switched back on the old Johnny returned. Wrapped in a towel he swiftly headed back over to Jackie who remained in distress. Only then on seeing him did the tears start to fall. All malice vanished, Johnny's only thought now was for his friend to recover.

Later, he and Jack Bates knocked on Jackie's dressing room, but at first received short shrift from his corner men. However, on walking away they heard the door opening. Stood there, covered in fresh cuts, plasters and very much bruised and battered, was Jackie with a rueful half-smile on his face. He went across and embraced Johnny who, with tears in his eyes, held him tight. Jackie offered up congratulations on a great fight. The pair shook hands and hoped that bygones would be bygones were raised. Sadly, the two would clash again in equally bitter circumstances.

Back in Blackpool, Harry Fleming had shown no emotion when ringing Belle Vue from the Tower Ballroom to find out the result. Relief, however, flooded over him when he was told both had come through without serious injury. Later, when he was informed the full extent of what actually occurred, Fleming was furious. To him it was like brothers fighting in the ring and it was something that would haunt him for a while. Events, however, would soon occur that finally helped to ease such feelings of guilt.

In 1937, after just one loss in fifteen at Bantamweight, Jackie Brown was officially named as number one challenger to Johnny King's British title. Meanwhile, the two intervening years had seen Johnny defend his crown successfully. At that weight he remained a class above all other British fighters. Now the rankings demanded another meeting against his old foe. After the brutal mauling by Johnny first time round, Jackie's pride saw him leave the Collyhurst gym and join Ted McGuire's gym on Stockport Road. He became obsessed with revenge. His manager, Lumiansky, realised a rematch between the two was still the biggest money spinner in town, "You've got to needle him Jackie," he would say, "get people talking. Rattle King's cage and we can make some real cash."

As Jackie rose up the rankings, the cries from the Manchester boxing public resonated. He had settled at the weight and many of his supporters firmly believed Jackie could provide a serious challenge to King's British title. The bad blood returned; it was unwarranted and cruel from Jackie, who simply, when in front of an audience, whether it be a pub crowd or a huddle of newspaper hacks, could never help himself. He belittled Johnny at every occasion, even to the extent of mimicking his speech impediment.

Such had been the clamour for tickets that the Belle Vue syndicate decided again that the only venue big enough to host such an event was the Speedway ground, last used for Johnny's epic bout against Panama Al Brown. As the fight drew closer, the animosity between the pair increased tenfold. When asked to pose for the usual pre-fight photo, Jackie refused point blank, "I'll see him in the ring," he snapped. Even Johnny, unlike last time, failed to hide his disdain for his former friend. When asked by a newspaperman what he thought may happen he replied with a worrying coldness that shocked even the reporter, "He shouldn't even be fighting me. I will shut him up again and no messing around, he will get hurt." As for Fleming, this time he declared himself firmly in Johnny's corner along with Jack Bates. Jackie was not considered family anymore after he left for another gym. Fleming, though still immensely fond of Jackie, despite his antics, no longer felt a clash of loyalties.

Come the night of 31st May 1937, a summer breeze blew across a packed Belle Vue Speedway ground as 20,000 spectators held their breath. All were aware of the feud that had erupted between the fighters. You were for one or the other. The atmosphere was tense. Threats had been made beforehand to Johnny's camp, said to be from local gangsters laying bets on Jackie and the police were brought in to protect him.

That night, under the stars, Johnny King finally rid himself of the thorn in his side called Jackie Brown, but it took thirteen rounds of boxing savagery before this torrid affair could truly be laid to rest. From the opening bell both men went for each other with a snarling passion. Each punch was thrown with the intent to cause damage. Jackie started the better; fast on his feet, he threw swift barrages of punches but this proved to be a mirage. Jackie's light soon went out as the magic in his legs had gone. Those few good early rounds could be viewed as the last hurrah for Jackie's career before Johnny upped the ante and went to work. Showing no mercy, King opened up and treated Jackie like a punch bag; time and again he trapped his old mate on the ropes and let fly a fearful amount of shots with nothing coming back in return. It was a never-ending torrent of hurt, yet still Jackie refused to yield. It was beyond barbaric as referee Jack Dare allowed proceedings to continue. Even the crowd wanted an end to the madness.

Jackie fought on, through nothing more than blind instinct and remarkable courage, but neither were capable of stemming Johnny's relentless and merciless attacks. Fighting off the ropes, hanging on for dear life, Jackie waved Johnny in and come he did. He wanted his best and was getting it. Finally, in the thirteenth round, a right cross slammed into Jackie's chin and put him on the canvas. Urged to stay down by his corner and, it appeared, the entire crowd, unbelievably Jackie was back up at the count of seven. Johnny stared over to the referee, as if begging him to end it, but instead he motioned to fight on. Moving in, looking to finish proceedings with one last shot, Johnny took aim and this time put Jackie out for the count. All was over. A deathly silence fell over the Speedway ground as Jackie lay still. A small huddle knelt around him and finally, as Jackie raised his head, a huge roar erupted that went on and on... There were many tears in the crowd, for it was definitely the end of an era. These fights between former friends had torn apart the Collyhurst gym and it would be many years before the "All for one, one for all" ethos of the club meant something again.

Johnny would defend his title one more time before war broke out and all minds turned from the ring to matters infinitely more serious. At Leeds' Headingley rugby ground, on 22nd June, 1938, he won on a disqualification against an old foe, Len Hampston. This after being put down in the third round by the Yorkshireman, to the delight of a hostile crowd. As Johnny struggled to get up, an over-excited Hampston hit him again, only this time well below the belt. As he sunk to his knees in pain, Jack Bates in Johnny's corner screamed "Foul!" To the horror of the partisan Yorkshire crowd referee Jack Hart immediately stopped the contest and awarded it to Johnny. Hart later told the newspapers that he had little choice, for it was clear to him Johnny was incapable of carrying on.

Just before the air raid sirens began to wail and the bombs started dropping on Manchester, Johnny and Wylma suffered an awful personal tragedy when their four-year-old daughter Marlene was knocked down by a car and later died in hospital. Both were left devastated. After the inquest Johnny became increasingly insular and moody. In time, the two grew apart and eventually divorced. Against the terrible background of Marlene's death, Johnny volunteered for the Royal Navy. Initially he was stationed in Plymouth as a PTI instructor and although Johnny knuckled down he wasn't happy. The war raged on and he was constantly in his superior's ear for a meaningful posting. Finally, Johnny became Able Seaman King aboard the ill-fated battleship HMS Prince of Wales. In December, 1941, she spent days stalking an enemy convoy off Malaya's east coast. Without any air support, The Prince of Wales was at the mercy of Japanese Zero fighter planes and those following close behind, the torpedo bombers. On lookout, in a crow's nest, Johnny clasped tightly to a Vickers machine gun staring for hours on end into a cloudless, crystal blue sky that stretched forever onwards. He was a long way from Collyhurst.

Suddenly, out of a blinding sun, the Japanese attacked, only their target was the Prince of Wales sister ship, The Repulse, alongside them. Johnny watched as she disappeared in white smoke and flames before going over on her side and then under. He braced himself, for sure as night followed day, they were next. Swarms of Zeros came first, then the bombers. Johnny blazed away on the Vickers, but clearly heard the shudder beneath his feet as the torpedoes struck and exploded. In no time the Prince of Wales was ablaze and sinking fast. The call was made "Abandon ship!"

For ninety minutes Johnny miraculously survived in shark-infested waters by clutching to wreckage while praying for all he was worth. Finally, a Royal Navy destroyer rescued him and he was taken to Singapore. However, any thoughts of Johnny's woes being over could not be further from the truth.

Shortly after arriving in Singapore, the Japanese attacked and all hell broke loose in the city. Desperate not to be taken prisoner, Johnny and a young lad from Glasgow, nineteen-year-old Paddy Scott, made a run for it. They escaped on a minesweeper to Batavia in the Dutch East Indies. After disembarking, Johnny and Paddy headed off into town looking for further transport, only to stare up at the skies in horror as they saw Japanese planes dropping thousands of white enemy parachutes. After travelling fourteen miles from the docks, a deserted car was found and the pair headed back to look for the minesweeper but it had already left. They noticed a tramp steamer being prepared to sail. Hearing the Japanese gunfire nearby and closing in, Johnny and Paddy swiftly commandeered a rowing boat and luckily were allowed on the steamer. From there they headed to Calcutta, then Colombo in Ceylon (now Sri Lanka) before finally making it home. Back in England, after extended leave, Johnny was posted to the aircraft carrier Implacable and saw out his final war years in the Pacific.

On returning to civvy street, Johnny, now aged thirty-five, and badly out of shape, was still desperate to fight. He met up once more with Harry Fleming, who had closed down the gym at the start of the war. Parts of Collyhurst had been reduced to rubble by Hitler's bombs come 1945, due to the district's closeness to Manchester city centre. At first Fleming was keen to help Johnny, but it swiftly became clear after just a couple of fights that his legs, punch resistance and the old King magic had waned beyond repair. However, Johnny was adamant that he wanted one last shot at regaining his Bantamweight title, now held by a fantastically talented and dangerous fighter from Glasgow, Jackie Paterson.

Their paths had previously crossed. When starting out as a teenager, the champion had met Johnny before the war and he had always been grateful for the advice given him. Feeling obliged to take the fight Paterson agreed to a defence and the pair met again and shook hands on the deal. Suddenly the old boxing war drums in Manchester resonated again. Johnny all but begged Fleming to stand by him this one last time and eventually persuaded him to do so. However, it was against Fleming's better judgement for he knew Johnny had little or no chance against the much younger and more powerful Paterson. There were no such thing as miracles in bomb ravaged post-war Manchester, but Harry would pray for one anyway.

Still retaining his star billing at Belle Vue's King Hall, Johnny had his last hurrah. In the seven thousand crowd that evening on 10th February, 1947, were fellow survivors of the battleship Prince of Wales. Sadly, as Fleming had feared, Jackie Paterson hammered Johnny into submission after just seven rounds, although he gave it everything. The opening of the fight saw Johnny roll back the years and box beautifully. In the corner, a hopeful Fleming thought for a moment that his prayers had been answered, but it was only a fleeting, short-lived moment. By the fourth Paterson found his range to cut loose and Johnny was repeatedly put on the canvas. No mercy was shown as he knocked the former champion around the ring with fearful ease. Still Johnny would not yield, he refused to stay down and as the crowd, many in tears, screamed at the referee to stop the fight, Paterson saved him the trouble by knocking Johnny clean out in the seventh.

Johnny King never fought again.

Just weeks after the fight, Harry Fleming died of a heart attack. One of the great characters of the Manchester boxing scene, Harry was an honourable man, a true gentleman in a thoroughly brutal business. He also had a huge heart, and perhaps his decision to help Johnny prepare for a fight he knew there was no chance of winning finally broke him. A Requiem mass was held for Harry at St Dunstan's church, followed by his burial at Moston cemetery. Collyhurst shed a tear and raised a glass to the man with the kind smile, who was happiest chatting boxing as he smoked his pipe. A man blessed with the shrewdest eye in the business.

As for Johnny, he went on to marry again, and with his second wife Mona they had a daughter, Jill. Life outside the ring was difficult and he, like so many before and after him, struggled once the last bell sounded. Johnny ran pubs and bought a sweet shop, but there was always something missing in his eyes. Johnny was lost without the sport he had graced in his prime.

Tragically he died a relatively young man from cancer in Christie's hospital, on 6th March, 1963, aged just fifty-five. He fought the terrible fight against this dreadful illness with the same quiet dignity and huge courage shown throughout his life. Whether it be in the South China seas or Belle Vue's King's Hall.

The king was dead… Long live the king.

6 - LANCE LEWIS
THE MAN WHO CAN'T BE MOVED

WEMBLEY ARENA: LONDON. 6TH DECEMBER, 1989. With a look that suggested they'd met somewhere before, a man nodded and then, as if a light had gone on in his head, there was that knowing smile.

Payback.

Suddenly, it was all over.

"I've been sussed, Billy" the fighter said to his cornerman, Billy Koyte. Still, he reflected, it had been a small miracle that the blag had lasted this long.

It had begun as a desire to right a wrong but he knew that after this there was no way back, his life in boxing was over. But once the dust settled and that last bell sounded, there were much more important matters to attend to than simply earning a crust wearing a pair of boxing gloves.

So it was farewell 'Tony Dore' - just another inexplicable twist in the extraordinary life of Lance Lewis. A boy brought up in Grafton Street in the shadow of the Holy Name Church…

LANCE'S MOTHER, DAPHNE, was six months pregnant with him when she arrived in London from Jamaica. His father, Luther, followed shortly afterwards. At the age of two, in 1964, the family moved to Manchester. Lance's home was on Grafton Street, Oxford Road. At school, The Holy Name Catholic primary, Lance was a quiet kid - introverted. It was a troubled childhood, his parents soon separated and he spent time in and out of care homes.

At that time in the sixties black faces were rare in the care system and the few there inevitably suffered racism. School was a nightmare and Lance was not able to read or write until the age of twelve. As the only black kid in the class, lessons happened around Lance. When he was at home the family spoke Jamaican patois, meaning he was viewed by the other kids like an alien from another planet. Outside the classroom life was even more difficult. On the hard Manchester streets, where no mercy was given to those who stood out from the crowd, trouble found him constantly. Despite being only small in stature, Lance was forever scrapping: he had little choice – the bullying and racism was as common back then as margarine on bread and sugar in tea.

The north of Manchester, like the rest of the city, was a hostile environment for a black face. The police were brutal, this was a white world that didn't accept outsiders. So it was that young Lance learned to fight his corner. To survive, the trick was to fight like a Tasmanian Devil. If anyone dared to bully him then they risked having their eyes ripped out and throat bitten. Soon word spread, 'Don't mess with the little black fella, he's nuts!' Job done.

The schoolyard became a place where Lance would be left alone. No one dared to pick on him. Instead he would just wander around on his own or stand in a corner watching the other children playing happily and ignoring him. Young Lance was content to contemplate the universe. Few could ever have imagined what was unfolding in that young seven-year old's head.

By the early seventies, as Lance began secondary school, he discovered martial arts. It all began when the family had moved to Ardwick. He and his one close friend at the time, Robert Murray, used to visit a sports centre to play table football. The Murrays were the only other black family in the area, meaning the pair naturally drifted together. Robert's mother was a white Irish woman while his Jamaican father, Les, had come over in the fifties. Les was a dangerous character not to be messed with. Locally admired, feared and respected, he had been around and knew people. Les had business dealings in Notting Hill and had travelled to the United States. When he spoke, you listened. Les took Lance under his wing and taught him how to survive on the streets. He told the pair the best way to act around the police, the best way to stay alive and out of prison as a black kid in what he viewed as a dangerous, racist society. All this apart, Les was a wonderful singer with the showbands and forever in great demand for his vocal talent in clubs and pubs. No more so than in Ireland where he was much loved.

Whilst playing on the table football at a local sports centre with

Robert, Lance became curious about the shouts and noises that came from the floor above. Finally, gathering the courage, he sneaked upstairs and watched in amazement through a half open door as the Karate club went about their routines. The moves were as strange as they were thrilling. Lance was mesmerised. The white uniforms, the hypnotic quality of it all. The ritual. This was in the era before Bruce Lee mania. Shukokai Karate was still an underground sport. It definitely wasn't taught in schools and was deemed unacceptable by the white middle classes. Having had their appetite whetted, the lads immediately rushed the instructor, "Mister, Mister, can we join, can we join?!"

They were told to come back with a karate kit, which they duly did and were given memberships. For Lance, this was a life-changing moment.

For his part, Les encouraged the boys to go together and keep it up for karate could only give them confidence. Ardwick was a battleground: one particular spot where it never failed to ignite was Zoo B Doo's disco at Belle Vue. With local rednecks looking for trouble, Lance and Robert's newly discovered skills always came in handy. Around this time another form of martial arts came to these shores from America, full contact Karate. One Sunday morning, instead of going to his normal karate class, Lance stepped into another teaching this new form of the martial art. Full contact karate included timed rounds, pads and gloves: another nudge for him towards boxing. He became hooked. The emphasis was more on fitness and the ability to move fast, kick and punch. Lance swiftly realised he possessed a special talent for this, but also realised he would have to work damn hard at it. Some aspects of the sport did come naturally though.

Lance had a gift of being able to read opponent's moves before they made them. He always considered this came from undiagnosed dyslexia (he was thirty-six before he was finally diagnosed a dyslexic). Lance was convinced that he was granted other gifts to make up for the curse of dyslexia, it was just a question of figuring out how to use them. Whatever the reason, Lance achieved remarkable success and, aged just fifteen, he reached the semi-finals of the British championships, being held in Manchester. Tragically, that same day a competitor had been killed in an earlier bout and the decision was taken, due to the step up in class at the higher level, that Lance would not be allowed to compete any further. Twelve months later, he was not to be stopped and took the title to the astonishment of all with a knockout in the final. Here indeed was a child fighting adults and beating them. A prodigy.

In 1976 Lance left High School with no formal qualifications. However, despite the dyslexia, in time he would go on to get his 'O' and 'A' Levels at Abraham Moss Further Education College. Teaching himself to read and write, Lance was determined that whatever the barriers, he would not be thwarted. Now newly crowned British champion, Lance knew he needed more boxing skills to remain at the top. There followed a short spell at Ardwick Boy's club, but Lance found the training far too limited for his needs. He viewed it in regards to chess, there they only showed him how to use the pawns and rooks, whereas Lance needed to use the entire range of pieces. He decided to look elsewhere. A friend, Carlton, a fellow martial arts fighter, who Lance always seemed to bump into at Zoo B Doo's disco, had an elder brother who was a professional boxer. He convinced Carlton to set up a meeting with him. The boxer's name was Kenny Webber. Kenny was a top Light-Middleweight pro who had won the central area title. At first Kenny was a little reticent, but soon warmed to the likeable little guy of whom he had heard nothing but good things. Finally, he relented and told him about a place across town that would suit his needs and about the man who ran it, but he warned Lance in no uncertain terms, "No messing around!" Passing him a phone number and directions to Lightbowne Road, Kenny used the words that over the years in Manchester would change so many young lad's lives.

"Just ask for Brian Hughes."

On arrival Lance recognised immediately that this could be his spiritual home. His first impressions of Brian were of him being strict about behaviour there. No swearing was allowed and bullying would see you shown the door. It was also obvious that here was a decent, fair minded man with a big heart and, above all, he was a brilliant coach. Such a working atmosphere suited Lance perfectly, for at this time he was also undergoing training to be a Junior priest…

Whilst still a practicing altar boy, Lance's journey into the priesthood had already begun. He was in the first stages with the YCW (Young Christian Workers.) Lance had always been a regular church goer. Soon that escalated from not simply just working on the altar, but helping out with other duties. He was learning on the job and his chief mentor was Father Rimmer, a local priest who would regularly visit Afro-Caribbean communities. Father Rimmer would call round to Lance's house every week without fail and soon they became close. A good and caring man, to this day Lance remembers him fondly. In time, in the gym, Brian would come to remind Lance of working for a priest. Knowing he too was a devout Catholic, Lance, quietly, without saying anything, bonded with him. It suited Lance that Brian attempted to run Collyhurst and Moston, like he says, "As a Catholic church!" Brian's regard for the welfare of his fighters combined with the scientific methodology of his training, meant Lance settled in wonderfully. He would drive home the defensive, technical aspects of boxing first and foremost, "Look after yourself at all times, Lance. but never forget when the time is right to go after your opponent."

Suddenly the Pawns and Rooks had been joined by the Bishops, Knights and the Queen. Every point ticked, he soon had all the right moves perfected for kickboxing. Here Lance found a home in Brian's seminary of boxing, it was a match made in heaven.

In Lance's first amateur boxing fight Kenny Webber was in his corner. Beforehand, whilst in the dressing room, the opponent came charging in and went off on a tirade of how he was going to beat him up! He and Kenny simply sat, watched and listened until the man disappeared back out the door. Come the actual fight Lance won easily, but after one more successful contest his amateur career came to a grinding halt when an anonymous letter was sent to the ABA informing them that an experienced kick boxing champion was fighting in their ranks. Immediately, without any right of reply, Lance was banned.

Refusing to let this derail his fledgling boxing career, Lance returned to the gym and Brian Hughes to continue his education. He viewed him, despite his gruff Mancunian, homely persona and fables about the good old days, as an intellectual. Not just on boxing, but life. Brian sensed with Lance that he needed to be quiet and just get on with things, if a lad was comfortable in his own space, why should he invade it? Despite not saying much, Lance adored Brian's company and loved nothing more than going along when he would show old boxing fights on rare 8 mm cine film to pensioners in retirement homes. It was here he made him aware of the great black American post-war Lightweight world champion, Ike Williams. Brian told Lance how much he reminded him of Williams. The way Ike moved and punched. So much that he suggested Lance changed his fighting surname from Lewis to Williams. This he did, duly echoing dramatic events that would recur years later.

Determined not to be bowed after being banned as an amateur, at just sixteen, on 19th August, 1978, Lance (now Williams) had his first profession bout. Lance had signed with famed boxing manager and also legendary cut man, Ernie Fosse, and with contests so difficult to come by, wherever the bell sounded he would travel, regardless of the distance or difficulties involved. For his opening contest against Surrey born John Cooper, at the 20th Century SC, Cliffs Pavilion in Southend, Lance would race from College, meet Brian at Manchester Piccadilly train station, get to the venue, fight Cooper, then head home, to be back in College the next day. Typically he would earn between £80 to £100 a fight - a club fighter's life was always a hectic one.

Lance's early professional career was rather scattered with a plethora of wins, draws and losses. However, arguably his greatest sporting achievement occurred out of the boxing ring the following year, 1979, when in an unofficial title fight at Belle Vue, Lance fought the then kick boxing world champion, Dutchman, Iwan Menes, and whilst still only seventeen, he sensationally beat him! Suddenly, Lance was being hailed as the greatest kickboxer on the planet by many in the sport. In time, he would make it official. His name and fame spread wide in the kick boxing world. Lance was invited to tour Colombia in South America with a demonstration team. When not staging martial arts shows, he went exploring the towns and countryside, picking up a sprinkling of Spanish on the go.

Lance came across a poor, almost destitute, poverty-ravaged people, who had little choice but to resort to crime, as he soon discovered to his cost. A first night scare came when out walking; a van pulled up and Military Police surrounded him. Lance was thrown against a wall and had a rifle placed to his head. Luckily, after checking Lance's passport and hearing his Mancunian accent, they realised it was mistaken identity! Two weeks later events got even worse when Lance was mugged at knife point, stripped of his money, camera and watch by a gang of machete wielding bandits and thrown down a small hillside. These incidents were a memorable, if frightening, snapshot of his time in Colombia.

On returning to England, he finally decided that the priesthood was not for him. After meeting with Father Rimmer, Lance explained his reasons. Instead he had a plan that would involve him going to the United States. It was a double-pronged attempt to help kick-start both his martial arts and boxing careers. Lance had martial arts contacts and family in New York. Being a black club fighter in England, he would be forced to scrap his way up from the very bottom to get anywhere near a title shot. Back then political and geographical issues loomed large. London, not Manchester, was the boxing hub of the country. It could take years for him to make progress from his home town. This was not somebody coming off a background of the Olympic Games or a flashy amateur career. Luckily, Brian had an idea. He had seen the potential in Lance and recognised that it would be a crying shame to see it wasted, so Brian decided to write a letter to a good friend. One day he put an arm around Lance's shoulders in the gym, "It just so happens Lance, that I know a man in Detroit who owns a boxing gym there. It's called the Kronk… You may have heard of it?"

On 2nd August, 1980, at the Joe Louis Arena, Detroit, twenty-two-year-old local boy Thomas Hearns demolished Pipino Cuevas in two rounds to claim the WBA Welterweight title and become the second world champion after Hilmer Kenty to emerge from the Kronk gym.

The following day Lance arrived in Detroit carrying nothing but his kitbag. He jumped in a taxi to take him to an address given him by Brian Hughes under the illusion this was where he would stay. Instead it turned out to be the home of the mother of Brian's friend and Kronk gym owner, the legendary boxing trainer Emanuel Steward. Appearing a little alarmed on opened the front door, Steward's mother was even more taken aback when Lance opened his mouth!

"A black Englishman!" she exclaimed, "ain't no god darn thing as a black Englishman!" After reading his letter and realising this was not some lunatic, she allowed him in before phoning one of Emanuel's sons who turned up and took Lance to the local YMCA, where he had been reserved a room.

The next day Lance got the bus to McGraw Street and looked for a while before finally finding number 5555. It was an old beaten-down building. He walked down some steps until reaching a closed door.

Lance entered and was hit with a blast of hot air. A large, dark, cellar-like room greeted him where fighters were busy working out. In time some truly magnificent talent would emerge from that gym. Kenty and Hearns had already won world titles. Milton McCrory, Jimmy Paul and Duane Thomas began as amateurs and became world champions. Then there were the likes of David Braxton, Dujuan Johnson, Caveman Lee Oba Carrand and Steve McCrory, who all challenged for world titles at some point in their careers. This was just the beginning, for in a short time Emanuel Steward's Kronk would become the boxing pride of not just Detroit, but all America.

Yet these talented star-studded names were not handcrafted in a pristine environment, quite the opposite. They learned their trade in a broken down, derelict building on the wrong side of the tracks in one of the most murderous and dangerous cities in the world. Indeed, conditions were so bad that they made the Collyhurst and Moston gym appear luxurious. The aesthetics of the gym were left this way on purpose by Steward to ensure his men were mean, driven and hungry to get out! This was the Kronk and at its heartbeat was a single ring in the centre. Dotted around the place were two scruffy punchbags, a pair of sit up benches, the odd spit bucket and a sparse changing room. On arrival Lance introduced himself to a trainer, Walter Smith, and was quickly shown the changing rooms, showers and lockers before Walter announced out loud, "Hey guess what? We got ourselves a black Englishman!" Everyone in the gym stopped and crowded around. At first glance, they must have looked the most terrifying bunch, their eyes blazing, bodies sweating, each one wanting nothing more than to rip the newbie's head off. There were guffaws of laughter on hearing Lance speak with the now familiar comment, "A black guy from England? No such thing man?" and a bewildered shake of the head.

However, when it came to facing him in the ring, all talk of fresh meat swiftly vanished, as did the smirking and jokes. What struck Lance first about the gym was the ferocity of the sparring and the intense, unending competition. So many boxers were desperate to stand out that they seemed intent on beating each other to death if it meant they rose up the gym's pecking order. It was like a production line to get in the ring. They would wait their turn on the benches and move up as the next two got in the ring and the last two got out. There would be three minute rounds of utter carnage, then... next! Two more would climb in. And on and on...

The sparring was specifically designed as a filtering system. There were so many good and desperate fighters to choose from that only the very capable survived the wars within the ropes. It was those who survived that received the vast majority of coaching and none more so than the legendary Thomas Hearns who emerged from this brutal system to win world titles in an incredible five different weight categories.

On the outside Lance was calm and collected, inside it was another matter altogether as he watched these slugfests take place. Before Lance realised it, the end of the line was almost in sight and he was up. The sweltering heat heightened the tension and became almost claustrophobic - there was no getting out of this now! He remembered little of that first sparring session, but must have impressed hugely for by the end Lance found himself surrounded once more, only this time the fighters were desperate to ask him questions. To the astonishment of the Americans he was doing stuff in the ring they had never seen before.

"Who the hell taught you that, man?"

"Hey you gotta show me how you do that combination thing."

Lance was shocked because he had come to the Kronk to learn and now there were fighters utterly bemused at his ability to slip and counter punch. Suddenly it dawned on him that Brian Hughes had no equal, for if this was reputedly the greatest gym in the world and they had not been taught this stuff, then just how good was Collyhurst and Moston?

While life was never dull in Manchester, Detroit took it to another level. Officially, at the time, one of the top five most violent cities in America, Lance was constantly warned when not training to be on his guard. Once he was out with a friend from the gym, Light-Heavyweight Lindell Holmes. As Lance walked on, Lindell stopped to make a phone call. Upon picking up the receiver he had a gun put to his head and was relieved of a wallet. It all happened so fast. Lindell ran and caught up with Lance. He explained what had just happened as the shocked Englishman listened on aghast.

"Do you know why they didn't kill me?" Lance shook his head. "Because, my English friend," he said, still shaking, "I am wearing a

Kronk tracksuit." The gym was a huge source of pride in the Motor City, even among its killers and muggers.

Another time, one afternoon after training, Lance was getting dressed in the changing room when a rather large fellow in front of him put a hand down the front of his shorts and pulled out a hand gun. As Lance stared in shock and raised both hands high, the man smiled, "Don't worry, I'm a cop. I have to carry this with me at all times."

Then there was the madness of the great Puerto Rican fighter and world champion Hector 'Macho' Camacho. It had always been widely thought that Hector trained exclusively in New York City. This wasn't true for in his early career, many times he trained at the Kronk. It was here that he perfected his flamboyant skills in a most dramatic manner, so much so that on first setting eyes on him, Lance could never make out whether Hector was the bravest or the most insane man he had ever come across.

Whenever Hector made his way down those steps, the entire gym would come to a halt as 'El Macho' announced his arrival. "Hey Detroit I'm back and I'm gonna kick all your black asses. Man, I'm so good and you lot are gonna get whipped!" he would announce. Faces would turn around on hearing this and the groans on seeing who it was turned swiftly to silent menace. Yet still Hector would not be silenced. Once he had their full growling attention, a smiling Hector would pull out a comb and run it through his hair.

"Man, I'm so beautiful and you lot are so god damned ugly!" Then came the sparring!

A stampede of needled Kronk Lightweights would form a disorderly line – ten fighters stretching from the ring corner to the centre of the gym, each more anxious than the next to commit GBH on Hector, who would be waiting.

"Line up you bums," he would laugh. "Hector has plenty for you all!"

Lance would watch on mesmerised as these Detroit boxers shouted back in gruesome detail just what they had planned for him once it was their turn in the ring! The tear-ups were a sight to behold as Hector took on the Kronk, each man determined to knock Hector's head off! Many a time he received a good hiding, but Hector always came back for more and he was getting fitter.

"Is that the best you got? Come on!" he would say as the next man was summoned to the ring. After a while it became clear to Lance there was method in Hector's madness - it was what he needed to get himself into the correct mindset and fighting condition. He described sparring between Hector and the ferocious Kronk fighters as a "Pit bull against a pride of lions!" Hector 'Macho' Camacho has since sadly passed away, but for Lance he truly was a one off! A legend of the Kronk.

After a year alone in Detroit, the time came for Brian Hughes and another boxer from the Collyhurst gym, Ensley Bingham, to join Lance. For Emanuel Steward, Brian was boxing royalty, there would be no more buses for Lance as the Kronk organised a car to pick all three Englishmen up for training in the morning from their YMCA lodgings. In July 1981, Lance Williams was properly recognised for what he had achieved over the past year at the gym when, in an impromptu ceremony, he was with the famous 'Kronk' jacket presented by Emanuel Steward. There was no higher honour in the sport and Lance Williams was now a fully recognised member.

Emanuel and Brian worked tremendously well together and it was clear to Lance they were cut from the same cloth. The American would pick the Englishman's brains and vice versa. It was a wonderful friendship. Two men steeped in boxing history and in love with the sport. Brian spent his time in the gym analysing the American fighters. He and Steward had written to each other quite often discussing the 'sweet science' but it was during his time in Detroit that Brian felt his ideas were gaining credence. The Collyhurst and Moston club rightly ranked alongside the Kronk and though their colours may have been different the similarity in styles could never be doubted. They were brothers-in-arms 5000 miles apart.

Finally, Lance said goodbye to the Kronk, but he would soon be back because on returning to Manchester, Lance walked into a battle of wills with promoter Mickey Duff. It was a tough period: his mother was ill in Ardwick and time was split between studying to be a teacher and looking after her. All this while trying to earn a living through the boxing, but the bouts were becoming far too infrequent. Any northern fighter who dared to dream of being a champion and having real pay-days was forced to sign with a London-based promoter. That was where the power and influence lay. Lance had signed with Mickey Duff, but he felt Duff wasn't promoting him sufficiently. By the time the contract came up for renewal Lance and Brian met with Duff in his London office to iron out their differences and start afresh. They finally came to an agreement with special clauses included for regular fights and a guaranteed shot at the title within a certain period. The three shook hands and a new dawn promised, but the song remained mostly the same.

Lance began having grave doubts and soon realised it had been a mistake to re-sign. There were notable performances, no more than against former World Lightweight champion, Ken Buchanan, at Wembley Arena, on 24th November, 1981, when, with only five days' notice, after Buchanan's original opponent pulled out, Lance stepped in and won deservedly on points. Brian always stressed the importance of being primed and ready for situations like this. Fights were hard enough to come across, especially for black fighters, so he made a point of keeping them at peak condition and alert for the chance. Finally, Duff delivered on his promise, a fight in Las Vegas for Lance on the under-bill of the soon to be four times world champion, the great Puerto Rican, Edwin 'Chapo' Rosario. Duff flew Lance and Brian out for two weeks beforehand and he trained alongside Rosario at Johnny Taco's gym. In temperatures of close to 120 degrees, Lance learned just how much the human body is able to adapt. As for Rosario, he simply blew away both the Englishmen up close. A bewildering talent, 'El Chaco' would go on to be three times World Lightweight and one time Junior Welterweight champion. Lance always related a line somebody told him years later that the magical Rosario could beat anything but drugs. Tragically, those words would prove true and he died suddenly in 1997, aged just thirty-four, from an aneurysm. Doctors, however, put Rosario's horrific narcotic addiction as one of the main factor.

Also at this time something occurred that would have devastating consequences for Lance's own boxing career. In the pre-fight medical a tiny cataract showed up in his eye. The American doctors said this in no way presented a danger to stop him fighting. Indeed, it was so small it hardly registered on their scan. They would though send the details to the British Boxing Board of Control. Finally fit and raring to show what he had on the big stage, Lance was left shattered when the Vegas show was cancelled at the last minute.

Luckily, old friends stepped in. The Kronk came calling and they flew Lance and Brian out to Phoenix, Arizona, where the whole team were there in support of fellow fighter Milton McCrory's world title fight. At this time, there was also chat about Lance and a contract with the Kronk. His second one with Duff was all but up and he had absolutely no desire to sign another. To maintain his fitness, it had been arranged for Lance to box a three-round exhibition bout against another Kronk fighter; soon to be IBF World Lightweight champion Jimmy Paul. Incidentally, making sure it was a family affair, the fight would be refereed by none other than Thomas Hearns! However, the venue raised eyebrows when Lance and Brian heard the fight was to be held in a top security prison at Perryville Penitentiary! A few days later they drove in stifling heat down to the prison, past one security gate, then another before seeing it. There was a boxing ring set up in the yard, with benches all around for the incarcerated audience. After changing, the fighters began the walk to the ring. As they exited into the yard in one-hundred-degree heat, the entire prison awaited their arrival. Lance remembers it like a scene from a movie. Huge muscle-bound monsters doing weights and glaring at you with looks of sheer hatred in their eyes and wanting nothing more than to cut you into a thousand pieces! Scuffles broke out ringside. On entering through the ropes some prisoners charged towards them but were beaten back. High above in the watch towers and along the walls stood a long line of guards in dark glasses with guns aimed down at the inmates. Against this surreal, torrid and tense backdrop, Lance and Jimmy touched gloves with one eye on each other and the other on their excitable audience.

Both had sparred many times before in the Kronk and Lance knew he had to watch out for Paul's dangerous, sharp right hand. The first round saw him deal effortlessly with the American and come the second he was catching Jimmy with his own left hook combinations to the jaw. So much so that Lance mentioned to Brian in the corner that, were it a proper contest he felt confident of knocking Paul out. Come the finish, Thomas Hearns raised Lance's hand, the two fighters embraced and with great haste the delegation from Detroit Kronk left the prison and never looked back. It was a memorable experience for Lance and one that proved to himself that he was more than capable of being in with the best. Jimmy Paul would soon be crowned world champion and

Lance Williams had his measure. However, he could not have dreamed what was about to happen.

On returning to England, Lance undertook another medical with the information from the Americans regarding his eye now available. Following this he was called before the British Boxing Board of Control and informed that because of the cataract discovered whilst in the States they were revoking his licence to fight. It was an astonishing decision and it left Lance reeling. Due to quality differences in the medical scanners, the cataract did not even show up on the English version and yet he was out. An equally shocked Brian arranged for him to see the very best; Moorways Eye specialists had passed Frank Bruno and Maurice Hope, but even with their recommendation the board refused to change the original decision. It simply did not make sense, there was no justifiable reason for the ban. Lance's boxing career had been brought to an abrupt halt. He sensed something underhand; it stank to high heaven, but it would be many years before he discovered exactly what had occurred. The boxer Lance Williams could not set foot in a boxing ring for six years.

Stunned, angry and perplexed Lance had to get on with his life. The option to return to the states with the Kronk was there, but personal issues in Manchester meant it was not viable at that time. As the years passed Lance gained a teacher's degree, got married, had kids and continued with his martial arts career. The dream of becoming official kick boxing world champion burned brighter than ever, He also helped Brian out occasionally in the Collyhurst and Moston gym and was in great demand as a sparring partner, although this at times did not go smoothly. On one occasion, he sparred with fellow Manchester boxer Najib Daho, and Lance ended up sending the unfortunate Daho to hospital. Because Daho was in training for a European title this was all covered up. Lance also spent time with Pat Cowdell but was not allowed to spar! Instead they just wanted him to talk and work with Cowdell on his confidence. This was all while holding down a day job as a PE and Design Technology teacher at Ducie Central High School in Manchester. Life, for the now once more Lance Lewis, was always full and eventful.

Six years passed, then, come 1988, it suddenly all made sense.

Lance was passed some information that for years he had suspected, but could never prove. Back in 1982, word had reached Mickey Duff from the States that Lance was going to sign with the Kronk when his contract with him was up. He had also been to the Kronk gym and must have known how much they thought of Lance, the first Englishman accepted into their inner sanctum. So it surely would have come as no great surprise to Duff when he was informed of their desire to sign him. Lance was told he then used his huge influence in British boxing at the time to ensure the tiny cataract that didn't even show up on a British medical scanner was sufficient to end Lance Williams' career. Wanting to right this wrong, Lance went to see Brian Hughes.

A meeting took place in Glasgow that included Lance, Brian, Scottish promoter Oliver Morrison and an unnamed solicitor. Morrison wanted to sign up two of Brian's top boxers; European champion Pat Barrett and Delroy Waul, however the solicitor insisted a third name be on the dotted line - Lance. The plan was hatched for him to use an assumed name. When asked which one to use, Lance thought back to some brothers who he remembered from kickboxing many years ago, Tony and Vernon Dore. Tony had also boxed a little, so would be on the record somewhere if checks were made. Thus, a legend was born, the contract was signed and Lance Lewis became Tony Dore.

The transformation into Tony began! Lance shaved his head and got rid of the beard. Whilst doing his day job as a schoolteacher in class he was Mr Lewis, when he was boxing he became Tony Dore. It was an elaborate sting and one that had never been tried before, but Lance felt it worthwhile. There was no real surprise for him when he went for a boxing medical and passed the eye test with flying colours to gain his licence. This only served to further fuel a desire to expose the truth and prove once and for all that he had had six years of his boxing career stolen from him. Finally, the time arrived for 'Tony's' first fight and typically, it wasn't all plain sailing.

On 5th September, 1988, at the Edmiston club, Glasgow, he was due to face Peterborough born Neil Legget, under his new guise as Tony Dore. However, all hell broke loose on the morning of the fight when it was discovered the referee was to be Manchester's legendary, MC, match-maker, manager, trainer, agent and promoter, Nat Basso. Lance panicked because he and Nat knew each other well. His cover would be blown before even entering the ring! So, a plan was hatched.

One that evolved from sheer desperation and Glaswegian ingenuity. They would get Nat so drunk that come the first bell he wouldn't be able to recognise himself in front of the mirror, never mind Lance! Incredibly, after Nat was wined and dined throughout the afternoon, the plan worked and Tony Dore won his first fight on points and a good evening was had by all. At times Lance remembers Nat giving him the odd strange stare, but he put that down to Glasgow hospitality!

From that nerve shattering opening night as Tony Dore, matters settled down a little in the ring. Over the next eighteen months Lance fought eleven times, including twice in Italy and lost only once. All appeared to be going well.

Too well.

On 6th December 1989 at Wembley Arena he was down to box an eight-round contest against a tough former silver Olympic medallist, the twenty-four-year-old Nigerian, Peter Konyegwachie. Top of the bill that night was British Heavyweight champion Gary Mason. The arena was full. All of London's boxing movers and shakers were present ringside, including a certain Mickey Duff. As Lance readied himself in his corner before the bout, Duff entered the ring and walked towards him. He just stared whilst wearing a knowing smile. Immediately Lance knew it was all over.

"Hello Tony Dore," said a smiling Duff before turning away. With those three words the whole facade came crashing down. Or so Lance thought. With his mind unsurprisingly elsewhere, he lost that night on points to Konyegwachie.

The next day Lance received a phone call from Brian. He had been contacted by someone claiming to represent Mickey Duff. The caller told Brian that if Lance took a fight in Liverpool against Duff's up and coming prospect, the young twenty-year-old scouser, Nigel Wenton, in five days time thenhis true identity would not be revealed. It was blackmail, pure and simple. Left with no option, Lance agreed. This despite the fact his hands were badly mauled from the Konyegwachie bout.

On the following Saturday night, at the Sports Centre, Kirby, a strange atmosphere filled Lance's dressing room. At one time when Lance was just sat quietly, somebody shouted his real name from outside in the corridor. This was clearly done to try and unnerve him. In his corner that fateful evening was Billy Koyte, he and Lance were close and Billy just wanted the whole night to be over with so they could go home, "It doesn't smell right Lance," said Billy.

Calling on all his experience and defensive skills, for Lance could hardly punch with two damaged hands, he made the highly rated Wenton appear clumsy. Lance would spin him so Wenton struggled to get his shots off. Here was an experienced pro, who had been there, seen it and done it twice over. Lance fought a magnificent rearguard action laced with guts and buckets of technical skill. At times Wenton couldn't lay a glove on him. That Lance lost on points hardly mattered, for he had proved a point. Brought in at the last moment to be used as cannon fodder, instead Lance had schooled Micky Duff's bright young thing. He had embarrassed him and despite a promise made, once again Duff dropped a grenade and blew the lid on Tony Dore.

The following morning, the tabloid headlines exposed it all! The fallout was incredible. It was carnage, total hysteria.

The *News of the World* ran the story for three weeks under the banner 'THE TONY DORE SCANDAL' Unsurprisingly, Lance was barred from ever entering a British boxing ring again, although now at least his side of the story was out.

So, it was a case of RIP Tony Dore, yet Lance Lewis's journey was just beginning.

As one door shut firmly in his face, Lance simply walked through another and returned to martial arts and within twelve months he became European kick boxing champion. It was also the year he started as a specialist teacher dealing with primary and high school pupils in an emotional and challenging behaviour school. Finally, in 1997, he achieved his ultimate dream by becoming martial arts world champion. Lance is recognised as the greatest pound-for-pound kick boxer to ever come out of the UK.

Meanwhile, his astonishing life outside the ring continued. The young kid who once stood in the schoolyard, contemplating the universe, in a world of his own, would now go to work. At the age of thirty-six, he was finally officially diagnosed with Dyslexia. Lance had faced many burdens in his life, but to achieve so much whilst also overcoming this was surely his greatest victory.

Lance's academic career led to him spending a considerable amount of time living in Manhattan. There he worked with African-American and Hispanic youths experiencing difficulties in education and at risk of gang involvement. It was from this he developed a number of successful approaches for working with similar youths of African descent in primary and high schools in England. In 1995, his work directly led to a school in Manchester becoming the first in the country to put African/ Black centred history on the curriculum for all pupils. Lance's immense research contribution in helping under-privileged kids also saw him earn a Doctorate and in 2002, a PHD from Manchester Metropolitan University.

In acknowledgement of Lance's achievements, despite the barriers faced, he is now one of the characters to feature in a school book that was launched in the House of Lords in 2007. This child friendly book is about black pioneers, ancient and modern called 'Did You Know?' Also, in honour of Lance, the Nigerian Royal family of Ekiti State, Nigeria, awarded him a chieftaincy in 2008. And there is more: so much more! Enough for his own book - all will be revealed in Lance's soon-to-be-released autobiography.

Today his special talents remain in demand across the world at international schools in places as far flung as the US, Saudi Arabia, Egypt, Jordan and Kazakhstan. As well as being a PE instructor, Lance teaches the teachers in specific subjects such as monitoring a child's well-being, motivation techniques, group work and leadership. When home he operates as a substitute teacher. Never off duty, his own upbringing in the brutal life of hard knocks means anything Lance can give back, he will.

"I treat every kid as one of my own" he says of his teaching, "It's a big family, and one that also still extends to Collyhurst and Moston."

Steeped in the spirit of Brian Hughes, on a recent trip back there he witnessed the gym's rebirth under the stewardship of Pat Barrett and Thomas McDonagh, the visit left him open-mouthed, emotional and proud. Lance joked that if somebody back in the day had asked him which two people were the least likely to have been in charge of the successful running of the place, he would have said Pat and Tommy! Never could Lance have been happier to be wrong!

"Watching the two work it's clear Brian's methods have stayed in place," he says, "but the lads have also taken the place forward. I couldn't be more proud."

And for the man who would not be moved, there is no better way to end.

7 - ALEC CLARK
FROM THE EAST END TO LIGHTBOWNE ROAD

He may not speak with a Mancunian accent or know the words to Collyhurst Road but Alec Clark (his family were so poor as kids they could not afford the 'e') is equally a part of Collyhurst and Moston Boxing Club as any world famous fighter that has ever walked up those steps. It is in his heart.

ALEC'S RELATIONSHIP WITH THE CLUB, and specifically Brian Hughes, began in the early 1970s when the club was based on Willert Street. Alec is a proud East London boy from Canning Town, an area of London very similar to Collyhurst, albeit on a larger scale. Upon leaving school, there were few opportunities available. It was either factory work or, depending on talent, a footballer, gangster, priest, or if blessed with the right ability, a boxer.

Like Collyhurst, great respect was given to those who fought between the ropes. Indeed, in every working-class city, whether it be Liverpool, Newcastle or Glasgow, the same applied. The *Sunday Times* once described Alec's birthplace as the 'Ashtray of London.' It was a description that inspired immense pride in the local populace! The legendary boxing writer Colin Hart wrote of it, that within a two and half mile radius of the docks there had been born more World, European, Empire, Commonwealth and British champions than anywhere else in the country. It was a remarkable fighting heritage, where every warehouse and factory had a boxing club. Alec's family was laced with the sport's history, the pugilist's art was an East End religion.

All the family boxed. Alec's grandfather, Paddy Clark, was a well-known East End character. He was a feared but beloved bare-knuckle fighter who would ply his talent on the old crofts. Once finished, Paddy would enter a local pub, one that had the old style Wild West swing doors, head straight to the bar and climb up on it. Then bloodied, but unbowed, whether in victory or defeat, he would loudly declare to huge cheers that the next round was on him and burst into song! Somewhere, in the heart of the East End, there still hangs a photo of the great Paddy Clark in full flow!

Alec met his wife Carole, a Newton Heath girl, when he was working at a holiday camp in Devon. Originally they were going to live in Bristol and Alec and a friend were going to sell cars back into London but circumstances saw them instead move to Manchester. They settled at 29 Hilda Street, off Lightbowne Road, with the rent at two shillings a week. Alec had heard of the Collyhurst and Moston club before. One of his closest friends back home was Jimmy Tibbs and Alec remained in touch with all the boxing news coming out of the East End. He had also seen some of the Collyhurst lads fight in the ABA semi-finals in Birmingham, "Those lads always stuck in my mind as being different" he says today, "They had a touch of style that fascinated me and made them stand apart."

In the early 1970s Alec wandered into the club on Willert Street with his youngest son. After a while he got to know Brian Hughes, as it became apparent they had many mutual friends in boxing. The pair shared a love of the sport and would chat for hours about fighter's styles past and present. Once Brian had got to know Alec, he asked him to help out about the club and a friendship began that would last until this day. Alec was swiftly hooked by the Collyhurst & Moston ethos and became passionate about the club, its colours and all they stood for; the red and gold. One of his greatest thrills was arranging to take a team to the East End to fight on his old patch. Six of them travelled down in a big Jaguar. There was himself, Brian and fighters Ensley Bingham, Kenny Dobson, Wayne Pritchard and Johnny Mills. Alec remembers that Brian was beaming, but as ever he remained laid back and underplayed everything. He epitomised the self-confidence that ran through the club. Brian rarely showed any aggression, but come fight night, the mask would come off as the gloves went on.

The show was a huge success for the visitors with all their fighters winning and impressing hugely. The Manchester lads were cheered to the rafters and it was a memorable moment for Alec. Here, in his hometown, he had made a triumphal return. As for Brian? He was treated like royalty and everyone made a fuss of him. His reputation was already well known amongst the aficionado London fight fans, at that time this area dominated boxing in England.

The promoter Terry Lawless once confided to Alec that during this period any boxer coming to fight in the capital from the north held little fear and no research was done on him - unless, that is, they hailed from Collyhurst and Moston Boxing Club! Then Lawless wanted to know all about the fighter. Alec still remembers with great pride the time he brought the boys back, his eyes well up at the memory of their performances and how wonderfully they were received.

The area was home to several renowned boxing clubs such as West Ham Boy's - once known as the most powerful amateur club in the world and their great rivals from across the river – Fisher Amateur Boxing Club. Then there were the famed black tops - The Eltham Boxing Club where Henry Cooper learned his trade and that infamous West Ham-Millwall rivalry stemming from a hundred years before when Millwall dockers failed to back up their West Ham counterparts in a strike that led to a simmering hatred that lingers on until today. However, the arrival of Collyhurst and Moston in London that night cut through all this as the visiting Mancs charmed the East End.

Journeys with the club were never boring. None more so than when Brian insisted on calling off at fish and chip shops and then proceed to rattle the staff terribly with his Manc sarcasm and wit whilst bartering away for the best deal. He would say, whilst pointing at the fish, "Look, it's splitting! No, no, look, look! It's splitting in two. You've got to give us a bit of discount on that broken one there!" On Brian went, not stopping until he was happy he had got a bargain!

Another high point occurred in 1972, a few weeks after the horrific Bloody Sunday massacre in Derry, Northern Ireland. At that period, no significant sporting event had taken place in the province for some time, with all professional sportsmen and teams refusing or not being allowed to set foot across the Irish Sea at the height of The Troubles - the situation was poisonous, the place was a war zone. So when a friend of Brian's, a trainer who ran the Derry Boxing Club, asked if there was the remotest possibility that he would consider bringing a team to the city to box, Brian talked it over with Alec. After much soul-searching and discussions with all involved, Brian decided to go. Collyhurst and Moston Boxing Club would rise above politics and show people, just as has happened recently in our own city, that life must go on.

It was a nervous group of Mancunians who arrived in Derry, only to find that the Irish people opened their arms to embrace them. The trainers and fighters from Collyhurst and Moston were treated as long-lost family and their brave action to make the journey was seen as an act of friendship never to be forgotten. They were taken to meet the Mayor and, much more importantly, Brian organised a trip to see the temporary Bloody Sunday monument. As their bus pulled up and the lads walked towards the site, the locals in the surrounding flats poured out to greet them. There was spontaneous applause, hugs, kisses and embraces that brought many of the young lads to tears, none more than Winston Cousins.

A black lad from Manchester, Winston had never experienced such a show of emotion from white faces. This reinforced Brian's decision to make the trip to prove that in the fight against bigotry, there can be no better weapon than sport. This was the same Winston who almost caused a diplomatic incident with the Soviet Union, and a possible long unexpected stay in Siberia. He had travelled to the USSR with the England boxing team having forged his own passport to make the journey! After originally lending it to a brother for a trip to Jamaica, where they simply swapped photos, he then had to place his own back in for the adventure behind the Iron Curtain. Happily, by some miracle, Winston made it home. It was an ashen-faced Brian Hughes who listened on in utter shock to Winston telling him all about it the next day! They teach you many things in Collyhurst and Moston Boxing Club but international espionage was never one of them...

Anyway, that same night in Derry, Brian received a phone call from a high-ranking British army officer, who told him, "We will be watching your every move." "Stay away!" Brian replied and put down the phone, for there was simply no need for army protection. And so it proved - for come the show it all went wonderfully well with the Manchester lads in red and gold, mostly prevailing and earning fantastic cheers from an adoring and thankful Derry audience. Shortly before the first fight was due on Brian was visited by a leading member of the IRA who thanked him for coming and reassured him that as their guests they would come to no harm. Where so many feared to tread, Collyhurst and Moston were received with open arms! The visit proved to be a triumph in every sense.

Closer to home, Brian Hughes was contacted by the manager of the local Ben Brierley pub football team in Moston. At the time these lads were winning titles and leagues for fun. It was a well-known fact in the Manchester Sunday leagues you did not mess with them. The manager asked Brian if they could have a few sessions training in the gym. Brian happily agreed and passed the task over to Alec. Knowing their reputation for being a little rum, to say the least, Alec was at first taken back but Brian swiftly calmed him, "Don't worry mate, with your cockney accent they'll be scared to death!"

Come the night they strolled up the stairs, cocky and thinking it would all be a piece of cake, Alec soon had them on the bags. Firstly, just for twenty-five seconds, which they found easy enough, but then for a full minute and down on their knees in between. Soon the feared Ben Brierley were close to a collective heart attack. Alec didn't ease up on them and once the session finished they all staggered out into the Moston night; breathless, coughing and red faced. They were cocky no more! The next day Brian received another phone call from the manager to inform him the Ben Brierley would not be coming back. "That f.....g cockney nearly killed my boys!"

In those early days money was always desperately needed for funding repairs to the gym and equipment. There was always something that needed mending whether it be gloves or a plumber to fix the toilet. They would put on dinner shows at places like the Lightbowne Club and make a couple of hundred pounds and a bit more off the raffle, but it was never enough. Alec hit on an idea – why not copy what the London clubs did? West Ham Boys would hold three huge shows a year at the West Ham baths hosting 2500 punters. There would be special guests, speeches, singers, auctions and quizzes, but it would ultimately be in aid of the boxing club. Alec argued this was what they had to aim for.

He began to organise similar nights at venues such as the nearby British Aerospace or the Bower Hotel and they proved hugely successful. The evenings were very up market and sponsors queued to be associated with Collyhurst and Moston. Some events made up to eight thousand pounds and every penny found its way back into the club. Alec was elected treasurer and made a point of ensuring he always got the best deal. Sometimes the parsimony of his treasurer worried Brian as his careful friend from the East End played hard ball with suppliers. Alec always paid in the end, but with bank interest in those days running at ten to twelve percent, every penny counted and it would always be at a snail's pace!

Another aspect of their friendship was the similarity in the pair's politics. But while Brian was a Labour man, Alec was a little more hard-line, he was a dyed-in-the-wool Communist from the dockyards of East London. Both hailed from similar backgrounds and had seen first-hand the heart-rending poverty, pollution and industrialisation wrought by market forces and pre-war governments. They would argue with each other for hours with unbridled passion, but they never fell out, for it was simply impossible to. Here were two men who wore the same working class traditional values like a medal around their necks and believed more than anything else in loyalty to family and friends – to your own.

These arguments often diverged into other unanswerable questions – such as why were there no great gymnasts or tennis players emerging from their parts of the world? From Moston, Collyhurst or Canning Town? The pair thought it was time to try and do something about it. They hated the tragedy that in the early eighties was afflicting Moston and so many similar areas. Huge local firms like Ferranti's and British Aerospace were laying off workers in huge numbers. Margaret Thatcher's Tory government was busy decimating working-class communities and Collyhurst and Moston was not spared. Unemployment spiralled as sons and daughters watched their parents lose heart along with their livelihoods. Hopes and dreams were wiped out at the same wicked speed as the Tories were shutting down factories and breaking the heart of a once unbreakable Cottonopolis. Brian and Alec, in their own way, wanted to try and help.

A committee was formed to help change the landscape, one that meant business. On it, alongside the two Collyhurst and Moston men, was politician Paul Murphy and friend of the club Bob Barlow. Then there was Billy Howarth, a well-known scrap metal merchant from Collyhurst and local businessman, Duggie Flood, who had made a fortune in the hotel and leisure business. It was rumoured that Duggie had changed the Kray twin's minds about staying in Manchester back in the sixties after they had arrived by train at Piccadilly station. He was said to have politely advised them to "Go home!" but not in so many words! Another member of the committee was a landlord from the Sparrow Pub in Collyhurst, Ray Carroll, also noted for other talents. They were desperate to help out the club in any manner possible and to round off the committee was Saint Dunstan's priest and the commander of Collyhurst Police station, Brian Eastwood. The power of politics, law, God and the dark side of Manchester combined to help the kids of Collyhurst and Moston.

"We want to produce battleships, not sprinters!" insisted Brian. "Hand them the tools to get through their lives, not just a small part of it." The plan was to expand: to produce champions for other sports, not just boxing and with the help of the committee, they set about doing so. To make this possible a bigger venue was required and Brian and Alec had one in mind, just a stone's throw from the present site. Across Lightbowne Road sat a large Methodist church that was perfect in size. It was the legendary Police commander James Anderton, who claimed to be on first name terms with God, who made the introduction. Whether Anderton did whisper into the almighty's ear can never be proven, but a deal was quickly sealed. Now, the only problem remaining was for Brian and Alec to come up with the £160,000 required to make their dream of a Mancunian sporting Camelot come true.

This was all happening in the aftermath of the Toxteth, Brixton and Moss Side riots. Community funds were being made available by the government, but when Brian and Alec approached them, they were told money could only be used for creating new jobs. The reply was simple and straight forward, "Collyhurst and Moston are not creating jobs, they're creating new people." Such was their refusal to go away and take no for an answer, they were eventually given special dispensation and £60,000 was grudgingly handed over.

Next on the hitlist for Brian and Alec was the Sports Council. This organisation was like a red rag to a bull for these two men steeped in working class culture. In their first meeting with the Sports Council they were curtly informed in no uncertain manner, nothing doing.

"No funds are available for a project such as yours," they were told. But Brian was prepared, "What about the money you recently handed over to the Oxford rowing squad for equipment? And what about the same amount you gave Cambridge as well?" At first the Sports Council refused to budge until Brian played their joker, "Fine forget it. We'll go elsewhere and find the cash, but you remember this. When we have our grand opening and reporters ask us about you lot, and trust me they will, I'll make sure that I tell the world that it took us so long to complete this project for the kids because the Sports Council said 'no' but thanks to the generosity of others we finally got it done and your name will not be on our plaque!"

The next day it was announced that the Sports Council were delighted to be working with Collyhurst and Moston!

And, so it carried on - Manchester City Council promised to match the funding when they reached £80,000. This they did and finally, the money was raised. Brian and Alec had worked miracles, to scratch, borrow, barter and beg to make their dream come true. It was a remarkable achievement and no expense was spared to ensure the kids had the very best facilities. Everything was top class, from the changing room, showers, a boxing ring, a state of the art sports floor, a five a side football pitch and a brand-new car park. Not to mention an extension to the original building. It was a brave new world, one created by men who wanted to change things and make life a little easier for kids nobody outside their families cared little about.

Sadly, it proved to be short lived, for the dream swiftly turned into a nightmare. Problems began when a strange smell rose through the building. Matters turned worse when the cellar flooded and dry rot was discovered. Despite calling in all kind of experts, the water continued to return and take a heavy toll. Nobody could figure out what was causing it? Whilst investigations were ongoing, Brian got the lease back for the old gym. Even the notion of ancient tributaries flowing beneath the building was checked out, but to no avail. Finally, with a heavy heart, the decision was taken to sell the building, lock, stock and soaking barrel, back to the council. The dream died and so they returned home, up those twenty steps back to work.

Alec never failed to be amazed at just how good a boxing coach Brian was. He was a driving force and fulcrum of the gym, a fountain of knowledge. He would always tell Alec that their job was to concentrate on a fighter's finer points, make them even better, whilst building on what they were not so good at. Brian was meticulous, verging on obsessive. He kept diaries on every boxer in the gym and missed nothing. Every training session would be logged and noted. Notes on sparring, time-keeping, weight and attitude were made. They were all essential to the overall make up of a Collyhurst and Moston boxer. Brian assessed whether they were improving, standing still, or deteriorating. Alec had been around boxing gyms and different coaches all his life, but he is adamant that none could lay a glove on Brian Hughes. The only one who could possibly come close to Brian, and stand alongside him, in his opinion, was Jimmy Tibbs. Brian's ultimate dream of finding a Heavyweight champion may never have come to fruition, for he simply never had the tools to work with, but that apart, his immense achievements with a whole host of champions at different weights means, for Alec, he stands alone today.

Over the years Brian would regular correspond stateside with some of the sport's all-time greats trainers such as Gus D'Amato, Jimmy Jacobs, Freddy Lynch and Emanuel Steward and there were times when Brian's love hate relationship with the realities of boxing was sorely tested. The dark arts that scarred the game made him abhor the sport at times. Shortly after the tragic death of Welsh boxer Johnny Owen at the hands of the ferocious Mexican world champion Lupe Pintor in 1980, Brian and Alec were present at ringside when another young fighter lost their life in a horrendous mis-match that stunk of corruption. It sickened both men, but for Brian in particular, it was enough to make him seriously consider giving up. In the end he carried on, but in an interview given to a journalist called Bobby Light, a sports writer for the Socialist Workers Party magazine, Brian opened his heart on the darker side of his sport. Both truthful and gut wrenching the words just poured out onto the page. They spat like bullets, sprinkled with tears - a symphony for the ring.

On completion Brian sent a copy of it to his good friend Emanuel Steward, who was so moved he put it in a frame and a pride of place in the Kronk gym. It was the first thing you saw when you entered the hallowed Detroit gym.

A lighter side of their relationship showed itself many years later when Steward was over in Manchester at a sports dinner with the legendary Thomas 'The Hitman' Hearns. Also present was Brian Hughes. Hearns had recently lost an epic fight against Sugar Ray Leonard and Brian could not help telling him how he could have avoided Leonard's lightning punches. After hearing and thinking it made so much common sense, Hearns turned towards Steward, "Hey Emanuel, why did you not tell me to do that?" The look on Steward's face was said to have been priceless!

We have already mentioned Steward's offer for Brian to go and work in the States in a previous chapter, what is less known is that Mike Tyson's trainer, Jimmy Jacobs, also wanted him to train his wonderful prospect Mark Breland. Jacobs offered Brian $1million a year, but again, for him, home was where the heart lay and he respectfully said no.

In 1985, the South London born American Golden gloves champion Michael Bennt travelled from New York to Manchester, with his good friend Tunde Foster, once of the Lightbowne parish, but by then known as 'Doctor Foster' and one of the most popular boxers fighting out of the 'Big Apple.' Tunde had emigrated years before, but had always remained in contact with his old mentor Brian Hughes.

The pair were crossing the ocean as a favour to Brian who, after corresponding with their trainer Jimmy Jacobs, came up with a novel idea and something different for a north Manchester boxing show. New York's finest in Michael Bentt versus Ireland's Heavyweight champion with the fight to be put on at Saint Matthew's RC high school in Moston. All of the city's major Irish 'movers and shakers' would be present and these characters were over-flowing in generosity of spirit for the right cause and none better than Collyhurst and Moston Boxing Club.

On first sighting the Lightbowne gym, Bentt was enthralled. He was a wonderful fighter, sheer class. Then Tunde took him over to Moss Side to hang out with old friends and train a little with them. These were different times in Manchester, there was a lot of gang-related racism both real and imagined and some members of the Moss Side gym were soon telling Bentt that he was being used by the 'white man' and that certain others were going to make a fortune out of him. It was all said to put doubt in his mind and was wide of the mark as Collyhurst and Moston was renowned as a place where all were welcome, regardless of colour or creed.

The next day Bentt returned to the Lightbowne gym complaining he could not fight because of a damaged hand. Although there was a slight injury, it wasn't anything remotely serious and it was clear to both Brian and Alec that somebody had got at him. This was where the genius of Brian Hughes once more showed itself. He took Bentt aside, "Now don't you worry, son. It just so happens that a very close friend of mine, a Harley street surgeon, is in Manchester treating a footballer. I'm going to ring him and we'll sort this." Bentt knew Harley Street as the fabled place where the doctors to film stars and rock idols had their surgeries. That was good enough for him!

A problem now existed... after consulting with Alec, Brian remembered there was someone else who could help them pull this off, the landlord of the New Moston pub, Tommy O'Malley. A great patron of the boxing club, O'Malley's best friend happened to be a vet! After explaining their predicament to him, Tommy rang the vet and with a little gentle persuasion, he agreed to act as the Harley Street doctor. Now, all they required was a nurse and the small matter of a hospital.

Another call was made to a mutual acquaintance, whose girlfriend happened to be a midwife at the now gone, but much beloved Booth Hall Children's Hospital. Again, the good will towards Brian and the club showed itself as the lady in question agreed to go along with their Mancunian sting! A pre-arranged time was set to meet Brian, Alec and Bentt in the hospital foyer. As the men entered, she stood there smiling wide and pointed down a nearby corridor.

"Hello Mr Bentt, please follow me."

Off they strode before entering a side room. "Make yourself comfortable gentlemen" continued the nurse. "The specialist will be with you shortly."

It was Oscar winning stuff.

A couple of minutes passed before the door opened and a man in a white doctor's coat walked in. Full of purpose he shook both Brian and Alec's hands. "Good to see you again Brian," he said before looking across at Bentt and nodding approvingly. "So, you're the next Heavyweight champion of the world, Mr Bentt? Let's get you fixed up." The vet was playing his role to perfection. He picked up Bentt's injured hand and checked it closely.

"Oh, there is no real damage here, young man, nothing that a little extra special bandaging won't take care of." He looked the boxer straight in the eyes, "Now then, there are very few people I would trust to do this, but Michael, this is your lucky day. Do you know why?"

"No" the fighter replied with a look of sincere respect and awe at this man's medical opinion, despite the fact that it would have carried much more weight in a stable or a cow shed.

"Because Michael," continued the vet, "the one man I would trust to do this is stood right there," and with that he points to Brian who smiles back at him.

Bentt grins widely, "Man! It truly is my lucky day."

Come fight night, in a Saint Matthew's class room acting as a changing area, Brian, with great care and putting on a wonderful play of applying extra bandages to his fighter's hands, finally finished, "There you go Michael," he said, "perfect!"

Content in the knowledge his hand was wrapped by a true master, Bentt went out and hammered the beleaguered and badly outclassed Irish champion in the first round. It was a happy ending and one typifying how, when pushed, Brian always found a solution to the greatest of problems.

"All for one!"

As the years rolled on work commitments saw Alec forced to spend less time at the gym, but he and Brian have always remained close. Today his heart still belongs to Collyhurst and Moston. The passion for the red and gold burns brighter than ever and the kid from the East End, lovingly christened 'Joe 90' by another great patron of the club, Bernard Manning, remains its biggest supporter.

A Cockney with a Mancunian heart, he is one of our own.

8 - PAT BARRETT
THE BLACK FLASH

SALERNO: ITALY. 24TH AUGUST, 1990: it was a punch they claimed resonated all along the Amalfi coast right up to Naples and probably echoed 1532 miles away in Moston, Manchester. The local hero and European Super Lightweight champion, twenty-six-year-old Efrem Calamati, was unbeaten in twenty-seven previous fights and the pride of all Salerno. On that still, sweltering evening, deep in the Italian south, Calamati was defending his title for a sixth time against an unfancied Englishman, Pat Barrett. It was always said in this part of the world that any successful challenger would need at least two knockouts to sneak a close defeat, but not on this evening.

It all happened in a black flash…

Calamati, if not quite sleeping with the fishes, was put on temporary first name terms with them as Barrett's right hook hit home. Consternation and shock reigned at ringside in this makeshift boxing arena built on a beach. The Mancunian had rocked Italy in no less a way than the nearby volcano, Mount Vesuvius, that loomed large over Salerno's big city neighbour Naples had ever done. With a sickening thud, both frightening and dramatic, Calamati dropped like a tree being felled and lay unconscious. Collyhurst and Moston had come to Salerno. It was a long way from Lightbowne Road.

North Manchester: 2017: as we move on through the years, it's time to take a stroll up Lightbowne Road, Moston, past FC United's red roofed stadium on one side and on the other Moston cemetery, a sea of past lives, hopes and dreams. Onwards, it is just a five-minute walk until you reach a set of traffic lights and there above you looms a large Victorian building. At floor level is a food store, the gym resides above. Looking upwards you see the sign emblazoned in red: Collyhurst and Moston Lads Club. The entrance is on the corner, up two sets of winding steps, until you reach a small corridor. There are ripped posters on unwashed walls and silence, broken by the echoes of leaking water. A door stands ajar. Ten yards away a half-hidden punchbag can be seen. In the back room is a full-size boxing ring and on entering an open training floor is separated by a small walkway where an office sits. Hanging pride of place behind a desk, in the midst of poster bills, certificates, old Polaroids and club memorabilia, is a photograph of Brian Hughes with the words 'The Godfather' beneath it. The message is obvious, he may not physically be at the gym anymore but his spirit and philosophy lives on. One of those striving to ensure Brian's legacy remains enshrined in all who wear the colours of Collyhurst and Moston is Pat Barrett. The office now belongs to Pat and this is his story.

Born in Moss Side, on 22nd July, 1967, Pat is one of five children - three sisters Barbara, Martha and Sonia and elder brother Michael. Their mother, Iris, was a firm disciplinarian, a strong-minded lady. A single parent who loved, fought and protected her kids with everything she had. When Pat was just two years old, Iris moved the family to Foreland Avenue, Collyhurst and they became one of the first black families in the area. Back then Manchester was a different world, racism was everywhere - monkey chants and banana jokes were the norm on telly or at the football. Casual racism was a national disease with its own apologists. Of course, Collyhurst was no exception. Pat's elder brother Michael was constantly fighting, if he wasn't sticking up for his family, then he'd be sticking up for himself. Born with a hole in his heart, Michael refused to let that curtail his love of sport, so much that at nine years old he walked into the Collyhurst Lads club on Willert Street run by Brian Hughes and took up football and boxing. It was only when his mother found out and pulled the plug that Michael took the gloves off although, when he was away from his mother's all-seeing eyes he would always have a dabble! Today Michael is fifty-four and fit as a fiddle which is a minor miracle when you consider that doctors at the time of his diagnosis told his mother that people with his condition rarely lived past thirty-two. It must be the north Manchester air…

The family moved once more, this time just a mile down Rochdale Road to Harpurhey, a place best known at that time for the comedian

Bernard Manning's, 'world famous' (so he claimed) Embassy club. Here the family again found themselves in a minority and facing the same problems they had suffered in Collyhurst. It was only natural then that Pat should gravitate towards nearby Cheetham Hill. To his relief this place felt different, for there existed a large black community and he made friends there that would last a life time, through exceedingly good times and horrifically bad.

Back in those days Pat was Michael's shadow. The pair were inseparable. Pat started off as a kick-boxer, which all seemed to be going well until one particularly memorable encounter when a talented young girl embarrassingly put him down on the mat - a career in the martial arts was swiftly forgotten. He would try elsewhere. Locally, Michael was a respected figure, always in and out of trouble and with a well-earned reputation as a hard man. To keep fit he would go to Collyhurst and later, Moston lads club and by this time the original club had been flattened and relocated to Lightbowne Road. There Pat would go and watch him train. He would take everything in. A slight kid, fearless on the streets, Pat had been in plenty of fights, but rarely won. He described himself like Popeye without the spinach! Muscles were needed. Pat had a big heart and was 'game' but ultimately always left on the floor. Something had to change.

So, after leaving school at sixteen, he started making the daily one-and-a-half-mile pilgrimage from Harpurhey with his gym bag, determined that life was not going to beat him down. Little did Pat know that while training he was being scrutinised very closely by Brian Hughes. As Michael says today, "Our Pat was a natural though he would never admit it."

Brian recognised the talent early on. Upon removing Pat's gloves after every session, he would say quietly, but constantly, "You're going to be good Pat, you have something. You can be a champion." Thinking he probably said that to all his fighters, Pat humoured him, "Yeah right Brian, course I am," after all, Pat barely knew Brian. He assumed he was just being polite. Yet, just as Harry Fleming had recognised the talent of Brown, McAvoy and King years before, Brian now saw something in Pat that, if harnessed correctly, could see him go all the way. He urged Pat to take his medical and give it a go. Pat did and slowly what started as a hobby became a bug; an all-consuming desire. Everything came naturally to him. Pat had found something he loved. In the amateurs, his early record was impressive, which was surprising because at Collyhurst and Moston, Brian stressed defensive skills. Whereas amateur judges looked for points scoring and an upright, all action style, the defensive aspects of the Collyhurst and Moston lads, although technically brilliant, largely went unnoticed and more than likely ignored. It was all about movement, countering and slipping punches. Brian would pull Pat aside beforehand and utter the words all those who fought under him would instantly recognise.

"Go and look in the mirror and, after the fight, I don't want you to look any different."

However, Pat was learning and listening in the gym. He was soaking everything up. Brian's word became law and when the time came to go professional, Pat was ready.

Sadly, nobody in the Barrett family was prepared for what happened next. In 1987 they lost their beloved mother Iris, who sadly passed away to break the family's heart. It was under this dark shadow that a nineteen-year-old Pat, still grieving, decided to try and make a career in the ring. His early fights were drama-filled as he took up with boxing promoter Harry Miller and went on the road. Miller had a reputation for supplying 'cannon fodder' and beefing up the bill if needed with journeymen, new meat and last-minute replacements. Pat was never expected to win and the many times he impressed in upsetting the odds meant word began to spread amongst punters. For just £600 a fight he was more than value for money. Like an unexpected bar brawl, he was guaranteed to ruin the favourite's night.

Incredibly fearless for one so young, Pat was up for boxing anybody, anywhere. Miller fixed him up a bout in Interlaken, Switzerland on 1st July, 1987, against a popular local fighter called Iskander Savas and nobody expected this scrawny black kid from England to upset the odds, but they never counted on an old pro from Collyhurst who knew every trick in the proverbial boxing book. On reaching the ring there were two pairs of gloves, one, the old-fashioned straw gloves, the other a nice set of eight ounce gloves. The fighters tossed for them and Pat lost. However, seemingly not interested in the result, Brian picked up the nice gloves. "Brian, we lost the toss," implored Pat, but he was away! The Swiss were bemused and kept pointing towards them. "I speaky no

English," smiled Brian, as he began to put them on Pat and as the Swiss crowd raged at the foreigners' antics with the gloves, Pat shut them all up in the first round when he knocked Savas clean out.

"Cheers Brian" said Pat, as his gloves were taken off by the old maestro afterwards.

"Don't mention it, Patrick" replied Brian with a smile and a wink. "Let's go home, son."

The 'Black Flash' moniker was bestowed by Brian on Pat as a tribute to Ghanaian fighter Roy Ankrah, a former Commonwealth Featherweight champion who specialised in knockouts. Pat reminded Brian so much of Ankrah and it was a nickname wholly suited to his modern-day successor. There was one disappointment when, in only his third professional bout, Pat was surprisingly matched against a much more experienced opponent, the classy Preston born Paul Burke. On 1st June, 1987, at the Norfolk Gardens Hotel, Bradford, Pat fought well after being put down in the fifth round, but was finally beaten on a close point's decision. It was his first defeat and hit him badly. Suddenly this wasn't a game anymore. Despite Brian's urging that every great fighter loses at some point in their careers (and it was certainly no disgrace against someone of Burke's class who would go on to become a British champion) Pat was utterly determined to never suffer that losing feeling again. From that night he went unbeaten in the ring for five years.

It is strange how so much more is learnt in the aftermath of bitter defeat rather than glorious victory. A boxer's pride and ego can never be underestimated. The next day Pat was back in the gym and would go on a great run of twelve fights, wining eleven and drawing just one, and that against a tough and skilled Liverpool boxer called Sugar Gibiliru, a name that haunted Pat for some time. It all stemmed back to his early days as an amateur when he felt like nobody could get near him in the gym ring. Brian sensed outside help was needed just to calm his lad down and to make Pat realise that it was best he walked before he tried to run. To do so Brian brought in a professional fighter to spar with him.

Pat hit Sugar Gibiliru with every punch in his armoury, but he just kept coming. He walked through Pat's shots with alarming ease and unleashed his own thrusting the youngster on to the back foot and he was clearly hurting. It was simply a case of a professional schooling an amateur. A mismatch. All eyes in the gym fell on the ring as Pat was hammered mercilessly by Sugar on the ropes. From pillar to post, he was cowering and covering up. Finally, Brian had seen enough, "All right, come out now Pat, that's it, son. Time." A hushed silence descended on the gym, broken with occasional calls of encouragement, though it was clear many were shocked at what had just occurred. A smiling Sugar stood in the centre of the ring enjoying his moment. This irked Brian who motioned to another fighter, the much more experienced, retired professional, Lance Lewis to recover the gym's pride.

In went Lance who in no time at all was hammering Sugar and making it known with every punch thrown that in Collyhurst and Moston you show respect, whether in victory or defeat. For Pat, the mauling he received at Sugar's hands left him reeling. Heartbroken, his eyes welled up and tears of frustration started to fall and soon he was sobbing uncontrollably. This from a young man who later admitted he couldn't cry at his mother's funeral. No words from Brian could console him as he realised just how far there was still to go. From that moment on, Sugar Gibiliru would be someone Pat measured himself against and until the day came when he could beat him, Pat's eyes would always see Sugar coming towards him like a mechanical robot – a relentless demon that haunted his every thought.

On 1st March, 1988, the time finally came to fight Sugar Gibiliru once more at the Midland Hotel, Manchester. Following the fight, Brian had arranged for Pat to travel to America and train at Sugar Ray Leonard's gym in Baltimore. On first being told of the bout with his nemesis, Pat was riddled with self-doubt, but as the first bell rang, it soon became clear that his past worries had disappeared as he tore into Sugar from the off. Brian's advice to pick his shots had been lost in a wild flurry of punches all designed to knock the Merseysider into tomorrow. His words to Pat at the end of all the early rounds sounded like a stuck record, "You'll stop this kid Pat. You'll stop this kid. You'll stop th…" and yet, as the fight wore on and Pat continued to hit Sugar with everything, reality dawned that he was not going away. Indeed, his own shots were starting to get through. Pat's mind started to drift back to the sparring session: the tears, the embarrassment, the sheer frustration. Sugar just kept marching forward and he clawed his way back into the contest, so much that the contest was called a draw.

A furious Pat was left gutted, but luckily, to keep him sane, America was calling. The kid from Harpurhey was off across the ocean. For Pat his time at Leonard's gym was an eye opener: he got to meet the great man a few times, and spar with truly world class fighters, like the formidable Super-Flyweight Eugene Speed. When the 'Flash' met the 'Speed' the entire gym would stand and watch. Pat fought once in the States against Donnie Parker at the Teamster Local: 557 Hall and impressed hugely to win on points. He was turning heads, not just in the ring, but the gym. So much that when time came to go home, Dave Jacobs, who was Leonard's first trainer as an amateur, decided to return with him. After Sugar Ray Leonard lost to Roberto Duran in 1980, Jacobs resigned because he didn't agree with Leonard's decision to have an immediate rematch with the Panamanian. The legendary 'No Mas' fight. However, the pair had since made up and Jacobs rejoined Leonard when he came back to fight Marvin Hagler. On seeing Pat Barrett up close, Jacobs was taken aback, "I ain't never seen no Englishman fight like you Pat!"

Pat's time in the States did not necessarily improve him as a fighter, but instilled unbelievable confidence. On return he reeled off five consecutive wins, four by knockout, before challenging Doncaster's tough and durable southpaw, Kevin Plant, for the vacant Central Area Super Lightweight title at Bowlers in Manchester, on 29th November, 1988. The drunken Moston 'barmy army' led by Pat's brother Michael and good friend Dave Crompton cheered wildly as he beat Plant well on points to claim the title in a ten-rounder, despite fighting from the second round onwards with a broken hand. Wild celebrations ensued and an emotional Brian urged Pat to enjoy the moment and travel home on the coach with his mates. Despite being desperate to do so he always felt a little guilty about leaving a man he now viewed as a father figure, "Are you sure Brian?" he would always ask. Onto the coach Pat would go to be greeted by his ecstatic band of mates hoisting him high, many of Pat's followers were down on their luck and struggling with jobs and opportunities scarcer those days than a sun in a Mancunian sky.

On 11th April, 1989, in a first defence of his Central Area Super Lightweight Title, a familiar face reappeared, one that had haunted Pat. It was Sugar time again! As number one contender Sugar Gibiliru arrived from Liverpool at the Sports Centre in Lord Street, Oldham, confident he had Pat Barrett's number. However, Sugar had badly underestimated what lay in wait ever since he had been told of the fight, Pat had lived, slept, trained and ran thinking of nothing else but beating this man. It was time to put an end to bad memories. Come the night and from the opening bell he schooled Sugar. His spell in the States had supplied the confidence and Brian had designed a perfect plan with which Pat could lay his demon to rest. The perfect moment arose in the eighth round, Pat ensured Sugar wasn't so sweet by flattening him with a vicious, but perfectly timed left hook to end the evening's proceedings. As Sugar lay flat on his stomach with his arms hanging onto the bottom rope, the referee went through the motions of counting him out. Pat had finally cast away the demons and as he recalls, "beating Sugar was like winning two world titles!" For in that moment as Pat danced around the ring and fell into Brian's arms, he now felt anything was possible.

He proved this when, after being given just two weeks' notice, he fought the much lauded twenty-nine-year-old Tony Willis for the vacant British Light-Welterweight title. Willis had represented Britain at the 1980 Olympics and had already won a British title himself, albeit at lightweight. Pat learned of the opportunity, as a late replacement for Clinton McKenzie, when Brian called round at his home in Harpurhey, "I've got good news and I've got bad news," Brian began, "The bad news is that it's a British title fight at short notice. The good is I am convinced Willis is there for the taking. Chances like this come along once in a lifetime son and they can't be passed up!" Pat had just come off fighting Sugar so it was simply a matter of ticking over in the gym. "You've done the hard word Pat," smiled Brian. "the title's ours." He went on to explain Willis was fighting out of his weight, he was not a natural and had been "looked after". But most importantly had never fought anyone like him.

Pat's reaction to Brian's enthusiasm was as expected, "If Brian said it was possible, then it will be done."

On 9th May, 1989, at the City Hall, St Albans, Pat knew as soon as he entered the ring that he wasn't going to get beat. He recalled Brian's words when first entering the gym at sixteen of, "You could be a champion, Pat." For eight rounds, the fighters went toe-to-toe and then, with just ten seconds left in the ninth, and with Willis ahead on points, Pat landed a brutal left hook on the Liverpudlian's chin that dropped him to the canvas. Willis lay on his stomach, eyes shut, he was out cold. The roar went up from the travelling Mancunians. Chants of 'Champion' echoed loud across the arena. Clearly concerned, Pat went across to make sure his still laid out opponent was okay. After a few worrying moments with a huddle around him, the brave Liverpudlian came around. However, after being knocked out that night, Tony Willis retired and never fought again. Before leaving the ring, Pat placed the title belt around his waist and hugged a tearful Brian tight. For a moment, the two were alone in their own world, despite the spotlight being on them. Also at ringside was Pat's brother Michael and there was no prouder man in the arena.

After winning the British title and a £6000 cheque, thoughts turned to bigger things. First, though, came the matter of defending the newly won belt. On 24th September, 1989, at the Civic Hall, Wolverhampton, Pat met Scottish Champion Robert Harkin. Going into the contest Pat was on a seven KO streak. Following the stunning victory over Tony Willis he fought three times, each ending with the same savage finale. Pat's punching power was beyond belief. The fights were not so much bouts as executions. The knockout of his opponent not a matter of if, but when. Twenty-seven-year-old Glaswegian Harkin, however, proved a tougher nut to crack. He had a superb defence and although Pat ultimately prevailed, it was only through a very close points decision.

Any disappointment he must have felt at not being able to stop Harkin was eased in his next fight by knocking out New Jersey's Joey Ferrell at the Kelvin Hall in Glasgow, to close out the eighties. Craving a world title shot, Pat signed with manager Mickey Duff whose influence at that time may have been waning a little, but still remained influential within boxing. Rumours were already rife of a 'superfight' across the ocean, one that would catapult Pat into the boxing stratosphere, with the great Mexican Julian Chavez, mentioned as a possible opponent. People were already whispering in Pat's ear that such a clash could be made, he simply needed to maintain his rise through the division and he couldn't be ignored.

Duff delivered by negotiating Pat a shot at the EBU European Super Lightweight title against Efrem Calamati, who had an unblemished record with twenty-seven unbeaten fights, twelve by knockout, including that of the highly rated Clinton Mackenzie - a defeat that had ended the Londoner's career. Calamati was a serious operator and with the defence against Pat set to be hosted on his home soil of Salerno, deep in southern Italy, many experts claimed this was a step too far for the Mancunian 'Black Flash.' However, there was one man who believed in him. Once the fight was made, Brian pulled Pat aside and what he said has stayed with him since...

"Some fights are won by sheer heart, Patrick. If you are ever gonna do this, it will be for the love and not the money. If you have not got the passion inside you, then forget it." With these words ringing in Pat's ears, Collyhurst and Moston's finest prepared for his very own Italian job.

They arrived in Salerno four days before the fight. Pat was ready, it was just a case of staying calm and focused. He found conditions difficult. Pat hated the food and hotel rooms that were less than luxurious. However, as the fight drew closer, a strange peace came over him. He wasn't in the least bit nervous. Indeed, Pat was looking forward to getting in the ring with Calamati and becoming one of the rare band of British fighters who have won titles on Italian soil, joining such boxing royalty as Lloyd Honeyghan and John Conteh.

All the time, Brian was in his ear, "You can do this Pat. You can make history."

Despite it being a well-known adage that in this part of the world it took two knockouts for a foreign fighter to earn a draw, neither Pat or Brian were unduly worried. For in reality, if a champion is flat out on the canvas, he can have no argument in losing his title.

On 24th August, 1990, the day of the fight, Salerno was baking hot. A thick mist rose from the Tyrehnnian Sea. This city on a dusty coast was hardly one of the southern pearls, but it was rich in character and history. In 1830 the first textile mill was established by Swiss entrepreneurs and by 1877 the city was the site of twenty-one more employing around ten thousand workers; in comparison with a mere four thousand employed up north in Turin's textile industry. As a consequence, Salerno was named the 'Manchester of the Italian south'. In 1943 the Allies landed at Salerno as part of 'Operation Avalanche.' Winston Churchill's plan to attack the Axis powers via a perceived 'soft underbelly'. The population and city itself suffered terribly. As the Italian campaign drew to a bloody close, between February and July 1944, it hosted the Government of Marshal Pietro Badoglio. During those historic few months, Salerno had the honour of being the temporary capital of the kingdom of Italy and King Vittore Emanuele III lived in a mansion on its outskirts. Now, a young kid from the streets of north Manchester, trained on Lightbowne Road, and fighting for the colours of Collyhurst and Moston, prepared to add his own little place in the history of this far off southern Italian outpost.

Despite being a huge underdog with the odds makers, Pat had good reason to be confident as he had a remarkable record of nineteen knockouts in just twenty-five bouts. That afternoon, just a few hours before the fight, Pat and Brian went for a walk along the beach front. The stifling heat was being given temporary reprieve by a soothing breeze that swept in from the sea. As Brian was talking he turned to find Pat had laid down on a wall with a towel covering his face and appeared to have fallen asleep. He let him be for a while, but as thirty minutes turned into an hour and Pat showed no signs of waking up, Brian gave him a shove. As his eyes opened he was greeted by a smiling Brian with the words, "C'mon lazy bones, we've got a European title to win!"

The fight would take place on a specially built arena on the beach. As the evening drew on and the night skies turned black and became littered with a million stars, the atmosphere in Salerno suddenly took on a wholly different feel. Their boy was fighting and the entire city would be in his corner. It was unthinkable to the locals that Calamati could lose. In Pat's dressing room Brian was busy wrapping his hands and administering last minute advice, "He's the champion Pat, let him bring it to you. Let him play to the crowd. You've got nothing to lose. Just fight your fight."

On the ring walk the hostility of the locals rained down upon Mancunian heads - a sea of vitriol, a lot of it racist, though luckily Pat could not understand it - "Ci prendiamo cura la nostra," as they say in that part of the world, "We look after our own". The abuse continued and grew louder once Pat reached the ring.

"They love us really Patrick," whispered Brian.

In the distance car lights sped past on a nearby busy sea road making for truly surreal surroundings for a European title fight. Calamati, in white shorts, waved to the crowd, smiling and appearing like he did not have a care in the world, this was his stage. Pat, in black shorts, was merely a minor obstacle before the night's partying could get underway. From the first bell Calamati came out in showboating mode then, suddenly, a shower of vicious fast right hooks from Pat shook him and it was gloves up, all business. However, despite little flashes the Italian was clearly outgunned and early on Calamati was hit with an almighty right hook that put him on his backside. Forced to take a count of eight, it was apparent this Englishman possessed the power to do their champion damage and come the fourth round, the crowd already seemed in a lynching mood. As Calamati tried vainly to keep the Englishman at bay, Pat unleashed a shattering right and left hook combination that sent the Italian crashing to the canvas. It was over before he hit the floor. The execution was as chilling as it was magnificent. The local lad was knocked clean out and the immediate worry was that Calamati had swallowed his tongue. Back in the corner Pat was surrounded by his cornermen as the Italians vented their spleen at him. Their night was ruined.

Any notion of celebrating was swiftly forgotten as Pat glared across at the worrying sight of a stricken Calamati. Thankfully he came around and was helped to his feet, but by that time Pat and his entourage had been forced to leave the ring for their own safety. A police escort saw them back to the dressing room as an outraged crowd abused them.

As for Calamati, with his title now gone, he waved to the crowd once more as they applauded back. Only this time he wasn't smiling and clearly wondering what had hit him…

The 'Black Flash' had hit him.

One man there in spirit, if not body, was Pat's brother. Unfortunately, Michael was detained at Her Majesty's pleasure at the time and spent the evening pacing his cell praying his younger sibling would come through unharmed and become European champion. Suddenly the door opened and two wardens stood smiling wide after listening to the fight on the radio. Telling him the good news Michael Barrett, despite the grim surroundings, could not have been happier or prouder. Pat had done it!

Meanwhile, feelings still ran high back in Salerno and an even larger police presence was required to get the victorious band of Englishmen from the venue back to their hotel in once piece. However, tempers had calmed by the morning and suddenly Pat had gone from being public enemy number one to a local celebrity. Everybody wanted a photo of the champ! On the plane home, the Captain announced over the intercom: "Ladies and gentlemen, we have a champion on board!" As the title belt was passed around among the applauding passengers, it suddenly dawned on Pat what he had achieved. Here, high above the clouds with Brian alongside him, they had touched the stars. Now all bets were off, there was talk of a fight with Julio Cesar Chavez. Mickey Duff promised him it would happen, it was just a question of time.

And so Pat waited, first patiently then later he mithered and demanded answers. Nothing happened and finally his patience snapped. Instead he signed with another guaranteed match-maker, promoter Frank Warren. Frank promised Pat a world title shot and typically, in a short time, duly delivered. Meanwhile, staying busy in the ring, Pat produced a trio of impressive European title defences. Salvatore Nardino was dropped in the sixth with a short but blinding left hook. Mark McCreath fared little better, despite catching Pat in the second to put him on the floor, the Black Flash roaring back to pummel McCreath. Finally, Racheed Lawal was beaten in six rounds.

Pat was clearly coming to a fighting peak. All seemed to be bubbling over perfectly and when Frank Warren announced he had negotiated a deal to bring world champion Manning Galloway over to defend his WBO World Welterweight title in Manchester against Pat, the boxing stars appeared to have aligned for a happy ending.

Nicknamed 'The Spoiler' Galloway was a southpaw who specialised in making fighters look bad whilst beating them. Though delighted to be handed the opportunity, Pat was a little worried about moving up to Welterweight, but realised it would be more than worth it for the shot at a world belt. Although in hindsight he would later claim that the hassle that awaited him in the lead up to the fight was the most frustrating time of his career. Galloway was as divisive out of the ring as he was in it. Three times the fight was postponed: whether through mitigating circumstances or simple mind games, it served to demoralise Pat, so that when the time finally came to fight, he was all but broken. There were many who claimed Galloway did it on purpose to deflate his opponent and stall as he worked on a way to overcome Barrett's style. It was either that or Galloway endured some incredibly bad luck!

By the date of the original fight Pat had been in the best shape of his life and was thoroughly convinced he would not just beat Galloway, but knock him out. Special preparations had to be taken in the gym, for such was Pat's power that Brian called in outside help in the form of heavyweight John Fury, the idea being for Pat to concentrate solely on movement and speed in the ring, hit and run fast, for he knew if Fury caught up with him it would be a painful experience! Fine-tuned mentally and physically, it was all systems go, only to see his dreams crash and burn when it was called off at the pre-fight press conference.

Instead, Pat fought a swiftly arranged ten rounder against the American Mike Johnson at the Sports Centre in Oldham on 19th December, 1991. It was a strange evening, for though he finished Johnson in just two rounds with a crashing left hook, it was a listless showing from Pat, it was almost as if he didn't want to be in there. It was a payday, nothing more, for Pat's mind was still focused on that world title.

The fight had been rescheduled by now, but Galloway pulled out citing gastroenteritis and when his brother was shot before the third scheduled date, he quit again. Galloway seemed content to play hide and seek forever which perplexed the Collyhurst contingent.

Finally, over 8 months after the original date, Galloway showed up. But on 25th July 1992, at the G-Mex in Manchester, what should have been the best night of Pat's life turned out to be the worst. Ultimately Galloway retained his title on a narrow points decision, but this was a contest lost by Pat even before he made it to the ring. An example of Pat's psychological state occurred on the afternoon of the fight when, after leaving his protector at home, instead of sending someone else to pick it up Pat went himself. The fire in his belly had been all but extinguished. It was only on doing the ring walk and looking around at a packed G-Mex and seeing family, friends and fans roaring out his name that Pat suddenly came to life and realised this really was happening. Yet, so haunted had he become by Galloway's antics, a small part of him still believed, even at that late stage, Galloway would find a way to drop out and continue his torment. In the ring, everything Pat and Brian had worked endlessly on in the gym went hurtling through the G-Mex doors and out into the Mancunian night air. "Don't chase him" Brian had said. "He'll make you look stupid. Play a waiting game. He's the champion so let him bring it on. Be smart Pat!"

Needless to say, Pat did the exact opposite.

Just as the great Floyd Mayweather possesses the ability to turn world class fighters into seemingly average plodders, Galloway, though nowhere near Mayweather's class, had a similar ability. As Pat chased down 'The Spoiler' Brian's instructions went out of the window and he became ever more frustrated and eventually dropped his gloves in frustration at not being able to get off shots. Despite at times managing to nail Galloway, Pat later admitted that even though his body was willing, his heart and soul wasn't really in it, he simply wasn't hungry enough to go that extra mile. To this day Pat Barrett sees the fight as a curse. It wasn't so much that he lost for the first time in five years but that the real Pat never showed up. There could be no excuses, just the simple truth - The Spoiler had done his job and the 'Black Flash' had been dimmed - no matter how hard he tried, Pat would never again be able to fully re-ignite it.

The dying embers of a fighter's career are always painful to watch and none more so than in Pat's case. His had been a meteoric rise, rich in memorable moments and explosive knockouts. The defeat to Galloway was by no means the end, but all the messing about had taken something from the fighter's armoury. Pat fought on; on 22nd September, 1993, at the York Hall, Bethnal Green, he took on Nottingham's Delroy Bryan for the vacant British Welterweight title. In a closely fought contest Bryan came out on top after twelve gruelling rounds. However, it was clear to all, even though he was only twenty-six years old, that Pat's best days were behind him. Yet pride is a powerful tool and the fires still burned within him and refused to die.

Handed a last opportunity for glory in the most random of places, Pat fought Congo-born Patrick Vungbo for the vacant WBF World Super Welterweight Title in West-Vlaanderenm, Belgium. Beforehand Pat had struggled terribly to make up the weight, to the point that at the weigh-in he had weights hidden in his pockets. Again, giving everything, Pat lost out on a split decision, one that left him convinced that he had done enough to win. It was around this time Brian advised Pat to hang up the gloves, not so much because of any lack of belief in his fighter's ability inside the ring, but what was happening in Pat's life outside it.

As mentioned, ever since he was a young lad Pat had gravitated towards the black community of Cheetham Hill and he had always maintained those same friends. His loyalty was unyielding, even when the area became notorious as a centre for one of the gangs who vied for control of the city's drug scene along with Salford, Moss Side and later Longsight. In the early 1990s, 'Gunchester' exploded and made front page news. Police were under pressure to put an end to the open warfare that had erupted between the gangs and now acted as a bloody background to much of Pat's boxing career.

Refusing to give up old friendships, it was only natural that Barrett would become a target for the police. Pat still looked the part and he continued to visit friends on 'The Hill' dressed in gold chains and the street style of the day. Despite not caring what the police thought about the company he kept, Pat was by now getting pulled three or four times a day by the GMP and was told that, as a role model, he should distance himself from the very friends he had made when just a kid on the street suffering racist abuse in lilywhite North Manchester.

Needless to say, Pat told them that wasn't how it worked. They would remain his friends, regardless of the consequences. It got to the point where Brian would joke, as a police van roared past the gym with its sirens blazing, "Pat is on his way in!"

Now, with the light of his stellar boxing career finally dimming, Pat and his mentor had a parting of the ways. Brian didn't want to see a lad he regarded as a son get hurt in the ring because he wasn't fully focused on his preparation and told him to end it. Pat disagreed and moved on…

He joined up with Lennox Lewis's trainer John Davenport in the hope of securing a multi-fight contract and a possible second shot at a world title. Davenport took him off to a training camp in the States. Pat landed in Pennsylvania in mid-November, the coldest time of the year and freezing even for a born and bred Mancunian. Here, away from all distractions, he was under absolutely no illusions that this was his last chance saloon. From day one conditions were tough and Pat missed home. Davenport's set up was unforgiving: rules had to be adhered to and anyone daring to take liberties was shown the door. It was nothing but boxing for breakfast, dinner and tea. At five o'clock every morning Pat would be out pounding the roads in the pitch black, with the snow piled up high on each side. He would see the headlights of a car coming towards him and have to move to one side through the slush and ice to let it roar past. This was just the start of a schedule that went on for days and weeks. Pat tried like hell to convince himself and his new trainer that he wasn't a busted flush.

Whilst there Pat fought once, on 11th March 1994, against Donnie Parker, the same fighter he had boxed many years before in Baltimore and beaten on points. This time it was a third-round stoppage, but again Pat appeared to be chasing ghosts. Shortly after he returned to Manchester, resigned to the fact that the last bell had sounded on his career.

Once back on home soil, in no time, Pat was arrested, charged with outstanding driving fines that mounted to almost £6000 and for failing to produce his vehicle details – he was forced to serve a three-month spell in Risley. Though released on twelve months' probation, Pat came out a lost soul and, needing to keep his nose clean, thought there was no better place to do that than in the ring. The opportunity arose for one last fight, this time in Belgium on Christmas Day 1994. Pat spoke to Brian in an effort to get him to join him one last time but his old mentor dismissed the idea. Not just because Brian didn't want to leave his family over the festive period, but more so because he felt it was a terrible idea. Brian wanted to convince Pat that the time had really come to hang up the gloves but, as ever, the fighter never knows when to quit!

So, he travelled alone and, far from home, it was time for the last act. The 'Black Flash' was up against Belgian Marino Monteyne and despite winning on points, Pat would remember it as the worst day of his life. In years past the limited Monteyne would not have been allowed in the same arena, never-mind the same ring, as the former European Champion. Performing from mcmory and with the fires inside now well and truly extinguished, Pat won a hollow victory and ended his career. He finally accepted the truth. And so, as the last bell finally sounded and the crowd's roar fell silent, the rollercoaster in the ring ended for Pat – the gloves were off and he was back where he started.

On the street.

There was a time when even Pat's friends would say to him that he shouldn't be around them, but come the end of his boxing career, that no longer mattered. However, in time Pat missed the camaraderie of the Collyhurst and Moston gym badly. The sounds, smells and the laughter. And he so missed Brian. Pat started to help out, an older head amongst a special crop of emerging young fighters set to take boxing by storm. This crèche of future champions being reared above the Co-op on Lightbowne Road was the club's finest harvest since the days of Brown, McAvoy and King. Thomas McDonagh, Michael Jennings, Michael Gomez and Matthew Hall were just four of those being talked of, but there were more. Whenever one of his starlets was playing up and he felt a word was needed, Brian would designate Pat to have a word.

Pat watched how Brian dealt with every little problem. His old mentor understood that, as with any problem in boxing, the answer could be found in its rich history. There was nothing in the ring that had not happened before. Training techniques used in decades past were as relevant then as they were now. Fascinated, Pat listened and learned. The time came when he felt confident enough to ask Brian for permission to train an exciting new fighter who had arrived at the gym, Olympic Bronze medal winner Robin Reid. It proved a perfect marriage and in 1996 Robin became the first fighter from Collyhurst and Moston to win a world title since Jackie Brown back in 1932. On a memorable Italian evening in Milan, he stopped Vincenzo Nardiello to win the WBC World Superweight title. It appeared Pat had found his niche.

Yet life outside the gym was proving equally dramatic and with his old loyalties still in place, trouble was never far away. On 7th February, 2003, it exploded in his face. Pat, now thirty-six years old, had booked into the Holiday Inn Express in Chingford, Essex. He was staying there before attending a funeral the next day. After a tip-off, armed officers raided his room and drugs, a revolver and ammunition were found. Pat denied all knowledge claiming he had been set up.

His trial was held at Snaresbrook Crown Court, London and he was jailed for three years. However, if it hadn't been for Brian Hughes, it could have been so much worse. Brian stood before the judge and spoke well of a lad he considered a son.

"Patrick was good enough to be world champion. It was just bad luck that stopped him. He was the undefeated British and European champion. He was a leading light in the sport and is a wonderful man. This is totally out of character for him. He has been doing a great job training our young boxers at the club, including one who is already a world champion" Brian told the court. It was a wonderful speech. The heartfelt words clearly affected the judge's thinking when it came to Pat's sentence, for the way the system usually worked was a year per bullet, plus one for the gun. Thanks to Brian he only got the three and ended up doing twenty-two months.

Life inside taught Pat a lot about himself, "In a strange way jail was probably the best thing that could have happened to me," he admits today. "I had got caught and it opened my eyes." Pat knew he was getting off lightly and that something had to change - life on the street had no happy endings. Just endings. It was time to make a choice.

On leaving prison, Pat applied for a trainer's licence, but his reputation preceded him and he was turned down. Not being put off Pat tried again. His mission in life was set and he wouldn't be denied. Whilst continuing to assist Brian in the gym, Pat also set up his own security company to pay the bills. Finally, after five years, he was granted a licence. Initially Pat worked alongside local promoter Wally Dixon helping him set up shows. This was a huge learning curve and it was Pat who played a part in helping Scott Quigg's career get up and running.

When, in 2011, Brian finally retired, it was felt he would leave shoes far too big to fill. In his immediate wake many left the gym for pastures new and it seemed like the gym had come to a natural end. However, determined to carry on Brian's legacy, Pat and former boxer and now trainer Thomas McDonagh decided the show must go on and starting with little more than an empty building they went to work. Slowly, from small acorns, they got it all back.

Now confident to venture out on his own, whilst remaining on good terms with Wally Dixon, in 2014 Pat launched Black Flash Promotions and helping him were trusted friends Thomas McDonagh and another former pro Paulie Da Silva. On 26th October, 2014, in Middleton, Pat held his first show entitled 'Homecoming.' It was a sell out with a card featuring six Collyhurst and Manchester fighters: Matty Ryan, Justin Newell, Zahid Hussain, Reece Cartwright, Curtis Gargano and a gifted, classy young kid with tremendous fast hands and a touch of stardust, Pat's nephew Zelfa Barrett - otherwise known as 'The Brown Flash'!

It was Zelfa's pro debut. A Super-Featherweight, he lacked nothing in confidence. Trained by Pat, Zelfa could not wait to get started, "I'm excited. It's always been my dream to be a pro boxer," he tells me, "the way Pat trains me, I'm ready for anything and for anyone. I seriously feel I can go all the way. I live the life, I've got a great trainer, I'm talented and have the skills. I want to be world champion. Pat's experience has rubbed off on me, I will follow in his footsteps. I can do everything in the ring, not wanting to sound big-headed! I just have belief in myself."

The Barret legacy appears to be in safe hands.

Today Pat all but lives in the gym. The club is booming once more. Together with Tommy they are creating the next Mancunian boxing legacy – perhaps bigger and better than any that have gone before. The pair still view themselves as Brian Hughes' disciples and his spirit has never left the place - it is soaked in the walls as you climb to the first floor and enter this humble workspace above a supermarket. And the words once spoken by Brian have their echoes in the advice Pat and Tommy dish out on a daily basis to the latest generation.

In Pat's office, Brian's portrait is a reminder of the glory days, of heartache and sadness, laughter and joy. When the gym is in full flow, Pat loves nothing better than watching proceedings from the office door, keeping an eye on the potential future champions. This is his special place, Pat's world. He made a choice and it was the right one.

The sixteen-year-old scrawny kid who used to walk everyday with his gym bag from Harpurhey may not have appeared to have moved far, but as he looks out over his boxing kingdom from his office door, the smile on Pat's face only means one thing.

He's home.

THE CHAMPIONS

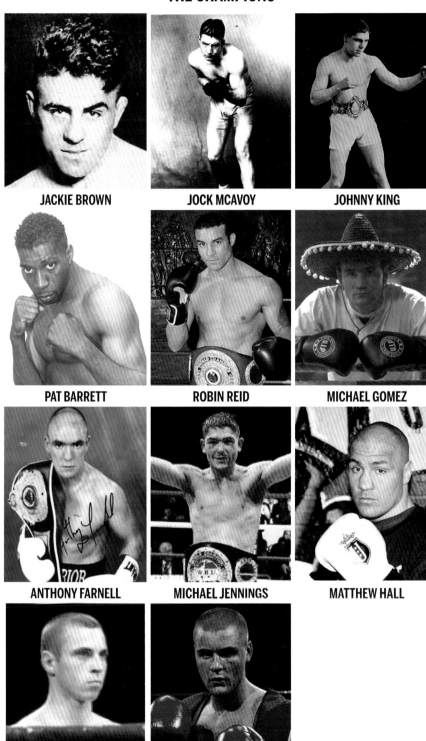

JACKIE BROWN

JOCK McAVOY

JOHNNY KING

PAT BARRETT

ROBIN REID

MICHAEL GOMEZ

ANTHONY FARNELL

MICHAEL JENNINGS

MATTHEW HALL

SCOTT QUIGG

THOMAS McDONAGH

THE PRINCE OF COLLYHU
The club's first world champ
Jackie Brown was famed for
gregarious lifestyle: flash ca
wine, women and song.

MENTO
Johnny King with trainer an
manager Harry Fleming

Dave Lumiansky the
American promoter
who talked his way into
control of Jackie Brown
and Jock McAvoy but
failed to persuade
Johnny King.

STATESID
Jock McAv
poses with
Henry Lew
before thei
Heavyweig
world title
Madison S
Garden in 1

MURDER INC.
Frankie Carbo, the New
York gangster said to have
run Lumiansky and Jock
McAvoy out of town.

THE COCK OF COLLYHURST

Johnny King knocks out Jackie Brown to retain his British Bantamweight title at Belle Vue, May 1937.

IN HAPPIER TIMES

LEFT TO RIGHT: Jock McAvoy, Jack Bates, Harry Fleming, Johnny King and Jackie Brown at a training camp in Rawcliff Hall, Lancashire in 1934.

COLLYHURST ROYALTY

Brian Kidd was a regular at the club in the early 1970s.

ALL FOR ONE...

Like Harry Fleming before him, Brian Hughes instilled an 'All for One, One for All' attitude among his young hopefuls, to get them to look after each other out on the streets as a band of brothers. This photograph from the 1980s typifies his approach with trainers, professionals, amateurs and youngsters all pictured together.

MAN OF MANY TALENTS

Lance Lewis aka Lance Williams aka Tony Dore was a World Kickbox champion at the age of 17 before taking up the colours of Collyhurst & Moston as a club boxer.

Lance was the first British fighter to be accepted at the legendary Kronk gym in Detroit, coming under the tutelage of Brian Hughes' close friend Emanuel Steward

THE BLACK FLASH

Brian Hughes was crucial to Pat Barrett's rise to European champion. Here he hugs his mentor after another victory.

Pat flanked by mentor Brian Hughes and Ghanian boxer turned trainer Billy Kotey during a photo op at the

GHOST

Craig Dermody was one of the best prospects to emerge from the Collyhurst and Moston gym. An elusive fighter with God-given talent he was quickly pursued by promoters who saw him as the next big thing but after a meteoric rise his appetite for boxing suddenly waned and he left the sport.

THE ICEMAN

A pensive Mike Jackson watches the action - in the interval between rounds there could only be one voice, that of Brian Hughes, but Mike's thoughts on the fight were always invaluable to the maestro.

WORLD CHAMPION

In 1996 Robin Reid became the first Collyhurst and Moston world champion since the pre-war glory days of Jackie Brown and Jock McAvoy when he upset the odds by beating Vincenzo Nardiello in Italy.

DEDICATION

Brian Hughes would often cite the dedication of Robin Reid to training to young hopefuls. Here trainer Mike Jackson puts Reid through his paces during a session at the gym.

RAINBOW MAN

Michael Gomez was a talented fighter who attracted trouble outside the ring. He could have had it all...

WARRIOR

A tough upbringing meant Anthony Farnell often had no option but to fight, but a fateful decision to try his luck at Collyhurst & Moston led to a stellar pro career.

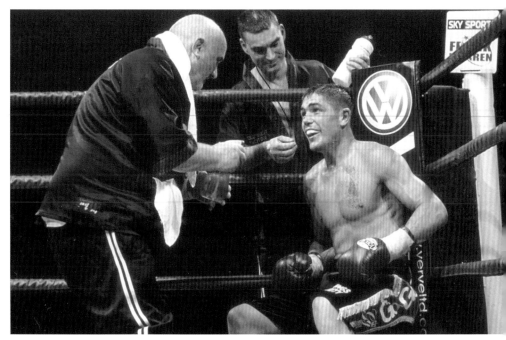

RETURN TO MADISON SQUARE GARDEN

Michael Jennings captured British and World titles at Welterweight, here defeating Jason Rushton (above) in his last defence.

In 2009 he got an unexpected shot against Miguel Cotto in the legendary surroundings of Madison Square Garden conjuring up memories of Jock McAvoy in 1935.

Below: the pre-fight tension is palpable as Mike Jackson and Brian Hughes go through the final preparations.

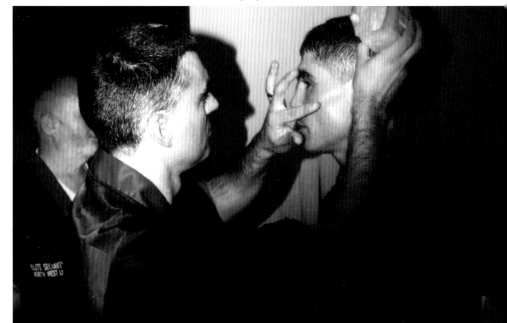

EL TORITO

Matty Hall was a rising star until he was stabbed in the stomach. In a career dogged by bad luck he was later diagnosed with Candidiasis which hastened the end of his career.

A disciple of Brian Hughes since the age of 14, Scott Quigg has risen to the very top of the sport starring in nine world title fights to date.

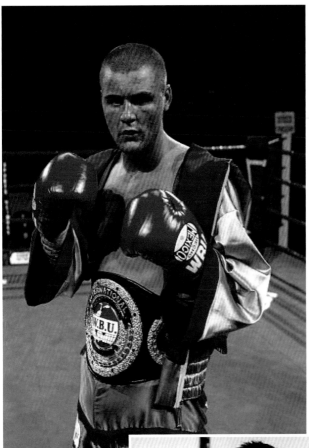

JOKER IN THE PACK

Known for cracking jokes between rounds, Thomas McDonagh was a talented fighter, the pugilist art coming very naturally to him during a stellar amateur career. Often infuriaturning to his coach Brian Hughes, his professional career was a rollercoaster affair that eventually led to his early retirement.

ARISE SIR THOMAS

From cheeky chappy to ambassador, Tommy helped open a Harpurhey youth club in 2013 and met a very special guest. It is not recorded whether Her Majesty asked for an autograph.

PHOENIX FROM THE FLAMES

After taking over the lease of the gym following Brian Hughes retirement, Thomas McDonagh and Pat Barrett have gone back to basics and returned the club to its former glories. Here training with unbeaten Light-Heavyweight Lyndon Arthur and (below) alongside former boxer-turned-trainer Paulie Da Silva.

THE BROWN FLASH

Among the hottest prospects at the gym is Pat Barrett's nephew Zelpha, nicknamed 'The Brown Flash'. The Super Featherweight made a nineteen-fight unbeaten run to the start of his pro career.

LYNDON 'KING' ARTHUR

The Light-Heavyweight is going places following an unbeaten ten fight start to his career. Between Lyndon and Zelfa the future of the club is in safe hands.

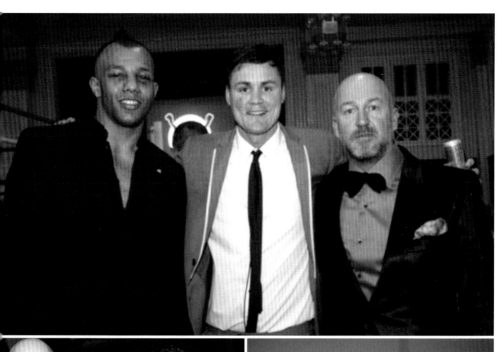

GIO-GOI

Following the retirement of Brian Hughes and the loss of many of its professionals, the club urgently needed to raise funds. Enter club regular Christopher Donnelly, founder of the Gio-Goi fashion label, who persuaded his sister Tracey to organise an annual white collar boxing event.

Sprinkled with star names from stage and screen, alongside Collyhurst and Moston's star boxers from past and present, the event has become a fixture on the Manchester calendar.

BRIAN HUGHES MBE

The man without whom all this would not have been possible...

"Up these steps walk future champions"

BRIAN HUGHES MBE

9 - CRAIG DERMODY

GHOST

For twenty years his name has haunted Mancunian boxing conversations and arguments. It is very easy to throw in the age-old adage of "What if" when it comes to fighters who, for whatever reason, failed to reach their full potential. Yet when the question relates to somebody whose talent was so immense that the mere mention of his name can bring those who shared a gym with him to tears, then we are talking about somebody truly special. It takes an awful lot to bring the Collyhurst and Moston Gym to a halt, but back then, when he entered the ring, everybody stopped; Brian Hughes, Pat Barrett, Lance Williams; amateurs, professionals, the younger boys and older pros, even the cleaning lady – they would all stop what they were doing and watch on in disbelief. If the lad been caught in a snowstorm he could dodge every flake and smile whilst doing so. It all came so naturally to him that it was a mystery how he did it and no one was more mystified than the boy himself.

From the age of eleven Craig had been walking up those stairs until it all ended with the finality of a sniper's bullet through the heart. Back in the day a smiling Brian would shake his head and say quietly almost to himself, "This kid could box on a handkerchief and not make a crease." He didn't so much move but glide, slipping punches with ghostlike ease. Later, as promoters queued, phoned and begged for the next big thing, he simply did what came naturally. When sparring in the ring it became more a stage than an arena. But there would be no pot of gold at rainbow's end for him, just another rainbow and another and another and in between storms a plenty.

This is a ghost story. Let me tell you about Craig Dermody.

★

★

CRAIG ENTERED THIS WORLD in 1970 in Hulme. One of four sons; Steven, Dean and Warren, born to parents Ann and Neil. As a kid, he went to North Manchester High School for Boys and was described by one teacher as a "likeable imp"! It was his late brother Steven who introduced Craig to boxing. One day he took him to Lightbowne Road and pointed up the steps, "Up you go our kid, see you later." From taking that first walk Craig never went back to anything else. Back then, in the early eighties, fighters such as Lance Williams, Tunde Foster, John Green and Kenny Webber were at the gym and attendance fluctuated depending on how boxing was perceived by the local kids. Attendances shot up with the rise of the Rocky films and slumped when movies and popular culture moved on. At the peak periods gangs of local lads would swamp the stairs, yet for the vast majority it was a brief flirtation. Once reality dawned that boxing wasn't like it appeared in the movies, the vast majority didn't hang around! It is not called 'the Hurt Business' for nothing. One of Craig's earliest mentors in the gym was Billy Kotey. With tremendous patience, the wily old former African champion taught Craig the very basics. Craig loved Billy's kindness and what would now be described as 'tough love'. When stern words were needed Craig knew they came from a huge heart. A constant welcoming and warm presence around the gym, he remembers Billy in the same tracksuit helping him every day for ten years. They may have been his first fledgling steps, but he was also aware of being closely watched by Brian Hughes, who missed nothing. This kid would definitely be worth keeping an eye on.

Craig's first amateur fight came aged eleven against Wayne Kelly, at the Tudor Lodge hotel, Blackley and not surprisingly it passed in typically Collyhurst and Moston style! Come the end of the evening, the takings were snatched and none other than compere Bernard Manning gave chase. After a gallant effort, a gasping Bernard finally admitted defeat, but was given a rousing ovation when he staggered back into the club. Also present that night were some members of Manchester's legendary Quality Street Gang who were not impressed at the going's on and passed the word locally that they wanted the money back. It came as no surprise that first thing next morning it was left on the Tudor Lodge door step by an ashen-faced thief regretting his actions!

Craig's amateur career is best described as mixed but this again came down to the styles in which the Collyhurst and Moston lads fought. Taught to defend themselves from day one in the gym, amateur judges were slow to notice their more technically refined skills and tended to reward fighters for action. The ability to slip a punch was always seen as being equally important to Brian Hughes as landing one, for everything else came in time. This was the case with Craig and by the age of seventeen he started picking up medals at the NABC's. Something had suddenly clicked as the endless hours spent in the gym, all the training and advice from Brian and Billy started to bear fruit. A talent was being harnessed into something quite remarkable. Craig was becoming harder to hit than a gust of wind. If you asked him how he did it, Craig could never tell you, it all came so naturally. Brian would smile as he sparred and with an arm around his mentor declare, "Billy lad, what have we got ourselves here?" Both knew Collyhurst and Moston had discovered a pearl. Craig Dermody was special and his talent was already in great demand.

With this in mind Brian arranged for him to spar with a promising up and coming Turkish fighter, a Flyweight training out of Denmark. Staying at a top hotel in Copenhagen and away from Brian and Billy's all-seeing eyes, the "likeable imp" had a whale of a time! Although he only earned £200 Craig thought "why not" and ordered caviar and champagne on room service!

There were also trips to the United States. Craig flew over three times whilst still in his teens after Brian had told Emanuel Steward how good a prospect he was in phone calls and letters to his good friend. Knowing well his British pal was not one prone to exaggeration, the excitement and wonder Brian held for this young lad's talent shone through. So it was that plans were put in place for Craig to travel under Steward's care. For a young Manc - quiet but streetwise and living at that time in a rundown area of the city, White Moss, where jobs and hope for the future were in short supply, America was not so much a different world but an alternative universe.

These journeys across the ocean came littered with memorable incidents, although the vast majority were out of the ring. Craig stayed with a childhood friend of Steward's and Sugar Ray Leonard's, who at that time was in training to fight the long blond-haired, Danny Lalonde at Caesar's Palace, Las Vegas. Craig met Leonard and a photo of the two together is still among his most treasured possessions. Also training with Craig were a number of Filipinos and one in particular stayed in Craig's memory after their sparring session turned into a war. "A vicious little bastard" was Craig's description! It took all his skills to keep him at bay. Only after it was over somebody told him that his opponent was just sixteen years old and had already done time for murder!

Steward watched Craig close up in training and swiftly came to the conclusion that Brian was not over-hyping this kid, who did not so much move around the ring but haunt it. He made a point of telling his own fighters not to go easy on the Limey and they didn't, yet like their English counterparts, no one could lay a glove on him.

"Dear Brian" began Steward's letter back across the ocean, "I do believe you have found yourself a genius."

There was though one time over the pond when not even Craig could have ducked what was in front of him. One morning when out on his daily five-mile run, Craig left the large palatial home of Steward's friend and headed off, but before he had gone ten yards he heard somewhat shout "Freeze!" As Craig stopped he found himself surrounded by armed policemen all training their guns at him. Wrestled to the floor, he was handcuffed and read his rights. In a state of shock, he thought for a second it was a movie scene! Next moment more police vehicles turned up with sirens blazing and hurtling through the residential gates. Dragged and placed in the back of a car, Craig had absolutely no idea what was going on! It was only later at the station that he was informed his 'landlord' was a notorious drug lord and that Craig was thought to be one of his gang! Finally, when a background check was done and it was realised that he was not, as first believed, a member of the mob, Craig was released back into Emanuel Steward's care and before he could take in what had actually occurred, Craig found himself on a plane home to Manchester. Once back and recovered from the great American dream, Craig met up with Brian who smiled and told him life was all about experiences, "If they had tried to shoot you would have ducked them anyway, son". Meanwhile, three weeks later, whilst out on bail, the drug dealer was shot in the head and died instantly.

At age twenty-one Craig turned pro and on 31st January, 1991, debuted at Quaffers in Stockport. He took on Northampton based Karl Morlin and stopped him with consummate ease in the fifth. Beforehand there had been a huge clamour to sign Craig up. Rival promoters Frank Warren and Mickey Duff had been competing in a desperate race and were constantly on the phone with Brian, bickering and trying to out-scheme the other for Craig's signature. The fighter himself was aware of all this but concentrated on his boxing. Money, though important, was secondary at that time, Brian assured him further down the road if he continued in the same vein, riches and all that came with it were just around the corner, "The golden rainbow is there for you, son". Craig was content to be patient and trust those around him.

Around the time that Craig's professional career was taking off, elder brother Warren also found huge success as lead singer with North Manchester band Northside. Formed in 1989, they released their first album Chicken Rhythms on Factory Records in 1991. Manchester had become a city reborn and Northside released a song that caught the mood, "My Rising Star". Warren's lyrics could easily have been written about his younger sibling who, while most Mancunians were witnessing the renaissance of the world's first industrial city into its number one party destination, was busy cutting a swathe and taking collective breaths away at ringside. The genie was out of the bottle.

Ten consecutive victories followed before the opportunity arose to fight for the Central Area Featherweight title. On 13th November, 1992, at the Castle Leisure centre in Bury, Craig took on the holder from across the water in 'Dirty Old Town' Salford, the tough and durable thirty-year-old Russell Davison. Although it was a night that would never register in the highest echelons of boxing, it gave the world a heart-breaking glimpse of what could have been. As shouts of 'Dermo' rang out from ringside, Craig's performance was poetry in motion as he badly outclassed Davison. The older pro just could not get anywhere near him. With his gloves held low he was as slippery as an eel and as light as a feather, Craig tormented the plucky Salfordian and when he opened up in the closing stages there was enough power to leave Davison dazed. Like a blind man staggering from a train crash and then being hit by a passing car, Craig would not let him off the ropes. The legendary veteran boxing television commentator Reg Gutteridge, not known for superlatives, gushed lavish praise upon him, "This kid is reminiscent of both Ali and Sugar Ray Leonard." There is surely no higher accolade. Come the final bell, Craig had clearly won all ten rounds and the referee walked across and raised his hand. Into the ring came a beaming Brian Hughes who embraced Craig. It felt like the first step: a stairway to boxing heaven. The fighter himself appeared slightly embarrassed by the whole scene. He was simply doing what he loved. Post-fight talk among boxing journalists was of just how far this kid could go. Already Frank Warren, who had ultimately won out in his duel with Mickey Duff to sign him, talked of a possible WBU title shot. As for Craig, he wasn't the slightest interested in boxing politics. As is still the case today, when someone shows up blessed with a supreme talent, the first thought in this often dark, ugly sport is how to make money. Whereas for Craig, all he cared about "Who's next?"

Craig next fought in February 1993, at the Free Trade Hall in Manchester against twenty-seven-year-old Brummie Karl Taylor. A fighter from the Nobby Nobb's stable who specialised in providing fighters to pad out bills, Craig finished off Taylor in the fifth of six rounds, with the ease of somebody perfecting his craft and operating simply in a different stratosphere to an outgunned opponent. Just seven weeks later the two met again. This time it was a fight to keep Craig ticking over for the WBU title shot that had all but been agreed. However, at the Broadway Theatre in Barking, London, it went horribly wrong when for reasons unfathomable to both himself and his corner, Craig lost on points. A state of shock existed in the Collyhurst and Moston corner. From the opening bell, Craig appeared drained of all energy and by the end, many at ringside were speechless.

For Craig it was unknown territory. From eleven years old, he had known only one thing - boxing was his life. Since turning pro, he hadn't looked like losing a fight and now, aged just 23, his first proper defeat hurt him deeply. Once back in Manchester Craig retreated deep into himself - foremost in his mind was that he needed time to think, to be on his own and work out just what had gone wrong but 'they' never left him alone. His manager, promoter and even Brian - they constantly knocked at his door... "Sort yourself out lad, we're relying on you. Don't you dare let us down."

The reality was that his mind was tired and Craig needed a break, but they simply never gave it him. For in reality, as ever, it was all about the money.

Three months passed and feeling sufficiently confident to try again, Craig rang Brian and asked if it was okay to come back. He agreed, but it was never the same. Something had changed. No one knows if it was in Craig's head or the atmosphere towards him. Either way, it didn't feel right. A coldness existed that was never there before and finally he walked back down those steps for the last time and never went back... At the age of twenty-three it was all over.

Lost and not knowing where to turn, life for Craig become more than difficult. He missed the respect and camaraderie that existed at Collyhurst and Moston gym and a career in dead-end jobs where you were made to feel like a number saw Craig appreciate what he had lost and it really did break his heart. For how do you go from being the next big thing to being the guy in the pub with the "What if" story?

Knowledgeable and respected boxing experts claimed that if he had continued then Naseem Hamed might never have even been allowed to proclaim himself a prince for Craig would have dethroned him before he set foot on his magic carpet ride to boxing stardom. He really was that good. He really was that special.

Let me tell you about Craig Dermody....

The ghost.

10 - ROBIN REID

MAN IN THE MIRROR

ITALY, 1996: When it comes to art and culture, the vast majority will argue that Milan may have the upper hand on Moston and Collyhurst. However, on the night a relatively unknown English fighter mauled their world champion and much loved local hero, Vincenzo Nardiello, into bloodied submission in the seventh round, it appeared that the Mancunians had stamped their own particular brutal brand of sophistication on the 12,000 stunned Milanese fans in the Medilanum Forum. Born in Sefton, Liverpool, but raised in Runcorn, it was all simply an accident of birth, for Robin Reid had climbed the Mancunian steps of boxing heaven to hammer Nardiello to the canvas, snatch his belt and take it home. As mayhem reigned in the ring and the victors hugged and embraced, a dark brooding atmosphere took hold. The referee went over and told the Mancunians to calm down. Italy was not a country that took the defeat of their fighters lightly. Thoughts turned to safety and getting the English back to their changing room in one piece. Such worries disappeared though with a quick bit of thinking by the new champion as he raised Nardiello's arm high to signal respect to his opponent. The cheers began and the animosity ceased. A proud Brian Hughes, close to tears, winked at his first world champion, who smiled and suddenly reality dawned. Robin Reid and Collyhurst and Moston had only gone and blown the bloody doors off - The Italian Job had gone to perfection.

IT IS SAFE TO SAY THAT ROBIN REID has been fighting since the day he was born. Put up for adoption at just six months old and in a children's home until he was two, before finally being adopted. Luckily, the foster family who took Robbie in offered him solid roots. Robbie's childhood years are remembered fondly, filled with warmth and kindness. His adopted mother Lyn was nothing but a loving, vocal and emotional lady and remains a strong influence on him to this day and remains a first port of call whenever advice is needed. A sporting child, it was thought he could have succeeded at any number of activities so Lyn took him to a local recreation centre in Runcorn where boxing caught his eye. A fledgling career began at eleven and as Robbie's talent evolved, it soon became clear here was a boy with a natural gift. One that if handled correctly could see him go on to great things.

In 1989, at the Bayamon Stadium, Puerto Rico, in front of a 10,000 strong crowd, Robbie reached the World Junior Championships Final, where he lost a close verdict to the Cuban Leonides Bedey. It was an early taste of the big time and the experience helped to put him on the road to becoming Britain's only boxing medallist at the 1992 Olympic Games. It was in the build up to the Games that Robbie had his first experience of Collyhurst and Moston. To help with his sparring it was arranged for him to spar with Pat Barrett who was by then back at the gym helping out Brian Hughes. It was a pensive Robbie who first walked up those steps that in time would for him, like so many others, become a second home. Robbie was a huge fan of Pat's and had followed his explosive career closely. "He didn't just beat opponents but he knocked them out flat," Reid recalls. The first impressions of those at the gym were that Robbie swaggered through the door looking like a million dollars - a cocky, good looking kid (an Oscar De La Hoya lookalike!) with a smile, a wink and a bit of a reputation as a rising star. However, inside Robbie's stomach was churning – he was a nervous wreck. So much so that he forgot his gloves. His swagger was a case of not wanting to appear cowed by the gym's reputation, it was all a bit of an act and one that apparently worked, at least until he entered the ring where Pat was waiting…

From the moment the Black Flash landed an opening left hook right on Robbie's nose to leave his eyes watering, the swagger disappeared. Welcome to Collyhurst and Moston! Nevertheless, as he settled into his rhythm, there was a style in the way Robbie boxed and moved that impressed all those who saw him in that first sparring session. Pat himself realised this kid was more than just a pretty face. Robbie had a natural talent, but also possessed real aggression and could dig hard. So it was that after winning his Olympic Bronze medal, nobody was more delighted when he decided to join Collyhurst and Moston, than

Brian Hughes. The old fox sensed this kid, who loved to talk the talk and couldn't pass a mirror without admiring his movie star looks, had the right tools to become a world champion. It would all be about harnessing his talent and adding them to the Collyhurst and Moston way. It could be a formidable combination.

However, in the beginning it wasn't all wine and roses as Robbie's persona irked Brian a little. Here was somebody, a boxing prodigy and an Olympic medallist, whose mindset was such that he believed he didn't need to train that hard or listen too much because it would all just come naturally. Brian thought that in order to unlock his potential, something needed to dramatically change. He spoke about this to Pat Barrett who suggested an idea, "Let me train him Brian".

Pat's line of thought was that Brian was just a little too nice for Robbie and a different approach was called for. As an outsider, although a hugely talented boxer with sharp intelligence, Reid lacked the street smarts of others at the gym. Surrounding Robbie were fighters of all ages that had been schooled in the Collyhurst and Moston way from being kids. Many were brought up in poverty and hardship whose only option, should boxing not work out, was the dole, a dead-end job or, more likely, a life of crime. Brian's boxing philosophy was their bible; hard work and determination the religion. For Pat, Robbie came over as a little spoilt for it all had come very easily so far. To succeed in the professional game he knew so much more was required – blood, sweat and tears would need to be shed in the gym and out on the road before fights were won. Pat's tough street mentality might just be what was required to drag Robbie's best out of him,

"The trouble is Brian" Pat said, "He's just not used to being told what to do." Brian agreed, it was worth a try and again at first it was a disaster! Pat's volatile temper compared to Brian's calm persona and his desire to rattle Robbie into producing more initially backfired, so much so that Robbie rang Brian on the telephone to complain! All Pat's shouting and swearing had got under his skin. On coming off the line a laughing Brian rang Pat and set up a meeting between the three of them. It was agreed Pat would be a little 'nicer' and they all went back to work. However, in reality nothing changed except Robbie slowly started to slowly shed his outsider's thin skin and began to grow a Collyhurst and Moston rhino hide.

On 27th February 1993, at the Groesbrook Leisure centre in Dagenham, Essex, Robbie made his professional debut with a first-round stoppage of Mark Lee Dawson. So began a twenty-two-bout unbeaten run with twenty-one wins, the only blotch on a perfect record being a draw against Danny Juma. Robbie had signed with promoter Frank Warren, but felt like it was close to impossible to get noticed. Warren's stable at that time read like a who's who of great British and Irish fighters: Nigel Benn, Chris Eubank, Frank Bruno, Naseem Hamed and Steve Collins - they were all superstars with regular fights on terrestrial TV. Robbie, though impressing many, was also receiving savage criticism from the likes of former world champion and Sky Sports pundit Barry McGuigan who claimed he amounted to less than the sum of his parts. Meanwhile, Robbie's part-time male modelling career irked those in the boxing community. It simply was not the done thing and when he did not perform between the ropes, the comments, many from McGuigan, were scathing, "Robbie is a one-dimensional fighter, he's too mundane at times and simply does not inject enough pace when needed."

The criticism hardly helped in his quest for a title shot and there were times he admitted that the performances suffered. The gut wrenching feeling of not getting anywhere and being pushed to the side-lines was killing Robbie inside. This made it hard to get keyed up for some early fights and clearly showed and were once again jumped upon by critics such as McGuigan. Brian Hughes, as ever, preached the positive side of this frustrating situation. He would counsel Robbie that not being promoted in a hurry was a good thing because it gave him time to properly develop as a fighter. Brian could see the improvement in Robbie's work with Pat and he was blossoming both as a fighter and person. The time spent together in the gym and out running saw the pair grow close as Pat realised that behind the wise cracks and cheeky scouse persona lay a fighter after his own heart. Also, unknown to Robbie, Frank Warren had not forgotten about him, he knew the work being done at Collyhurst and Moston, it was simply a case of finding the right fight at the right time…

With Robbie not having gone through the usual process of British and European titles, it meant outside the United Kingdom he was a virtual unknown in boxing circles. The recently crowned WBC World

Super Middleweight champion, twenty-seven-year-old Italian Vincenzo Nardiello, was looking for a first and relatively easy defence. Warren had spoken with Brian and both agreed that Robbie was primed, ready and more than capable of beating Nardiello. When negotiating the Italians had looked at his record and noticed he had not fought any recognised names and so a deal was struck. Their boy, it was felt, had nothing to worry about. Robbie was just a raw kid…

Nardiello had been around, he had fought and was stopped by Nigel Benn in the Dark Destroyer's first bout since his infamous clash against Gerald McClellan. Nardiello finally earned another shot against the man who ultimately beat Benn, the experienced and dangerous, if unpredictable South African 'Sugar Boy' Malinga. In a fierce, tight contest held at the Manchester Nynex Arena, Nardiello won on a split decision to take the belt back to Italy. Now, just three miles down the road at Collyhurst and Moston, plans were well in advance to bring a world title back to the city for the first time since the thirties.

At the press conference the day before the fight in Milan, Brian Hughes concocted a ruse to bring the hostile Italian journalists on board for the Mancunian's own means. Always thinking and looking for the slightest edge, Brian told them Robbie got his dark good looks from his father who was Italian, when in reality he came from Trinidad! Suddenly the poisoned penned questioning took on a friendlier feel. Brian had learned from his last title fight in Italy six years before with Pat Barrett in Salerno that the Italians were immensely proud of their rich culture and history and pandering to it, even if it meant telling a little white lie, might make things easier for all concerned. Yet it still meant that to win, Reid would almost certainly have to knock out his Italian opponent – at the end of the day, they looked after their own.

To prepare Robbie for the fight, Brian and Pat worked tremendously hard on his fitness, he had yet to go twelve rounds and it was a worry. In the gym, the concentration was on power, to get him to use his left hook to wear down the champion and ultimately finish him off. Their man undoubtedly had the strength, endurance and skill to win in Milan, however, come fight night, everything would rest on whether Robbie Reid had the heart. At the weigh-in tensions ran high with both fighters eyeballing each other. Words were exchanged, the eccentric Nardiello gave Robbie a look as if to say, "Who are you?"

On fight night, as they left their dressing room in the Medilanum forum to face the wrath of ten thousand Italians, Brian pulled Robbie aside in the corridor, "Good luck, son. Do your family and us proud." With Frank Warren leading, then Robbie, followed by Pat and Brian close behind, they headed into the arena. Greeting them was a huge laser show. Flashing beams lit up the walls and illuminated faces. Robbie wore a gown with the words 'Grim Reaper' emblazoned upon it. His face a cold mask, it was time to go to work.

Next came Nardiello, to the tune of "We are the Champions" and a cornerman holding his belt high behind him, the Italian entered to a crescendo of cheers. Nardiello had 'ICE' tattooed on the back of his head. If not smiling, there was an air of supreme confidence about him, he was cocky alright. A first defence against an English pretty boy, no problem…

Robbie watched on unimpressed but ready as the veteran referee, sixty-two-year-old American Frank Cappucchino from New Jersey, who had previously officiated Marvin Hagler and Mike Tyson, called the men to the centre of the ring.

From the first bell Robbie started well with chopping right hands forcing Nardiello backwards. An enthusiastic Frank Warren was off his seat immediately standing up in support of his fighter, "It's your fight Robbie. More body shots!" As early as the second round a tentative Nardiello was struggling with Robbie's punching power, so much that he went down complaining of a low blow that was clearly above the belt. It was play-acting of the worst order and immediately jumped on by Cappucchino who admonished Nardiello and warned him such pathetic behaviour would not be tolerated. Seemingly annoyed at Nardiello's tactics, Robbie went after him throwing lefts and rights and catching the champion. Brian sensed a possible loss of control, "Fight your fight Robbie. Calm down!" The third saw Nardiello finally come into the contest as Robbie's early fire appeared to wane. With a renewed bounce, confidence and swagger he roared back and the pattern continued in the fourth with the champion again winning the round. The devil had deserted Robbie for the moment, that early criticism of lacking the courage for a real fight once more entered minds. Robbie was standing off, not leading enough and needing to impose himself.

"You need to get busy Robbie" urged Brian in the break, "go to work, son." The fifth saw a much-improved showing as a series of left hooks and countering rights served to remind Nardiello that Robbie could still do damage. Then, a left-right combination caused the champion to buckle and down he went to his knees! Once back up the bell sounded to save Nardiello further punishment as the fighters squared up, Cappuchhino jumping between them before Robbie returned to his corner with arms raised. Suddenly, the realisation dawned in the forum that their champion was in real trouble. A bad cut had appeared over Nardiello's left eye and the tide of battle had now swung firmly in the Englishman's favour. The sixth saw Robbie again showing little respect for Nardiello as he chased him down, but there were more dirty tricks from the Italian as he dropped to the canvas once more claiming a low blow. Again Cappucchino shook his head in disgust and ordered him back up. The seventh began and the home crowd had clearly lost belief in their man. Another shoddy incident of bad sportsmanship by him claiming a low blow was all but laughed off by the American referee, who was clearly fed up with the Italian's antics. Sensing the time was right, Robbie went after Nardiello on the ropes. Two crashing lefts and a screaming right dropped the champion and this time he never made it back up. Cappucchino counted him out and the fight was over.

Robbie Reid had done it!

Immediately Pat Barrett raced into the ring to embrace the new champion and the pair jumped about like madmen! The long arduous hours spent in the gym and on the road had borne fruit. They were swiftly joined by Frank Warren and Brian Hughes as well as members of Robbie's family including his mother Lyn. As Robbie raised Nardiello's hand high as if to signal a sign of respect, the entire forum rose to its feet. The white lie fed to the home press by Brian that Robbie was half Italian almost certainly influenced the huge sporting ovation! The Milanese audience cheered loudly as the boxers embraced. Finally, Nardiello departed and the time arose to crown a new champion. As the belt was being placed on Robbie, he called across to a clearly reluctant Brian Hughes to join him. Never one for the spotlight, Brian joined Robbie and the men hugged. Together with Pat Barrett they had combined to win a first world championship title for the gym since Jackie Brown in 1932. The Collyhurst and Moston gym was back on the map. It really had been a team effort. A family affair. In the television interview with

Sky Sports, Robbie mentioned that the criticism, particularly by Barry McGuigan, had inspired him but it was more the belief shown by Brian, Pat and all back home in the gym that was a much bigger influence on him succeeding.

There was a welcome bonus when Marvin Hagler, one of Robbie's heroes, ducked through the ropes to shake the new champion's hand, "You did it the hard way, son," the former Middleweight World Champion told him, "you have the hunger. Congratulations."

As the Sky cameras entered the ring Brian lined up on one side of Robbie and Pat the other and the trio were also joined by Robbie's very proud mother - tear-stained and overcome with emotion, Lyn could hardly talk but simply held tightly to her boy. It was a wonderful moment. By the end a laughing Robbie stared straight at the camera lens to declare, "I've done it and I've still got my looks!" There was no doubt where that comment was aimed….

On 8th February, 1997, at London Arena, twenty-five-year-old Robin Reid prepared to make his first defence of the WBC World Super Middleweight title. His opponent was Johannesburg born South African Giovanni 'No Mercy' Pretorius. A clergyman's son, the South African was a brave but limited fighter, an ideal choice, Frank Warren believed, for a first title defence. However, his thirteen previous wins achieved by stoppages meant he was still a legitimate threat to Reid.

To a soundtrack of The Fugees 'Ready or Not' Robin Reid, the champion with the film star looks, made a grand entrance into the arena. Having been catapulted into the big league with one almighty audition in Milan, it's fair to say that to the general public at least, Reid had come from nowhere. A one-time Ladbrokes cashier, he was now a supremely confident fighter who had placed a hefty bet on himself to win inside seven rounds. Looking the part, Robbie roared loud at the adoring crowd, "Come on!" He clearly loved his sudden arrival in big time boxing. As promised, Pretorius had come to fight, but in the first round almost came unstuck straight away as he found himself struggling badly against the new champion's power. Being a natural Middleweight, Reid's superior power was evident in a flurry of rights and then a blistering left hook that rocked Pretorious and left him staggering. Robbie continued to catch the South African and a series of uppercuts again staggered the challenger, so much that the highly experienced referee Lou Filippo (Lou played the referee in four Rocky films) was already taking a close look at him. Robbie looked sensational; all aggression and power with swift and smooth movement he had a newly found ring confidence that came only with a champion's mantle. Another fierce left had Pretorious down on one knee, he took an eight count and although unsteady and clearly dazed got back up and only blind courage saw him survive that opening round. The huge roars from an impressed London crowd that greeted the bell were music to Robbie's ears. He had been nothing short of magnificent in his attempts to prove the Italian job in Milan was no one off.

The second and third round saw Robbie ease a little as he continued to pick his shots, but still hurt Pretorious. The word from Brian Hughes and Pat Barrett in the corner was for him to take his time as the right punch would eventually end his opponent's night. Robbie was much the stronger man up close, where the weight difference was clearly obvious, but brave and game, the South African came forever forwards as promised pre-fight and he was eventually forced to pay for such bravery. In the fifth Robbie let fly a right hand that almost put him through the ropes and forced Pretorius into taking a mandatory eight count. Now back in charge, a barrage of stinging punches left the South African close to going over. Yet still he managed to reach the bell. The clergyman's son needed not so much a prayer but a miracle to go further. The sixth saw both fighters appear a little laboured, but the song remained the same with Robbie's shots, landing like bombs, still finding and hurting their target. Pretorious' resistance was waning and in the seventh Robbie's first punch rocked his head backwards. No matter how much character a fighter has, they're only human and as more body shots flew in Pretorius was almost done. Treading water by now, the South African was caught by a fantastic countering right hook and his legs went. It was all over. The London arena erupted, Robbie raised both hands and smiled wide. Brian hugged his boy.

On Sky Sports, Robbie's long-time critic Barry McGuigan gave him praise almost through gritted teeth, whilst the-then reigning British Super Middleweight champion, twenty-five-year-old Welshman Joe Calzaghe, was not so forthcoming and hardly impressed, "Robbie is a one-paced fighter and when we fight I'll knock him out."

★

Life was never dull on Lightbowne Road. Even when the gym was shut there was always something brewing up those twenty steps to boxing heaven that could leave you open-mouthed. Characters straight out of a Dickens novel would regularly come and go. Events occurred that you simply could not make up. One night Robbie and Michael Gomez were hanging out in the gym and chatting in the changing room. Both were deep in training for forthcoming fights so the talk was all about making the weight and the qualities of their opponents. Suddenly, from above, a loud banging noise could be heard coming from the roof. Both left the changing room to check it out and over the gym stairwell they could see dust falling from the ceiling. Then, to their utter shock, a leg appeared dangling trying to kick a way through. This was obviously a burglar trying to break into the shop downstairs. Robbie tapped Michael on the shoulder and pointed towards a couple of broom handles stood up against a nearby wall, "Keep an eye on him" he whispered to the Mexican Manc, "I'll get the broom handles". Michael nodded, but no sooner had Robbie gone than the unfortunate stranger dropped down and landed before him. The look on his face must have been precious as Michael Gomez smiled wide.

"Evenin' mate," he said before head-butting him. As the would-be burglar staggered Robbie came rushing back over and cracked him with a broom handle. Lying flat on the floor he was advised that to get back up could be seriously bad for his health.

"Big mistake, lad" Michael informed him.

Robbie laughed, "Welcome to Collyhurst and Moston mate!"

The burglar never moved a muscle.

When the police arrived they asked Robbie and Michael how he had got the bruises on his face? They both shrugged their shoulders and answered in unison, "He fell!"

The policeman smiled, "What? On his head?" Later that same week Brian called them both into his office.

"Right, Batman and Robin. Sit down. I've just had Collyhurst police station on the phone."

The pair said nothing.

"So, he fell eh?"

Again, total silence. Brian leaned back in his chair and stared for a moment. He knew what had gone on...

"Well it might interest you to know that the villain in question has informed the police that he feels it would have been less painful for him to have landed in a pit full of Dobermans."

Again, they both said nothing. Even Brian, whilst pretending to be annoyed, looked close to a hint of a smile, "Go on, get back to your training." On walking out of his office door, he fired one last parting shot, "Oi super heroes!" Robbie and Michael turned around facing him. "From now on leave catching criminals to the bloody police!"

It was just another night at the gym.

On 3rd May, 1997, Robbie defended his title for the second time against the tough, hard punching twenty-nine-year-old Yorkshireman Henry Wharton. A former British, Commonwealth and European champion, Wharton had been in the ring with some of the best, with only two losses in his career to Chris Eubank and Nigel Benn - both times on points. The fight against Robbie would be his last shot at a world title and the granite tough Yorkshireman crossed the Pennines convinced he would prevail. Confidence was high in the Wharton camp and he was backed heavily by his promoter Mickey Duff who had a side bet with Frank Warren of £15,000 on the fight. At a packed Manchester Nynex Arena, hosting a show entitled 'Battle of the Brits,' Robin Reid fought out a furious, but skilful and intelligent battle against the experienced, huge-hearted Wharton, to win on points. He did so by using controlled aggression and Robin finally answered his critics regarding an alleged lack of stamina. For twelve rounds he danced, jabbed, hit and moved to produce the finest performance of his career. In training under Pat Barrett's watchful eye, Robbie had sparred for twelve rounds, but was only allowed to use his left jab. At times with gym mates, such as the brilliant Michael Gomez coming at him, it proved a torturous experiment, but by the time he faced the ferocious Wharton it all proved worthwhile. That night Robbie truly arrived to silence even the strongest of critics, none more than Barry McGuigan who lavished high praise on him, "Maybe I've been hard in the past on Robbie, but tonight against Wharton he's been immense." Brian Hughes placed a towel around Robbie's shoulders and whispered into his ear, "Well done son." Such simple words, but to Collyhurst and Moston fighters, and even world champions like Robin Reid, it was praise that amounted to winning the lottery.

Robbie mounted his third title defence against the experienced Lyon-born Hacine Cherifi on 11th September, 1997, at the Leisureway Centre in Widnes. A former French and European champion, Cherifi pushed him all the way and come the end only a split decision saw Robbie retain his title. It was a tough watch for the Reid camp as he struggled throughout the contest to impose himself on the troublesome and wily Frenchman. Robbie looked jaded, the fights against Pretorious and Wharton had clearly taken a toll. Also, in the post-fight interview Robbie claimed the recent death of Princess Diana the previous week had affected his mindset, comments that baffled many and sounded like a poor excuse. Critics of Reid were out in force again after the fight and it had been a case of just getting over the line. In the end, he had managed to do so. Robbie was still champion.... Just.

Despite the struggles against Cherifi, Robbie's star still shone brightly and nowhere more than at Collyhurst and Moston gym. Brian Hughes would constantly use him as a role model to the younger kids. Robbie offered hope - a way out. Brian would point over to where he was training, "You can be like Robbie. Be a world champion, be made for life. Have respect. It's not just about talent, you have to work hard and you have to listen." Brian would then motion towards the stairwell entrance, "Through that door there walk future world champions. Robbie has proved it." Outside, his sleek, blue low-slung sports car sat parked on the road looking entirely out of place in its grim inner-city surroundings. Normally any such vehicle around Moston would have had its wheels removed and replaced by bricks in a quicker time than it took an F1 pit crew to send Lewis Hamilton back on his way. But not Robbie's motor. Even the area's most notorious characters issued a hands off warning where their world champion was concerned. Brian also preached to his lads to look after their own. Whether it be in the gym or on the streets. An example of this occurred when one of the few non-locals, whose son was training at the club, came to watch him and left his motorbike outside, only to discover on leaving that it was gone. Being pretty certain who the thieves were, some of the boxers formed a posse and within twenty minutes they had found the bike and returned it. The guilty party was also brought along and made to apologise.

This was Collyhurst and Moston.

All for one.

Sadly, disaster was just around the corner for Robbie as sugar would, for once, not prove sweet. On 19th December, 1997, at the London Arena, his world fell apart when he lost the world crown on a unanimous points decision to the dangerous and much travelled veteran South African, forty-two-year-old 'Sugar Boy' Malinga. Though a huge underdog, Malinga's impressive record should have been sufficient warning for what followed. In 1992 he had got a shot at the WBO Super Middleweight title against Chris Eubank during which Malinga was dropped in the fifth round and lost a close decision. Three months later he also went close — losing by just half a point to Nigel Benn. After more fights in his native South Africa, and a further loss to the great Roy Jones Jnr in the United States, he landed another shot at the title in March 1996 against Nigel Benn. Despite suffering a knockdown, Malinga fought back to grab a points win, but ended up losing the belt in his first defence against Vincenzo Nardiello. Then came Robin Reid.

This was no fluke, Malinga won deservedly as a terribly under-performing Robbie simply never got going. There were mitigating circumstances, a bad cold pre-fight had definitely affected him to the extent that there was talk of pulling out. However, the decision to fight was made and the result was a disaster. There was no spark and Reid seemed to be a shadow of the young man who so gloriously blew away Vincenzo Nardiello on his own home soil, or who fought with courage and brains to defeat the hard-hitting Henry Wharton. The announcement of the judges' cards was unanimous - 117-113, 115-114 and 117-112 all to the South African. As the decision was announced Brian placed both arms around an exhausted and bloodied Robbie and hugged him tightly. This was a father consoling a son. Both he and Pat Barrett were devastated. Brian told everybody that for the next week he simply did not want to talk about boxing. The highs and low were extreme, but the feeling of losing was especially nauseating. For Robbie, it would be a long road back. The critics once more circled and they had a field day. Malinga had regained his title and done a job on him. There could be no complaints.

Robbie's comeback began in earnest on 18th April, 1998, at

the Manchester Nynex arena against Surrey journeyman Graham Henderson. How the once mighty fall fast in this, the toughest and cruellest of sports, for Robbie was now sixth on the bill. Superstars such as Naseem Hamed and Chris Eubank were now operating in a different stratosphere. The dark game took no prisoners and Robbie was another victim. A sixth-round stoppage of Henderson was maybe only a tentative first step back in the big time, but it was a start. Elsewhere, the pride of Wales, the 'Italian Dragon' Joe Calzaghe had become WBO Super Middleweight title champion and the war drums had begun to sound for a fight with Robin Reid. There was huge dislike between the two. Rumours that Robbie had refused to give Calzaghe a shot at his WBC title saw him resent the 'Grim Reaper' for this. The fact Robbie was fast tracked to a world title shot, whilst Calzaghe was forced to take the long and winding, sometimes never-ending, road drove the Welshman to despair where Robbie was concerned. Jealousy was all consuming. Matters were made even worse when Calzaghe won the WBO title in an epic scrap with Chris Eubank and lengthy negotiations for a unification bout against Robbie were finally completed. The Welshman always blamed Reid for it taking so long when, in reality, like almost everything in boxing, politics, egos and money overruled a fight that the public and both fighters wanted. However, now confident he had Robbie's number, Calzaghe had no qualms about letting him share the big stage once more.

On 13th February, 1999, in an electric atmosphere at the Telewest Arena in Newcastle, Robbie and Joe Calzaghe fought out twelve brutal rounds with neither giving, nor asking for an inch. In the end Calzaghe won a split decision, but it was a result that is still bitterly contested today by Robbie and many others. Coming into the ring Reid appeared so fired up as to be close to meltdown. Wired from the endless insults Calzaghe had hurled at him in the build-up, he was a sight to fear. Screaming loud, he was emotional and ultra-aggressive, it prompted the Sky commentator Ian Darke to worry if Robbie was just too hyped up. Fourteen months had passed since the Cherifi fight. During that period his male modelling career was showing signs of prospering, but once the fight with Calzaghe was confirmed, Robbie dropped it like a stone to get into what Brian Hughes described as "The best shape of his career". Robbie had one thought, to beat the cocky Welshman, who at every opportunity chose to tell the world "I'm going to knock out Robin Reid."

Ultimately, Calzaghe prevailed in the battle between the two and, as so often in boxing, they came together at the end with a new-found respect. Though they were never going to become close friends, Robbie and Calzaghe would no longer be sworn enemies. Possibly the defining moment came in the eighth round when referee Roy Francis docked Robbie a point for a low blow and, even though he came roaring back in the final four, genuinely hurting Calzaghe with two huge right hands in the ninth, the damage was done.

Immediate comments from Frank Warren that a rematch was most definitely on the cards came as no surprise, for the fighters had put on a great show. However, as the months passed and arguments persisted over purses it never happened. Feeling undervalued Robbie refused to lower demands for a rematch. His pride allowed him to take what he considered 'rubbish money' for the first fight because of the prize at stake, alas, the same pride stopped him taking the second fight. And so Robbie drifted, a year passed and doubts were raised about whether he would ever be the fighter of old or even get back in the ring. Finally, on 24th June, 2000, at Hampden Park, Glasgow, on the undercard of the Mike Tyson-Lou Savarese bill, Robbie returned to take on the Roman born fighter Silvio Branco for his WBU World Super Middleweight title. A decent fighter with a good record, he was one hardly expected to trouble someone of Robin Reid's class. Or, at least, the old Robbie. Sadly, in a turgid twelve-round encounter against the much taller Branco, Reid laboured badly and come the end cut an exhausted, broken figure. As Branco was lifted high by his corner, Brian wiped down an emotional Robbie. This really felt like the end of the road for the adopted son of Collyhurst and Moston. Shortly afterwards he was advised by Frank Warren to retire. All appeared to have come to a natural end, but there was one man who would in time think differently… Robin Reid.

As the boxing income dwindled to almost nothing, Robbie was persuaded to develop his modelling work by posing for 'top-shelf' magazines. He had few qualms about this for like anyone else Robbie had bills to pay. However, when the opportunity arose to regain his status in the ring the time came to once more put on the gloves. Determined to claw his way back up the rankings, there was an acrimonious split with Frank Warren. During his time out Robbie had refused to fight on the undercards of Naseem Hamed and was still holding out for a Calzaghe rematch that never came. Robbie finally signed with new promoter Jess Harding. So began a series of ten wins to re-establish his career and prove he was far from done. Harding secured him another world title shot and he was scheduled to face American Ron Martinez for the vacant WBF title. Yet disaster struck when Martinez failed his pre-fight medical. To save the show at the Crystal Palace Sports Centre, London, a disappointed Reid fought a late replacement, Mike Gormley and took out his frustration with a first-round knockout of the brave, but thoroughly outclassed Salfordian.

Whilst it had been an easy passage to his second world title, Robbie enjoyed a successful reign as WBF champion. He made a first defence by impressively stopping a tough Russian, Roman Babaev, in just three rounds. Next up was a demolition of South African Soon Botes in the fourth. Only two months later and determined to stay busy, he took out South American champion Jorge Andres Sclarandi of Argentina. Robbie even managed a fourth title defence before the end of 2001, putting on a superb performance to win a unanimous decision over another Argentine, former WBA world champion Julio Cesar Vasquez. Taking a much deserved seven-month break, he eventually returned to the ring taking on a third Argentine opponent, the tough and durable Francisco Antonio Mora. On 10th July, 2002, at the Wembley Conference Centre, 'El Chino' Mora, survived knockdowns in rounds three and six to go the full distance, but in the end Robbie was on another level and retained his crown with a clear unanimous decision. This would be the last defence he made of the WBF world title. His next four opponents were all stopped in what was a case of merely ticking over. Finally, a pot of gold appeared when Robbie came within sight of a bout against thirty-six-year-old IBF and WBA world champion Sven Ottke.

The German was a veteran of twenty world title fights and on 13th December, 2003, in the Nurnberg Arena, Nuremberg, Robbie experienced an outrageous decision that verged on the scandalous. In one of boxing's most infamous 'home' robberies, Robbie himself commented afterwards, "At least Dick Turpin had the decency to wear a mask!" There had been no doubt that he had beaten Ottke on points but the referee Roger Tilleman's disgraceful officiating of the bout and the judges blatantly biased scorecards left the visiting English reporters and neutrals speechless. Robbie won at least eight of twelve rounds by a distance and even scored a knockdown, which the scandalous Tilleman remarkably refused to acknowledge. He instead called it a 'slip' and deducted a point off Robbie for a phantom head butt! Something was dreadfully amiss.

Back in Manchester before the fight, Brian Hughes and Robbie had worked on a game plan to beat Ottke and after five rounds it was all working to perfection. Brian was hugely optimistic. Shortly before they set off for Germany he confided to British journalists that thirty-two-year-old Robbie was going to roar back into the world title reckoning, even joking with some of them who were set to go and speak with him, "He'll be up at the gym working out and then having an hour or so in front of the mirror!"

Sadly, Brian's confidence was to prove cruelly misguided. That something untoward was in the air became clear when a worried looking Jess Harding came rushing towards the corner and told Brian that Robbie had only won one of the opening five rounds on the Judge's scorecards. Suddenly reality dawned that the Manchester contingent were being mugged. Realising the sheer scale of cheating that was occurring Robbie appeared to lose heart. Some accused him later of not going for the knockout, but in reality, it was a ridiculous criticism for every time Robbie attempted to open up, Tilleman barged him. Watching the fight again, the referee is constantly warning Robbie for fouls that did not occur and threatening disqualification. At one stage he appears to chastise him for having the nerve to punch Ottke! In the end Robbie simply stopped throwing shots and the German won the last four rounds. In the post-fight interview Robbie, though incensed, appeared shell-shocked and was even laughing at the absurd favouritism. Following that disgraceful decision in Nuremberg, Roger Tilleman was pilloried, but sadly for Robbie the damage had already been done.

Now aged thirty-three, time appeared to have run out, but luckily an opportunity arose to challenge the twenty-nine-year-old unbeaten Irishman Brian Magee for his IBO World Super-Middleweight title at the legendary King's Hall, Belfast. General consensus was that the

Englishman had longed since peaked and would be a decent scalp to add to Magee's previous twenty-two consecutive wins. So far in his career Magee had alternated between flashes of brilliance and lengthy stretches of mediocrity. He had defended his title eight times but had yet to truly impress. The Belfast southpaw had been a world-class amateur and the time had arrived to prove he was worthy of joining the elite in the professional ranks. Magee's last fight had seen him once more under-perform and it was felt that a boxer of Robbie's class, albeit seen as 'over the hill' by many, would prove a perfect opponent to bring Magee on.

Many experts predicted a tactical battle between two technically gifted fighters, but what actually occurred was a strangely scrappy, yet volatile encounter. On 26th June 2004, in a hostile Belfast atmosphere, with 6000 locals roaring on their boy, Robbie won a deserved unanimous points decision over Magee, even though at times he appeared to struggle badly to find his form throughout the fight. Matters were not helped when Magee caught Robbie with his head and cut him badly on the forehead. Robbie's superior punching power had the Irishman on the canvas four times and the Irishman survived a nightmare eighth round after suffering a double knockdown, when seemingly out on his feet. And yet other rounds were harder to call as the pair slugged it out. As the bell signalled the end of the twelfth many in the King's Hall felt it would still be close, despite the four knockdowns. The Mancunian contingent feared another hometown decision and prepared for the worst. It had been a tempestuous affair that lacked in real quality, but Robbie took the decision on all three judges' cards; 115-112, 114-111 and 113-112.

It had been a fight of unrelenting action, if at times it was all a little messy with theatrical antics from both fighters. The fun and games began in the opening round when Magee was deducted a point for hitting and holding Robbie at the same time. American referee Tommy Kimmons required less than a second to decide Magee had landed an illegal punch. He settled down in rounds two and three by adopting an ugly but effective tactic of throwing a single punch and then grabbing hold of Robbie, who was becoming increasingly infuriated with the tactic. Here he was fighting for his future and Magee's spoiling tactics were proving beyond maddening. The first knockdown came in the fourth: a short right from Robbie that connected with Magee and saw him go over. In round five the Irishman was sent tumbling to the canvas again, but Magee came back to win the next two. In the eighth he was knocked down twice more, but remarkably, the judges gave this round to Magee! It was that kind of fight. Come the finish justice was done and as the blood was finally wiped off Robbie's body, the judges declared, somewhat reluctantly in volatile surroundings, for the challenger. It was a third world title for a man who simply refused to go away.

The desire still burned within Robin Reid and he craved more: a career that had suffered from some blatantly poor decisions, some would say outright cheating, was added to a desire for proper respect from a press and media that seemed very reluctant to recognise his achievements. The loss to Calzaghe still cut deep, but boxing politics meant a rematch was an impossibility. There was another avenue to go down, though arguably against the most dangerous opponent Robbie had ever faced who many thought it madness to even consider taking on, especially at the age of 34. However, it suited both parties to make the fight and a deal was done. At stake would be two world titles – the IBO and IBF World Super Middleweight belts. Reid's courage and desire to prove himself at this late stage against a truly world class fighter meant Collyhurst and Moston was heading to warmer climates; Tampa Bay, Florida was the destination and Jeff 'Left Hook' Lacy the opponent.

Few gave Robbie much hope against the much-hyped, unbeaten twenty-eight-year-old Lacy nicknamed 'a Middleweight Tyson' by the American boxing press because of the power of his punching. Lacy could be devastating when in the mood and he had an eye on a money spinning unification contest against WBO champion Joe Calzaghe in the near future. The American's camp felt Robbie was little more than an irritant to be dealt with before the main act against Calzaghe. It showed a lack of respect and one that irked Robin badly in the build-up as Lacy appeared to mention Calzaghe more than him. Reid's mood hardly improved in the first press conference when Robbie was handed a tee shirt from Lacy's camp emblazoned with the words: "I visited the United States and all I got was knocked out by Jeff Lacy". Such antics only served to further antagonise Robbie, so much so that although normally a chatterbox beforehand, he refused to participate in the final conference promoting the fight.

With Robbie's temperament wholly unpredictable it was impossible to know which fighter would show until the first bell, although he was confident of causing a major upset. Having watched Lacy's previous five bouts closely, the Mancunians were of the belief that he wasn't really all that and distinctly beatable, especially with Lacy's mind already drifting towards a clash with Calzaghe. Also, after his problems in Ireland and especially Germany, Robbie was convinced the American referee would at least allow him to hit back… or so he thought, for some things it appeared, never changed.

On 6th August, 2005, at the St Pete Times Forum, Tampa, Florida, Robin Reid fought bravely against all odds, both fair and not and ultimately was pulled out of a brutal encounter by Brian Hughes to avoid further unnecessary punishment against an on-fire Jeff Lacy. There was no argument that Lacy was the superior fighter, but he was helped along the way by a clearly biased referee in Jorge Alonso, who looked to constantly pick Robbie up on discrepancies both real and imagined. The controversy began in the first round when Lacy turned his back for no reason and Robbie was warned and was then pulled for throwing kidney punches and when Lacy did similar nothing was said. In reality, the American hardly needed such help – as the fight progressed it was obvious he clearly outgunned Robbie. In the second Robbie was cautioned for supposed use of the head though both fighters were equally guilty before brutal clubbing rights from Lacy ended the round as he appeared to be seriously warming up. Sensing the ante was being raised, Brian told Robbie to stay calm, that he was doing okay, "Don't get into a brawl son!" Come the fourth, Lacy was running away with the fight, he hit Robbie with a low blow and whilst Alonso gave him time to recover, nothing was said about it. The tide was not just turning, but starting to overwhelm him as Lacy started to open up with left hooks. It became apparent what all the fuss was about. The hype was real: come the round's end Robbie's legs were close to buckling and the bell came to his aid like ambulance sirens wailing. With the crowd screaming for their boy it was starting to heat up in Tampa Bay. "Come on son," urged Brian, as Robbie sat bruised and breathing heavily, "get control of yourself and get back to what you're good at."

It got worse as Lacy started to unleash a ferocious barrage of hooks.

Stirred by this and led by his cheerleading father, Hydra, himself a former fighter, the crowd raised the tempo and the arena shook with noise. They knew Lacy was ready to explode. Their man was coming. At the end of the fourth Robbie was reeling. Lacy had come into his own and Reid simply could not handle him. Watching on, a pensive Brian knew this. For the first time in his career Robbie was knocked to the canvas and then forced into taking an eight count. Also, the ref had fined Reid a point for holding, but when being admonished by Alonso, Lacy took a free hit and got away with it! Notwithstanding this, the American had won every round so far and it was in serious danger of becoming a mismatch. Back in the corner Brian laid it all on the line for his fighter, "If you don't do what I say, I'm gonna stop this fight, I mean it. Rob, are you listening to me?"

"Yeah" replied a shattered Robbie.

"You're getting hit too many times son, now come on."

Roared on by a frenzied support, now sensing blood, round six saw Lacy continue to open up and become even more menacing. Though Robbie fought on with tremendous guts, it appeared only a matter of time and two huge right hands saw him down once more. He was in dire straits. Showing courage and battered to a pulp, Robbie made it back to the stool.

A worried Brian was close to ending it, "I'm gonna stop this."

"No please Brian, let me…"

"No, no you're getting hit far too often."

"Brian please, no. Brian."

"No Robbie I don't want to see you get hurt, I mean that."

Yet Robbie insisted and got off his stool for round seven. Again Alonso took another point off Robbie and threatened him with disqualification after both fighters were clearly holding. Still he fought on, only to be felled again when Lacy cut loose with uppercuts that landed smack on his chin. Forced to a nine count, exhausted and clearly close to the end, Robbie survived to the bell. This time Brian had seen enough, "I'm stopping it Robbie. I'm not gonna see you get knocked out." He called for the referee. "We're stopping it ref."

As Alonso signalled to end the fight, Robbie continued to plead, but Brian was not having it. He had seen enough.

"I'm okay Brian, please!"

"No, no you're not son. I'm not having you getting badly hurt."

As the crowd erupted and Lacy jumped onto the ropes to take his bow, Robbie sat quietly, head down with Brian in his ear, "You could not have done anymore, son." It was an appropriate action, one typical of Brian who cared passionately about his fighters and was not prepared to see them get seriously beaten up or even worse. The staggering power of Lacy, as he ripped into a shattered Robbie, meant such a scenario could easily have occurred. For the first time in forty-three fights Robbie had been stopped, but it was never a question of lacking courage. Like so many fighters he was now up against an enemy who took no prisoners.

Father Time.

A crutch with many great fighters is the belief that they always have one more big fight within them. The mind tricks the body into believing everything is well. Two years on from losing gallantly, if badly, to Jeff Lacy, Robbie fought once more for a major title. On 9th October, 2007 at the Nottingham Arena, Robbie took on British Super Middleweight champion, thirty-year-old local boy Carl 'The Cobra' Froch who was looking to extend his unbeaten record to twenty-two professional fights, Froch was in merciless mood and finished Robbie off, who retired on his stool at the end of round five. After the fight he announced it really was all over. By then just a mere shadow of the boxer who stormed to victory many years previous against Nardiello in Italy, retirement was the right decision. Against Froch he had fought with typical bravery. Ever the showman, Robbie attempted to intimidate Froch as he stepped into the ring, blocking his entry at the ropes, then shoulder-barging him. Froch's eyes never left his and this behaviour drew a hail of derision from the 6000 strong Nottingham support. Robbie shaded a cagey first round with Froch intent on simply stalking his man, but the signs of an early night in Froch's favour were there when he had Robbie down with a ferocious right in the second and after another assault in the third, he was dropped again. With Froch set to finish it off the ailing challenger looked to survive. The inevitable end came at the end of the fifth when Froch hit Robbie flush in the face with a right hand that dropped him to his knees. He opted for a mandatory eight count from referee Dave Parris. The old pro was looking for a breather, but ultimately his body, strength and will had been broken by a much younger and stronger man. At the bell Robbie was in his corner and with Brian urging him to stop, he opted to retire from the fight. Later that evening Robbie would claim it to be permanent... but do they ever really say it's over in their head?

Four years on and now aged forty, he attempted one last comeback in a fight for the vacant British Super Middleweight title. On 20th October, 2012, at the Sheffield Arena, against Edinburgh-born Kenny Anderson, the curtain finally came down on Robin Reid's professional career. Stopped in five rounds by Anderson, it was simply too much to ask. Boxing was not averse to huge upsets, but when it came to performing miracles, Father Time normally refused to go along. So, it proved to be in Robbie's case. A boxing career littered with wonderful highs and lows that had truly been a rollercoaster ride.

An adopted son of Collyhurst and Moston and even today a regular visitor up those steps, Robbie still sees the gym as a second home. The young boy with the movie icon looks who achieved the ultimate dream in boxing may have been born and raised on Merseyside, but his heart belongs to Lightbowne Road in Moston. Now, when Robin Reid looks at the man in the mirror he can afford a smile and a wink because staring back at him is a world champion.

"Robbie was born under a star" Brian Hughes once claimed.

There can be no higher accolade.

11 - MICHAEL GOMEZ
DOWN ALL THE DAYS

In 2001, Michael Armstrong Gomez died on the operating table for forty-eight seconds. An allergic reaction to anaesthetic caused him to stop breathing. Michael was twenty-four years old, of Irish gypsy blood and proud of it. He was told beforehand by a reassuring surgeon that the chances of such a scenario occurring was a million to one. It seemed it just wasn't his night. Stabbed over a stupid drunken argument in a nightclub, it was just the way Michael lived his life, and really came as no surprise. To him the only time the world really made sense was in a ring, for at least between those ropes rules existed with a referee and his mentor Brian Hughes keeping a close eye on him from the corner.

In the operating theatre, there was a kind of calm, but organised chaos, "He's gone!" shouted out a startled voice. "We've lost him, he's flat lining!" The seconds went past... ten, twenty, thirty, forty. The count went on until it reached forty-eight and then he came back. There were sighs of relief all around, as Michael breathed once again. The truth be told, that night as he stared out a waiting Grim Reaper was not really so extraordinary, for down all the days there had been worse. Heaven could wait. Michael Armstrong Gomez had been fighting for his breakfast, dinner, tea and the clothes on his back since he was eight years old. The candle had not even burned halfway down. There was much more mayhem yet to cause.

IT MAY COME AS LITTLE SURPRISE that Michael Armstrong was born in a car crash. Back in the summer of 1977 his expectant mother, Mary, was being thrown around in the back of a battered old Austin Allegro, driven by his partially blind father, Michael John Armstrong. As they careered onwards at a crazy speed along the winding ribbon roads that sliced through the beautiful rolling fields of County

Longford, Michael senior was forced to swerve and skidded, smashing into the signpost of an old person's nursing home. A shaken Mary's waters broke and pretty quickly it became clear that she was going to have to deliver the baby there and then, amid the smoking, smouldering wreck. Luckily, a member of staff from the home came rushing out and, with her help, Michael junior entered this world kicking and screaming.

Michael was one of ten children. They were always on the move trying to stay one step ahead of the rent man. Mayo, Kerry, Galway – the Armstrongs were constantly roaming, living in slum accommodation and moth-ridden bedsits before eventually turning up in Ballymun, Dublin where they stayed at a Catholic church hostel. Whilst there Michael attended the Holy Spirit school run by priests and nuns - the rules were many and had to be adhered to at all times or God help the poor kids. Retribution was swift and usually involved a smack over the head, punch in the face or, in more formal circumstances, the favoured standby for folk of the cloth – a whacking with a leather strap. Michael suffered more than most. A little gypsy kid dressed in rags and hand-me-downs whose personal hygiene was never the best, he drew the ire of one staff member in particular called Father John. As the mutual antagonism between Michael and Father John grew, this dirt-faced little eight-year-old made it his mission in life to wind up the priest at every opportunity. Finally, with his patience exhausted, Father John snapped! He dragged Michael by the collar and took him to a nearby boxing gym where all eyes fell upon them as they entered. The speedbag stopped and the skipping ropes hit the floor. The owner came over – he was a big man with a lifetime of taking punches clearly written upon his face. It was obvious even to a blind man he loved that place, there was an angel's smile amid the war wounds. It was his church and he spoke with true reverence. "A good day to ya Father, what can I do for ya?"

"I was wondering if ya could teach this little maggot here some good manners?" Father John began.

The owner looked at Michael and then back at the priest, "No problem," he replied.

Michael was gloved up and made to fight a much larger and bigger kid who knocked him around the ring like a spinning top. Bruised and bloodied, he was returned to the school and it was assumed by Father John that Michael had learned a costly lesson, "Away with ya Armstrong and be a good lad now!" Little did he know the tears of that little boy whose alleged sins Father John was trying so hard to cleanse were simply of rage. Michael had loved it and all he could think about was going back to the gym and getting his revenge. Michael trained himself for a couple of weeks then went back. He called out that same kid from before and this time around he beat him to a pulp. A little scrag, knee high to a grasshopper, was pummelling this much bigger opponent. He kept punching and didn't stop until the boy fell to his knees crying. Only then was he dragged off him. Suddenly Michael realised this was to be his vocation. Inadvertently Father John had done him a favour. He was going to be a fighter.

Tragedy struck the Armstrong clan when they lost two-year-old Louise from Sudden Infant Death syndrome. It was horrific for all the family, especially Michael's mother who was, unsurprisingly, utterly distraught. Something had to change and so she came up with an idea, they would start afresh by going to England. Gathering their tattered belongings, they set off for Manchester!

They arrived just as the Madchester music scene erupted like a supernova over the city – yet the arrival of the Armstrong's provided explosions of a different kind. Their first port of call was Longsight where they waited until a council house could be found for the family in Moston. True to form, trouble followed them around like a bad smell and after a fall out with some small-time local gangsters, they were forced into a midnight flirt after threats of a serious beating from an avenging mob! However, practice made perfect and doing runners was something in which the Armstrong's specialised. Next stop was a homeless refuge in Moss Side where they stayed for a short while until re-housed. It didn't take long before they were fixed up and a house was found in Miles Platting. As a young teenager, when Michael was not out shoplifting or causing mayhem he would be playing football for Collyhurst and Moston boys. "Playing" might have been pushing it a little because he wasn't very good. Michael had bundles of enthusiasm and could run forever, but his short fuse and frustration meant this would often get the better of him and he would erupt! No matter the size of the opponent, if there was a single word said in return - smack! Then a red card would be flashed and inevitably it was Brian Hughes who dismissed him. Clearly livid, but quietly impressed with the left hook.

It was on a Lightbowne Road pavement where a fuming Brian saw Michael knocking lumps out of a much larger lad that was to prove another defining moment in the youngster's life. Michael felt an arm on his shoulder as he was dragged off, "If you want to fight Armstrong, then you come to the gym tomorrow morning and learn how to do it properly. Not out on a street swinging your arms around like some yobbo annoying nice people." The next day he walked up those steps at Collyhurst and Moston and sheepishly approached Brian who passed him a pair of boxing gloves and smiled, "Now let's do this properly without worrying about getting arrested."

One day in the gym word got back to Brian that Michael wasn't going to school so he pulled him aside to ask what was going on? Michael explained the other kids were always taking the mickey and calling him names because of a thick Irish accent and lack of schooling whilst travelling meant that he could hardly read or write. Brian told him to make sure he went in the next day and promised the bullying would cease. Come the next morning Michael did as he was told and on entering his class was shocked to see Brian and then current European champion Pat Barrett, stood waiting in front of a very hushed audience. Brian, with arms folded, was short and succinct when addressing the other kids, "Everybody, meet Michael Armstrong. A very good friend of mine and Pat's. We stick together at the boxing gym. It's all for one and one for all. You would do well to remember that." Young Michael was never bothered again.

At that time there was a picture on the gym wall depicting the sacred heart of Jesus. Brian used to point at it all the time declaring, "He's the gaffer here!" Good manners, discipline and behaviour were not so much asked for but demanded. This mob of streetwise Manc kids respected Brian and dreaded letting him down. Whenever one was fighting, the others would be at ringside in support. Time passed and Michael developed as a boxer to the point where Brian suggested he turned amateur. He did so and impressed hugely. Brian was putting him in championships and Michael wasn't just winning them, but blowing fighters away. When he did not get the decisions, Brian always thought it was political and claimed in those days when fighting London boxers his boys needed to knock them out for a draw. It was a north v south business - boxing politics.

By age seventeen, Michael had won two national titles, but really should have had five or six more. A trainer called Ray Flannagan helped look after him. Ray, like Brian, was a fountain of boxing knowledge. At that time Michael soaked up all their advice and was being viewed as a rare talent. However, some decisions made against him in the amateurs defied belief. Michael, in his own mind, began to put this down to being a traveller. He lost faith and wondered what the point was in carrying on. He went off the rails and stopped coming to the gym and was getting in trouble. Finally, Brian tracked him down and listened to his point of view. It was clear Michael was never going to be a priest or a politician, more likely a bank robber! So, Brian decided it was time to take him professional, otherwise he would have ended up in Strangeways in less time than it takes to boil an egg. Brian spoke to boxing promoter Frank Warren, who already had Robbie Reid on his books, "If Michael is brought on slowly then he could be something really special, Frank." Warren reluctantly agreed. He knew of the excellent amateur record, but was also aware Michael was trouble; a grenade without a pin, with only a thumb on the detonator. All things considered Warren decided he was worth a punt. After all, there were few better judges than Brian Hughes.

Brian would often tell Michael how much he reminded him of the legendary Puerto Rican Featherweight, Wilfredo Gomez. Like Michael, he too came from poverty – a street kid who fought and clawed his way up from nothing. Brian gave him videos to watch so he could study his style. The way he moved and prowled like an alley cat until the chance arose and then bang! Michael loved him as well so, when Brian discovered there was already a Michael Armstrong registered in the professional ranks it really didn't take much persuasion.

"You're going to have to change your name, Michael."

"Alright then, I'll call myself Michael McGuigan!"

"I've got another idea. How does Gomez sound?"

"Yeah Gomez Armstrong sounds sweet."

"Not Gomez Armstrong, soft lad," Brian laughed. "Michael Gomez" and so the paperwork was sorted and Michael Armstrong Gomez was born. It would never be boring.

Eleven days before his eighteenth birthday, on 10th June, 1995, Michael stepped through the ropes at what was then the G-Mex centre in Manchester for his first professional fight, a Frank Warren promotion. He was pitched in against a decent twenty-one-year-old kid from Bournemouth called Danny Ruegg. Michael won on points and afterwards in the dressing room Frank Warren made a point of shaking his hand. He would be keeping a close eye on Gomez. However, any delusions of grandeur Michael may have been suffering from came crashing down in his next two contests which he lost. Michael was hardly setting the boxing world alight. Happily, matters soon improved dramatically as he won his next five fights impressing both Brian and Frank Warren but tragically for Michael, events were set to take place that would leave him reeling and a young man dead.

Michael and two friends had gone to the Fifth Avenue nightclub on Princess Street, Manchester. It was a Thursday evening, student night, good music, cheap drinks, two-for-one. They were drunk and clowning around on the crammed dance floor when a scuffle broke out with a gang of four lads. Immediately the bouncers turned up and with one of them knowing Michael, they threw the others out. Come the end of the evening on leaving through the main door, these same lads were waiting and all hell let loose. Seeing a friend elbowed and punched to the floor, Michael hit one, two backed off and as the fourth came at him, he was dropped with a left hook and cracked his head horribly on the pavement.

Immediately Michael knew this kid was hurt badly for he appeared to go down in slow motion. As police sirens were heard they made their escape. After worrying all weekend about him, come the Monday he switched on the television news and there was a police officer stood outside Fifth Avenue nightclub asking for information about a young man lying critically ill in hospital.

"We know who you are" he said, staring at the camera, "Just come forward to help with our enquiries." After finding out the other two had already turned themselves in, Michael had no option. He was charged and put in a cell overnight. The next morning two CID officers entered and told Michael that Sam Parr had died and he was being charged with murder.

The trial looked like an open-and-shut case, especially when Michael's solicitor managed to get the charge reduced to manslaughter – he was looking at seven years.

A beggarwoman who had been in a doorway opposite the club on Princess Road said she saw everything and that Michael acted only in self-defence. As had a hot dog man who was working nearby. Added to the testimony of Brian Hughes speaking as a character witness, Gomez was found not guilty. It had been a close-run thing but the death of Sam Parr would haunt Michael for the rest of his life.

In an effort to forget what had occurred Michael threw himself back into boxing. A series of fine wins saw him finally challenge for the vacant Central Area Featherweight title against Scunthorpe's Chris Jickells. On 27th February 1999, at the Oldham Sports Centre, the soon-to-be-familiar shouts of "Gomez" crashed off the walls of the dressing room. All his supporters had taken to wearing sombreros: a loud, rowdy bunch of fans, friends and family who offered great noise and colour at all of Michael's fights. On his boot he had tied a Holy Mary medal sent by his grandmother during the trial. A win would be dedicated to Sam Parr, everything he ever won would now be for Sam. A smell of cordite always hung in the air for a Gomez fight, this was no different. Michael's Mexican dance tune started off and into the arena he appeared to huge cheering. Jickells was experienced, he had been around but simply could not live with Michael, who had pummelled him into bloody submission by the fifth round. He fell to his knees, then stood up and blessed himself before bending down to touch the medal. The message clear – that was for Sam. A sombrero came flying into the ring and Michael put it on. The madness was under way!

Three months later he stopped twenty-nine-year-old Yorkshireman Nigel Leake in Halifax to claim the Inter-Continental Featherweight title. Once more the sombreros flew into the air. Two titles fought for and both won. Next was a date across the ocean, an Irishman on the Boardwalk. Michael Gomez was off to Atlantic City, New Jersey.

Brian Hughes convinced Frank Warren that the experience Michael could gain in the States would be priceless in the long term. At first the promoter demurred, uncertain on whether he was trustworthy before finally agreeing. Also going was another fighter from Collyhurst and Moston, Anthony Farnell, and Robbie Reid would help Brian out in the corner. Michael and Farnell were way down a showtime bill being staged at the Taj Majal Hotel and Casino in Atlantic City. Topping it was a Heavyweight clash between Francis Botha and Shannon Briggs and the legendary Mexican Marco Antonio Barrera against Pastor Maurin. Six thousand people were packed into the arena with Barrera drawing huge support. It was loud and chaotic. Brian warned Michael that his opponent was a decent boxer from Alabama but that he was better. In the dressing room shortly before it was his turn to go on, something strange started to happen. Farnell had already fought and won by knockout in the third round. He was singing, excited about impressing, but was shocked into silence by the noise coming through the walls as shouts of "Gomez, Gomez" could clearly be heard.

"You Armstrong's get everywhere," smiled Brian. "How many relatives have you got over here?" Something wasn't right. Michael had no idea what was going on. Then it dawned, the name - Gomez. The thousands of Mexicans who had come to support Barrera must have thought one of their countrymen was up next!

Brian, by now a little anxious, looked at Michael, "You're the whitest Mexican I've ever seen, son. We'll have to tell them you don't go out a lot." On arriving into the arena with Michael wearing the sombrero there was a further eruption of cheering! It was a bear pit. The newly formed Michael Gomez Mexican fan club screamed out his name like a war cry. The atmosphere was electric and deafening as they climbed into the ring. Then, as Brian removed the robe and sombrero it was like turning the noise off with a switch and one almighty silence descended upon the arena. This pale and scrawny little Irish lad stood before them shadow-boxing, and it was pretty clear he hadn't been born in the backstreets of Mexico City. "I feel like I'm in the bloody Alamo," muttered Brian.

Luckily, this misunderstanding was swiftly forgotten because that night, for six rounds, Michael fought at his best. Slick, fast and hard hitting, he moved, crouched, danced, bobbed and fought like a Mexican. Come the end he received a standing ovation off one of the hardest crowds in world boxing and was mobbed for his autograph. The reaction to this performance by the American boxing journalists was staggering.

Mike Tyson's ex manager, Bill Cayton, pulled Brian aside and told him he hadn't seen anyone fight like Michael since the forties.

"Where's this kid from Brian?"

"He's from Moston in Manchester, Bill."

"Manchester, Massachusetts?"

"No, Manchester, England."

"You're kidding me," replied Cayton. "A god damn Limey? I ain't never seen a Limey fight like that before." When Brian mentioned this to Michael he was not particularly happy, "I'm not a limey Brian. I'm an Irish Mexican."

"You're a Mexican, Irish Manc," he replied, "and don't you forget it!"

On hearing how well Michael had performed in the States, Warren negotiated a shot at the British title. From the moment he was born in the car crash it had been a struggle to survive. Nobody had ever given him a thing, everything he owned, he had either stolen or fought for. Down all the days, Michael never gave in. He erred, wronged, fell and got back up. Done good, bad, loved and hated. Down all the days. Michael had lived on his wits, he fought, scratched, punched, robbed and survived. Then, Michael Armstrong Gomez, an Irish traveller, a boy from nowhere was fighting for the British Super Featherweight title.

Down all the days…

On 4th September 1999, at the York Hall, Bethnal Green, the East End cradle of boxing, Michael stopped tough scouser Gary Thornhill with a furious second round assault of left and right hooks that had the place in uproar. Thornhill, dazed and beaten, never knew what hit him. Michael was in the centre of the ring celebrating when Brian grabbed and almost threw him back onto the corner stool, "You're a British champion now, Michael Armstrong," he declared standing over him. "Be proud and act like one, both in and out of the ring." Brian kissed Michael on the cheek and then they hugged, "Now go and take your salute, son." After posing for photographs, Michael got the nod from Sky that they were ready to interview him at ringside. Ian Darke began, "Michael, what an amazing success story. You seemed to find that finish out of nowhere?"

"First of all, I'd like to dedicate this belt to a young lad who died in my company, in Manchester, two years ago. Sam Parr. This is for you

Sam, I'm sorry for what happened and I love you."

Riding a tide, the title opportunities kept coming and on 6th November 1999, at the Kingsway Leisure centre, Widnes, just two months on from becoming British champion, Michael fought a Mexican warrior from Baja California, for the vacant WBO Inter-Continental Super Featherweight title. If he won it would be his fourth belt in twelve months. Pre-fight he was up to his usual tricks to rile Jose Manjarrez and failing miserably. A puzzled Michael tried the usual pushing and head-butting attempts, but the Mexican simply smiled. Frank Warren went crazy at him, "Michael what the hell are you doing? You don't wind these Mexicans up. They are difficult enough characters!"

The thirty-year-old Manjarrez had been around, an old pro who took Michael the full twelve rounds in a gruelling contest, fought at a ferocious pace. It was a war. In the end Michael got the decision, but at times it had felt like going back to school in the ring. Manjarrez simply walked through every punch he threw. They breed them tough down on the Rio Grande, but then again, equally so on the back streets of Moston and Dublin.

Later, in the home dressing room, a smiling Frank Warren appeared and told Michael he'd just spoken to Manjarrez's trainer. It turned out that as his man entered the arena and saw all the Mancunians in sombreros, Manjarrez thought they were cheering for him! He couldn't understand where all those Mexicans had come from?

Just forty-three days after beating Manjarrez, Michael was back in the ring at Liverpool's Everton Sports Centre, defending that same title belt against another Mexican. Twenty-two-year-old southpaw Oscar Galindo, incidentally the brother-in-law of Jose Manjarrez. He spoke tough at the press conference, whilst Michael was his usual self, nearly starting an international incident with Mexico and wanting to kick off right there and then. Another war broke out as Galindo matched Michael for every punch, headbutt and sly, low dig. The early rounds were a slog: there had been too many ring hours for the champion. Fit, but jaded. As the fight wore on towards its bitter end, Michael finally caught up with Galindo in the eleventh round and unloaded upon him. As he buckled, the referee, Mickey Vann, stepped in to stop it. Michael was exhausted and as the crowd roared, he simply fell to his knees, now fully aware that Mexicans did not do rollovers.

Michael was two defences away from owning the British Lonsdale belt outright. Despite a tough schedule, the decision was made to keep going, to strike whilst the iron (and money) was hot. Any extended time out of the ring inevitably, despite best intentions, led back to the pub and endless sessions on the lash. Worse was the drugs. What Michael needed more than anything was the incentive of another fight. It came against Coventry's Dean Pithie, again in Widnes, on 29th February, 2000. Frank Warren wasn't too keen on Michael fighting Pithie, for he was a dangerous character and had beaten Naseem Hamed in the amateurs. It was only Michael's mad desire for the Lonsdale Belt, plus Brian arguing his corner, that saw Warren ultimately back down and do the deal, helped of course by the number of tickets Michael shifted. This was also a big reason why he got away with so much more than any other fighter in Warren's stable.

It was only a concoction of sheer power, guts and determination not to lose that got Michael through the twelve rounds, for too many fights in too short a time drains any boxer, no matter how talented or fit. Pithie had him over in the first round and the look on Frank Warren's face at ringside as he hauled himself back up was simply, "I told you Gomez!" Michael levelled it up in the fourth by putting Pithie on the canvas with a crashing right. A real scrap broke out and in the eighth Pithie broke his left hand and was obviously in a lot of pain. He showed real guts by not quitting, but from that moment, a few rights apart, Pithie was a broken fighter and Michael won comfortably on points. This left him just two wins away from retaining the Lonsdale belt – it was a hard night's work and money well-earned, but one that had left its mark. Brian promised him a decent break afterwards. "Put your feet up Michael and do me a favour? Please stay out of trouble!"

There was more chance of him becoming a priest.

Five months passed and on 8th July, 2000, Michael stepped into the ring once more at Widnes to take on Carl Greaves. For the entrance, the Manchester City mascot Moonchester led him into the ring, "Good luck, Mike," it said, "Knock his head off!" Michael just stared back. The Mexican music began and from the part of the arena where his supporters were there was an eruption of noise and the sombreros went up! In round one Michael had a good look at his opponent who had come to fight. Come the second he moved up a gear and caught the game if unfortunate Greaves with a peach of a left hook on his temple to knock him flat out. It was a blow similar to the one that floored Gary Thornhill. Like Thornhill, he was not getting up and with feet flailing, Greaves was all but dragged back to his corner stool. Michael didn't celebrate immediately because he knew it was a bad knockout and had no intention of dancing on anybody's grave. It was a great relief to be told his opponent was okay. Huge cheers erupted across the arena as the pair embraced and Greaves, along with Michael, donned sombreros. He was one win away from entering the annals of British boxing history.

The third and final contest came against Edinburgh-born thirty-one-year-old Ian McLeod. A tough character with a decent record, McLeod was a former IBO Super-Featherweight champion. On 11th December, 2000, in Michael's adopted boxing home of Widnes, he entered to a fantastic reception: the sombreros flew high and music started up. It was hysterical: a scene of Mancunian/Mexican madness had descended upon the arena. Shut your eyes and you could have been in Mexico City! McLeod, in tartan shorts, was already in the ring. His eyes met Michael's from the moment he climbed through the ropes. So began an enthralling, brutal twelve-round contest that Michael ultimately won, but was forced to go through boxing hell to get there. The pair stood toe-to-toe throughout: it was a slugfest. For the first time in his career Michael got cut but finally prevailed. Come the finish, referee Richie Davies, his shirt dripped in blood, raised Michael's hand and the arena erupted! The fight was savage. Never had he suffered so much to win. Sombreros flew into the ring and a badly bloodied and bruised McLeod also put one on. They embraced. Finally, the Lonsdale Belt was handed over for keeps and was fastened around him. Today Michael has it safe, a reminder to his children and grandchildren that once upon a time he was not just a fighter, but a champion.

Afterwards, in the dressing room, as the doctor was treating his cut, Michael started to think who next? He was twenty-three years old and had promised himself that he would retire at twenty-six. To do this bigger fights and purses were needed. Naseem Hamed was by far the biggest star of the day, the one they all tried to knock out of the sky, but there were other world champions who were much more beatable in Michael's eyes, notably the Brazilian Acelino Freitas, and Hull's Paul Ingle. Brian wasn't so sure. It was too much of a risk. He was utterly determined that Michael should wait until he was one hundred percent ready for that world title shot. Michael trusted Brian inherently because this man was like a second father. He knew a wrong career decision could end everything. It was right to be patient, for boxing was a cruel sport that took no prisoners, and if not careful, it would chew and spit you out.

It was announced that Michael would defend his WBO Intercontinental Super-Featherweight title, as ever, in Widnes, against a well-travelled, thirty-two-year-old Hungarian fighter called Laszlo Bognar. A tough character with thirty fights and twenty-five wins on his record, Bognar was a step up in class. He had been around and if Michael wasn't firing he could end up in serious trouble. Five weeks before the fight he turned up at the Collyhurst and Moston gym after endless partying looking like death warmed up. Shattered through lack of sleep, horribly overweight and with bloodshot eyes, although he knuckled down and trained like a madman, the excess body fat proved hard to shift. Michael lived in the gym. He ran, sparred and skipped. There were endless saunas and swimming sessions, but the nine stone-four-pound weight limit felt like over the hills and very far away. Feeling like all that effort was pointless, he continued his crazed lifestyle right up until the week of the fight. As the bout drew nearer he started to panic, eating tiny mouthfuls of baby food then making himself sick. The age-old problem of training to make the weight and not the fight was a time bomb, one that exploded in his face when in round nine Bognar, after treating Michael like a rag doll the previous round, finally let fly another combination and down he went. It had been a brave, almost suicidal performance by Michael. That he lasted so long was down to sheer guts and a fierce Irish pride. Bognar's trainer picked up a sombrero that had been thrown in and placed it upon his fighter's head. It was the ultimate insult. He stood in the middle with arms raised shouting "Champion!" It was Michael's first defeat in four years and a warning that if you don't live the life, then you pay the price. Michael Armstrong Gomez paid it that night. However, this would soon pale into insignificance with what happened next.

A night out in Manchester ended up with both Michael and fellow boxer Michael Jennings getting stabbed and rushed to hospital by ambulance. The immediate concern was for Jennings due to the amount of blood lost. But, luckily, he was deemed out of danger. Michael had been knifed in the arm and at first it was viewed as nothing too serious. Then, after a nurse took a closer look, panic set in and it was explained that if they didn't act quickly he could lose his arm. In typically dramatic Gomez fashion Michael flat-lined. An extremely rare allergic reaction to the anaesthetic caused him to die for forty-eight seconds. Luckily, he came back.

Once he had recovered Michael was called down to London for a meeting with Frank Warren who tore a strip off him. His chances were running out. He wasn't so much burning the candle at both ends, Michael had set fire to the church and razed it to the ground. He was told to sort himself out and Michael hit the gym with a desperate fury to impress once more. Finally it paid off, a rematch with Laszlo Bognar, on 7th July, 2000, at the Manchester Velodrome - it was the last chance saloon with bells on for the Mexican Manc. This time, despite a first and second round scare when Bognar again put him down twice, he roared back and come the fourth the Hungarian was finished as Michael let fly a flurry of punches, all dipped in doses of sweet, brutal revenge. Laszlo Bognar would not be donning a sombrero that night. Gomez had quite literally come back from the dead to regain his title. Even for him that was quite a feat. However now something wasn't right between him and Brian. A coldness now existed between them and Michael believed the ring was the only place he could win back his trust.

Five months later, on 7th July 2001, at the MEN Arena, a short tear up followed against unbeaten Glasgow fighter Craig Docherty for Michael's British Super Featherweight title. It lasted only two rounds before Docherty, too brave for his own good, was taken apart. It took Michael just four minutes and forty-two seconds to retain his title. At the post-fight ringside interview with Sky he thanked both Brian and Frank Warren for sorting his life out. All sounded positive when Warren declared, "We're going to give Mike two more fights then look at a world title."

Then, outside the gym, Michael, seemingly cursed to shoot himself in the foot, fell from grace again. The months passed and there was no sign of him at the gym. Finally, a shadow of his fighting-self, Michael made his wary way back up the steps. He was greeted warmly by the lads, but eyed with obvious suspicion by Brian. Called into his office,

DOWN ALL THE DAYS

Michael was urged to retire yet he somehow persuaded Brian for one final chance. "My prodigal pain in the backside, that's what you are Michael. No more. This is the last chance for you!" After speaking to Frank Warren, it helped that Michael remained, despite all his antics, a huge ticket seller – a Mancunian licence to print money. Damaged goods he may have been, but one that possessed a touch of box office gold dust. After a month of working like a Trojan, it was agreed Michael had got himself in decent enough shape to fight again. Warren lined up twenty-five-year-old undefeated Londoner Kevin Lear for the vacant WBU World Featherweight title at the MEN Arena. Sadly, despite promises made, Michael simply could not help himself and drifted back into his old ways. It was a curse, an affliction. Training was not taken seriously and come the fight with Lear, he was Gomez in name alone. Lear's jab was fast, accurate and painful and cut Michael over the left eye early on. It had been an old wound from the MacLeod fight. Showing typical bravery throughout, he found himself constantly being caught, and despite believing Lear was growing tired and could be had with one punch, Michael was simply taking far too much of a beating. So much that despite him arguing, almost pleading to carry on, Brian stopped the fight at the end of round eight. It was just too much punishment on someone he cared about. One of his boys. The dressing room was quiet afterwards. Michael was seething over being stopped. He said nothing. Brian tried talking to him, but the damage had been done. Sadly, it was to be a parting of the ways between the two. Michael Armstrong Gomez would never fight for Collyhurst and Moston gym again, though it was no means the end of his story. Michael's finest moment in the ring was still to come.

Desperate to fight on, Michael knew there was only one place he could possibly find redemption in the ring, but would they take him? The word in boxing at that time was Gomez had become *persona non-grata*. A lost cause not worth the risk. But Michael had to try so he rang the preacher man. Along with Brian Hughes, Billy Graham was Manchester's most prominent boxing trainer. From his Phoenix gym in Denton, great fighters were starting to emerge. None better than soon-to-be world champion Ricky Hatton. It had a great reputation with some fantastic talent and Michael felt that if anyone could save his career it would be him. They met and talked with Billy saying he would sleep on it. The following morning Graham rang and agreed to give Michael a chance, but laid down ground rules that were non-negotiable. One strike and out.

"I hate bad eggs, Michael. You're more than welcome to come to the gym, but you need to cut the partying down between fights. When you're training with me pal, you don't mess about or you're out. We have a laugh at the right time, but no screwing around when it's business. Agreed?" The law laid down, Michael agreed – he could not wait to get started.

He was determined to impress. Michael trained hard, listened and sparred like a warrior. The fire was being rekindled. Billy told him to keep it up and there would be some gold at the end of the rainbow. The Preacher Man had spoken and that was good enough for Michael. Billy proved true to his word and on 28th September 2002, at the MEN Arena, Gomez time returned when he put away the hard hitting Brummie Jimmy Beech in the fourth round with a shot that knocked him off his feet! More fights followed to prove Michael was far from finished. Finally, there began to be whispers of a British title shot. Edinburgh's pride and joy Alex Arthur was the up and coming golden boy of British boxing. Scottish and proud of it, he was being groomed for great deeds by Frank Warren. Arthur was viewed as a prodigy by Warren's Sport's Network. The experts were saying he had the tools to go all the way. No one, however, had counted on Michael Armstrong Gomez. They simply never saw him coming… Once the fight against Alex Arthur was confirmed, Michael became like a man possessed in training. His team of Billy, Kerry Kayes and Bobby Rimmer were soon convinced it was no simple pipe dream. Their man had a chance. The rest of the boxing fraternity were predicting that Gomez's time had come and gone and Alex Arthur, in his own backyard, with all Edinburgh in his corner, would wipe the floor with him. Frank Warren, boxing magazines, internet forums, Sky Sports commentators, the odds makers – they were all convinced it was a mismatch and Michael would be simply a good name on the new golden boy's record as he went on to conquer the world.

On the eve of the fight Michael, in the shape of his life, got a message through from Collyhurst and Manchester, passed on by Thomas

McDonagh that wished him luck from none other than Brian Hughes.

"These are Brian's words Mike," said Thomas, "'If Michael is fit… he wins.'"

If any further incentive was needed Michael now had it!

What followed at the Meadowbank Sports centre was five rounds of unadulterated carnage, now widely regarded as one of the finest British title fights of all time. On 25th October 2003, Michael Armstrong Gomez ripped the championship belt off Arthur in unforgettable style. In an atmosphere where the words torrid and intimidating did not do it justice, the Mexican Manc, in a fury, went left hook happy to shock the boxing world with a stunning display. Come the fifth, Michael was blowing heavy, whilst Arthur cut a bloodied, staggering mess. Though his bravery could not be doubted, the sheer arrogance in under-estimating Michael had proved mind-blowing. A heavy price had been paid and Arthur was fighting through fog and memory. Finally, Michael sent him to the canvas with yet another crashing left hook. Astonishingly, Arthur got back up, smiled and talked to the cameras, as if trying to convince everyone that all was well. The referee's count reached three and they were signalled to fight on. Here on his own patch this man was being taken apart. All he had left was blind courage and a fighter's heart. Two right hooks later Arthur went over once more and again he got up, this time on a nine count! It was a fool's courage blinded by pride. With the referee seemingly content to give him a last lash they fought on, but two more left hooks followed by a right and this time around Alex Arthur hit the floor and stayed there. It was all over. Carnage under the Edinburgh stars! Michael Armstrong Gomez had produced a miraculous boxing comeback that was on a par with anything Lazarus ever pulled off. Immediately, a sombrero came flying into the ring! A Mancunian victory dipped in Irish tricolours! Billy came over and hugged Michael tight. His entire life had come down to one fight and he had pulled it off. Mayhem reigned in the ring. Michael was not too keen celebrating because Arthur appeared still in a bad condition on the canvas. Despite any bad mouthing and hostility beforehand, all became forgotten and finally a dazed Arthur got up and the fighers embraced. As for Frank Warren, he bore the appearance of someone attending his own funeral.

Gomez had taken apart his prodigy.

Then the announcement for the Edinburgh bells to toll. "Ladies and gentlemen, after two minutes and fifty-eight seconds of round five, your referee John Coyle has dispensed with the count. The winner by way of technical count out. He is the new Super Featherweight champion of Great Britain. From Manchester, Michael Gomez!" Boos and jeers rang out, apart from Michael's supporters who remained defiant and sang loud. "And a round of applause please for a superb ex-champion, who I'm sure will come back from this defeat. Alex Arthur!" Cue wild cheers and mass applause. Michael's crowning was kept short and sweet in an arena that would soon be looking to vent their frustration and anger at seeing their man beaten to a pulp. The sombrero wearing Mancs, still dancing and singing, were a likely target and were swiftly escorted out as the mood changed from utter bewilderment to raging fury!

And so Michael Gomez had finally climbed to the top of the mountain - not knowing then that he had reached his rainbow's end. What happened from that moment onwards was a drop into a deep abyss, but one he refused to be ultimately drawn fully into. Sadly, that night in the Scottish capital proved Michael's defining moment in boxing, but as a one-off snapshot it proved a glorious sporting epitaph.

Following the Arthur fight there were more blood and guts contests in the ring, but many, far too many, out of it. Gangland Manchester, alcohol and drugs took a hold and for a time Michael's life fell apart. A comeback in Dublin for the vacant Irish Lightweight title, on 28th January, 2006, against Peter McDonagh, ended in farce when Michael appeared to just give up and walk away in the fifth round. Rumours of a fix were rife in Ireland and for a while controversy raged. What came to light in time were the personal reasons behind Michael's decision to quit in the ring. The Dublin scandal, despite him being found innocent of all wrong doing by the authorities, brought about his retirement, but allied to a serious cocaine problem and the loss of any discipline that boxing brought, he soon hit rock bottom and attempted suicide. Luckily he failed, but life for Michael appeared destined to end in tragedy.

A brief illusion of the old Gomez fire appeared when he fought an upcoming superstar called Amir Khan at the Birmingham NEC, on 21st June, 2008. It was a shot at yet another Frank Warren prodigy. Taking the fight knowing he was being used as a mere stepping stone, it had echoes of the Alex Arthur saga and the similarities roared ever louder in the second round when Michael put Khan down. That he finally ran out of steam in the fifth and was eventually stopped was the last act of a potentially great career that never quite reached the heights it should have done.

The last bell sounded on Michael Armstrong Gomez's professional career on 27th March, 2009, in a Glaswegian bearpit against Scottish champion Ricky Burns for the Commonwealth (British Empire) Super Featherweight title. A highly charged atmosphere did not do the Bellahouston Leisure centre justice. Over the years Michael had specialised in decimating Scots, sadly that fighter had disappeared some time ago. As a fanatical home crowd bayed for revenge and blood, it all came to an inglorious end in the seventh round. There had been too many storms outside the ring as Burns let fly with a blinding combination of a dozen punches without reply and Michael was finally finished. No drum roll or trumpets sounded, it was just a weathered old boxer whose time in the ring was brought to a brutal halt – a warrior who would not have wanted it any other way.

Afterwards in the dressing room there were very few people present. It felt like a funeral. Only those who truly loved Michael were present. He got a text off Billy Graham, "You owe Manchester nothing x"

Nobody dared speak. Sky's Adam Smith came in to see how he was. Adam had followed Michael since the early days. He had witnessed the mad, bad, good and utterly crazy times. Adam sat down next to Michael and put an around him, "Jim Watt has always told me it isn't our job to tell fighters when to retire. I don't disagree with Jim on many things but I do on this. It is over. Get out whilst you can, son. Thanks for the memories Michael."

With that it finished…..

Once back in retirement, drugs and drink again took hold. Depression cut deep. Few now craved the once blinding limelight in Manchester that was to be seen alongside the Mexican Manc. As Michael himself remembered, at that time he was invited to plenty of funerals, but never weddings or christenings. The hangers on and supposed friends had disappeared. Nobody wanted to know. Michael felt like he was drowning and a concerned family, fearing for his health and convinced he was close to killing himself, ensured Michael was admitted into care and sectioned. For six weeks he was watched like a hawk and with the help of medication and talking to specialists, finally Michael came back. Suddenly he could see a future. A new day no longer brought dread. Gomez time was far from over....

Today a small, stocky shuffling figure makes his way up the steps of Collyhurst and Moston gym. He pauses at the door. Inside the sounds are of those this man knows so well. Organised bedlam! He enters and gazes around. So many memories. The man makes his way towards trainer and old friend Thomas McDonagh, who is overlooking a group of young boxers being put through their paces. The man shakes hands with Thomas and they share a joke. Both laugh loud. Thomas points over to a young girl of whom he has high hopes. She is a possible Olympic medallist and then the world is her oyster.

"Have ten minutes with her mate."

"No problem," comes the reply.

The young girl watches with disbelieving eyes as the man shows her best how to hit the speedbag. He demonstrates a flurry of ferocious left hooks that rock the bag like it has not felt for many years. Finally, after talking to her, they share a small hug. The man walks back over to Thomas, shakes his hand and leaves the gym. The girl comes over to Thomas almost in tears.

"I can't believe it," she says. "He actually took time to help me. I have only ever seen Gomez on You Tube. The fight against Alex Arthur! Wow! A legend."

Down all the days, so many fights, so many storms and yet Michael Armstrong Gomez is still around.

For that we can only be thankful.

12 - MIKE JACKSON

THE ICEMAN

Whenever the bell rang to signal the end of a round, there could only be one voice. In that short respite from battle where the fighter sits breathless, hurting and desperate for advice to help him through the next three minutes, the last thing they need is people screaming in their face. For Brian Hughes, the corner was sacrosanct, like a confessional, a brief refuge from the storm, where advice was passed clearly and concisely in words of few syllables.

As the crowd bay for blood and the seconds count down to restart, there was no time to waste, no time to break it down, analyse or explain.

"Don't get sloppy."

"Fight your fight."

"Cover up, son."

Alongside Brian for so many years was a slim, dark-haired figure who always remained cool, calm and collected. And silent. Almost like a ghost at Brian's side. His much-appreciated observations on the fight before them had already been passed onto Brian before the bell rang. For fifteen years this figure watched and learned from the best around, soaking up knowledge like a sponge until today there are few better to have in your corner as a trainer. His name is Mike Jackson, but around the fight game he possesses another title - The Iceman.

BORN IN 1965, MIKE GREW UP in the Collyhurst flats opposite the Electric Circus club and he remembers watching many a lively Saturday night there as drunken mayhem erupted outside. As a small child he was fiery and game but where Mike had no problems hitting people, especially those much bigger than him, he was averse to being hit back. The same reasoning existed on the football pitch, he was happy enough to get stuck into a tackle, but Mike found it utterly annoying when someone ever had the temerity to take the ball off him.

Wanting to ensure that he concentrated fully on schoolwork, to get him away from friends and bad influences, his mother Patricia sent Mike to a school in far off Longsight and not the local one at Moston Brook. There his life was never boring. Being one of only a dozen white kids, matters were hardly helped being called Michael Jackson as the legendary singer's Off the Wall album was all the rage! One black kid who bore a remarkable resemblance to the great man took a particular dislike to Mike because of this. The dude had the hair, moves and even the white jacket off the cover, but what he did not possess, most importantly, was the name. He approached him to see if Mike fancied swapping names so that life could be complete, but he was not having it. Absolutely no deal, especially when he realised his nemesis's name was Critchlaw! "You must be joking and I get called Coleslaw!" laughed Mike. Critchlaw smiled and could only agree, "Fair point mate," he said and the pair shook hands.

Leaving school at fifteen with eight CSE's, Mike's first job was on a YTS scheme at a butchers in Monsall. This was the early eighties, and the area was in depression. Manchester was a grim uneconomical northern outpost at odds with the shiny new world of Margaret Thatcher's Tory government. A scarred city wracked with unemployment, crime and drugs, there were few golden tickets and his CSE's guaranteed nothing. After a few weeks at the butchers Mike developed a constant niggling cold that refused to shift and it was only after five months that he discovered he had an allergy to feathers. A job that included plucking turkeys meant there could be little future as a master butcher, so Mike looked for employment elsewhere. A job on Debenhams' loading bay came next until he finally started a twenty-year career at OMG chemicals based where Manchester City's training facilities now stand. Mike always found it ironic that his beloved football club were ultimately responsible for making him redundant!

After moving to Moston, a chance meeting occurred with an old friend, Pat Barrett, who at the time was preparing to take on Robert Harkin for the British Super Lightweight title in Wolverhampton. Pat invited him to the fight and it wasn't long before Mike started training at Collyhurst and Moston, purely to get fit, there was never any intention to box. He soon got to know the other fighters who trained there including Wayne Rigby, Delroy Waul and Ricky Burton. More importantly, as the weeks and months went on, Mike found himself spending a lot of time with Brian Hughes, until one-day Brian threw him a curve ball and suggested that he could help him out around the gym. Mike could not believe his ears.

"Brian what are you talking about? I have never even boxed amateur or pro?"

"Mike, I don't want an outsider coming in with his own ideas and diluting everything I'm doing here. You're calm, collected and can talk to people and the lads here like you. This gym stands for something. I trust you to do a good job." With that seal of approval Mike began to learn the ways of Collyhurst and Moston that had stood them in good stead since 1917. It would prove to be a fruitful partnership for both men. One of the first things Brian taught his new apprentice was that all fighters were individuals, "What is good for one lad is not necessarily right for another," Brian would say.

Twelve months went by during which Mike watched, listened and learned through the everyday trials and tribulations that went on inside the gym and with individual fighters. Finally, after a series of small hall shows, he got the nod from Brian that his apprenticeship was over and Mike would be alongside him in the corner for a very special fight - Robin Reid against Joe Calzaghe in Newcastle for the WBO World Super Middleweight title. However, events changed shortly beforehand when Brian asked Mike if he could stay in the dressing room and look after a nervous Darren Rhodes who was turning pro that same night. Himself and Darren watched on a television screen as Reid lost controversially on points. Sadly, due to the schedule running over, Darren was not allowed to box after being prepared, sat with his gloves on from eight o'clock onwards.

Mike's first time in the corner alongside Brian at a big show finally arrived at the York Hall, Bethnal Green, when Michael Gomez blew away Gary Thornhill to win the vacant British Super Featherweight title. A memorable night made even more unforgettable when he shared the Mexican Manc's 'lively' sombrero donning supporter's coach back home to Manchester!

Something special was occurring in the Collyhurst and Moston air. It was the era of the Italian jobs. In 1990, Pat Barrett's pulverising punch pole-axed Efrem Calamati in Salerno to win the EBU European Super Lightweight title and then six years later in Milan, Robin Reid hammered Vincenzo Nardiello into submission to claim the WBC World Super Middleweight title. The wonderfully charismatic 1930's golden era of Harry Fleming's magical trio of Jackie Brown, Jock McAvoy and Johnny King was in danger of being eclipsed.

The age old adage of success breeding success proved true once more as a young stable of fighters emerged from Manchester that stood alongside anything this country has ever produced; Michael Gomez, Thomas McDonagh, Michael Jennings, Anthony Farnell, Darren Rhodes, David Barnes and Matthew Hall to name a few…They had all been schooled since they were youngsters in Brian Hughes' traditional values and it was a production line of talent that seemed never-ending. Unlike other gyms that were reliant on outside help to bring in sparring partners, Collyhurst and Moston bred their own, for each fighter possessed different gifts that could be put to use in the ring against each other.

It was during this period Mike earned the nickname of The Iceman. It occurred one time at Wythenshawe forum when the club had five fighters appearing. One of Mike's task was to ensure there was sufficient ice available. That particular night the ice machine broke in the building causing utter mayhem beforehand. From that moment on Mike was convinced such a scenario would never happen again and always took his own ice to venues. So it was that around the gym this mantle swiftly struck and The Iceman cometh! When asked about this Brian would always tell everybody the name came around because of how cool Mike was in the corner. This was indeed true for one of the many boxing commandments Brian had taught him was to never let your concerns show beforehand because a boxer will latch onto them. They can sense nervousness in those around them and if this happened, the fight could be lost before he entered the ring. If things went badly Brian would say it was pointless discussing it on the night when emotions were running high. It was best to sleep on it.

Mike had become close to Charles Lawrence at Sky Sports who would film every undercard fight on a bill even if it wasn't shown on TV. If asked, Charles was always happy to send the club copies. These would be watched by Brian, Mike and the fighter in question. On first viewing the trio would concentrate on his left hand, in the next the right. Then his feet, the day after they watch how his head moves. Everything would be analysed and dissected. They would never watch the whole fight but instead broke the action down into these small components, the disparate elements coming together to form one picture. With most boxers this worked, they would listen and take it all on board. Others seemed simply disinterested and Brian's philosophy then was always, "If it does them good and they are interested, then happy days. If not, your conscience is clear because you couldn't have done anymore. It's all about guidance, Mike. This way they can never accuse us of failing them."

Mike has never earned a penny whilst working at Collyhurst and Moston, but due to having a job that involved shift work, he always ensured enough time was spent at the gym for the boxing education he received from Brian was priceless. It was knowledge earned that no wage packet could match. "It was a privilege just to watch how Brian was with people," he says, "even those he would only ever meet once. Brian had a gift of making everyone in his presence feel special. He was a mix of social worker, politician, psychologist and boxing trainer all rolled into one."

Mike was always amazed that wherever they were in Great Britain, somebody would recognise Brian. One time the pair of them were driving through Bridgend in Wales, they were completely lost. It was the middle of the night and in desperation they flashed a police car for help. Over comes an officer and the first words, after a huge smile appeared on his face whilst pointing at a bemused Brian were, "Ah, Mr Boxing!" Mike adored travelling with Brian and hearing his tales of times gone by.

When it comes to choosing a most memorable fight, Mike has no hesitation in nominating the time he took to the corner of the most famous boxing venue in the world - Madison Square Garden. It came on 21st February 2009, when Michael Jennings took on the devastating Puerto Rican Miguel Cotto for the WBO World Welterweight title. Going to London fighting was always a big deal for Mike, but The Garden is the sport's spiritual home. It really was a dream come true and it all began on the Wednesday before the fight with a huge press conference. Then there was the weigh-in that actually took place at the Garden – "You could feel the history of the old place," he recalls, "so many legends have fought there, the ghosts of the ring."

On the actual night of the fight, as Brian sat with Michael Jennings in the dressing room bandaging his hands, it was always a very personal moment between fighter and trainer, as both gathered their thoughts for the waiting storm. Suddenly the door burst open and in walked Miguel Cotto's veteran cut man Joe Chavez to watch, or more likely to unnerve and wind them up. He began a monologue of who he had worked with and how good his man was. Chavez was trying desperately to get under Michael's skin, but was shocked when Brian sprung up and got right in his face, almost touching his head, "Get out of here now or it's me and you!" he growled. Or words to that effect! Taken aback Chavez, who was no shrinking violet himself, was led out. As Brian turned back to Michael he winked, while Mike watched on astonished. The ploy from Chavez had failed.

1-0 to Collyhurst and Moston!

As Michael made his ring walk to a Sex Pistols soundtrack of "Anarchy in the UK" the ten thousand crowd, mostly hostile Puerto Ricans, went crazy. Vitriol rained down on the Mancunians, but Michael appeared utterly focused, staring straight ahead and The Iceman could not help but smile at the thousands of manic screwed up faces in the crowd roaring abuse at them! They were a long way from Lightbowne Road.

Sadly, Michael was eventually stopped in round five after a brutal Cotto put him down for a third time, but that did not tell the full story of what had been a truly heroic effort by the thirty-one-year-old Chorley born fighter. Nobody had given Michael a prayer against the lethal Puerto Rican, although Brian and Mike seriously believed he could win – with Michael's superb fitness and movement there was always hope but ultimately he was up against an upcoming all-time great. A true sign of Michael Jennings' guts that night came after the fight when he was mobbed by those same Puerto Ricans who had been won over by his bravery.

Also, Joe Chavez sought out Brian and the two embraced and shook hands, "You're damn good, man," smiled Chavez, "a real tough Motherf…".

Mike became aware very early on that sometimes fighters have to be protected from themselves. Robin Reid was one example when he was up against Jeff Lacy in Florida. Robbie was being taken apart by the much younger American and his vicious punching. In the corner, Brian, Mike and fellow boxer Matthew Hall were of the opinion to stop the fight, but Robbie was adamant he wanted to continue. It ended shortly after when Brian called it off to avoid further punishment. Later, again when some time had passed, Robbie confided in Mike that he felt Lacy was tiring, but The Iceman coolly replied that the only reason the American was growing tired came from hitting him! A smiling Robbie couldn't disagree.

Then there was Thomas McDonagh. Mike recalls Thomas was the only fighter he had ever seen telling jokes between rounds! Brian would be trying to talk to him, only to be asked, "Have you heard the one about the two Irishman…"

"Thomas be serious!"

As a defensive fighter, one of the finest this country had ever seen, what Thomas had could not be taught. He was one of the main reasons Mike dislikes amateur boxing, as so many good kids are robbed of decisions and tend to drift away from the sport because of the at times absurd scoring system. This is especially true for boxers trained the Collyhurst and Moston way. An example of how ridiculous the system can be occurred when, in his formative years, Thomas went off to an England training camp. When sparring and doing his normal thing of making fighters miss, he found himself pulled by a coach, "Stop boxing, what are you doing? No, you duck down and take the punch on top of your head." Needless to say, when Thomas reported this back Brian had him on the next train home to Manchester.

Thomas and Mike grew close and even today when visiting his old haunt, he will smile at the irony of seeing Thomas admonish someone over their training! "If you said the word 'work' to Thomas it was like showing a cross to Dracula!" Mike recalls.

Always believing he was up to something, it made Brian paranoid about the craziest things. No more than when himself and Mike were in Cardiff, Brian's phone rang and it was his wife Rosemary.

"Is that you Brian?"

"Yeah."

"Brian, you have had a letter from Buckingham Palace."

"Oh, it will be nothing just put it in the bin."

"No Brian, it looks very official. Should I open it?"

"Oh, go on then."

"Brian, you have been awarded an MBE!!"

"No, no I'm not having that!"

"No Brian it's real, it's serious!"

"No, it will be that bloody Thomas McDonagh messing about. Put it on the sideboard until I come home!"

Mike always believed strongly that Thomas should have won a split decision against Wayne Alexander when the two fought for the WBU World Welterweight title at the MEN Arena. Also, two years later when up against Andrew Facey at Manchester City's stadium for the English Super Welterweight title, the fight was called a draw. Mike was speechless. He felt so sorry for Thomas that evening because all he wished to do was get home and see his baby daughter, who had been born at nine o'clock that morning. Mike had no doubts Thomas should have left with the belt to show his new arrival.

A little-known fact is that Tyson Fury trained for a while at Collyhurst and Moston and Brian mentioned to Mike after an early viewing that one day Tyson had the raw materials and potential to rule the roost. They worked tremendously hard, if ultimately unsuccessfully, to ensure he got his right hand up. Initially, they had no intention of even letting him box until Tyson insisted and finally a fight was arranged in Huddersfield against a tough and durable German, Hans Joerg Blasko. Disaster almost struck in the opening twenty seconds when Tyson left his defence wide open and he was caught with a huge right. That he came storming back to stop Blasko just two minutes later meant little to Brian and Mike – Tyson had not fought to orders and the ride back to Manchester was not a happy one. The future Heavyweight champion of the world is remembered fondly around the gym. Indeed, Mike recalls him as one of the most hard-working fighters they ever had during his time there. More importantly, he was a genuinely nice person and not the cartoon bad-guy character many try and make him out to be.

Trying to pick the best boxer from Collyhurst and Moston is an impossible call for Mike. Whether it be for personal reasons or, more likely, that it is too hard to call, instead he went for a potent mix of Pat Barrett's knockout power, Thomas McDonagh's defensive abilities and Michael Jennings' speed and movement, for him that would be a truly formidable combination. As for the one that got away? Mike has absolutely no doubt that Craig Dermody could have conquered the world, "Just watching Craig spar was better than watching boxing on the television," he says. "When I saw what Marcos Antonio Barrera did to Naseem Hamed, I was convinced that in time Craig would have done the same and much earlier. He was an exceptional talent and his loss to the sport was a crying shame."

After Brian Hughes stepped down from running Collyhurst and Moston gym in 2011, it was never the same for Mike and although he remains on the best of terms with Pat Barrett and Thomas McDonagh, who continue Brian's legacy, he joined Ricky Hatton. Today Mike works at the Hyde gym full-time and those years at his former mentor's side have proved vital. Equally close now to Ricky, as to Brian, their gym has developed the same family atmosphere that existed at Collyhurst and Moston. The old rules still stand. It isn't about money and if they don't like the fighter, he does not get trained. The Iceman continues to maintain his silence in the corner. If he has something to say it will be passed onto Ricky beforehand. As always there is only room for one voice during those vital moments between rounds. Besides, if you have prepared your fighter correctly there is no need to go mad on fight night. You can't teach in one minute what you have not done for weeks before in the gym.

For Mike, the Collyhurst and Moston gym still holds magical memories that will stay with him forever, "It is always so special walking up those steps and whenever I go back it still feels like a second home. It was an honour and a privilege to have worked alongside Brian and so many other wonderful people." One can only assume that after meeting Mike Jackson the feeling is mutual.

13 - ANTHONY FARNELL
THE WARRIOR

Red Mist: Manchester, 2001. Sometimes the urge to fight and show your true worth can so overwhelm a fighter that the last thing going through their mind is that the other guy can punch as well. At a packed Velodrome in Manchester, he started the walk to the tune of Queen's "We are the Champions". Wearing a number sixteen shirt of his beloved Manchester United, with KEANE emblazoned on the back, it was the fighter's tribute to another warrior. On he went as they roared his name. Six thousand Mancunians, drunk on alcohol and fight fever; screaming and demanding victory. The heat inside the Velodrome was almost unbearable, sweat poured from every face, the tension gripping the audience. It became hard to breathe for spectators, never mind the ones expected to carry their hopes into battle. Suddenly, in front of him on the walkway appeared a huge figure, face contorted with passion, tears rolling down his cheeks roaring loud. With shirt open, a gold chain glistening so bright it blinded, suddenly the realisation, the noise rose higher, the furore increased, it meant so much. So, so much. He could not lose that night. Nothing would stop him.

No time for losing, for we are the champions....

BORN ON THE 1ST OF JULY, 1978 and raised in north Manchester, Anthony Farnell loved to fight as a kid, even if he'd never yet seen a boxing ring. After attending St Edmunds primary, he moved on to St Matthews High School. One day heading home with a group of friends someone mentioned a place nearby where they could all go for a tear up, somewhere they could do some proper training, it even had a ring, not to mention boxers they had seen on television. Plans were made the next day for all to go and try it out. It was unanimous. Putting on gloves beats having scraps in the school yard or against lads from neighbouring schools such as North Manchester for Boys on nearby Broadhurst Park. However, come the moment of truth only one lad bothered to bring kit. So once school ended, off he set down Lightbowne Road, up those twenty steps, down the short corridor and into Collyhurst and Moston Gym. From that first day Anthony was hooked.

Surrounded by a plethora of the finest fighters Britain had to offer, Anthony started on a learning curve that began the moment he walked through the door. Delroy Waul, Ricky Burton, Robbie Reid, Thomas McDonagh, Michael Gomez… they were all experienced fighters, the last two already veterans of thirty amateur fights. From that day onwards it was a painful, but truly enjoyable education for Anthony. He swiftly found his way, working desperately hard to improve technique, whilst already blessed with the toughness required and the owner of a fighter's heart, essentials in this pugilistic university.

In no time at all Anthony impressed the only man who really mattered around those parts. Brian Hughes had seen enough and after just three months he put Anthony in for his first amateur bout. He was thrown in at the deep end against Salford's Jamie Moore at Pembroke Hall, Walkden. It was a true baptism of fire in which, despite losing a close fight, Anthony also ended the contest with a broken nose, cut eye and bleeding badly. It was a ring war, merciless and brutal. As Anthony remembers himself, "It was a really good hiding!" Afterwards, his father, Gary and mother, Teresa, suggested that boxing might not be the best career move, but his heart was set on it. Anthony thought he was a hard case, well he might have been back at school or on the streets, but the cruel realities of boxing showed him that there was so much more to learn. So, it was a case of going back up those steps and starting all over again; the sparring and the bags, listening and learning, watching those around him. The school of hard knocks had begun and Anthony had taken an early one, but he would return. In just his fourth bout, Anthony fought Jamie Moore again and it was another no holds barred, fierce contest that this time he won on points. A photograph of the two fighters together after that contest still sits proudly on his gym wall today.

Whereas the traditional Collyhurst and Moston adage of defence as taught by Brian had the fighter side on with his left hand low, for some boxers it simply was not in their nature to fight like that. Matters came to a head regarding this in the amateurs when in his fourteenth fight Anthony went up against Ashley Delancy from Blackpool and Fylde boxing club. In the corner that night was dad Gary and another highly respected trainer in the world of amateur boxing, Ray Flannagan. In the opening two rounds Anthony was being handed a real beating by Delaney who, in the second round, dropped him with a right hand over the top when his left was low. Once back on the stool he had taken enough, "This isn't me he" pleaded, "I just can't fight like this."

"Okay then," replied his dad, "go fight your fight."

As the bell for the third sounded, Anthony was on his feet, his stance adjusted and in no time had Delaney down three times and ultimately knocked him out. After just twenty-five amateur fights he had a 22-3 record and won the NABC class C National and Junior ABA titles. Anthony was not just succeeding in the amateur ranks he was leaving a trail of mayhem and destruction behind him of spectacular stoppages and knockouts. Then, at just eighteen, Brian Hughes advised Anthony to turn professional. Looking back now with hindsight he thinks it was all too soon, everything was happening just a little too fast. From being on a learning curve he was now taking a turn onto a much more dangerous road.

He had already experienced the quality of the Collyhurst and Moston gym. Such was the class of the fighters there that it was like a war every day. Between those four ropes, no prisoners were taken. He became close with Michael Gomez and they were inseparable in the gym and also ran and swam together and shared experiences whilst boxing in Germany and the United States. Anthony watched and sparred with Gomez and never failed to pick up useful tips. This was something the gym became famed for – the most minute detail or skill performed by a fellow boxer would be watched, scrutinised and practiced by others. As an example, when Pat Barrett helped Anthony out, it might be a word of advice in the ear or a painstaking lesson taught in the ring, he took it all on board. Pat helped shape Anthony as a fighter and is remembered with fondness by him today. Also Anthony was blessed to share a ring with the 'Ghost' Craig Dermody, even though by this time Craig had all but given up boxing. Anthony remembers it with awe, "Trying to hit Craig was like trying to hit a gust of wind."

Something occurred just after he turned pro that would have a profound effect on his career and for the better. Whilst in the gym sparring with top professional and tough Welshman Craig Winter, Anthony was suddenly in trouble when Winter caught him with a ferocious right hand over the top. Watching on Pat Barrett realised that for Anthony's sake this could not go on. Once back in the corner Pat did not mince words, "Right, hands up, and smash the body, do it now!" The realisation dawned that if Anthony was to have any chance in the pro game, he had to develop his own natural attacking style. Anthony was never going to be able to dodge salt like Thomas McDonagh or dance through raindrops like Craig Fleming, he was a warrior and would have to stand or fall as one.

On 3rd May 1997 at the Nynex Arena, on the Prince Naseem Hamed-Billy Hardy undercard, Anthony took on tough Scouse journeyman, twenty-seven-year-old, Lee Molyneux. Again, just as in the amateurs, he experienced a tough maiden fight and in a vicious battle, in which Anthony was cut once more, he edged it on points. The grim realisation that the amateur and the pros were vastly different sports soon dawned, here the referee does not break you, he just lets the fight go on inside. This was serious business - the hurt game. Next up at short notice was the former Irish Commonwealth silver medallist Martin Renaghan who fought out of Brendan Ingle's gym. Anthony was given a video of Renaghan and went over to Pat Barrett's house to study the Irishman. After watching it only once Pat turned to Anthony and smiled, "You'll stop this kid with a left hook mate". So it was that on 2nd August 1997, at the Metrodome, Barnsley, after being floored in the first by Renaghan, Anthony returned the favour in the second and then come the third, as forecast by Pat, finished him with a left hook!

Back in the gym Anthony had been receiving little one-on-one training, but slowly a bond was forming with Pat who took him under his wing. So began a long winning run in which Anthony was rarely involved in a dull contest. Soon he was twenty-six fights unbeaten, his popularity grew to such an extent that he became the biggest Mancunian ticket seller, outdoing crowd favourites such as Ricky Hatton and Michael Gomez by some distance. Anthony signed with Frank Warren meaning Sky Sports were always on hand to cover his fights and, given he was rarely in an average bout, they were always covered and shown.

Explosive fighters such as Anthony were like gold dust. Fame and popularity beckoned and duly arrived. Of all Manchester's new wave of exciting boxers around that momentous period, Anthony was at the fore. Along the way, on 29th May, 1999, at the North Bridge Leisure Centre, Halifax, he stopped the American John Long in the sixth round for the vacant WBO Inter-Continental Super Welterweight belt, a title he would successfully defend eight times. All appeared to be going swimmingly and then, like everything in life, when he least expected it the wheels came flying off.

It was one of the biggest fight nights in Manchester boxing history. 7th July 2001, at the Velodrome, Manchester, it seemed like half of of Collyhurst and Moston had turned out for the fight. Top of the bill was Ricky Hatton defending his WBU Super Lightweight title against Jason Rowland, but there was as much interest in the under card. A large majority of the crowd that, warm and extremely humid evening were there to roar on Anthony in his quest to win the vacant WBU World Super Welterweight title. His opponent was the dangerous twenty-six-year-old Iranian Mehrdud Takaloo. Born in Tehran, but by then residing in Margate and calling himself The 'Margate Rock', Takaloo was a refugee from Iran and had arrived in Britain when he was just six years old. Bullied and taunted at school, this all ended when he discovered a passion and talent for boxing. Coming into the fight with Anthony, Takaloo had a 16-2 record. He was a decent opponent, but most experts thought Takaloo wasn't near good enough to ruin The Warrior's big night. None in the Velodrome were more confident than the man himself, for he had come across his opponent before. Only twelve months previously Takaloo had turned up at Collyhurst and Moston gym to spar with Anthony and after being in the ring with him that day, he believed no way could this man ever beat him. So, when the fight was announced a worrying amount of over-confidence filled the air.

Pre-fight, Anthony had met with Manchester United Captain Roy Keane, who passed on a shirt for him to wear on the walk-in to the fight. As the contest drew ever closer the normal anxiety a fighter should go through to bring him to his peak before that first bell rang was missing. In Anthony's mind he had already won the fight, it was just a question now of turning up and knocking Takaloo out, smash right through him.

Sadly, boxing is a deadly business that thrives not just on destroying flesh and blood, but also has a habit for breaking hearts.

As Anthony walked from the dressing room into a wall of noise, the entire arena was chanting his name. Stood wearing his United shirt, his eyes blazing, he looked ripped and ready to take on the world, not just Takaloo. Defeat was unthinkable. As Freddie Mercury started singing, Anthony began his walk. The noise from the crowd only increased in thunderous tones as Anthony set foot in the ring. Before doing so he saluted the adoring crowds still singing. Among the masses now on their feet roaring, many were locals of his aunt's pub, The Clarendon, in Manchester. On entering through the ropes Anthony made his way over to a red robed Takaloo, who appeared not in the least intimidated by such hostile surroundings or his opponent. Indeed, there was a worrying smile that appeared to suggest he was enjoying it! A kid whose earliest memories were of being bombed and strafed by machine gun fire back in Iran was hardly likely to be perturbed by a sing-along in Manchester!

Favoured at 2 to 5 on by the bookies, Anthony's confidence appeared contagious and at the announcement of his name, the Velodrome exploded with cheers from every corner. Manchester was on its feet for one of their own. Takaloo was considered a major underdog, but as the first bell rang he attacked from the off. Straight away Anthony appeared to tense up behind a tight guard. Something was not right - Takaloo had nothing to lose and began hurling huge right hooks into Anthony's body and nothing was coming back. Immediately the crowd sensed their man was ill at ease and the concern transmitted itself to the ring.

Bad tidings.

Anthony attempted to move forward with a jab, only to miss and Takaloo, cool, calm and calculated, exploded with a savage right uppercut that he simply did not see coming. It was a sickening shot. His legs fell beneath him, Anthony went down heavily in the corner. The referee Dave Parris began the count and although still shaky he made it up at eight and was declared good to fight on. Sensing his opportunity Takaloo went to work and opened up on Anthony with nine unanswered punches, Farnell was like a rag doll being mauled. It was like he had been struck by some wizard's potion that made him unable to fight. Anthony was reeling, stage struck. Blinded by the lights and his own inability to fend off Takaloo, it wasn't that he lacked courage, what happened that night had more to do with the stuff going on inside Anthony's head, than who was hitting it. Left with no option Parris stepped in and ended the contest after just two minutes and three seconds of the first round. As Anthony stood like the lone survivor of a plane crash, Takaloo's corner came rushing in whooping and hollering and a sense of total bewilderment cut across the Velodrome. A twenty-six-fight unbeaten run had ended in a manner so brutal and shocking few could believe their own eyes. Howls and insults rained down, mainly from people unable to believe what they had just witnessed. Anthony's legions of supporters were left open-mouthed. Takaloo had conquered and nobody, least of all Anthony Farnell, saw it coming. What followed next proved equally explosive outside the ring, as what went on in it. That night a frustrated, embarrassed and broken Anthony left the Velodrome sobbing, unsure of what the future now held, but certain of one thing. It was time for a change.

To this day, Anthony remains convinced that the fight was lost before he even got into the ring. His state of mind in getting so worked up ultimately worked against him, although he also admits that Takaloo's punches did not help! Yet believing everything happens for a reason and determined to exorcise Takaloo's ghost, Anthony acted quickly and left the Collyhurst and Moston Gym almost immediately following the fight. There was bad blood between himself and Brian Hughes that had lingered through the years. Boxing is, was and always will be littered with such relationships, such is the complexity and emotions that come with the business. Anthony felt the best way to move forward was a complete break. He contacted the 'Preacher Man' Billy Graham and The Warrior took flight to another of Manchester's boxing churches, The Phoenix gym.

At the beginning, he missed the lads from his old haunt. Anthony would always say that Brian Hughes created something special within those four walls. He raised street kids, got in their heads and made them into champions. It was that kind of tough love in a small ring where there was nowhere to run that helped create a special bond between the younger fighters. They were brothers in arms through good times and bad. But boxing stops for no one and he had to make the best of his new start.

Two months later, on 15th September, 2001, the chance arose to restart his career after the Takaloo debacle. At the MEN Arena Anthony defended his WBO Inter Continental Super Welterweight title against the six-foot two southpaw Lee Blundell. The thirty-one-year-old from Wigan was an awkward opponent, but Farnell made light work of him, ending the fight with fifty-two seconds left of the second round when he caught the shaven-headed Blundell with a wonderful left hook that electrified the MEN! Anthony's relief was obvious, his wide smile signalling a return to normality.

The following month, on 27th October, the comeback continued. Again, it was another defence of the WBO title, this time his opponent was the twenty-four-year-old Russian Pavel Melnikov. He was a durable character, but Anthony finally caught up with him in the last round to win a late stoppage. On 9th February, 2002, a third fight at the MEN against the tough twenty-nine-year-old Matt Galer, lasted until round three, when Anthony ended proceedings with a vicious body shot.

Suddenly the opportunity arose to fight for another world title. After moving up a weight it was announced that on 1st June, 2002, he would fight for the vacant WBU world crown against twenty-five-year-old South African Rueben Groenewald. Anthony appeared a more relaxed figure beforehand and spoke well of events past, "I've learned from the mistakes I made before the Takaloo fight and I'm determined not to come a cropper this time. My feet are firmly on the ground and I'm not getting carried away." However on an extremely disappointing night, with expectations again sky high before an 18,000 crowd, Anthony lost out in a foul-filled bout on a unanimous points decision, although one desperate last effort in the twelfth to finish off the South African almost came to fruition but come the bell there could be little argument. During the fight Anthony had cracked a rib, but never used this as an excuse. The truth was that once more he had become too intense and ignored Billy Graham's pre-fight instructions. Anthony instead tried to turn it into a street fight and ultimately paid the price.

A swift shot at redemption swiftly followed three months later when, boxing politics being what it is, Groenewald received a lucrative offer to fight a rematch against Anthony. His camp was confident, with Groenewald's manager Eugene Maloney confident and cocky, "I see no reason not to give Farnell an immediate rematch, what can he do better? He has reached his level. This time around my boy beats him a lot easier, believe me."

During the short build-up sparks flew between Anthony and Groenewald, the animosity mostly springing from immediately after the fight as the South African was hanging on for dear life at the end, the pair nearly went at it again when the points decision was announced. Bad blood was boiling. As the re-match grew closer, Anthony pleaded with fans to stay claim and let him do the fighting. Alleged threats had been made to his opponent's entourage in messages to a boxing website. Billy Graham stepped forward to calm matters, "We will tell the fans beforehand there can't be any trouble. I have nothing at all against Ruben - he has shown courage as a fighter and deserves respect." All said it was time once more for Anthony and Groenewald to settle matters in the ring.

On 28th September, 2002, at a packed MEN, screaming loud and on its best behaviour, Anthony Farnell, the kid who remembered his kit and made that first walk up Lightbowne Road to Collyhurst and Manchester, captured the WBU Middleweight title and became a world champion. This time around both fighters provided a much better contest with Anthony sneaking home on a split decision. The realities of boxing showed itself post-fight, even amidst celebrations when Anthony realised he had broken a rib and was urinating blood, a snapshot of the dangers boxer's face spoke volumes when away from the spotlight. "All boxers are liars," Anthony admits today, "they will say and do anything for a fight. They have courage and blind faith that everything will be alright on the night."

On 18th January, 2003, at Preston Guild Hall, Anthony defended his newly won title with a tenth-round stoppage of another no-nonsense Russian, twenty-nine-year-old Nikolay Talalakin. It was a rough and gruelling evening in which Talalakin cut Anthony in the first and proved a wily opponent until he was finally worn down and broken. Five months later, just six days before Anthony was due to defend his world title, once more, this time against twenty-nine-year-old Brummie, Wayne Elcock, at the MEN, his girlfriend Natalie had a particular traumatic time giving birth to their son, Frankie. Happily, all ended well, but Anthony's mind was not on his opponent. Friends urged him to postpone the fight, but he would not hear of it. As mitigating circumstances go, Anthony would never use this as an excuse but come 5th April, 2003, he simply never got started and lost his title convincingly on points. Despite making only eleven appearances as a professional, the unfancied Elcock had Anthony in trouble on numerous occasions and floored him heavily in the fifth. Despite being hopelessly outpointed Anthony refused to give up and by the eleventh both men had blood splattered across their faces from nasty cuts. That he actually made it to the final bell was a kind of victory in itself, but the result was never in question and Elcock won deservedly by a unanimous points decision.

Something was not right at the Phoenix. Despite having the utmost respect for Billy Graham, Anthony found himself training alone most days on the bags and bars, whilst Billy concentrated almost solely on Ricky Hatton. The Hitman's career was starting to ignite and despite some assurances that he would receive more one-to-one help from Graham, it proved impossible and finally both decided to shake hands and Anthony moved on. Following the split with Billy Graham he teamed up with trainer Oliver Harrison and after an eight-month absence, on 13th January, 2003 at the MEN, Anthony stepped into the ring once more to beat the Brazilian born, London-based Tomas Da Silva on points. Elsewhere, in the boxing world, fate decreed that he would be handed another shot at the WBU Middleweight title when Wayne Elcock suffered a first-round knockout in his first defence of the belt by Scotsman Lawrence Murphy.

This time around Anthony was on a mission and come 6th March, 2004, at the Braehead Arena, Glasgow, Murphy never knew what hit him! Fighting like a man possessed, Anthony swarmed all over Murphy and with his very first decent punch had the Scotsman on the canvas with a clean right to the jaw. Unloading everything in his armoury he had Murphy rocked again in the second when another huge right hand forced him to take a standing eight count. Another right hook appeared to demoralise Murphy, whose defence simply fell to pieces and he was forced to cling on for dear life until the bell. It was now a matter of when, not if, for the champion was almost out on his feet, yet Murphy was somehow able to clear his head and his fans raised a cheer when he began to land some telling blows of his own and opened a cut on Anthony's face. The bell to end the second saw a brief respite giving Murphy precious time to recover. As the third began, Anthony poured on the pressure and a sweet but deadly left hook had Murphy down once more. The referee Dave Parris had seen enough, for as Murphy turned his back, it was clear he needed protection. Showing mercy Parris intervened and it was all over. The title was going back to Manchester!

Just three months later the opportunity arose for Anthony to take the place of Joe Calzaghe who had pulled out of a Ricky Hatton undercard. The down side was that he had only nine days to prepare. What Anthony didn't mention when accepting the fight was that he was eighteen pounds overweight and went into almost suicidal mode trying to make the weight. It was utter madness and proof fighters have to be saved from themselves. That Anthony finally succeeded was bad enough because in doing so he had become totally dehydrated and a walking time bomb.

'All fighters are liars…'

On 12th June, 2004, at the MEN, the Preston-based Portuguese fighter, Eugenio Monteiro beat a shadow of a man in the midst of developing a potentially fatal condition. After an opening first round that Anthony thought he had won comfortably, problems began on trying to stand for the second. Suddenly Anthony felt like his head was going to burst. All strength drained from him, his legs turned to dead weights and what started as a fight between two boxers swiftly turned into one of them almost praying the other would knock him out to ease the pain. For Anthony, like warriors of old, he was determined to go out on his shield. Call it blind pride, a strange kind of madness that exists only in those brave or foolish enough to climb through those ropes. Finally Monteiro, after toiling throughout, even against a broken opponent, put Anthony down in the tenth and the fight was stopped by referee Dave Parris. Immediately it became apparent as he clung to his corner man that something was not right with Anthony. Once back in the dressing room as he sat preparing to have stitches, Anthony felt the desperate need to lie down and the next thing he remembers was waking up on a stretcher with Sky Cameras following him out to hospital. When admitted Anthony was checked for everything, including brain damage. He was also given a lumbar puncture that went wrong and left him paralysed for four days. Soon it was confirmed that Anthony was suffering from viral Meningitis. The virus had lain dormant after first catching it when he was just eighteen, but with Anthony running down his body to the point of collapse in losing the weight for the fight, the Meningitis returned with a vengeance. For two weeks he remained in hospital, slowly, but surely recovering. With his family around him, they were all just relieved that Anthony was going to be okay.

Secretly, without saying anything, Anthony realised that this could not go on. Retirement beckoned, if not for his sake, then for those closest to him. In such a short period of time there had simply been too many wars, brutal fights and ferocious sparring sessions. They had all taken their toll and finally done for him. At just twenty-seven years of age, The Warrior hung up his gloves.

It was all over.

A sad post note to the Eugenio Monteiro fight occurred when the Portuguese failed a drug test. It was reported that they found his system contained illegal substances including steroids. For this he was banned for twelve months. Years later Anthony read of something similar happening in *Boxing News* and the fighter was stripped of the win. This didn't happen in his case and he contacted Robert Smith of the British Boxing Board of Control. However, Smith claimed because it happened so long ago they could not do anything about it and the loss remains on his record...

Struck by the fighter's curse, on finishing boxing Anthony fell into a deep and dark depression. For close to a year he spiralled downwards. It was horrific. His family despaired. Anthony was drinking up to ten pints a night and he was unrecognisable from the person they knew and loved. Out of control, a danger to himself and others, there seemed to be no way back. Finally, a chink of light emerged as the realisation dawned that he was in big trouble. With the help of family and professional guidance Anthony came back and one day the dark clouds passed.

Anthony's father pulled him aside, "Right what do you want to do with the rest of your life?"

"I want to stay in boxing."

"Okay," replied Gary, "We'll find you a gym."

"When it comes to family they are in your corner for life," Anthony says now.

A grimy relic of Cottonopolis stands on Oldham Road – it is the original home of Manchester United football club - Newton Heath. To enter, you walk through a grimy courtyard, up four flights of stairs until finally you see the sign on a door. Inside you can hear the sound of music and fighters training. Welcome to Arnie's gym. On walking in there is a wall of photographs, a who's who of boxing memories; friends, foes and legends. Facing you at the far end of a once broken-down warehouse floor sits a state of the art boxing ring. It is home sweet home for Anthony as he stands watching, eyes focused but content as two of his lads spar, shouting instructions, encouragement and passing tips.

There is no bullshit: these are his rules. They listen hard as he offers advice, sometimes with a smile or when necessary a scowl that would make a wild dog head for cover and call the RSPCA. His was a colourful career etched with wonderful highs and bitter lows, but it has left Anthony rich in knowledge and anecdotes for almost everything he now sees in the ring. Anthony has been there, done it, worn the Keane shirt and world championship belt. The fighters are weighed, he listens with a knowing smirk to their tall tales - nothing gets past him. For Anthony this is a love supreme. A special place. One even Natalie is content for him to be in all day and night if needs be, for she knows it is here that her man is content with something no amount of money could ever buy.

Peace of mind.

In coming through after retirement The Warrior has faced his toughest opponent - life itself. He ensured there was no last curtain call. It has been no bed of roses or pleasure cruise, but Anthony Farnell has kept on fighting till the end and is still standing....

14 - MICHAEL JENNINGS
ANGELS ON MY SHOULDER

For the first time since 1935, when Jock McAvoy destroyed Babe Risko in the blink of an eye and left the mob bosses at ringside open-mouthed and seething, Collyhurst and Moston Boxing Club made an impact in Madison Square Garden. The fighter looked around for friendly faces, there were a few hundred, but the 12,000 Puerto Ricans screaming for blood made the film Zulu look like a fifty-fifty contest. Miguel Cotto stood across the ring: a future hall of famer, an ominous opponent, who everyone in the boxing world (bar a handful of Mancunians) believed was going to hammer his latest challenger into the canvas inside one round.

As the crowd howled for his head, a smiling Brian Hughes put an arm around Michael Jennings' shoulders, "Ignore them, son, it's just noise." Never one for the limelight or titles, Michael fought only to keep winning. The pressure of winning always spurred him on and if belts, glory and fame came his way, then so be it. There had already been enough drama and tragedy in Michael Jennings' thirty-one years to ensure that whatever happened against Cotto, it was simply just another night in the ring. And, once the bell sounded, two angels would still be resting on his shoulders.

It was time to go to work.

BORN 9TH SEPTEMBER, 1977, in Preston, Michael was the youngest of eight children and they lived with their mother, Margaret and father, Raymond, in a three-bedroom house. As a pupil at Holy Cross High School, he was never any trouble, more a dreamer! Decent at most sports, Michael played football, threw the shot-putt and ran cross-country for Lancashire schools. The calling for the ring took hold when he started following his elder brothers into Chorley amateur club and in no time it became a passion. At fourteen Michael had his first fight and was swiftly recognised as someone to keep an eye on. He found boxing a great discipline to have at an early age, so while most of his mates were on the streets smoking and drinking, Michael was living for his next fight. He would win three national schoolboy titles, the Junior Amateur Boxing Association national title twice, the National Association of Boys' Clubs title and the Golden Gloves team event for England against Scotland, Ireland and Wales. Michael has no doubt that without boxing his life would have gone down a much more mundane or perhaps even a darker path.

To earn money, and also have one eye on another career if the boxing option went awry, he worked a twelve-hour shift at a slaughterhouse and studied electronics at night school. Hard graft away from the ring was never something he backed away from, in fact Michael relished it, but it was boxing that he lived and breathed for.

Despite the sixty-mile journey there and back from his hometown of Chorley, Collyhurst and Moston gym swiftly became a second home. Michael arrived as the gym was flourishing. Robbie Reid had conquered the world in Italy and a new breed of young and hungry quality fighters such as Michael Gomez, Anthony Farnell and Matthew Hall were set to be unleashed on the boxing world, all watched over by a man who missed nothing. Michael loved Brian Hughes straight away because he had a way of explaining things that made it so easy to understand. There was nothing complicated, his was a simple genius; practice, practice, practice, over and over until it becomes natural. Firm but with a fatherly hand, Michael was taken under Brian's wing until the time was right to make a decision. A defining conversation with his mother saw Michael decide to take the plunge and on 5th May, 1999, by the seaside at the Winter Gardens, Blackpool, twenty-two-year-old Michael Jennings turned professional.

He took on twenty-four-year-old Tony Smith, a southpaw from Sheffield, and made short work of him with a first-round knockout. Michael was up and running. As was nearly always the way with Collyhurst and Moston, he wasn't rushed and he learned his craft with victories over tough, hard-bitten journeymen such as Lee Molyneux, Brian Coleman and Paul Denton.

It was around this period that Michael lost the second of his brothers,

Raymond, to a drugs overdose. This after losing another, Stephen, years before to Leukaemia. Both left him distraught but somehow boxing enabled him to carry on. A good friend and fellow boxer from Collyhurst and Moston, Thomas McDonagh, remembers those sad days and how Michael somehow managed to hold it together to the astonishment of all. None more than Brian Hughes who would shake his head at his courage in putting on such a front, whilst inside, no doubt, Michael's heart was breaking.

Soon, he was also involved in a stabbing incident when out one night with Michael Gomez in Manchester. They were walking down a street when two guys on motorbikes kept shining lights at them. At first the boxers thought it was just a couple of idiots, so they ignored it. Then all hell let loose and the next thing he recalls were people screaming for an ambulance.

"Before I knew what happened I felt like I'd been punched in the back. When I looked down I realised I'd been stabbed with a Stanley knife. I found out later the blade had snapped off inside me and I had to have an operation to get it out."

Once back in the ring he continued to impress, going eighteen fights undefeated and his chance at a first professional belt arrived. On 8th May, 2003, at the Guild Hall Preston, he stopped the Wolverhampton born Jimmy Gould in six rounds to win the WBU Intercontinental Welterweight title. The success continued. By the time he had gone twenty-three fights unbeaten, Michael claimed the English Welterweight championship at the MEN Arena, on 1st October, 2004, this despite being dropped in the first round by the then champion, hard-hitting Yorkshire veteran Chris Saunders. Shaken but unbowed, Michael admits that back then, sometimes, he needed a wake-up call to get totally switched on. In round five he cut loose to turn Saunders into a bloodied mess before finally he retired on his stool. It was a sweet victory, for in the gym with Brian Hughes, beforehand, Michael had been working on his accuracy and as Saunders's face swelled with the power of the punches, it was obvious all the hard work had been worthwhile. It was an impressive performance from the Chorley boy.

More glory, albeit unexpected, was waiting around the corner, for just eight months later he earned a shot at the highly prestigious vacant British Welterweight title. It came up after another former Collyhurst and Moston fighter, David Barnes, had beaten the champion Jimmy Vincent. After a rematch was cancelled, due to Barnes taking on a Commonwealth title fight, Michael was offered the opportunity to step in at just four weeks' notice. When asked by Brian Hughes if he wanted it the reply was short and succinct, "Yeah dead right I want it!"

Always in the gym keeping fit for a title defence, it was a no-brainer for Michael, only a month before he had beaten the tough and durable Gavin Down with a ninth-round stoppage and had remained in fantastic shape. This was an opportunity not to be missed and on 16th July, 2005, at the Bolton Arena, Michael took on the thirty-four-year-old Brummie Jimmy Vincent. It was top of the bill and the event was being shown live on ITV. Interest in this contest was huge. General consensus was that it would go twelve rounds and even Michael, who admitted he dreamt the fight a thousand times beforehand, was of the opinion a long night lay ahead.

The bell for round one sounded and in the first minute Michael threw a sweet one-two, the right of which connected with Vincent's eyes and all but shut them! His legs buckled. After around fifteen seconds, and in a daze, Vincent hit back with a left hook and Michael backed off. Then, attacking again, he hit Vincent with another vicious combination. It became relentless and in the closing moments of the opening round Michael let fly yet another vicious right and left hook to drop Vincent and it was all over! What a sensation! Few British title fights have ended so quickly and in so spectacular a manner.

Brian Hughes came into the ring and hugged Michael tight. It was yet another champion for Collyhurst and Moston! Once back in the dressing room with the historic Lonsdale belt, Michael gave a short interview to ITV that ended with him saying direct to the camera, "Cheers Chorley! Yeah!"

Reminiscing today Michael admits just thinking about that night makes the hairs on the back of his neck stand up. He had prepared for a difficult soul-searching twelve rounds, so nobody was more shocked when Vincent was down and out inside three minutes. "It was amazing, but the first right hand I caught him with, I saw in his eyes that I had hurt him. As a boxer, you instinctively know that. He threw a left hook back, and I thought he'd recovered, so I just stepped off, moved around the ring again, and threw a punch over his left guard. His legs went. I caught him again with a powerful right and then a left hook. I remember praying. Don't get up, don't you get up! He was gone. Obviously, I was glad Jimmy wasn't hurt too badly and recovered. Nobody wants that."

Three months later, on 25th October, 2005, at the Guild Hall, Preston, Michael's first defence of his coveted British title was against Welshman Bradley Pryce, and it almost matched the previous opening round, but this time it was the Chorley boy who was almost down and out. Michael entered the ring grim-faced but bristling with confidence and in the shape of his life. Pryce also appeared relaxed and fit after a recent return from a two-year break, now back under the guiding hand of fellow Welshman and experienced trainer Enzo Calzaghe.

Normally content to turn every fight into a brawl, Pryce adopted different tactics for Jennings, he was happy to fight off the jab and use his long frame and reach advantage to keep him at bay. The Welshman appeared poised and in control, but it couldn't last! Just one minute in a ferocious exchange of blows culminated in a left hook-right cross combination by Pryce that clearly shook up the champion. The 8-1 underdog sensed glory and as the Guild Hall rocked, a thunderous right hand had Michael on the floor. Swiftly up, Jennings quickly reassured his worried corner that all was okay. As the eight count was completed, Pryce flew at Michael, who remained in desperate trouble. Caught cold, disaster loomed – his legs looked gone, his eyes glazed over and the strength seemingly drained from both arms. Michael's head was jolted as he clung on for dear life. A stinging series of jabs from Pryce looked to have done for him. Michael looked close to going down again as his gloves touched the canvas, but somehow he survived and luckily the referee, Ian John-Lewis, didn't call it.

"Those were the longest three minutes of my career in the ring," Michael recalls today. Staggering back to the corner for a moment's salvation, few at that moment gave him much hope of retaining his title. ITV Commentators John Rawling and Duke McKenzie were both in raptures after what they had just witnessed. It was enthralling, but brutal.

Clearly still stunned as the second round began Michael ever so slowly regained his senses and deferred from his preferred tactic of boxing at distance. Against the on-fire Pryce, he needed to get closer to negate the Welshman's natural reach advantage. He became much busier with hooks to Pryce's body that in time would take effect, yet still he continued to take powerful shots off the challenger that clearly hurt. The rounds went on and the battle raged. Three, four and five saw Michael roar back to take control of the fight, but Pryce was always one big punch away from breaking the pride of Chorley's heart. As the crowd roared for the champion, few believed the furious pace could be maintained. Throughout the middle rounds Michael began to dominate. Physically stronger, he began to bully the clearly waning Pryce, who looked increasingly forlorn, desperate even. Come round eight Michael was letting fly his own shots, catching Pryce with one particular storming left hook. Now clearly three or four rounds up, it became obvious Pryce's only chance was a glory shot. Fatigue had clearly taken its toll, the failure to finish off Michael in the first when he had him at his mercy, was now just a bitter memory.

In the ninth Pryce enjoyed a brief rally. Michael though still throwing the better punches, was also now tiring. It became a question of who wanted it more. Again Jennings won the round but belief remained in the Welsh corner that their man still possessed the capacity to nail the champion. In the eleventh Michael was in unchartered territory. The bell rang, the crowd roared and the fighters went back to war. The final two rounds on this dramatic night of boxing took an even greater twist when from somewhere Pryce found a right hand that sagged the champion's knees and knocked the wind out of him! As the seconds ticked down in the twelfth the improbable still felt possible as Michael continued to go toe-to-toe with Pryce, risking it all knowing that one crazy haymaker from Pryce could end it. Whether it be pride, sheer courage or just the love of a good scrap, to the horror of his corner screaming for him to cover up, Michael refused to take a backward step and went for it.

Finally the last bell sounded and as the two warriors fell into each other's arms, it was obvious to all in the Guild Hall that Michael had retained his title. The champion had ended the fight as he began it, on the ropes and out on his feet, but had dug deep and despite the acclaim for the challenger, it was Michael who came roaring back to ultimately win the day. Chorley still had its British champion even if, at times, they had come close to losing him.

Speaking afterwards Michael summed it up in his own straight forward style, "It's not the sort of fight you want every night, I'd rather box and not get hurt. But sometimes you get caught and have to take good shots, get over them and come back. Fair play to him, it was a hard fight."

After the gruelling contest against Pryce, Michael was back defending his title only three months later on 28th January, 2006, this time at the Nottingham Arena against a truly dangerous 'banger' from the Black Country, Lee Woodley fighting under the name of 'Young Mutley.' It was an evening when everything turned sour for Michael, as Mutley dug deep and ripped away his coveted British Welterweight title in controversial circumstances on a split decision. The scoring 116-113 twice for the challenger and 115-113 for the champion, shocked many, none more than Michael, who despite being far from his best believed he had done enough to win. It was a view shared by many at ringside and the vast majority of the boxing press. There were mitigating circumstances that Michael didn't mention at the time. He had ridiculously over trained and knew almost immediately after the opening round that he was drained. Michael's twenty-eight fight unbeaten run had finally come to an end to leave him devastated, upset and not wanting to leave his house for fear he had let people down. Nothing could appease him. After the fight his friends tried everything to cheer him up, but only a fighter can explain a loss such as this. No amount of bearhugs or family and management around him saying how unlucky he was and how bad the decision was could help. The fact remained Michael's title had gone and it broke his heart.

Eight months passed before Michael returned to the ring. It was with unreserved venom that he knocked out the Czech Republic fighter Rastislav Kovac in the third of an eight-round contest on 22nd September 2006, at the Bolton Arena. Michael was brilliant throughout, despite the bitter disappointment that a world title shot against Mehdrud Takaloo had been cancelled. As for Kovac, he was deemed a tough opponent for the Chorley man, but was left looking outclassed as Michael took him apart, bit by bit with machine gun style punches that knocked Kovac's head back constantly. It soon became clear demons were being vanquished and the third round was only seconds old when a blistering left hook knocked the wind out of Kovac and the Czech fell to the canvas only to beat the count. Sensing his moment Michael let fly another left, this time catching the his opponent's solar plexus and down he dropped once more. Brian Hughes' pre-fight advice was pretty straight forward, "Throw plenty downstairs" and it worked a treat. His trainer was a happy man afterwards, "Michael boxed superbly. These Eastern Europeans can be tough and obstinate, but Michael took his time, placed his punches in the right spots and got the right result. He was down, but he will now rest and have a holiday, before starting to prepare for the big one against Takaloo."

For another shot at a title now dawned, this time against an old adversary of Collyhurst and Moston. On 7th April, 2007, at the Millennium stadium in Cardiff, on a Joe Calzaghe bill, Michael took on Takaloo for the WBU Welterweight title. Four hundred fans from Chorley were present to cheer their hero on. Preparation had gone to perfection for Michael, he had been not just under the watchful eyes of Brian Hughes but also Pat Barrett. Nothing was left to chance and a battle plan to beat Takaloo was put in place. Every day Michel ran five miles in the Rivington area and then fought near wars in sparring sessions with good friends Robin Reid, Tommy McDonagh and Matthew Hall. Everyone was aware of the importance of victory over Takaloo. He could ill-afford another defeat. On the night Michael proved simply too good for the Iranian - fighting with style, blistering speed, intelligence and wonderful technique, he won impressively by a unanimous decision. Once more Chorley could celebrate a champion - as for Michael, a life beset by tragedy and triumph and an unswerving desire to keep on fighting, whatever cut across his path, was veering ever closer to a date at the Garden and a place in Mancunian history.

A series of four more victories catapulted Michael into a scenario he could hardly have dreamt about. Firstly on 28th September, 2007, at Michael's spiritual home of The Guild Hall, Preston, he beat Ukrainian Volodymyr Khodakovskyy on points. Three months later, at the Excel Arena in London, Michael took apart Alan Minter's son Ross in a scintillating performance. That it took him nine rounds mattered little, for he appeared at the peak of his powers. From the off the difference in class was evident and when a right hand caught Minter flush in the first minute, it appeared more a matter of when, not if, the brave but outgunned Londoner would go down. Michael boxed beautifully in the opening five rounds, picking Minter off at will. A slight easing off in the sixth and seventh was met by a furious if controlled retort by Brian Hughes when Michael returned to his corner, "You're not doing what we trained for in the gym, son. Now get back to your boxing." This was taken on board and come the tenth it was clear Minter, after being caught late in the ninth, was on borrowed time. His head had not cleared and sensing this Michael cut loose looking to end proceedings. The end was clearly nigh and a huge left hook put Minter down. Though back up at eight, referee Micky Vann let him carry on and Michael, utterly relentless, cut loose again forcing his by now almost defenceless opponent into a corner. Finally, not prepared to see their man suffer further, Minter's corner threw in the towel and it was all over. Minter had shown he had heart and courage and following the post-fight formalities he made his way over to his father, Alan, at ringside to apologise. Although really, it wasn't necessary because he had been beaten in a good battle against what many were claiming now to be a truly brilliant fighter. Michael Jennings was back! The kid from Chorley had come to the East End and had shown his worth. All bets were now off as to what could happen next.

Further victories followed, first against George Ungiadze from Georgia. In a non-title fight at the Bolton Arena, Michael hammered the defenceless Ungiadze into submission with a flurry of punches that led to referee Phil Edwards stepping in to halt the bout. The Georgian had taken a pounding from the opening and for Michael it took him to a record of 33-1. The fights kept coming. On 14th November, 2008, at the famous bearpit of the Kelvin Hall, Glasgow, the now thirty-one-year-old Michael took on Doncaster-born Jason Rushton and won comfortably on points. What happened next was beyond Michael Jennings's dreams.

It was announced that Michael was to fight for the WBO World Welterweight title at the historic Madison Square Garden against the savage punching and lightning fast Puerto Rican, twenty-nine-year-old Miguel Angel Cotto. Devastatingly intense and already hailed as a future hall of famer, Cotto was a truly dangerous fighter who operated at the highest level. He had been beaten only once, an eleventh-round brutal stoppage in his last bout against the Mexican Antonio Margarito. However, this was later deemed to be in controversial circumstances when Margarito was suspended for having his hands illegally wrapped before a fight with Shane Mosley. Cotto's previous list of victims read like a who's who of boxing royalty as he left a trail of destruction in his blistering path; Shane Mosley, Zab Judah, Oktay Urkal, Paul Malignaggi and DeMarcus Corley. Widely regarded as the hardest punching fighter around, in 2006 he left Malignaggi with a fractured jaw. When the fight was first announced many believed Michael would not last a single round against the lethal Cotto. It got to the point where he stopped reading the boxing forums and magazines. At Collyhurst and Moston no negativity was uttered, Michael Jennings was entering the lion's den and as far as those closest to him believed, he had no inclination of just going over there to get hit, go down, take the money and run. He was going to the Garden to win.

In boxing anything is impossible. Michael may have already been written off as a no-hoper, a hapless underdog, but lightning had a reputation for striking more than once in boxing rings of the past. Five years before Danny Williams was a 15-1 outsider against Mike Tyson and yet effectively ended his career. Before that Lloyd Honeyghan had dethroned the mercurial Don Curry, Alan Minter beat Vito Antuofermo and the days when Brits travelled across the Atlantic to be dismissed as mere 'horizontals' were thankfully over thanks to the achievements of Lennox Lewis, Ricky Hatton and Joe Calzaghe. However, if Michael could pull off a victory over Cotto he would top the lot.

The plan to achieve this centred on somehow dragging the Puerto Rican into the latter rounds. Brian Hughes instructed Michael he had to tire Cotto out with movement. Then, hopefully, the demons from his last time out against Margarito may return. Brian urged Michael constantly that he needed to have total belief in his ability to pull this off. Although the old guru also stressed that if things went awry he was never going to allow Michael to get hurt. Deep down Brian secretly feared for a lad he had nothing but respect and love for.

Before setting off for the states, Michael made a quiet visit to his brothers' resting places in Chorley. Placing flowers on Raymond and Steven's graves, he knew that whatever happened in the Garden, they would be like angels on each shoulder. Both were never far from his everyday thoughts and if Michael could pull off a miracle against Cotto, then he would dedicate the win to them. Although, win or lose there was no doubt Raymond and Steven would have been so proud of their little brother.

On arriving in the Big Apple, Michael swiftly made friends in New York. His quintessential Lancastrian drawl, quiet demeanour and easy smile impressed the American fight writers. Michael appeared confident, but also showed huge respect for Cotto. "I'm not so stupid not to acknowledge that he is a great fighter, but my preparation has been terrific and I'm going to give it one hundred percent. I'm here to win the vacant WBO belt. I will give it everything and I don't feel overawed. My entire career has led to this. All I know is I have to weather the early storm and then finish him off in the later rounds. I know I can do it, and I will do it."

And he believed every word.

This was Michael's first test at such a heady level against an opponent fighting in his fourteenth successive world title contest. Yet, before the media Michael appeared unfazed. He had a personality that simply exuded stoicism, no doubt stemming from the criminally unfair slice of tragedy that fate had so far dealt him. It meant that for Michael, the forthcoming night in the Garden was not a matter of life and death. He had experienced enough of that, it was just another fight, albeit in extraordinary surroundings.

New York: 21st February, 2009. Madison Square Garden, the boxing equivalent of a Roman Amphitheatre. Jennings is a 12/1 underdog viewed as mere cannon fodder by almost all but those closest to him. Michael arrived at the Garden with the boxing world's spotlight upon him. The previous evening all the fire alarms had gone off at half past three in Michael's New York hotel. Typically, he ignored them and stayed in bed and choose to sleep through it! If it had been a ploy by Cotto's camp to unnerve him, they had picked on the wrong man. Nothing mattered to Michael more than family and with the money earned from the forthcoming fight he intended to buy his parents a home. On this night of nights, in the place where Muhammad Ali and Joe Frazier went to war, Michael could feel Raymond and Stephen on his shoulders more than ever and like all fighting men who simply cannot resist that one shot at everlasting glory, he prepared for the fight of his life.

As the minutes ticked by ever so slowly, Brian Hughes began the final acts in the dressing room. That of bandaging his fighter's hands. It was a private moment between boxer and trainer. A chance to gather their thoughts. Talk in whispers: exchange advice that was intended for their ears only. It is an intimate process that needs to be done slowly and with real care, the unwritten law in the dressing room is to leave them to it.

A quite literal calm before, in this case, a Puerto Rican storm. When a title and huge money are on the table a representative from the opposing fighter's team can oversee the bandaging process to ensure nothing untoward takes place. Though while observing this sacrosanct act, a respectful distance is kept and, more importantly, the observer watches on in complete silence. Sadly, there were those such as veteran cut man Joe Chavez who, when the stakes were so high, viewed it as a last chance to cause upset and gain a psychological advantage. The wily old Chavez was Cotto's cut man. For Chavez, when it came to his fighter, all was fair in love and war and he had no qualms in attempting to ruffle the Brit's feathers.

As Michael fought to control his pre-fight nerves, matters were hardly helped when Chavez expressed dissatisfaction at Brian's wrapping of his hands and insisted it be done again. Keeping calm Brian agreed, only for Chavez once more to complain. Refusing to become rattled Brian did it a third time and again Chavez was not happy. He even threatened to cancel the fight unless Brian repeated the process. On noticing a slight shake in Michael's hand, only then did the great man play Chavez at his own game. He turned to face their tormentor and as Chavez screamed in his face, Brian went for him! Sixty-nine-year-old Brian Hughes faced off the Puerto Ricans in Madison Square Garden on behalf of his fighter! Toe-to-toe Brian went, inches from Chavez's face. In the ensuing chaos, a shocked boxing official jumped in to separate the elderly warriors and a ranting and swearing Chavez was escorted out. His bullying tactics were seen off by a man who had been there, seen it and written multiple books about it. Once relative calm had been restored, Brian turned to Michael and winked at him, "We won't let anyone bully us tonight, Mike," he said. Michael smiled and nodded, understanding Brian's actions had been as calculated as Chavez's.

"What helped me was not the fact that Brian had squared up to him, but when he turned and gave me a wink! He kind of made a joke of it and that definitely helped. By giving me that wink and saying what he did reassured me and then it was just a case of let's get back to business."

Michael was convinced that Brian was one of only a few people who believed that he could actually win, and goes on to add, "If Brian didn't believe in me that night, then he was a bloody good actor!"

For his ring walk Michael picked the Sex Pistols, 'Anarchy in the UK.' Made painfully poignant after his best friend Ned Hardy had been killed in a road accident the previous year. He was taken to hospital, but tragically passed away shortly afterwards. They had both played in a Chorley Punk Rock band, The Shoks. Michael was the drummer and Ned a talented bass guitarist. Outside the ring, along with family, music had always been Michael's other true love and so with angels on his shoulders and the Sex Pistols playing loud in memory of Ned, Michael Jennings made his way into the Garden.

As he came into sight, 12,000 Cotto supporters began hurling abuse on his head. The lyrics of 'God Save The Queen' a little piece of England in this Puerto Rican bear pit, were drowned out amid the deafening noise. The few hundred who had made the journey from England found themselves hopelessly outshouted in the midst of such furore and sheer passion for Cotto. In a wonderful gesture, Michael had Collyhurst and Moston Lads Club emblazoned on the back of his red, gold and black robe. It was only right, he thought, for this was for them. Boxing maybe the loneliest sport in the world, but until that moment, when the bell rings, there exists great camaraderie. Nowhere more so than up those twenty steps on Lightbowne Road.

Boos and hisses greeted the song's ending and a smiling Michael, shadow boxing in the ring, found himself the centre of the crowd's attention! Then the resonating of a drum beat and entered Miguel Cotto and Madison Square Garden exploded with excitement! Wearing an orange robe with FEARLESS inscribed on the back, Cotto reached up and entered through the ropes to a cauldron of his fellow countrymen going wild with delight! He saluted them and all this time Michael stood patiently with Brian Hughes and cornerman, Mike 'The Iceman' Jackson alongside him. A boxing historian, undoubtedly Brian's mind must have drifted back all those years to Jock McAvoy and his sensational win in this same ring against Babe Risko in 1935. It had taken seventy-nine years but Collyhurst and Moston were back!

The legendary MC, Michael Buffer, made the introductions and the atmosphere, already seething soared to boiling point.

"Let's get ready to rumble!'"

Again, the Garden went into raptures! People were off their seats, flags were waving as Puerto Ricans made one finger gestures at the cameras, the inclination being that was how long Michael would last. All the time the man in question had a slight smile on his face, seemingly content to soak up everything and just get on with the fight.

The opening round was a cagey affair with Michael keeping a safe distance from Cotto as the Puerto Rican dominated the centre of the ring. Cotto seemed content to take his time and find the measure of the man in front of him. Michael was not running, it was a case of avoiding being caught cold. He threw occasional shots, lone jabs and flashing one-twos, but it was the murderous Cotto who won the round. On the prowl he was like a caged lion, waiting. His corner was happy, telling him he was doing a good job, but to not overlook Michael's dangerous right hand. Meanwhile, on the other side of the ring, Brian was busy at work doing similar, "You're doing cracking son! Remember, just stay out of bounds and jump in when you feel the time is right."

The beginning of the second saw little sign of the phoney war erupting into life. Michael continued to hit and move, whilst Cotto's shadow stalked him ominously, Finally, midway through the round the Puerto Rican caught Michael on the chin with a ferocious short upper cut that made his eyes water. As the Garden roared, Cotto launched a barrage late in the round, but Michael managed to tie him up for the last ten seconds. Brian urged his man not to get caught on the ropes, to spin off and upset his rhythm. The third saw Michael begin with more aggression, but that only seemed to torment Cotto, suddenly he was like a lion with toothache as he sought the chink in Jennings armour. Yet still he preferred to wait, picking shots, knowing that the right moment to catch his opponent would inevitably arise. Early in the fourth Jennings was caught with a crashing straight left on the nose and suddenly Cotto sensed this brave Englishman was there for the taking. Michael was rocked back into his corner with a left hook and then was put down for the first time with a body shot, again Cotto's left. He took the count, but was swiftly back on the canvas as Cotto's immense power was now on full show. This was truly one of the fighters of his generation and although Michael survived the round, Cotto celebrated with his corner as though it was already over… meanwhile Brian was telling Michael that he had no intention of letting him get hurt, but Michael wanted more.

The fifth started with another left jab from Cotto that whipped Michael's head back but, still refusing to yield, Michael continued to try and stay in the fight, even though by now he was being repeatedly mauled. Cotto exploded into action once more, sending him reeling onto the ropes with a crunching right to the head, followed by an equally fearsome left. Another straight right was the final blow as a near done Michael went down on one knee again. Though bleeding freely from the nose and knowing surely the game was up, he still got to his feet only for the referee, Benji Estevez, to have seen enough and call the fight off. There had been no disgrace in defeat for Michael Jennings, he had simply lost to one of the greats and, as the Garden let loose in joy and glee, the night belonged to Puerto Rico and their favourite son.

Following the fight there were fine words from Cotto, "Michael had a lot of strength and courage inside the ring. Everyone saw it. He should be a proud man."

"Cotto is a great fighter" said Michael. "The hardest puncher I've ever faced. He's very deceiving. You think you're out of range and yet he strikes and connects. He really surprised me. I thought I had distance from his firepower."

Despite being down after such a crushing loss, Michael's mood was lifted when he re-appeared from the dressing room and found himself mobbed by Cotto supporters. The Puerto Ricans recognised bravery when they saw it and as he was hugged and backslapped within an inch of his life, Michael Jennings's night in the Garden drew to a memorable, heart-warming close. He could not have done any more against the three times world champion.

There was to be one last throw of the dice for Michael when, the following year, he challenged Sheffield's rising star Kell Brook for his WBO Inter Continental Welterweight title. On 18th September 2010, at the LG Arena, Birmingham, Michael failed after being stopped in the fifth round with a horrific cut. It was an unsatisfactory finish and, though promised a rematch, it never came to pass. Further recurring problems with his shoulder required surgery and proved impossible to overcome. It could not go on. These battle scars and wear and tear saw him finally make the decision to retire. A fine career in the ring came to an end but for Michael it was simply the closing of one chapter and the beginning of another.

Using his connections in boxing he began running a security business that operated at nightclubs, building sites and sporting events. Michael swiftly built up a reputation as someone to trust and it proved successful. He helped provide the security for his friend Ricky Hatton's brave if ultimately doomed comeback against Vyeschlav Shevchenko in November, 2012.

However, as always seems the way, a quirk of fate intervened to set Michael off on a much more recognised path. Initially appearing to accept that a life outside boxing awaited him, circumstances prevailed to make this not so. Michael got a call from his brother Dave and some friends to help them out with their training. They were amateur boxers and asked him if he would go down and just hold the clock, do a bit of timing. It did not take long for Michael to end up being the one training them!

Soon this snowballed into something bigger. Michael had the bug. Along with Dave they opened a gym to help get local kids off the street. Then things really began to take off and from small acorns... Today Jennings Gym thrives and has truly made its mark on the boxing landscape. Not just in the North West but the entire country. Champions are now emerging, recently the British Cruiserweight Matty Askin became the first to make the brothers proud and undoubtedly there will be more.

The twelve years spent working with Brian Hughes have clearly had a guiding effect on Michael. The manner in which he explains points to fighters and gets his ideas across has echoes of another voice many years before saying similar to him! "Keep it simple, break it down, take it to pieces and then build it back up." Michael realises that it is important to teach things so anyone can grasp them. The true key to being a good trainer is communicating the basics and building on that and, above all the mantra. Practice, practice and practice!

"Only then can you move onto the technical aspects of boxing," Michael says. He is a chip off the old block!

Highly respected among his boxing peers, Michael Jennings is a credit to his family, fiancé Zoe and their three children, Mikey, Jack and Macy, Collyhurst and Moston boys club and his home town, Chorley.

Raymond and Stephen, the two angels on his shoulder, would be proud men today. There was one special night at the Garden, but also so much more and the story is far from over...

15 - MATTHEW HALL

THE FIGHTER

On 12th November, 2004, at the North Bridge leisure centre in Halifax, twenty-year-old Langley-born Matthew Hall was making his ninth professional appearance, against a forty-year-old journeyman from Watford, Ojay Abrahams. Ricky Hatton was top of the bill and Collyhurst and Moston, as ever, were well represented. In Matthew's corner was Brian Hughes and Mike Jackson. "Good luck son," said Brian as the bell rang to signal round one. "Remember all you've been taught". Two minutes and forty-one seconds later, poor Ojay did not know what had happened as Matthew pole-axed him. Later, back in the dressing room, Brian was a little worried about the state of Ojay and he insisted they go and see him. After knocking on they entered and in walked Brian, Mike and Matthew. There he sat, dazed, he didn't have a clue what was going on.

Brian sat down next to him, "Are you alright, son?"

"Have I fought yet?" replied Ojay.

The Collyhurst and Moston trio all stared at each other.

"Yeah mate," says Mike.

Ojay scratches his head, "What happened?"

"You got knocked out," Brian explained.

"What by him!" exclaimed Ojay pointing at Matthew.

"Yeah me" smiles Matthew.

"Yes, son" Brian says smiling and nodding, "unfortunately, you've just met the bull - the Langley 'El Torito!'"

★

S OMETIMES IT'S NOT ABOUT being able to fight. Sometimes the environment you're brought up in and the people around you mean you have no choice. Matthew Hall was born and raised in Middleton on the sprawling Langley council estate and he grew up having to look after himself. Langley was nobody's paradise. Being streetwise and having an eye for trouble served you well. Like anywhere there were the good, the bad and the downright nasty.

Matthew comes from a loving family; his mother, Shirley, worked all hours as a cleaner and his father, Jimmy, was a glazer and was known to his mates as Jimmy Glass! Jimmy is a fanatical Manchester United fan and Matthew was named in honour of Sir Matt Busby. However, Jimmy also loved his boxing and most of all the formidable Mike Tyson. At the time Tyson was tearing a legendary, blood-curdling, chaotic path through the Heavyweight ranks and every fight became a must see event, despite being shown on television in this country at three o'clock in the morning. It was a tradition, as in so many households of British boxing fans, to come home from the pub on a Saturday night, settle down with a take-out and watch 'Iron Mike' attempt to rip his opponent's head off in a thunderous assault. Matthew's home was no different. He would lie in bed waiting for the shout, "Oi Jimmy Glass, get the lads up, let 'em watch the fight!"

Downstairs, he and his elder brother Karl would come running and, as the adults watched enthralled on the screen, Tyson, with his deadly snarl and menacing lisp went to work as Matthew and Karl staged their own version of fight night in the living room! Jean Claude Van Damme movies were also all the rage back then and their mother would go mad on seeing her boys move the couch aside and turn the room into a fighting ring and go hell for leather at each other! Karl also boxed, but it was more out of necessity than a passion! Matthew recalls he was extremely talented, but was more bothered about his looks than a professional boxing career, ultimately Karl went on to study at university where he earned a chemistry degree.

Matthew went to Cardinal Langley School. A boisterous kid, clever, though interested only in football and boxing, he was at Leeds United academy from eleven years old, but once the boxing bug bit a choice had to be made. All Matthew's energy became channelled through boxing. Here Jimmy, strong on discipline and determined to guide his son the best way possible, felt he had to speak up. Jimmy didn't pressurise Matthew, but stressed to him that when it came to boxing you had to give everything. There could be no short cuts as you would be found out if you had not lived the life. Miss one training session because you can't be bothered and forget it because that means the hunger has gone and the sport becomes dangerous.

Matthew began his career at Boarshaw boxing club with a trainer called John Cusick who later moved to Wales. However, before he left Cusick ensured Matthew's emerging talent in the ring would not be lost by placing him in the safe hands of a man and environment he deemed perfect for his young thirteen-year-old star to shine - Brian Hughes and Collyhurst and Moston Gym.

The first walk up those twenty steps left Matthew in awe. On stepping through the gym door he witnessed a dazzling, rich array of talent with the likes of Robbie Reid, Michael Gomez, Anthony Farnell, Thomas McDonagh and Michael Jennings all working out. What struck him most about those early days was that it did not matter who you were, a world champion or an eight-year-old kid from around the corner, Brian Hughes treated everybody equally.

"There are no stars in here," Brian would tell Matthew many times over the years, "we're all the same". From the off he adored the training, the atmosphere and the friendship. It was like one big family. Brian's advice to Matthew was always to keep his head moving and don't stand still. He stressed the need, first and foremost, to have a good defence. Brian explained it in football terms,

"It's like the Italians, Matthew. They love to defend and if you have a great defence you can always nick a goal." Whilst Brian was busy with the pros during the day he would leave a blueprint for his assistant, Mark Campbell, to follow with Matthew when he arrived in the evening. Mark was a huge influence upon him and not only helped Matthew perfect his deadly left hook but played an integral part of him winning four national schoolboy titles.

Matthew was sensational in the amateurs and is the last decorated amateur champion from Collyhurst and Moston. His last twelve fights were won by knockout. The finale of that period came when boxing for England in a four-nation tournament in Scotland. Matthew knocked out the Scottish boxer, the Irishman did similar to the Welshman and it was all set for an England-Ireland final. Here was where Brian came into his own, he pulled Matthew to one side.

"Now listen, you have to win this, not just for England, but more to impress this crowd. The Scots love a fighter like you." He pointed towards them, "Rod Stewart is out there. How great would it be to show Rod how good you are?"

Taking every word Brian said as gospel Matthew, wound up and roaring, came flying out and nailed the poor Irish lad in no time. Was Rod out there? To this day he isn't sure!

It became apparent to Matthew that Brian was a master of mind games, he was not only a walking encyclopaedia of boxing tactics, but knew how to handle people to get what he wanted from them. He likens him to Sir Alex Ferguson in the respect that he possessed an ability to get inside boxer's heads. His fighters would do anything to please him – the words "Well done" were received with the same gratitude with which a thirsty man would accept a cold beer on a sweltering day. The reverse of that was the dread and fear of letting him down and that also drove them on. Matthew was never short of sparring partners, for in the gym there was such a wealth of all styles. Robbie Reid, Anthony Farnell, Gary Lockett, Michael Jennings and more. Sparring was always ferocious but, once over, the animosity would be switched off like a light. Matthew used to be picked up by Thomas McDonagh and they would be laughing and joking on the way to the gym and even walking towards the ring. However, once through the ropes sparks flew. If caught with a hard shot the other would hit back harder and absolute mayhem would ensue! These proud young men wanted nothing more than to knock the other out. Those sparring sessions in the gym provided better entertainment than many fights put on at the huge boxing shows. Many times Brian was forced to intervene – "Stop fighting and box!" he would say but when it was all over it was soon forgotten and they were friends once more. It was the best days of their lives, ask any fighter from that era at Collyhurst and Moston and they will tell you the same.

With Matthew being a short and stocky fighter, his sparring with Brian always took on a David and Goliath feel, for he loved an underdog. Brian adored nothing more than going to an opponent's back yard and beating them. When they would travel to London it was always Collyhurst and Moston against the cockneys!

"Frank Warren's lot think they are doing us a favour by bringing us here," Brian would begin, "well you show 'em boys. Let's get the job done and go home!"

Each lad was told the same story before going in the ring, "You're better than him, you're gonna be a world champion." Any snide comments about northerners in the big city would be met by Brian's instant retort, "Do you think we're idiots coming here to just get beat? We've come to win!"

After watching Matthew pound mercilessly away on the bag one day a thought crossed Brian's mind. He handed Matthew a video of the legendary Tony Ayala nicknamed 'El Torito', 'The Little Bull.' He was a magnificent but controversial fighter whose style matched that of Matthew. In a 1981 issue of *Sports Illustrated* promoter Bob Arum called Ayala, "The best young fighter I've ever seen in my life". Legendary trainer Angelo Dundee said of him, "There's no telling what he can do. This kid is going to be a champion." It was the start of the Four Kings era - Sugar Ray Leonard, Roberto Duran, Marvin Hagler and Thomas Hearns. It should have been five but fate decreed otherwise and a life of crime and drugs destroyed any hope 'El Torito' ever had of fighting alongside boxing royalty. It was a tragic waste for Ayala was truly special and nobody recognised this more than Brian, "This tape is worth $1million dollars Matthew. Go home and study it, son."

On finishing school, Matthew trained full time at the gym whilst learning Physical Education at college in the evening. Though there was never really any doubt that when he reached eighteen, he would be joining the professional ranks. Then came the moment of truth on 28th September, 2002, at the MEN Arena, on a Ricky Hatton undercard, Matthew took on forty-year-old veteran Pedro Thompson, from the Nobby Nobs journeyman stable. He was ready and primed to go - Matthew had sold all his tickets with Langley's finest off the estate roaring his name out amid the sold-out crowd. Desperate to make a good impression on his opening night, Matthew did so by finishing off Thompson in the first round. Job done, all appeared set for him to start building a long winning run, but trouble lurked around the corner.

Just five wins in, Matthew was stabbed in the stomach during an altercation in a Middleton pub while selling tickets. Rushed to North Manchester hospital, he spent a month in a High Dependency Unit.

Matthew had his bowel perforated in the attack losing huge amounts of blood, yet he couldn't feel sorry for himself, Matthew was more devastated for his mother and father seeing him so ill. Even on the darkest days Matthew remained positive and never looked back. He just wanted to fight again. To keep moving forward was his mantra from a young age and five months after being stabbed, in the December, he was urging Brian to let him fight but to no avail, "You're nowhere near ready, son," Brian advised, "you need to get well".

Finally, Matthew was allowed in the ring and somehow, despite being far from one hundred percent, he continued to get his boxing career back on track. A series of wins helped push him into the limelight as the old Matthew slowly started to reappear, only for disaster to strike once more when, almost two years to the day he was stabbed again. Matthew had refused to walk away from trouble on his estate and suffered a grim price. This time he was caught in the chest causing a collapsed lung. The injuries were becoming a major concern. They may have been enough to retire a man with an ordinary job, but for a fighter who earned his living through his strength and fitness it looked like Matthew's career would be over before it ever really began.

His body gave up and no amount of courage was sufficient. After stopping Kevin Phelan in the first round on 8th July, 2006, at the Millennium Stadium, Cardiff, Matthew was out for a year. His immune system was ravaged, he had drained every last drop from his system. Driven by sheer determination and a ferocious desire not to be taken down by either bad luck or circumstances, he came back. Remarkably, despite all that had gone on, Matthew was still sixteen fights unbeaten, if there were belts for bravery Langley's 'El Torito' would have been a pound for pound all-time great.

On 14th July, 2007, at the O2 Arena, London, Matthew returned and took on twenty-six-year-old Leicester born Martin Conception. It was a disaster, as he was clearly still not right. Matthew was dropped twice by Conception in the first round before the referee stepped in to halt the fight. Alarm bells would have sounded for most fighters, but not for Matthew who picked himself up off the canvas to go again. Still, all was not right, he had breathing problems that continue to this day. There were more trips to see doctors and specialists, but no proper or helpful diagnosis was ever forthcoming. And yet, despite it all, Matthew was not yet ready to quit. It appeared the best medicine for him was being in the gym amongst friends. There Matthew trained like a madman, finding comfort and solace in the sweat, tears and camaraderie of Collyhurst and Moston.

Just five months after the loss to Conception, Matthew was back in the ring. On 3rd December, 2007, at the Piccadilly Hotel, Manchester, he beat twenty-six-year-old Tyan Booth on points after an eight-round contest. It was a confidence booster for the young man who simply would not give up. Matthew fought next on 22nd March 2008, at the International arena in Cardiff. His opponent, twenty-seven-year-old Welshman Kerry Hope, who was in the same situation as his Mancunian opponent - neither could afford to lose. It turned into a slugfest with Matthew cut badly in the sixth by a clash of heads, but he was always on the front foot. Throughout the fight Joe Calzaghe had been shouting instructions to his stable mate from the front row. The behaviour of Hope's corner, specifically Joe's father Enzo, who was constantly screaming at their fighter, infuriated Brian Hughes, who deemed it unfair. Finally, in the seventh, despite the cut re-opening, Matthew nailed Hope and dropped him for a standing count. Sensing blood, Tysonesque, in black shorts and boots as always, Matthew went swinging punches in a style reminiscent of 'Iron Mike.' Come the next round an on-fire Matthew let fly once more with a flurry of low flying hooks that had Hope in desperate trouble. Looking ready to fold, the referee Grant Willis showed mercy and stopped the fight. 'El Torito' had blown the Welshman away and as Matthew went across to Enzo remonstrating with him at his behaviour, Brian Hughes turned his attention to Enzo's son Joe. Leaning through the ropes, Brian tore a strip off the young Calzaghe, who had Frank Warren alongside him. Brian was not having it, "It isn't your business to shout instructions," he raged, while Calzaghe listened stone-faced.

Three wins followed in swift succession setting Matthew up for a surprise title shot, as he cut loose igniting the kind of firepower visible before the stabbing incidents. The previous February Matthew had been promised a shot at the British title, but when Andrew Facey withdrew, Frank Warren moved fast and offered him another lifeline. On 14th March 2009, at the MEN Arena, on the undercard of the now legendary Amir Khan - Marco Barrera clash, Matthew took on Welshman Bradley

Pryce for his British Commonwealth Super Welterweight belt. Before the fight Pryce, another member of the Joe Calzaghe camp, said he was out to avenge the defeats suffered by three of his countrymen at the hands of Hall in his last four fights, most notably Kerry Hope.

"It's sweet sugar time. Hall has been talked up as the next big thing, but everyone I fight is supposed to be going places. He's a good puncher, but so am I. I love to go to war." Not surprisingly this cut little ice with Matthew, "I can't wait for the first bell to ring. I have heard all his boasting and what he's going to do to me. Well, we will see".

On the greatest night of his life Matthew Hall became the pride of Langley when he finished off Pryce with a right hand after forcing him into a corner at the end of round two. Matthew had him over three times before referee Ian John Lewis ended the bout on the bell. It was a stunning performance that electrified the MEN audience as they roared in salute to one of their own. Matthew had been threatening this kind of big-time performance ever since he first walked up those twenty steps aged just thirteen. Later that evening the party moved back home to the estate and the Woodman's pub. And, yet, there was a part of him, although ecstatic, that did not enjoy the attention. This only got worse as the days and weeks wore on. The constant focus on him proved overwhelming. Matthew's phone never stopped ringing, he was a local celebrity and invitations to open pubs, bars and restaurants wasn't for him - it was all about the fighting, not the adoration and the slaps on the back.

The reluctance to accept the plaudits came from Jimmy, who in turn had inherited it from his father and embedded it in both sons. He couldn't be doing with the mither, wasn't one for resting on his laurels, Matthew just wanted to get on with life. He was an ordinary, quiet guy from a council estate who simply wanted to go home after fighting. The following Monday, after the Pryce triumph, he was on the phone to Brian asking about the next fight. It was an addiction. People like him needed goals. Again, no matter how great or bad the moment, especially boxing, he had to keep moving forward. Always forward…

That period between winning and the next bout was a living nightmare for Matthew. To this day he has only watched the Pryce fight back once. Away from the ring Matthew ran a Sunday league football team with his good friend Johnny Joyce. It was simply a group of mates who got together and said let's win a few trophies and enjoy ourselves. They called themselves 'Langley Celtic' and came from the New Broom pub and played in the Middleton league. Though only midfield, Matthew tended to score lots of goals and this created a problem as all results and scorers were listed in the following week's local newspaper. Thus, he had to let somebody else take credit to avoid getting into trouble with Brian Hughes!

Matthew was not immune to being put upon by the gym's biggest wind up merchant, Thomas McDonagh. One time, while at home with his girlfriend Amy, he received a phone call off Thomas urging him to put BBC Asian network on the radio straight away because Brian was due on there to talk about him in an interview. Matthew did so and settled down to listen to the Punjabi speaking host, having absolutely no idea what he was talking about. An hour passed and no Brian, so he rang Thomas back,

"Tommy, he hasn't been on yet?"

"Just keep listening Matt, Brian is due on in the next hour."

"Okay mate, speak to you later."

Another hour passes and no Brian, so once more he rings Thomas. By this time a fed-up Amy has sent him to listen in the car!

"Still nothing Tommy, what's going on?"

"He's definitely on in the next half hour Matt. Keep listening, it will be well worth it."

Thirty minutes more go by and an English-speaking host comes on air, "Here we go" thinks Matthew. "At last!" Only for him to announce the next show will be the Punjabi top ten!

Again, he calls Tommy who simply burst out laughing....

Matthew had been done!

Next in the ring for 'El Torito' was a man he genuinely could not abide. On the 18th July, 2009, at the MEN Arena, Matthew took on twenty-eight-year-old Londoner Anthony Small for the vacant British Super Welterweight and his own Commonwealth title, chief support bout on the Amir Khan-Andreas Kotelnik bill. In a bitter build-up Small attempted to belittle Matthew from the moment the fight was made, "You're just a bully of a pub man who gets his mental strength from being stabbed twice."

Matthew now admits he let Small get inside his head with all his antics. It was a dangerous place for a fighter's opponent to be before the fight. Matthew trained hard, maybe too hard, as the all-consuming urge to rip Anthony Small's head off his shoulders became a worrying obsession. It was too much. After a week's postponement, the atmosphere at the final press conference slowly burned as the smell of sulphur and the desire in Matthew's eyes to shut the motor-mouth Small up electrified all present. One comment from him summed what was going on in Matthew's head. Said quietly but the intent was clear, "I want to dance on his face". Later, at the face off, the tensions continued as the Londoner carried on his clown act. Matthew, though clearly fuming, kept calm, only again to let slip his true feeling when finally letting fly, "I want to bite Small's nose off and strangle him with his title belt!"

Sadly, for Matthew, Small backed up his tirade of boasts by winning with an eighth round stoppage. From the off Matthew went after him but Small's unorthodox style proved maddeningly frustrating – the Londoner was full of feints and turns, a poor man's 'Sugar Ray' but grimly effective. Still gibbering on as the two fought inside, Small showed he could fight by taking some full bloodied shots on the ropes from Matthew before firing back with his own punches. As the fight reached the halfway stage it was too close to call.

The fight had failed to ignite as the bad blood in the build-up appeared to have affected both boxers. Matthew, whilst always going forward, at times appeared drained, while Small simply did not look fully committed to going for the kill. Content to posture, hold and maul, he threw few clear shots. Then, it all changed when a clash of heads opened up an old wound over Matthew's left eye. Whilst certainly no classic the fight was gripping as Matthew, clearly tiring badly, got another cut in the seventh, this time deeper and over the other eye. It proved just the encouragement Small needed as he finally showed his class and shook Matthew twice with vicious right hands. As the bell rang to finish the round, Brian Hughes bore the look of a worried man as he fought to stem the blood from Matthew's cuts. Knowing he was all but done with the injuries and being close to exhaustion, Matthew came out swinging, only for a slashing jab from Small to open his left eye, leaving it gushing blood again.

Bravely fighting on through a red mist, Matthew was caught by a perfect right hook that shook him badly. Sensing an opportunity to end it Small unleashed a combination that had the Mancunian wilting towards the canvas and in big trouble. Having seen enough, referee James Davies stepped in. It was all over. While Small won two championship belts he did not win many friends in Manchester that night. As Small came across to see how Matthew was, a seething Brian, furious at his behaviour pre-fight, told him in no uncertain terms where to go. It was only the intervention of cornerman Mike Jackson, who pulled Brian back, that prevented the potential of a Collyhurst nut on Small. Neverthless it was a bad night for a bloodied 'El Torito' despite a brave showing.

Devastated as he was by the defeat and the loss of his title, there was a part of Matthew that felt relieved. The phone didn't constantly ring anymore and there would be less hassle as he was left alone. It was a huge price to pay for a bit of privacy, but it provided some small comfort. Matthew's believed that, as sad as it was that he had lost the belt, there would always be another fight. His environment, the world he inhabited on Langley estate, had taught him that. Yet Matthew knew something wasn't right. His fighting talent inside the ring was on the wane. Matthew had peaked before the stabbings at around twenty years old. That would have been the time to strike. You can have all the will and courage in the world, he was testament to that, but if the body was not willing, then what occurred against Small would happen again. Never one for excuses, Matthew's thoughts turned to the next stage of his life.

Nobody wanted to listen to a hard luck story, all that mattered was what appeared in Box Rec. They look at wins and losses. Something drastic was called for and that included him leaving Brian Hughes and Collyhurst and Moston to join Anthony Farnell's gym in nearby Failsworth. Matthew did it the right way by going to see Brian at his home with Pat Barrett and explaining he needed a change. Matthew thanked him for everything but that he was twenty-four years old and it was time for pastures new. The pair shook hands and although they were both hurting, there were no hard feelings. How could there be?

Was it the right thing to do? Matthew looks back now and thinks perhaps not. Twelve years were ending on what he would also later recall as the best times of his life, a special place where he learned so much more than boxing. They were a group of friends who had grown up together and knew each other's lives inside out – they shared their hopes and fears training every day under Brian's watchful eye. Working, laughing and at times crying together, sharing victories and defeats.

All for one.

On 15th May, 2010, at West Ham's Upton Park and now under new management, Matthew returned to the ring and knocked out Tony Randall in the third round. This handed him a surprise crack at the vacant European Light-Middleweight title against the classy and vastly experienced Czech boxer, Lukas Konecny, following the withdrawal of Ryan Rhodes. Typically, Matthew had no hesitation stepping into Rhodes shoes when he was offered the shot at the last minute. However, on 18th September, 2010, at the LG Arena, Birmingham, the brilliant Konecny proved what a class fighter he was by stopping Matthew in the sixth. It was a blistering toe-to-toe contest that saw Konecny finally come out on top after both fighters stood in the centre of the ring for six rounds simply going for it. The wily and exciting Czech always appeared to have just that little bit extra. From the fourth onwards Konecny dominated and staggered Matthew with a left hook, then sent him to the canvas shortly after. Shattered, hurting and stung by the knockdown, Matthew came blazing back, looking for a miracle shot, only to walk onto a right hand that finished the fight. It was a blood-curdling contest. Afterwards Matthew said he really was ready to retire, for he felt there was nothing left to give. If this was to be a last hurrah for 'El Torito' it was one of which he could be proud. Matthew had given everything, but ultimately come up against an opponent who was just better. He paid tribute to Konecny calling him the best fighter he had faced, but what next?

In Matthew's personal life things were going well. He had become a father to two daughters who he claimed were what made his mind up to box again. Besides, what else was there for him? It was all about putting money on the table and now with children, the only place that guaranteed income was the ring. He made a phone call and in 2011, now being trained by his long-time friend Pat Barrett, he returned to Collyhurst and Moston. Once more he walked up those twenty steps, but what did he have left? By this time Brian Hughes had retired and the gym was now in the hands of Pat and Thomas McDonagh, students of Brian who were determined to carry on the traditions that had gone before them. On 28th September, 2011, at Bowlers Exhibition, Manchester, Matthew came dreadfully unstuck against an average Bulgarian, Alexey Ribchev and lost on points over six disappointing rounds. He looked a shadow of the fighter who once caused mayhem in the ring and it was sad to witness for those close to him. Not long afterwards Pat Barrett advised Matthew it really was time to retire. The kid from Langley who would always give anyone a fight was still willing, but the chances were that he would get hurt in the ring.

Matthew knew something else was not right. He was training harder than ever and was still only twenty-seven? Something did not add up. How could he suddenly be over the hill? The stomach problems still persisted, but not to the extent of affecting what occurred against Ribichev. After seeing a specialist Matthew had an operation on his nose that hopefully would cure the fatigue that affected him during fights. However, as one problem was solved, another showed itself when, after allergy tests, they found Matthew was now suffering from a fungal infection in his stomach called Candidiasis. Given medication and placed on a strict diet by specialists, the results were instant. After feeling he had finally got to the bottom of the problems that were affecting him in fights, Matthew, though respecting Pat Barrett's opinion, decided to fight on. After a heart to heart with Pat, he decided to return to Anthony Farnell's gym. Now a successful trainer, Farnell welcomed him back with open arms and the journey continued on a hope, prayer and the sheers guts of a fighting kid from Langley.

On 25th November, 2011, at the Ravenscraig Sports Centre, Motherwell, Matthew took on twenty-seven-year-old home town lad Kris Carslaw in a British Light Middleweight Title Eliminator. He appeared reborn; the fitness, strength and power had returned and finally Matthew looked to have overcome the problems hindering him in past fights. Rolling back the years he boxed with real authority and won deservedly over ten rounds to claim a unanimous decision. 'El Torito' was back.

That impressive victory handed Matthew the opportunity of a final British title eliminator. On 28th April, 2012, at the Royal Albert Hall,

Matthew took on thirty-two-year-old former champion Sam Webb, but on a bitterly disappointing night, when most present thought he had done enough to win, Webb took it on a split decision. Even though his hand was not raised, the performance made Matthew realise that he had regained the lung power to go the distance and looked forward to fighting on. Just three months later on 14th July, 2012, at West Ham's Upton Park, he took on the unbeaten twenty-six-year-old Irishman Gary O'Sullivan for the vacant WBO International Middleweight title. Even though it was a step up in weight to fight O'Sullivan, Matthew was extremely confident he had the talented Cork man's measure. Again, on a terribly disappointing evening, Matthew lost on a unanimous decision. This loss hurt him more than the Webb fight, for he had convinced himself his performance had been good enough to win.

The hunger and desire to fight on after two almighty kicks in the teeth remained and that November at the MEN Arena, Matthew beat Lee Noble on points. Yet something was wrong, mentally he was a mess and had been for a long time. The stabbing injuries had left him not only physically impaired, but mentally Matthew was still struggling to deal with it. Nobody goes through that without lingering consequences, especially a professional boxer who puts his life on the line every time he stepped into the ring. There remained fuel in the tank, but the engine was starting to stutter badly.

A last chance came when Matthew was offered the opportunity to fight one of Frank Warren's up and coming superstars, the gypsy warrior – twenty-five-year-old Billy Joe Saunders. At stake would be Saunder's British and Commonwealth Middleweight titles. On 21st March, 2013, at the legendary boxing venue of York Hall, Bethnal Green, the kid who fought with his brother, whilst Jimmy Glass and his mates cheered on Mike Tyson at three in the morning, gave everything and more against the brilliant Saunders. That he lost on a unanimous decision mattered little, Matthew had shown, despite all that had gone on before in his career, that 'El Torito' had come to fight, never taken a backward step and at the last bell he was still standing. Billy Joe Saunders said himself after the fight, "He's a tough fella, and the hardest fighter I've boxed in the pros."

Yet still the fighter wasn't finished. Two years later on 18th April, 2015, at the Sports Centre Oldham, Matthew took on Dan Blackwell and despite severely damaging his knee ligaments in the ring, he won a points decision. Still not officially retired, this remains Matthew's last fight. Will we ever see him climb once more through the ropes? Never say never.

In 2016, Matthew was involved in an incident that saw him serve twelve months at Her Majesty's pleasure. Although missing his family dreadfully, he found the solitary lifestyle almost a relief from the world outside. Matthew trained constantly, whilst many inmates did it to look good, he was getting ready for war. "Always be prepared to fight" was his personal motto. Endless hours were spent on the treadmill. Looking around Matthew realised what he believed was wrong with the world. There was no discipline inside, the legal high 'Spice' was taking over. Everything was changing and not for the better.

On his release Matthew found himself unable to switch off from this fighting mentality. Psychiatrists and doctors struggled to help as he tried to adapt to life outside. It was only then that he realised that there really was no place like home - therapy could be found on Lightbowne Road, so Matthew started helping out at the gym.

Still only thirty-two, he adores boxing. Matthew is a walking encyclopaedia of boxer's strengths and weaknesses. He regularly receives calls from fighters with upcoming bouts asking his advice. This was the kind of hassle on the phone he could handle! However, when it came to the subject of becoming a trainer, Matthew felt himself too old school and his manner too 'abrupt' to suited the modern fighter. The truth often hurts and his brand of advice would not go down well with today's generation. Hearing young boxers talking of three months to prepare for a journeyman fight drives him to despair. Matthew would pull them aside, "Three months? What happens if you walk out the gym today and are surrounded by ten guys who want to attack you? You have to be ready today. Not tomorrow or the week after. Now!"

What does warm his heart is the emergence of two young fighters raised from the Collyhurst and Moston crèche in the old ways: Zelfa Barrett and Lyndon Arthur. Here are two local kids blessed with natural talent, but more importantly learning their trade in the best place possible. They were prepared to listen and stick to a formula that is now one hundred years old. History never ages, it just grows with riches. Endless hours spent in sweat-stained sessions improving their technique until it came naturally. Like smiling at a beautiful girl or enjoying a wonderful song. Most importantly they are both hungry and prepared to take everything on board and then to practice, practice and practice some more. They know the riches in store tomorrow for today's sacrifices.

Zelfa and Lyndon have been raised on what can be achieved if you dream the impossible dream. Recently Matthew was overlooking a twelve-round spar with Lyndon who finished almost on the floor, "Not good enough son" he declared. Swiftly Lyndon was back in the ring doing another two more! It was all about the present. If they do not go onto great things Matthew will be the first to tell them to their faces that they have under-achieved.

When it came to the best fighter Matthew has seen coming out of the gym, he does not hesitate, "Robin Reid. Robbie was somebody who struggled doing a press up, but put a glove on him and he was on a different level." When Matthew started as a seventeen-year-old he was desperate to impress whenever sparring against Reid, but had his head jabbed off. However, it all proved worthwhile for when up against fellow amateurs Matthew would simply destroy them, for they were never in Robbie's class.

And then there is Brian Hughes, undoubtedly the greatest trainer in Matthew's eyes, "They talk of Emanuel Steward and Angelo Dundee, but both possessed a huge pond of fighters to pick from. They were already made, it was just a question of refining and improving them. Whereas Brian got the scraps. Robbie apart, whoever walked up those twenty steps dreaming of a pot of gold were gloved up and given a chance."

For Matthew Hall the fight goes on, but these days he is blessed with the thought that while Brian Hughes may no longer be in his corner, there are people much more important behind him, no matter what - his family: fiancée Amy and his daughters Oliveay, Lola and Ruby.

With those by your side, no fight is ever lost.

16 - SCOTT QUIGG

DISCIPLE

Although born and bred Mostonians may beg to differ, there is little comparison to be made between sun-drenched Los Angeles and the rainy murky, damp Mancunian air. that surrounds the environs of Collyhurst. In terms of climate and lifestyle they are a world apart. However, there is a trait that links them, one that can't be measured by distance or surroundings – for both possess a fighting heart. There may be 5281 miles between The Collyhurst and Moston gym on Lightbowne Road to Freddie Roach's legendary Wild Card gym at 1123 Vine Street in Hollywood but both institutions train their fighters in a manner that does boxing proud. They are run along similar values in belonging to the community as well as hosting elite fighters. As at Collyhurst and Moston, everybody who enters there is greeted warmly. You pay a small fee but are expected to train hard. Whether you are an overweight window cleaner struggling to get up and down his ladder and desperate to lose weight or the hottest prospect in the world of boxing, all are treated with the same cordial respect. One kid, born in Bury on 9th October, 1988, has been blessed to experience both gyms. Once a disciple of Brian Hughes, he made the journey to LA to tread the same path as the greats. So how did a kid from Bury end up being a stable-mate of modern day legends such as Manny Pacquaio and Miguel Cotto?

AGED JUST FOURTEEN, sports mad Scott Quigg recognised that despite working hard in lessons, school work at Elton High Boys was just not his forte. It was beyond maddening. Nothing was working. It all came to a head during mock exams when in his favourite subject of maths, after studying so hard and revising for weeks beforehand, Scott's exam paper was returned to him littered with red crosses.

So, he took a chance. After a heart-to-heart with his mother, Lindsay, and father, Kenny, Scott explained he was desperate to make it as a boxer or a footballer and the more time there was to train, the better his chance of success. He promised them to give it his all. Scott knew he wasn't cut out for academic pursuits but he could box and play football better than anyone in the school and most in the district. Wanting only the best for their son and proud to hear him talk sense, they went to see his head teacher. After listening to them he agreed to let him go, so long as Scott agreed to attend a part-time college course. He happily went along and walked out of the school gates for the final time.

True to his word, Scott threw himself into sport especially, at first, football. Scott was outstanding in the league in which he played and scouts soon lined the touchlines at games. Trials were forthcoming with Barnsley, his home town club Bury and Manchester City but it was Burnley who decided to take him. All was going to plan. Working feverishly, it became apparent even at just fifteen that he gave everything and more. However, disappointment arrived when after just a year at Turf Moor Scott was released. The excuse given was that he was too small and prone to being knocked off the ball far too easily, this in an age when clubs were throwing their hat on six foot plus teenagers and going for power over skill. Refusing to be bowed Scott threw himself into his beloved Muay Thai (Thai boxing). He had been attending classes since he was ten at GFC Muay Thai boxing club in Bury and returned there many times during his spell at Burnley in an effort to build up his strength. Driven in everything he attempted, Scott excelled and became undefeated British champion. At just fifteen he fought professionally on live television against a former European champion and won. Great things were expected, but the boxing ring was now calling.

One day when out running he was spotted by the brilliant amateur boxing coach, Mick Jelley. He asked Scott about doing some work with him and from that moment there was no looking back. Though Scott adored Muay Thai, he had only concentrated on it because their gym was closer. To box had always been a first love. After just seven fights Scott entered the ABA's and won them, it was an astonishing achievement. He enjoyed a decent three-year amateur career, capped by boxing for England and by eighteen Scott was ready to go professional. Just to ensure there were no lingering doubts in his son's mind, his father

Kenny took him to the window-making factory where he worked and handed him a sweeping brush. For three days at £20 a day, Scott swept the floors. He was told by his father to look at the faces of the other lads working there. Dead eyed – they already appeared resigned to a lifetime of crippling boredom, "See how miserable they are Scott. Is that what you want?"

Kenny Quigg had been a promising footballer, but a lack of dedication cost him dear, "Don't spend your life doing something like this, son. Go and chase your dream and give it all you've got."

From that moment on Scott would never give anything less than one hundred per cent and he was heading for a place where that was not just expected, but demanded. Towards the end of his amateur career Scott was already training with pros in a place heaven sent for a lad who did not just live for boxing, but ate, slept and drank it, making the transition to professional ranks a relatively smooth one. His natural good manners, respect and almost fanatical desire to become better made the Bury youngster a perfect fit to train full time at Collyhurst and Moston. Brian Hughes took to him from the off. Extremely polite and with a willingness to learn, Scott had wonderful talent, "You'll make it Scott," were some of Brian's first words to him.

Examples of Brian's sage advice continued to drip into Scott's consciousness and stick in his head, "You can have a nice-looking house son, but if the foundations aren't solid, it won't last long." He taught Scott the art of boxing, when to throw and when not to, how to slip a punch, it was a boxing education priceless to a lad desperate to learn and who soaked up every bit of advice and worked like a Trojan. Training the youths, Brian would get one of the lads to throw a jab first of all and the other had to slip it from left to right, like a windscreen wiper with his arms held behind his back. This would be for three three-minute rounds. Then blocking, where most boxers made a salute, Collyhurst and Moston boxers were trained to do it the old way - put the left hand out and it dropped like a hook, this would be used to block or parry their opponent's right.

Brian also recommended to his boxers to watch the all-time greats on DVD. He would stretch back into the sport's history and pluck out the best it had to offer. His favourites were Americans like Willie Pep, mainly for foot and head movement, while the Frenchman Johnny

Famechon was a genius at blocking - the former Featherweight world champion would wait, patient like a cat stalking a mouse and then always counter beautifully. Everything was about focus, total concentration and discipline. Brian knew boxing was a brutally savage sport, but beyond the blood and thunder and the desire to hurt your opponent, you had to be able to defend yourself at all times. To him boxing was a science. A beautiful, if dangerous one at that.

For Scott's personal viewing Brian picked a selection of Hispanic greats: Wilfredo Gomez, Ruben Olivares and Alexis Arguello. He would point out certain aspects of each fighter, how they moved their head or set up opponents before letting fly, how all three hit from incredible angles. Scott would sit dazzled, absorbing it all. This was boxing's version of splitting the atom or solving apparently impossible mathematical equations.

Scott also watched wide-eyed in awe when Brian was around people. Whether they were young or old, rich or poor, famous or anonymous, it mattered little. He treated them all with such respect, "Always treat people, how you would want to be treated. It costs nothing to be decent" was another Hughes motto. Absorbing these lessons in life were equally important as learning about fighting techniques – such was life up the twenty stairs to heaven.

On 27th April, 2007, at the Piccadilly Hotel, Manchester, Scott made his professional debut against Gary Sheils, winning comfortably on points over six rounds. It was a good start and kick-started a further eighteen victories over a three-year spell. One of his biggest fans was Manchester boxing legend and former world champion and by then promoter, Ricky Hatton. He signed Scott on in 2009 and spoke highly of him, "Scott is sensational. I see a lot of myself in him. He is an exciting fighter, a body puncher - a crowd pleaser and a great ticket seller. Scott is also a great trainer and that's vital. There is no point in having the talent if you've not got the will and determination to put in the training. On top of all that, he's a nice kid, down to earth and when you add that to everything else he's got, you're going to have a chance of going all the way."

Scott didn't stop trying to improve. At just twenty years old, he demonstrated the true extent of his ambition by paying £5,500 for a month's training at Freddie Roach's fabled Wild Card Gym in Los Angeles. Roach would rave about him. A proud Brian Hughes spoke with a father's pride when asked how his young prodigy was coping Stateside, "I've had brilliant reports back about Scott. They're saying he's a future world champion. He's got all the attributes, but Scott also listens and wants to learn. Anybody who sees him, like Freddie, agrees he is an outstanding prospect." Scott had to grow up fast at the Wild Card, for sparring sessions were like wars and so much harder than any professional fight he had taken part in at that time. In many ways Roach shared the essential values of Brian Hughes, they were kindred spirits in Scott's eyes and though he was on the other side of the world, he felt strangely at home.

Finally, a shot arrived at the vacant WBA Inter Continental Super Bantamweight title against Argentinian Santiago Allione. With Brian and Mike Jackson in his corner, Scott hammered Ollione into a third-round stoppage to delight his home town. Over a thousand fans, including all the fighters from Collyhurst and Moston, raised the roof as one of their own was handed the belt. "Well done," whispered Brian at the finish, "This is just the start". Along with his proud parents who watched through tear-filled eyes, their boy living his dream, Brian was the one he so wished to please.

In the first defence of his title, on 26th November, 2010, at the De Vere Whites Hotel, Bolton against the tough Daniel Kodjo Sassou, Scott impressed hugely to win on points and easily outclass the Frenchman over twelve rounds. He had him down on the canvas in the eighth and dominated throughout and never looked like losing. Immediately afterwards, Scott thanked Brian Hughes for his meticulous planning to see off the cagey, resilient Sassou, who had lost just once in four years, "Brian is a genius. I'll probably be looking for a British title fight next year, but I am still learning and couldn't have better people around me for advice. When Brian says the time is right, it will be right."

What happened next shocked everyone and none more than Scott. In April 2011, seventy-one-year-old Brian Hughes MBE announced his retirement from the sport. It was all over, a lifetime's painting on a never-ending canvas of a boxing ring, was finally left to dry. Fifty years spent dedicated to helping youngsters off the street and giving them a dream of something better came to an end. Not that the pot of gold up those twenty steps had disappeared, it had merely been handed over to the next generation. For once, thinking of himself, Brian declared he was sad to leave the club, but he wanted to spend more time with his family.

"For the past fifty years I have devoted my life to the club and unfortunately it has had to end for me, but I wish the lads all good wishes and pray they become a credit to their families and themselves."

Then, with a last walk down those fabled steps, Brian bid the empire he had built a final goodbye. It was a fitting and typically classy departure by the man.

As for Scott, he was left devastated by Brian's departure. Losing such a huge influence on his life was eased by the fact that Pat Barrett and Thomas McDonagh carried on the day-to-day running of the club and some experts believed the loss of his long-term mentor might affect his prospects. It was a case of the show must go on and Pat took over Brian's role as Scott's trainer. They were good friends and it worked well - six months on from beating Sassou, he defended his belt in Bury once more against a dangerous thirty-year-old Venezuelan, Franklin Varela with Pat Barrett and Mike Jackson now in his corner

From the opening bell Scott was relentless, almost methodical, in wearing down the tough Venezuelan. Come the seventh a vicious series of left hooks to the body finished off the South American and an elated Scott took the acclaim of his home crowd. Heads were being turned. Scott Quigg was proving to be the real deal and it sure beat sweeping up for a living.

The impressive victory over Varela would be the last time Scott would fight out of the Collyhurst and Moston gym. He left to join the Joe Gallagher camp across town that included superb boxers such as Anthony Crolla, Joe Murray, Paul Smith, Liam Smith and Stephen Smith. It wasn't a case of any problems with Pat Barrett and his training methods, just a feeling that he had gone stale after being in one place for too long. Also, Scott was the only professional left training there regularly, at this stage of his career and he needed regular top-class sparring partners. Huge fights were on the horizon. When Scott first arrived at the gym fighters such as Michael Jennings, Thomas McDonagh, Matthew Hall, Tony Doherty and Gary Lockett were all regulars and every day was a battle. Suddenly everything had changed –

after Brian's retirement there was an exodus from the gym and Pat and Thomas had to start from scratch.

In terms of his career it was the right choice for Scott - boxers have to be selfish, anyone who has the guts to climb through those ropes has the right to think about themselves first and foremost in this toughest and most dangerous of sports. It was their life, their risk; they took the punches and faced the consequences. Knowing exactly how Scott felt, Pat and Tommy wished him nothing but the best, there were no hard feelings. Collyhurst and Moston remained in Scott's heart. It wasn't so much 'goodbye' but until we meet again. because, like the vast majority who have walked up those steps, something will always pull them back.

Scott's rise continued against reigning British Super-Bantamweight champion Jason Booth; a stunning display saw him stop the thirty-four-year-old in the seventh as he dominated the dangerous Nottingham fighter from the off. Sharper and quicker, Scott also possessed more power, his punches were snappy and body shots troubled the older fighter badly. Scott hunted Booth down relentlessly until finally it was all over when his corner pulled him out of the fight. Twenty-two-year-old Scott Quigg was the British Super Bantamweight champion and was full of respect for his opponent, "To win this British title means a hell of a lot and to beat Jason and share the ring with such a great fighter makes it even more worthwhile."

Not long after his victory, Scott went to see his old mentor, now settled into retirement - as they embraced in Brian Hughes' living room, an emotional Scott handed him the title belt, "I would not have been able to do this without you, Brian." Clearly moved, Brian went on to tell him that if he ever wrote a book on how to make a fighter become great, then Scott would be the ideal student for he had all the right ingredients, "The only thing stopping you Scott is yourself. One day" he claimed smiling, "One day when you are world champion they will not only make you Lord Mayor of Bury, but it will be Sir Scott Quigg!"

Just four months on from winning his British title, Scott defended it in a stunning manner against proud Welsh warrior Jamie Arthur. After being dropped by Arthur in the fourth and taking an eight count, Scott survived the first major crisis of his career by storming back in the eighth and stopping the gutsy Welshman from Cwambran. Well on top going into the defining eighth round, he landed a series of ferocious body shots and cut Arthur, prompting referee Mark Green to end the fight. Arthur's corner were in uproar, but their man was already well beaten and Green's prompt actions made perfect sense.

Finally, the opportunity arose to challenge for a world belt and on 16th June 2012, at the Velodrome, Manchester, Scott faced twenty-two-year-old Leicester born, Rendall Munroe, for the WBA Interim Super-Bantamweight title. Sadly, for all, it ended in bitter disappointing circumstances after a horrendous cut stopped the fight in just the third round. An accidental clash of heads opened a huge gash above Munroe's right eye, resulting in a technical draw being called. Munroe's frustration was obvious, but the encounter simply could not go on with his eyebrow completely split. It was a real shame as the contest had shown signs of developing into a classic, but as Munroe's wound poured with blood, the doctor ended proceedings. There were immediate calls for a rematch and five months later, on 24th November, 2012, the pair fought once more at the same venue. This time it proved conclusive as Scott outgunned the Leicester man to claim the title. The fight was stopped at the end of the sixth after he twice had Randall on the canvas with sharp body punches. The referee stepped in and the pride of Bury celebrated with new coach Joe Gallagher. It was merciless from Scott, showing that despite all his technical prowess, there was power to finish fights at this elite level.

Suddenly the drums began to beat loudly for a huge unification fight with the pride of Belfast and Scott's bitter rival Carl Frampton, the-then reigning IBF World Super Bantamweight champion. This was a clash all boxing fans were desperate to see. To ease the path to the fight, Scott left Ricky Hatton and signed a five-fight promotional contract with Eddie Hearn's Matchroom Promotions. On 29th June, 2013, at the Bolton Arena, on his debut for Matchroom, Scott took out the tough Brazilian William Prado in three rounds. He dropped Prado in the second before finishing him off with body shots in the third. Punch-perfect from the opening bell; Scott was getting better with every fight.

The following September he was elevated to the status of world champion by the WBA, this came ahead of his first title defence that took place on 5th October, 2013, at the O2 Arena against Miami based Cuban Yoandris Salinas. Scott was forced to dig deep to keep his title and come the end the judges declared him a winner by majority decision.

Against a world-class opponent in Salinas, Scott was happy enough with his performance, "I've proved now I belong at world level," he said afterwards.

Next time around he did not dare risk leaving it to the judges, taking out the tough twenty-eight-year-old Argentine Diego Oscar Silva in the second round in Manchester. It was a clinical, no-nonsense showing as Scott put the struggle against Salinas behind him and continued onto a journey towards the Frampton fight. On 19th April, 2014, again at the Phones4U arena, against thirty-four-year-old, South African, Thisifiwa Munyai, he topped the Manchester bill for the first time in his career and proved to be on another level to the outclassed veteran - Scott had him on the canvas in the first and ended proceedings in the second.

The command performance continued unabated. On 13th September, 2014, Scott returned to the Phones4U Arena to fight former European bantamweight Champion, twenty-five-year-old Belgian Stephane Jamoye. Viewed as a dangerous character, Scott broke him in just three rounds - body shots did the damage wearing down Jamoye until it all proved too much. Two months later at the Echo Arena, Liverpool, seven-year unbeaten Japanese Super Bantamweight champion, thirty-three-year-old Hidenori Otake, proved a much tougher opponent for the now, well-established WBA World Champion. Quigg won a unanimous decision as the brave Japanese fighter survived the last few rounds with a seeping cut over his right eye. Scott's power had troubled him throughout, but come the end Otake survived to leave the ring beaten, but unbowed. Yet there was bad news for Scott as during the fight he tore two tendons in his right hand that caused him to undergo an operation in December 2014.

Scott recovered and seven months later on 18th July, 2015, at the Manchester Arena, he entered the ring for the most important fight of his career against former IBF Super Bantamweight world champion, twenty-nine-year-old Spaniard Kiko Martinez. Win this and Carl Frampton and a genuine super-fight would await. Martinez had previously come unstuck and lost his world title to Frampton, but in their two previous fights it had taken the brilliant Irishman a total of twenty-one rounds to bring Martinez to heel. A tough contest was expected but, as ever, Scott rose to the occasion when he destroyed Martinez in just two rounds. It was brutal. A savage body shot caught

Martinez that put him down in the second and although he managed to beat the count, the Spaniard was met by a flurry of ferocious punches to head and body that ended his night and set up the golden ticket for the boy from Bury who had given everything for the sport he loved.

After the phony war, the tension and the name-calling, emotions overflowed as Carl Frampton and Scott Quigg finally entered the ring on 27th February, 2016, at the Manchester Arena to do battle for the WBA and IBF World Super Bantamweight titles. There had been heated words and minor skirmishes between the camps at both the final press conference and the weigh-in. It was clear that the boxers disliked each other. There was an intensity in Scott's eyes that many had not seen when it came to previous opponents and amid the pre-fight nonsense a dispute arose about who would use the biggest dressing room on fight night? Frampton's manager, the great Barry McGuigan, who had been there seen it and done it all twice, was looking for every possible edge before that first bell rang. Both fighters stood their ground over this clearly psychological move to unsettle Scott. Frampton even hinted, with a glint in his eye, that he might walk away from the contest. With the Irish claiming rightful use of the larger room because they viewed their boy as the real star of the show, Joe Gallagher was equally adamant that as this was Scott's hometown it should be his. Finally, the matter was dealt with by locking the said room and neither man used it - however, McGuigan appeared just a little too pleased with this solution and it appeared to be a victory for the 'Jackal'.

Ultimately, it turned into a disastrous night for Scott as he lost out to Frampton on a split decision. For the first time Scott tasted bitter defeat. The Northern Irishman sent his vast and vociferous army of travelling fans amongst a twenty thousand sell-out crowd, into ecstasy as he deservedly won on the night. Frampton got the nod courtesy of two 116-112 counts in his favour with the third judge giving it to Scott 115-113. Whilst never the epic many predicted, it became a real spectacle in the last quarter as Scott fought desperately to claw back points after a terribly slow start. Despite all the pre-fight hype, the opening rounds failed to catch fire as both appeared apprehensive and neither landed anything of note, although Frampton was always on the front foot. As the contest evolved Scott improved, but by this time he was fighting with a broken jaw sustained in round four. By the eighth a proper fight broke out with both opening up and the ninth saw Scott land a thunderous right hand that for a fleeting moment shook Frampton badly. Suddenly the contest everybody had hoped for broke out and at the final bell, all the bad mouthing and hyperbole was forgotten as the fighters embraced. The decision of the judges was fair, it had been Carl Frampton's night.

As for Scott; the old adage that you can't keep a good man down proved itself again when, ten months on from the Frampton heartache and with his broken jaw now fixed, he returned to the ring like a man on a mission. On 10th December, 2016, at the MEN Arena, Scott took on twenty-nine-year-old Mexican Jose Cayetano for the vacant WBA international Featherweight title. Typically, Scott had chosen no easy route back, for the man from Tijuana had been around. Mexicans don't do rollovers and so it proved once more before Scott finally caught up with him in the ninth. Fighting at a higher weight did not seem to affect Scott as he went about his business against the brave and resilient Cayetano. Rounds six and seven saw Scott move into overdrive as he began to catch the Mexican. Cayetano settled on the ropes, hitting back with decent counter punching. Remaining patient, Scott bided his time and come round nine he opened up to leave his opponent reeling. His power overwhelmed a brave opponent as he finally cornered and outgunned him. Talk of a rematch with Carl Frampton remained on the lips of most British fight fans, but what happened just two months later brings our story full circle.

After six years together Scott split from trainer Joe Gallagher in a move that was described by all as amicable, "I believe I need a fresh challenge to help me grow. Over the last few weeks I've been in America training and I'm delighted to announce I will be basing myself in Los Angeles at Freddie Roach's Wild Card gym."

With warmer climes and different dreams, Scott was still the same kid from Bury, who had gone from gloomy, rain-lashed Mancunian mornings, walking up those twenty steps to heaven at Collyhurst and Moston, and was now staring into Hollywood sunsets.

Brian Hughes would be proud.

17 - GIO-GOI
WHERE ANGELS PLAY

Forever associated with their world famous GIO-GOI fashion label, what is less known about the Donnelly family is that they have a huge interest and love for boxing stretching back to the seventies when Uncle Jimmy (the Weed) Donnelly, was involved in promoting a series of shows. So, on hearing that Collyhurst and Moston's WBU Intercontinental Welterweight champion Michael Jennings was a huge fan of their clothes, they simply could not resist the chance to sponsor him. It was Christopher Donnelly who was first introduced to the delights of the gym. On reaching forty, after doing some boxing as a kid, he fancied jumping back in the ring and it was Michael who suggested going to the gym. At first Christopher was unsure for he knew of its reputation and the calibre of fighters who trained there. Happily, Michael put him at ease, "Don't worry," he said, "I'll have a word with Tommy McDonagh and let him know you're coming down." Feeling a little comforted by this, Christopher had no idea what lay in wait!

THE FIRST DAY HE WALKED UP THE STEPS Christopher was nervous but determined not to show it. He entered the gym bold as brass, acting like he did not have a care in the world and suddenly the stereo music was turned off and all eyes were on him. Trying hard not to look intimidated he called out loud, "Mike, Mike, where are you?" Suddenly Michael Jennings appeared and introduced Christopher first to Pat Barrett and then a smiling Thomas McDonagh.

"Come with me Chris," Thomas said, "let's go play hide the sausage in the changing rooms!" A penny for Christopher's thoughts at that time as Thomas led him away. Later he would come to realise this was a rite of passage line used by Thomas to welcome all newcomers!

After getting changed Thomas returned, "Time to get you warmed up!" He took him to the bags – "on here Chris, mate". As he looked up Christopher saw a who's who of English boxing at that time; Pat Barrett, Matthew Hall, Tyson Fury, his father John and Robbie Reid. Luckily, as a youngster, Christopher had knocked a bag around a little so did not embarrass himself. However, after giving it everything for a minute, and being unfit, he was almost out on his feet! Christopher also remembers seeing Brian Hughes eyeing him with a little suspicion as if to say, what is this friend of Michael's doing here during the professional's time? On finishing the bag Christopher joined the others to train, but could sense a little distance. It would take a few sessions before he felt really comfortable and that came when the others started taking the mickey! It took Brian a little longer to acknowledge him not even as a boxer, but just as one of the lads' pals trying to get fit, but it came in time. Even in those early days Christopher could feel the history and heritage that surrounded everything at Collyhurst and Moston. He knew his fight history and Brian's status in the sport and felt it was a privilege to be allowed to train in such company at such a boxing institution.

Years before Christopher's brother Anthony was involved in serious trouble at a Manchester nightclub. Events had turned nasty and it was Pat Barrett who helped him out of a potentially sticky situation. Unknown to Christopher, for the first twelve months, Pat wrongly believed he was Anthony and mentioned in passing to Michael Jennings, "I can't believe how ignorant Anthony is after what happened? He comes in here every day and just waves." Finally, the situation was cleared up and Pat pulled Christopher for a chat, "Bloody ell," he said laughing, "I thought you was your kid!"

When it came to sparring Thomas never had any problems putting Christopher in with the top professionals because he knew they would go easy on him. Whether it was Michael Jennings, or another top prospect, there was enough respect in the gym to ensure Christopher never came to any harm. It simply wasn't that type of environment. However, one time when sparring with Lyndon Arthur, he caught the brilliant youngster and watched in mortal horror as Lyndon's face changed before his very eyes! Immediately, a worried Christopher grabbed hold of him in a bearhug, pleading, "Come on now Lyndon! Remember I'm old enough to be you dad!" Luckily, a laughing Thomas rang the bell and it all ended peacefully with an embrace! There were many other times Christopher would spar and his opponent would not be allowed to hit back. He was simply in there to work on head movement. Again, this was something Christopher considered an honour and he felt so proud just to share a ring with these fighters.

He was there when Brian retired and remembers how all of a sudden it went from a proper, mad-busy boxing gym to total silence. Loyal to Thomas and Pat, Christopher remained training there when many left, but in all honestly, it appeared back in those dark days as if there was little future for the gym. An endgame loomed and it was something he simply could not stomach. Suddenly, after racking his brains thinking how he could help out, Christopher had an idea. His expertise lay in creativity, giving people something different, but with its own particular style - streetwise with a touch of class.

Gio Goi went to work.

Christopher approached Thomas and Pat about arranging white collar boxing tournaments. The plan was to put the fights on in Manchester hotels such as the Midland and the Palace using Collyhurst and Moston during open hours for the public to let the competitors train and hold meetings. Not surprisingly, Thomas McDonagh had an interesting way of greeting the new arrivals, "Hiya lads! Now you've all got normal jobs and so what you have to remember is that there can be no sex because you're now in training. So, I will do you a favour and deal with all your wives and girlfriends on condition that after the fights have happened, you tell them to stop ringing me."

Welcome to Collyhurst and Moston!

This influx of fighters gave the club an immediate new lease of life and fantastic energy. To help organise this Christopher brought in the only person he knew who could possibly make it all happen, his sister Tracey. She swiftly went to work. They needed something that would give not just boxing fans but couples a fantastic night out. Thomas and Pat took her to a professional show in Blackpool and Tracey could not believe how bad it was. There was no build up, the whole thing was dour and dull - outside the ring nothing happened. This was not Gio-Goi, but she knew what was. They would make their shows flamboyant. There would be huge television screens where fighters would be interviewed and shown beforehand. These were just normal lads who wanted their fifteen minutes of fame, so a dramatic entrance with fireworks and smoke machines was essential – the same treatment the pros get. It was an attempt to bring white collar boxing into the twenty-first century.

Unsurprisingly the events were a huge success, playing to audiences of 700 to 800 people. With Robbie Reid refereeing and a stylish if drunken audience roaring on the fighters, they were spectacular nights – innovative, sexy and Manchester to their core. There can be no doubt whatsoever that these events electrified and brought something new to boxing. Sky Sports took note. Tracey adored being involved, but more for being able to help out Thomas and Pat. She loved the gym and just being privy to "lad's time" as she called it - the energy and the banter and the friendships. Treated as just one of the gang, her love pretend hate relationship with Thomas remains the same today. His greeting of Tracey, as 'Princess' then followed shortly after by 'Fiona' (from Shrek) repeatedly giving him cause to need his famed defensive skills!

It was around this time that Christopher was sat in the Collyhurst and Moston changing rooms after just getting changed from a session. He was set to leave when in walked Michael Jennings. Known for being pretty forthright, Michael looked at Christopher and declared, "You've been training here for two years, isn't it time you had a f-----g fight!" The same thought had been playing on Christopher's mind for a while and he set about putting matters right. It was to be against someone he had a bit of history with and the same person was digging him out beforehand, in the white-collar world of website forums, whilst the two trained. Also, there was a huge weight difference with Christopher fighting at twelve stone while his opponent was three stone heavier. On the night, at a packed Midland, with Thomas McDonagh's brother Frank in his corner and friends and family screaming him on, Christopher won. It was a proud moment, made even more special on his next visit to Collyhurst and Moston, when entering, he was met by Robbie Reid, "Well done mate" he said as the former world champion shook his hand, "You can come in here now and say you're a fighter." That really touched him.

What a wonderful thing to hear in this place where angels play.

It cannot be underestimated just how much respect and love the gym is held in by the Donnellys and especially Christopher and Tracey. Christopher has seen youngsters like Zelfa Barrett and Lyndon Arthur grow from boys to young men and their talent, reared in the traditional

Collyhurst and Moston way by Thomas and Pat, is now set to explode on the world of professional boxing. For Christopher, walking up those twenty steps now feels like entering his living room. Over the years he thought nothing of turning up with boxes of Gio-Goi stuff for the lads, many of whom had nothing, but that gym, and the hope it offered to keep them going. Some would train with the same clothes they had walked in with. Training tops, shorts, trousers and trainers – Christopher would dress the fighters, no questions asked. Nothing was ever too much trouble.

Tracey recognises the impact Thomas and Pat have on kids from the local community, "A lot of them are close to being out of control and lost and they drag them back and offer a way out. Theirs' is a special relationship – Thomas and Pat don't just have each other's backs, but they also care about everyone in that gym and those who have helped them out through the tough times."

Like Christopher, Tracey views Collyhurst and Moston as unique. It is living and breathing Mancunian history – one hundred years not out. Gio-Goi recognise class when they see it, and make no mistake from up those twenty steps, the feeling is mutual.

18 - THOMAS McDONAGH
ONE FOR ALL

On 8th December 1980, the world mourned as John Lennon was gunned down outside his New York apartment by crazed madman Mark Chapman. Meanwhile, five thousand miles away in Crumpsall Hospital, Manchester, Thomas McDonagh entered this world. On his arrival, an emotional midwife turned to her nurses, "A legend may have died today ladies, but another has just been born."

Or so Tommy will tell you!

BORN THE PROUD SON OF IRISH TRAVELLERS, his mother Annie and father Thomas, both came from large families. Fighting had always been in the genes with grandfather Frank O'Donnell, a feared bare-knuckle fighter back in the auld country. Frank's fame has been confirmed to Thomas over the years as various older travellers spoke in awe about him. Sadly, Frank died when he was only in his early fifties.

Raised at number 17, Devonshire Street, Salford, their clan included his Grandmother, Catherine, elder brother Frank and sisters in descending age; Mary, Kathleen, Bridget, then came Thomas and finally the youngest, Anne Marie. However, there was more family next-door but one, and at the end of the street. Open doors! Not to mention regular visits from Ireland with so many first cousins whose names were always a mystery! One time eight-year old Thomas came home from school to find the house had been invaded by up to forty relatives, "Who are these people?" he asked his brother and sisters. Their large house was overrun by fellow McDonagh's and O'Donnell's. Some of Thomas's first fights were against cousins who had stolen his toast off the kitchen table or he would awake to find a couple of them sharing his bed. Cue unadulterated mayhem! One thing Thomas remembers fondly is that these scraps were always just one against one, nobody ever jumped in. Irish fair play!

Finally, after his Grandmother passed away, the family moved to nearby Blackley, which although only a stone's throw away, was in so many ways a world apart. In Salford, they were just like everybody else whereas in Blackley it felt like everyone had better clothes, schoolbags and cars. As a young teenager Thomas admits he was horrible! Not nasty, just terribly mischievous. He was always fighting on the streets and in and out of trouble with a wisecrack or a prank, but even at this time he could look after himself. With his sisters terrorising him and Frank at fifteen, already like a man in the bookies or the pub, Thomas was more or less left to his own devices.

At school he was constantly in trouble and that was when Thomas could be bothered to go. A fifteen per cent attendance record was little better than putting in guest appearances and he got in the habit of writing his own sick notes - "Thomas wasn't in yesterday as he was ill".

Also, there was always a wedding or christening seemingly happening on the home front where they would be away for a week. Astonishingly, he did this even though he was regularly on the back of the local *Moston Advertiser* newspaper at the same time due to his boxing exploits, yet he was never found out. Either that or, as Thomas himself admits, "The teachers were probably glad of the rest!" Soon the fights were more regular than maths and English on Tommy's curriculum. He wasn't the type of kid who ever bullied, his opponents always seemed to be older lads who Thomas would wind up to the point where they would snap and explode! On seeing this it was a case of job done and he would beat them up. Today, Thomas claims never to have lost a fight at Saint Matthew's and is proud of his unbeaten, albeit 'unofficial', five-year record. Many of these 'scraps' would often result in him being sent home to explain to his father what had occurred. Once he told his dad there was always the same question...

"Did you win Tommy?"

"Yes dad."

Content that the McDonagh honour had been upheld, he would get a forgiving nod and the call would go out to the kitchen, "Make sure our Tommy gets extra tea tonight, Annie."

He remembers that harrowing first day at secondary school when all the primary school kids met and came together. Like tribes they kept their distance in the playground and were wary of strangers having heard all the horror stories for months leading up starting 'big school'. But for Thomas this held no such fears for again, through the boxing and the club, he knew all the tough lads from elsewhere, Barry Smith from Our Ladies for one.

Also, fighting with near neighbours North Manchester High School was a regular concern back then, but for Thomas it held no fears as one of his best friends, John Barrett (Pat's nephew) was the 'cock' of that school and the two were close from the gym.

However, God forbid Thomas was ever excluded from school for reasons other than fighting. Giving cheek to a schoolteacher for example was deemed unforgiveable, meaning it was time to duck and run for cover in the McDonagh household! Undoubtedly Thomas's crowning glory came when deciding one day it would be a grand idea to let off a live detonator in the playground. The ensuing scene of bedlam with hordes of screaming children running for cover saw him dragged before Mr Ryan, the headmaster. It was a dire situation for young McDonagh that became infinitely worse when he was asked where he had got hold of the 'banger'?

"It's wasn't a banger sir, it was a detonator."

Mr Ryan spat out his tea! It has to be remembered that this was the time of the IRA bombing campaigns in mainland Britain which culminated in Manchester being the target of a huge attack in 1996.

"Thomas, are you mad?" exclaimed the irate headmaster, "With a name like McDonagh and everything that's going on, you're letting off detonators in the playground!" As one can imagine, Thomas senior had his son swiftly practising his famed defensive skills on returning home. Yet, remarkably, Thomas was always popular with teachers, especially in the last couple of years. Happy go lucky, he had a big heart and was always quick with a smile or joke. The trouble was that Thomas took high spirits to levels others could only marvel at. It was only in the ring that he was reined in.

At seven years old Thomas had started at Blackley Boy's Club and immediately fell in love with boxing. It was run by a man called

Jack Blackburn who recognised even then that this tiny kid who was knee high to a large traffic cone possessed raw talent. Also, there was Colin Jones, who became Thomas's first corner man. He remembers Colin going down on his knees to help him with the pads and telling everybody who was around that this kid was one to keep an eye on, "You're gonna be good Tommy McDonagh!"

When the club shut down for the summer it was Thomas's Uncle Michael, who lived on the Lightbowne Estate, that first introduced him to Collyhurst and Moston Boxing Club. At eight years old, with his mum and dad on either side, Thomas made that first walk up the twenty steps. On entering the gym they were met by the sight of two boxers, Wayne Rigby and Zenon Blackburn, knocking holes out of each other in a ring that in those days faced you as you entered. It was ferocious - sparring in name only! Straight away a horrified, open-mouthed Annie was adamant - "My Thomas is not coming here!"

Thomas senior acted fast, he told her to wait outside whilst he chatted with Brian Hughes. As the men spoke, young Thomas gazed in awe at a club photo on the wall containing Pat Barrett, Zenon Blackburn, Ricky Burton, Craig Dermody and Delroy Waul - warriors all. Happily, Annie's frayed nerves were calmed and she allowed her son to join and he very swiftly impressed Brian. So much that at just ten years old Thomas was given the privilege of training with the professionals. All was going well until one sunny Mancunian Saturday morning. Thomas's friends were playing football and he decided that there would be no boxing that day, "No gym today Dad, I'm playing footy." Thomas had decided he was having a day off, or rather that was the plan.

"Oh yes you bloody are!" Thomas senior replied, "you either go happy or you go sore, it's up to you." Off they went with his son crying all the way in the car. Once inside Thomas senior sought out Brian and quietly explained young McDonagh's tears and unusual foul mood. "Leave it with me" he replied smiling, "I'll sort him out"

As Thomas was gloving up Pat Barrett, one of the young boy's heroes, came across. He had watched Pat fight on Grandstand and to him this man was bigger than life itself. "Why don't you want to train Thomas?" There was no answer, just a grim silence. Pat continued, "everyone is talking about you. You're gonna be a brilliant fighter!" And that was enough! It was back to work for Thomas McDonagh.

Thomas was soon counting down the days to his first amateur fight. It came at eleven years old against Nicky Wolstenholme, at Haslingden. Thomas won on points and even then could not resist showing off with some fancy footwork. In his corner that day was Colin Jones, his old coach from Blackley boys club. This would be the first of sixty-six amateur bouts for Thomas. Once Colin left a man called Duggie Adair took over his corner, one of many unpaid volunteer coaches who, each in their own way, played an integral role in the history of the boxing club. Other volunteers included the likes of Gary Farnell, Ray Flannagan and Tommy Bennett.

Those days it was rare in club tournaments that Collyhurst and Moston suffered across the board losses, but one time at a club show in Stafford, Thomas, Anthony Farnell, Michael Gomez and Craig Blackburn all came unstuck. Thomas's opponent was called Joey Ellesmore, "there are some things you never forget," Thomas says now with a wry smile. It wasn't even a case of the fighters being unlucky, all got a pasting and there could be no excuses as they returned home fuming. It was a quiet bunch of lads who walked up those twenty steps the next day to be greeted by Brian Hughes. He said nothing, there was no need, the look was sufficient. They knew this could not be allowed to happen again. Shortly afterwards Brian arranged rematches for all four boxers, "You're all going back!"

Wired, and knowing they dare not show their faces at the gym again if they failed, they all won! It was essential this happened, especially in Thomas's case, because that had been a first defeat and made for a strange and unsettling experience. He had been fighting and winning constantly since eight years old, and losing for Thomas, at the time, was the worst thing that had ever happened in life and had to be put right. It was hard enough for lads such as Pat Barrett, who came into the sport later, to handle defeat, but when winning has been all you've ever known, and the kids in school only ever ask about the losses, it can be heart-breaking to an 11-year-old.

He also recalls, even back then when in the ring, being, in his own words a "cocky little shit!" In the heat of a fight a smiling Thomas would drop his hands, tell a joke in the corner or delight the crowd with an Ali shuffle! Despite being warned constantly by his corner and referees, Thomas simply could not help it! Talented enough to know when he was losing and being able to step it up and just do enough to win, the honours flowed – Thomas was soon boxing for England, won the boy clubs championships, became Junior ABA's champion and twice national champion. At this tender age he was a class apart and yet perhaps it had all come too easily? When winning, which was most of the time, Thomas adored it, but the odd loss killed him inside. The hard work required to bounce back was gruelling and took a heavy toll, for the dedication required was not for him. At fourteen years old he snapped and Thomas suddenly went missing. His career appeared to be over until Brian Hughes took time to write him a letter. Worried his young star was throwing it all away, Brian told him he was wasting his talent and that one day Thomas could be a world champion. His father also read the riot act, "If you don't box Thomas, what are you going to do, get a job? So help me God, I'll make sure you go in school every day and get some qualifications."

Only when looking back does he realise what a huge honour it was for someone like Brian to go chasing him. Thomas senior also played a huge part in changing the young boy's mind, "Brian is not wrong, son," his father warned, "he knows his boxing". Short and succinct, but never were truer words spoken.

Doubting Thomas lived only a mile and half away from the gym. Other fighters who trained and gave everything came from much further afield; Gary Lockett travelled in from Cardiff, Robbie Reid, Runcorn; Darren Rhodes, Leeds; Michael Jennings, Chorley and Tony Doherty, Wales. It was that level of dedication that Thomas had to find and so he went back. For a while it all went well, but at sixteen other problems arose. After getting into some local 'bother' it was Pat Barrett's turn to intervene where Thomas was concerned. He also delivered to him the kind of stern talking to that even today resonates. Pat also let certain people know Thomas was out of bounds. One day both boxers were in a Manchester store when a couple of lads came in and let on to Thomas. Knowing of their reputation, Pat looked at his young friend, "Do you know these two?"

"Yeah" replied Thomas.

Pat turned his stare to the said characters and told them in no uncertain manner where to go! After doing so he turned back to Thomas.

"You don't anymore!"

Off the back of this Thomas re-focussed; boxing came naturally to him. Even when he was not fully fit, life in the ring appeared more like a playground than a sporting arena. The clowning and joking around infuriated his corner, but the talent shown at times as he slipped punches with consummate ease could be put to music. Thomas could not be hit with salt. He could anticipate punches before an opponent had even decided to throw them. Everyone at that level threw a jab, followed by a one-two, then a hook. To make them miss for Thomas was child's play. Also, all his mistakes would happen in the gym, rarely on fight night, due to the class of fighter he trained and sparred against.

On the odd occasion when Thomas felt he had a serious fight on his hands, his much over-looked ability to bang came to the party. No more so than on one eventful trip to Ipswich when representing England boys against Ireland. An audience packed mostly with Irish supporters gave Thomas an unusually warm reception when they heard his surname, only to regret it a short time later when he dropped his much-vaunted opponent in one round! That extra ingredient of fear proved sufficient to end proceedings early, but that was a rarity, mostly it was a matter of coasting, even sleepwalking to victories. He was impossible to hit and a mixture of clowning, genius and supreme self-belief proved to be his finest asset and his own worst enemy. Thomas was only tested to the limit on home ground during sparring back at Collyhurst and Moston. They were the most difficult fights. There you concentrated, learned and daren't switch off, for doing so could prove a painful experience. In the midst of a battle you took your exams in that university of life.

At just fifteen, Thomas was deemed good enough by Brian Hughes to help out with Robbie Reid's sparring for the Joe Calzaghe fight. Here was a truly brilliant fighter, arguably the finest to come out of Collyhurst and Moston since the trilogy of Brown, McAvoy and King. He was one also you could never take liberties with. As Thomas himself recalls, "Robbie would never patronise or take the piss. All the fighters in the gym when in against Robbie behaved, for if you caught him with a decent punch it was like waking a lion. The lad in against him would see his face change and be more than aware that before the sparring session had finished, they would have paid for it. Robbie waited! He never got mad, just even!" Sparring Robbie was a valuable learning curve for Thomas and so different than when in against upcoming fighters like Michael Gomez or Matthew Hall, they knew nothing more than to come back tearing after you, whereas with Robbie, it was a case of revenge being a dish best served cold. In his own time!

On 9th October, 1999, John Lennon's birthday (that man again) the time arose to turn professional. At Bowlers Exhibition centre, Thomas took on seasoned pro, twenty-six-year-old scouser Lee Molyneux and beat him on points. The fight was shown live on Sky Sports and Thomas went down well with both the television people and audiences. These were learning fights for, unlike fellow Collyhurst and Moston boxers, Matthew Hall and Anthony Farnell who looked like men, Thomas was still a boy in appearance and strength. He possessed the skill, but had to be brought on slowly. In his second bout a month later, at the Kingsway Leisure centre, Widnes, also against Molyneux, he won on points once more. Brian was not about to rush his prodigy – it would all come in time. He understood Thomas was gold dust, but once more events outside the ring came in to play. At eighteen years old he met his girlfriend, and later to be wife, Lyndsey, and suddenly Thomas dropped another ten per cent. On the surface, everything appeared fine, but bubbling beneath was a whole heap of trouble. An opening ten fight unbeaten run was hiding the truth of what was actually occurring. Thomas was earning good money and allied to decent sponsorship, it added up to a tidy sum, but despite winning, he was taking his foot off the gas during fights and Brian was losing patience. There was no momentum. He would scratch his head when confronting him, "What are you doing?"

Thomas was skipping training for weeks at a time. Unusually for him, he was even boozing. If not out with Lindsay, there would be all-nighters with friends or cousins. The city was buzzing and Collyhurst and Manchester was thriving like never before. Sky Sports were regular visitors to the gym and the sight of Barry McGuigan and Adam Smith was the norm. The lads were fighting almost every week. either on their own undercards or Ricky Hatton's, who was set to explode on the boxing world. Yet for Thomas, the partying continued unabated, for in a busy gym there were always places to hide. The truth was he was bored with training, for it had become monotonous. The gym life was killing him inside. Practice, practice and more practice sounded fine as a motto, but if every day is the same from the age of eight then it is easy to become distracted. It all came to a head when Thomas's unbeaten run came to a stuttering halt with two successive draws against Mark Richards and Tomas Da Silva. It was time for a serious word. He received a phone call from Brian, "Thomas, listen to me, you have two choices. Either knuckle down or retire because if you carry on like this you're going to get hurt. You're not living like an athlete. You're coming in overweight and showing no interest. Just give it a go! Dedicate twelve months of your life to boxing and see what happens?" Thomas agreed and on 28th September 2002, at the MEN Arena, Manchester, he took on the hard journeyman from the Nobby Nobs camp, thirty-three-year-old Brummie Brian Coleman. A veteran of thirty-four fights, he very rarely got stopped, but this time around Thomas ended proceedings in the first round. Looking, sharp and focused, he followed this up with a revenge win against Tomas da Silva, before encountering an opponent he had met many years previously in the gym at just fifteen – Paul Wesley.

Back then he had originally been down to spar with Delroy Waul, but he couldn't make it so Brian immediately pointed to Thomas, Gomez and Farnell, "You lot! You're going in with Paul." All three climbed in and stood ready in the corners. On instructions, one would go up against the journeyman. Finally, when it came to Thomas's turn, a grinning Wesley rubbed the top of his head. An irate Thomas turned to Brian who was laughing, "Well are you gonna stand there and let him do that?" Immediately Thomas flew at Wesley, but could not get near him. Soon the three young colts had Wesley on the ropes together though none could get a glove past his defences. Now and again he would strike back with an unsuspected punch, and this infuriated them more. It was a master-class in the realities of professional boxing. All were made to look like blind men with sweeping brushes trying to swat a fly. On calling time Wesley was still smiling, he had clearly enjoyed himself! Brian called over his three youngsters, they were all frustrated and in utter disbelief at their inability to land a shot on Wesley.

"See that man over there," Brian pointed towards him and Wesley had a huge grin on his face, "What he's just done to you daft three, that's what pro's do."

Fast forward to 5th April, 2003, on a Ricky Hatton undercard, Thomas went up against the self-same Paul Wesley, now 41 years old and in his sixty-ninth professional contest. At one point in the fight, Wesley retreated to the ropes pretending he was hurt, but remembering those events many years before, a smiling Thomas realised it was a trap to simply lure him in and so kept his distance. Knowing the ploy had failed, Wesley gave him a wink! The two fought on with Thomas boxing wonderfully to win on points.

A first professional honour arrived on 27th September, 2003, once more at the MEN Arena, against Droylsden-based Portuguese fighter, Eugenio Monteiro. Thomas won on points to claim the WBU International title. The pre-fight word on Monteiro was that he was good, but Thomas was ready for him and on the night put in an impressive performance of counter punching with Brian, throughout, urging him to stick to the game plan.

Five months later Thomas took on the wonderfully named Bobby Banghor, and in a fight shown live on Sky stopped him in round two. To celebrate he did an impromptu Irish jig to earn a gentle cuff round the head from a smiling Brian Hughes. That May, Thomas defended his title and topped the bill against the dangerous Welshman, Bradley Pryce in Barnsley. Boxing beautifully, he won a unanimous decision after twelve rounds. Pryce seemed unable to land a punch on the kid from Manchester, he was just too fast, clever and slick for him. A quirky side-line to this fight occurred when Thomas's Mother, Annie, could not bear to watch, so instead waited outside in the foyer. There she met another lady who was too nervous to watch - Bradley Pryce's mother! Against a soundtrack of a cheering crowd watching their two sons battle it out, they spent the entire fight chatting away, talking about anything but what was going on through the nearby entrance!

Next for Thomas was an awkward contest against Leeds-born former Collyhurst and Moston fighter, Darren Rhodes. The fight came around when both had boxers pull out on them through injuries, leaving an opening Thomas and Darren stepped into. This being a business and both needing to put food on their family's table, it made for a difficult scenario as they regular texted and spoke on the phone. Suddenly all that had to stop. Come the weigh-in, there was a handshake and embrace before battle commenced on 12th November, 2004, at the North Bridge Leisure centre, Halifax. Thomas won on points over ten rounds, it was a fight both boxers were glad to get out of the way so that normality could resume!

Bad habits can be masked, but are truly hard to totally discard. On 3rd June, 2005, at the MEN Arena, Thomas fought twenty-three-year-old, Barry Lee. A southpaw, he was strong and could punch. The early rounds saw Thomas cantering to victory only to switch off momentarily and be caught by Lee. Suddenly reality smacked Thomas hard in the face, once more he was his own worst enemy. An irate Brian was not happy in the corner, "Thomas will you give over! Wake up son!" Knowing he had to shape up or get hurt, Thomas went through the gears to ultimately stop Lee in round seven, but the warning signs were there. Cruising through the contest and thinking he had no need to rely on a punch was a dangerous ploy in a brutal sport and the higher you went in the professional ranks, the more likely it was that that one mistake could prove fatal.

"You carried that kid," Brian complained afterwards.

However, Thomas was always afraid of burning himself out in fights. He had a way of winning that suited his mind and body, for the years of half training and not being fully committed had taken its toll. Thomas liked boxing, it was a job he was good at it, exceptional even, but what Thomas really loved was the attention; the training, dieting and sacrifices he detested. Now, there was not much left in the tank, boxing had gone from being a love affair to a loveless marriage – the end was only a matter of time.

In the background. a television dispute between Frank Warren, Sky and ITV meant fights were becoming much more difficult to make. Finally, on 25th October, 2005, at the Guild Hall, Preston, Thomas took on Dean Walker in a sixth-round contest. After dropping him early with a thunderous left hook and a badly, hurting Walker, it should have ended there with the Sheffield boxer looking beaten. However, once more, Thomas switched off, his mind drifted and he was clearly content to saunter home behind the jab for a points decision. Again Brian was left shaking his head and perplexed as he rubbed his fighter's face dry with a towel, "You never threw another left hook Thomas, what's going on?"

Suddenly it became a case of now or never for the young kid who once had to fight for his toast at the kitchen table. The opportunity showed itself with a fight against the brilliant and dangerous Londoner,

Wayne Alexander, for his WBO Super-Welterweight Title. On 4th March, 2006, at the MEN Arena, what could and should have been Thomas's defining night was lost, due mainly to him taking his eye off his game. In the opening six or seven rounds Thomas appeared to be in control, he was always aware not to switch off, for one mistake and Alexander would put him to sleep. Then came the demons, Thomas started to think too much, believing he simply just had to do enough to win. Fifty-fifty rounds went against him and in the eleventh he was docked a point for holding. Suddenly the fight had gone to the score cards and a devastated Thomas lost a split decision. It was all down to his own stubbornness, thinking he could not lose. Speaking later about his corner that night, Thomas said they were perfect – in Brian Hughes, Mike Jackson and Delroy Waul, a superb team, it was he who had blown it. Of all the fights Thomas lost or drew, that one hurts him to this day, for the feeling of letting Brian down more than anything. Against Alexander, he would try telling him what to do in the corner, but Thomas was not taking it in, preferring instead to do it his own way.

"Thomas, Thomas, can you hear me?" the old maestro said frustratedly to the point where he turned to both Jackson and Waul to take over, "You two speak to him. He isn't listening to me anymore, somebody else needs to do it."

Following the loss Thomas was down. He and Lyndsey had moved into a new home and were planning to get married, but everywhere Thomas went people appeared only too keen to remind him that he threw away the Alexander fight.

Deciding to get on with life, Thomas went back to the gym. What he needed more than anything was a fight to exorcise the ghost of Wayne Alexander. It finally arrived seven months later in the shape of Leicester-born Martin Concepcion. As if to add to the tension running up to the fight, *Boxing News* published an article claiming whoever lost would have nowhere left to turn. One of them would reach the end of the road. Well, on 14th October 2006, at the MEN Arena, Thomas and Concepcion simply nodded at each other beforehand and from the first bell went hell for leather in a proper six-round scrap. In that one fight Thomas got hit more than in the rest of his career put together. It was a question of pride. Thomas won by a point in a thrilling contest and he remembers a lot of people wanting to shake his hand afterwards. Brian, though, was far from happy, because Thomas had been involved in a tear up and was badly bruised. Pat Barrett was also concerned because he had been hit so much, but for once it did not matter to Thomas, it was all about exorcising demons. He had so much to prove, not just to others, but perhaps more to himself, that Thomas McDonagh was not just a boxer but a fighter too.

A huge event was closing in for Thomas, marriage to the love of his life Lyndsey, but a week before the ceremony, there remained a small obstacle to be overcome. A fight on 30th June, 2007, against a tough Ukrainian southpaw, Oleksandr Matviychuk. Thomas fought under orders from his wife-to-be, to not get hit in the face and ruin the wedding photographs! Not daring to face the wrath of his future spouse, Thomas beat Matviychuk on points, intent from the first bell to simply box his head off.

Once married, any love for boxing that he still possessed faded swiftly. Fights had become even harder to match, so much that it was a full ten months before Thomas fought again. Matters were made worse by the Rocky Hatton road show moving to Las Vegas. For his next fight Thomas took on London-based Yassine El Maachi, a tricky customer, but one he took care of easily enough to win on points. It was all becoming a little stale. Thomas seriously considered telling Brian that he wanted to pack it in. Then again, what else could he do? Now aged twenty-seven, Thomas was not just a husband, he was also due to become a father. Boxing paid the bills and put food on the table. In a career shift Thomas reluctantly left Frank Warren and joined Frank Maloney.

A good friend called Denis Marr helped with some extra cash by bringing him into work with local schools. There, Thomas would speak to the pupils about not just boxing, but life. He appeared to have the 'gift of the gab' it was this ability that helped Thomas further down the line once his career in the ring ended.

Then came the phone call he had been waiting for; confirmation of a bout against Andrew Facey for the British Super Welterweight title. If the fight was exciting, so was the venue, for Thomas would go from fighting in small venues on Sunday afternoons to Manchester City's stadium, on the undercard of Ricky Hatton's huge 'Homecoming' show against Juan Lazcano. The date was set for 24th May, 2008, however that day was to have much more meaning for the McDonagh's than a mere boxing match. The day before, after the weigh in, Thomas had dropped in to see Lyndsey at North Manchester hospital as she was about to give birth. He was staying at his parent's house to ensure a good night's sleep before the fight when the call came and baby Lola was born at 8.56, the following morning. Suddenly for Thomas everything was different. After seeing Lola and Lyndsey, he just wanted to stay with them. Brian had arranged for him to box early on the card so he could get back to his family, but the truth was that Thomas simply did not want to fight. His head had been turned. This was one punch he could never slip. His heart had been stolen.

Finally, after talking to Thomas senior, he decided to go ahead and under the most surreal circumstances imaginable he produced perhaps the finest performance of his career. And yet, despite Sky having him winning by eight rounds to two, referee Phil Edwards quite astonishingly declared the bout a draw! It was daylight robbery. Chaos erupted in the ring as Edwards strangely first raised Facey's hand and then after seeing the shocked expressions at ringside, grabbed Thomas's too. *Boxing News* later scored the fight 8-2 in Thomas's favour. Emotion overflowed. Both Brian Hughes and Frank Maloney were incredulous. Their boy had boxed brilliantly and did not deserve what had befallen him. Even the Sky commentators were left open-mouthed and called it a terrible decision. On the positive side, Thomas remembers this as being one of only four or five times in his career that Brian was truly happy with him, "I love the way you're boxing Thomas. Keep it up son." Thomas himself remembers glancing constantly up to the giant television screens showing nothing, it appeared, but all his best shots. It seemed impossible for him not to win…

Following the fight Maloney put in an official complaint, but it was to no avail. Also, Facey's manager Brendan Ingle pulled Thomas aside, "You're a brilliant fighter son". His trainer Dominic Ingle was also honest enough to admit the referee had got it badly wrong, "You won that fight well Thomas". It appeared the only person unaffected by the hysteria over the diabolical decision was Thomas himself, for he had much more important matters on his mind. Without even showering Thomas swiftly got changed and drove home to be with his wife and new baby. They were all that mattered now. He admitted it would have been nice to take the belt home to Lyndsey and Lola, but it was nowhere near the end of the world. Some things are just not meant to be.

After seriously considering retirement another fight showed itself that was impossible to turn down. British and Commonwealth Super Welterweight champion Anthony Small had controversial defeated Thomas's close friend Matthew Hall following a build-up during which Small had successfully got inside Hall's head and driven him to distraction. But against Thomas he simply never bit. Instead, at the press conference, it was Small who was being ripped apart as Collyhurst and Moston's biggest wind up merchant went to work! In the end Small simply gave in and shut up. On 27th November 2009, at the Robin Park Centre, Wigan, Thomas stepped into the ring for the final time. In his corner that night were Brian Hughes and Mike Jackson. Brian had been away and only returned on the eve of the fight. It had been Pat Barrett who had trained him and planned the tactics. The two had spoken at length beforehand. Though neither mentioned it, this was clearly Thomas's last shot. Pat knew that to go after Small, as Matthew Hall had done, was riddled with danger, "This is not going to be an exciting fight Tommy," he said many times in the gym, "You just have to win. If you chase this guy he will beat you with his shots and look good, but if he comes to you, then you've never been stopped or even dropped. If you get a lead, he can't beat you with your defence."

Tactically the plan was to get six or seven rounds ahead and then simply ensure Thomas did not lose. During the fight it was Pat's voice he heard above all others. In the end, it was a disappointing spectacle as Thomas lost a unanimous decision, he got too tired in the closing rounds, fell badly behind and did not do enough. There were no excuses. The game plan was fine, sometimes it was a question of simply holding your hands up and admitting it was not your night. If there had been any lingering doubts about his future they were laid to rest.

There were many tears in the dressing room afterwards, but none came from the fighter himself. He was surrounded by friends - Scott Quigg and Matthew Hall were crying, Michael Jennings was choked, Pat was devastated. Thomas sat with his head down, contemplating that it really was all over. No one had ever seen him looking so upset. He was the one who always brought people back from the despair after defeat. However, inside he was happy. Thomas was choosing when to go. He wasn't going out on his shield or being carried from the ring a bloodied mess.

Thomas looked up and saw all the gloomy faces and cracked a huge smile, "What's up with you, why are you all getting upset? I'm Tommy McDonagh, don't you worry about me!"

Thomas woke up after his professional fighting career and made a bacon sandwich! He went out for meal with Lyndsey, had a pint with his mates and for the first time they could book a family holiday together. As one door shut, another opened. And within a year Thomas took the walk up those twenty steps and became the new custodian of Collyhurst and Moston Boxing Club. During the previous year as fights became increasingly harder to find, he had more time on his hands. Twice Brian approached him to take over the lease but Thomas did not feel ready. Finally, after a third time, he agreed. One of his first tasks was helping Michael Jennings get ready for the Kell Brook fight. Life in the gym carried on as normal. Some weeks it earned a profit, on others it didn't. Thomas threw himself into it. He went out to local schools, youth clubs and colleges spreading the word and learning his trade as the spokesman for the club. When asked what certificate he possessed to speak to kids or students, the answer was simple and could not be argued against, "I run Collyhurst and Moston gym." Locally there was no better calling card.

It was on-the-job work experience. Whilst fantastic talent such as Michael Jennings, Scott Quigg, Tyson Fury, Rhys Roberts and Matty Askin were all the professionals, it was beneath that Thomas was concentrating his efforts. There was a young boy hanging around the gym, Zelfa, a nephew of Pat Barrett. Watching him spar onc day Brian turned to Thomas and smiled, "You've got a good one there Thomas. Keep your eye on him."

Finally, the time arrived when Brian officially retired and left the gym leaving it in the hands of Thomas and Pat Barrett. It was a new world, a strange world. Brian's spirit would linger forever in every corner of the gym and the two would always ensure his credo lived on. Though he now paid the bills, Thomas insisted it was still Brian's gym, he and Pat were simply carrying forward his mantle, "it is not my gym,"

Thomas says today, "It is our gym and it belongs to all the fighters who use it. It is a community gym."

After Brian's departure, dark skies soon descended over the gym. There seemed to be a lack of belief now that the old maestro was no longer around and it affected morale. Thomas called a clear the air meeting of all the fighters, and told them straight, "Anyone who wants to leave can do so". And leave they did, the long shadow of Brian Hughes, bathed in lost genius, already proving hard to escape from. So many left that Thomas later admitted he was glad they did not have a cleaner for she would surely have left too! Sky Sports dropped them and even the local newspapers lost interest – what is a gym without fighters? What was the point? People stopped coming in for a chat.

A few stood by them, like Brian Howard, who got his seconds licence to help out in the corner but the place still had that smell of decline, they were a sinking ship that nobody wanted to be a part of or seen near. On their own now, Thomas and Pat partook in their first amateur club show - Collyhurst and Moston had only three fighters. Thomas was forced to ask organisers to make up the numbers with other fighters. All lost. They were quite literally starting from scratch. He told a disconsolate Pat that what they wanted to achieve would be no quick fix. It would be five years or more before they could even get near what they had before, "It will get worse before it gets better Pat," Thomas told him, "but we'll get it back."

Then, just when things looked like they couldn't get any worse…

Pat's nephew, John Barrett, Thomas's friend from schooldays, was stabbed and killed. John had been a regular at the club for years, a part of the family. He would knock on the door every day between eleven and twelve like clockwork. It was like a large dark cloud over their lives. Zelfa and Lyndon were still just kids and were in abject shock, but Pat was inconsolable and disappeared from the gym.

Knowing his temperament, Thomas tried to track him down but to no avail. Finally he turned up - angry, cold and certain of what lay ahead, Pat told Thomas what he was dreading to hear, "You're not gonna see me in here anymore, Tommy."

This did not sit well with Thomas. He told him that together they could pull through it.

"No Tommy!"

Thomas stayed on him, "This is where you're best off being. It is you Pat. You need this gym more than it needs you! This gym keeps you sane, it keeps you happy. It keeps you alive, mate. It's our club. Just being in here, the air, the smell, the memories. It's what makes us. You're better being here because this is what we do. Come on Pal, y'know it. You'll be here for the rest of your life."

Eventually, after weeks of refusing to accept it, Pat finally returned.

Then, little chinks of light started to appear as word of mouth was having an effect. Footsteps could be heard once more on the famous steps. From an empty gym, now there were at least a handful of regulars. At the next amateur show there were five fighters, okay there were four losses, but the numbers were there.

They had to remain patient and keep finding their feet. Dividing the workload, Thomas ran the amateur side while Pat took the professionals. He set up Black Flash Promotions and Thomas reminded him to stay calm and promised to send over a professional every year – they were doing it the old way, the Collyhurst and Moston way. It would be their own kids, reared in the traditional methods who would be the gym's future.

On 25th October 2014, at the Middleton Arena, Zelfa Barrett made his professional debut against Kristian Laight. It was the dawn of a new era – the sinking ship was now afloat and people wanted to jump back aboard.

Collyhurst and Moston re-registered with the ABA and the shows continued – there were now eight fighters, five winners. The colours of red and gold were starting to fly again. The queue of local kids turned from a trickle into a torrent, Thomas and Pat would tell them all the same, "Either stay on the estate and get in trouble or be fighters and champions. Then years from now you can tell your own kids – 'I was a professional boxer.'"

Not all went to plan. One week Thomas would be mobbed by grateful parents for the great work he was doing for their kid, "We don't recognise him Tommy, his manners and everything about him is better." Then, the week after a defeat, he would suddenly be a bastard and the same kid would disappear from the gym. What he could never make them understand was you don't lose at that age, you learn. If they believed in what you were teaching them, then the kid was on the right path. Everyone gets beaten, it is how you came back and pick the bones from it that matters. Never stop learning and soak everything up.

It was all part of Brian Hughes' philosophy on not just boxing, but life itself. He changed lives and quite literally saved them. However, sometimes the environment and society simply overwhelms some and will not let them get away. Lose interest in the gym and prison or worse follows. Others lost faith and took up everyday jobs that sapped heart and soul, but it's a thing called life and living that has to be gotten on with.

Thomas always remembers his father putting it on the line for him, "I will get you anything you need for your boxing. Anything! But if you want to throw it all away and just exist doing something you hate and piss it all up the wall, then forget it." It was Thomas senior's unique way of saying don't give up on your dream.

Brian's ways remained sacrosanct. He taught them to keep sparring in-house. Stick to your own, why give your secrets away? What their fighters could not get in sparring, Thomas and Pat could teach them on the pads. Why let everybody know your business? No one ever puts the bad stuff on social media, just the good, who they sparred with, what they learned. This would be seen by those in the know; managers and coaches would use it for future reference. Styles could be sussed out and plans made. At Collyhurst and Moston there was a different feel, they took care of business their own way. Thomas and Pat became the last two originals. Brian, being the only one who had taught them and so they passed it on. One voice lost in the mists of time but forever present.

Thomas's sixty-six amateur and forty professional contests ultimately left him unscathed. This was not just natural talent and technique, but it also came down to courage. For never forget the thousands of sparring rounds in the gym against the best Manchester had to offer. Yet Thomas never got hurt, oh he took a beating, but next day, as was the way at Collyhurst and Moston, revenge would be had. When Thomas was caught, Brian always pulled him aside, "You got hit once - twenty press ups! But first go and look in the mirror. I'm not having you going home to your mum and dad looking like that."

Brian would say to all the lads when fighting an opponent with a broken nose or pug nose features that it spoke a thousand words, "This kid leads with his face. Give him what he likes." However, he also had another saying, "Always be wary of a guy who does not look like a fighter." It is reminiscent of the wonderful scene in the Magnificent Seven when a man with a horribly scarred face walks into the saloon and a comment is made by one of the Mexicans looking to hire gunslingers, "Don't worry about him. Worry more about the man who did it."

The next generation. Their two shining lights today in the professional game, Zelfa Barret and Lyndon Arthur have been around the gym since they were knee high to a spit bucket. They are reared in the club's philosophies, both in how they fight and conduct their lives. Each is blessed with huge natural ability and train like monsters. Therein lies the difference, for if you can combine the two, titles await. As they progress Thomas knows the gym will move in the same direction, for he witnessed it when Brian brought in Robbie Reid and he won a world title.

Thomas's proudest moment so far since taking over the gym came on 19th May, 2017, at the Bolton Whites hotel, when Zelfa, fighting live on Box Nation, against a tough and wily Nicaraguan, Eusebio Osejo, fought in such style, displaying everything they had preached to him, since he was eight years old. The jab, head movement, defence, left hook and almost equally important, humble acceptance of a magnificent knockout victory where his first comments in the post-fight interview thanked Brian Hughes. This was a kid with class and who came from good stock.

Collyhurst and Moston stock.

Pat used to shout and scream at Zelfa and Lyndon, sometimes to the point where Thomas would urge him to lay off a little, but it was all done with reason and love, and look at them now? He would grab them back in the day and shouting loud give them both barrels, "Listen to me, both of you. You don't know how good you are. Now come on!"

Those small acorns have grown.

One day, when Thomas was about twelve, Brian was looking through a window and noticed somebody messing with his car. He turned back towards the lads, "Thomas, go and belt that kid, he's trying to break off my aerial." So off he duly went, doing as ordered, down the stairs, over the road and smack! Off the kid ran, holding his nose and back to the estate. The next thing, when back in training, there is a loud knock on the gym door. Someone opens it and the same kid, well known locally as little more than a bully, is stood there with his mother.

Brian goes across and with his best shocked expression and concerned voice inquires, "What's happened, love?"

"One of your lads has just hit my son. Look at his poor nose!" Brian looks carefully, checking out the damage. Almost up the nostril.

"It was him!" the kid says pointing at Thomas.

Brian shakes his head in mock disgust, "Thomas! Come here now! Did you hit this poor child?"

"But Brian, you…"

"Don't you dare answer me back young man. Say you're sorry now."

A shocked Thomas did as he was told, "I'm sorry" he mumbled.

"There you go" says Brian to the woman, "I've told him. I can assure you it won't happen again."

"Right then," replied the satisfied mother. "Let's leave it at that." Off she went with her snivelling son in hand who was clutching tight to a bloodied handkerchief.

Soon as they had disappeared through the door a smiling Brian grabbed hold of Thomas and ruffled his hair, "You son, are gonna be a champion!"

All for one.

Sometimes, even today, Thomas will sit and think it is simply a privilege to just be a part of Collyhurst and Moston Boxing Club, never mind running it alongside Pat. There are still bad days, but now the good vastly outnumber them. Friendships made since he was a small child remain strong today. Matthew Hall and Michael Jennings are Godparents to his children, and he to theirs. Robbie Reid and Pat are still around of course. They were all taught by Brian Hughes to look after one another, both in the gym and out on the Manchester streets. His much-quoted phrase of "All for one, one for all" resonates as loudly today as ever.

As for Thomas, the gym comes only second to what awaits him at home. His wonderful family with Lyndsey and the children; Lola, Lucy and young Thomas, aptly named to keep up the tradition of his father, grandfather and great grandfather. They keep him relatively sane.

Though many who know him will beg to differ! And to end, as for the day job? Well, it has taken a while, but Collyhurst and Moston are back! You just can't keep a good gym down for on Lightbowne Road, up those twenty steps, there is a light that will never go out.

STATS

JACKIE BROWN

107 (40) - 24 (5) - 9

Date	Opponent	Record	Venue	Result	Method
1939-07-24	Benny Jones	57 22 6	King's Hall, Belle Vue, Manchester	W	PTS
1939-07-20	Richie Kid Tanner	40 6 1	The Stadium, Liverpool	L	PTS
1939-05-08	Teddy O'Neill	31 16 7	King's Hall, Belle Vue, Manchester	W	PTS
1939-04-24	Tommy Tucker Smith	29 4 0	King's Hall, Belle Vue, Manchester	L	PTS
1939-03-20	Battling Jim Hayes	51 22 8	King's Hall, Belle Vue, Manchester	W	PTS
			BBBofC Northern Area Bantamweight Title		
1939-02-06	Syd Parker	41 20 6	Victoria Baths, Nottingham	W	PTS
1938-12-06	Benny Jones	55 21 4	Villa Marina Ballroom, Douglas	D	PTS
1938-11-28	Ginger Murphy	18 3 2	King's Hall, Belle Vue, Manchester	W	TKO
1938-10-31	Pierce Ellis	27 5 2	King's Hall, Belle Vue, Manchester	W	PTS
1938-10-05	Dave Kellar	29 15 7	Devonshire Club, Hackney	W	TKO
1938-07-25	Battling Jim Hayes	48 20 7	King's Hall, Belle Vue, Manchester	W	PTS
1938-06-29	Joe Connolly	1 2 0	St Mirren Football Ground, Paisley	L	PTS
1938-04-17	Joe Skelly	23 23 10	Dillington Park Grounds, Barnsley	W	TKO
1938-04-07	Jim Brady	37 20 8	Harringay Arena, Harringay	L	PTS
1938-03-14	Freddie Tennant	59 65 33	Hippodrome, Darlington	W	PTS
1938-03-03	Pat Palmer	29 14 2	Earls Court Empress Hall, Kensington	W	PTS
1938-02-15	Joe Skelly	23 22 10	Villa Marina Ballroom, Douglas	W	PTS
1938-01-10	Battling Jim Hayes	46 18 7	Town Hall, Leeds	L	PTS
1937-11-24	Len Hampston	92 19 3	Olympia, Bradford	L	DQ
			BBBofC Northern Area Bantamweight Title		
1937-10-11	Pat Palmer	22 11 2	Earls Court Empress Hall, Kensington	W	RTD
1937-09-07	Benny Jones	54 16 3	Victoria Hall, Hanley	W	PTS
1937-05-31	Johnny King	140 31 13	King's Hall, Belle Vue, Manchester	L	KO
			BBBofC British Bantamweight Title		
1937-03-21	Juan Hernandez	21 13 4	Junction Stadium, Miles Platting	W	TKO
1937-03-15	Van Meensal	debut	Baths Hall, Rotherham	W	KO
1937-03-08	Bobby Hinds	62 34 8	Batley Carr, Batley	W	PTS
1936-11-30	Len Beynon	113 23 7	King's Hall, Belle Vue, Manchester	W	PTS
1936-11-16	Rafael Valdez	23 13 0	Kings Theatre, Cardiff	W	PTS
1936-11-02	Jim McInally	31 11 5	King's Hall, Belle Vue, Manchester	W	KO
1936-10-05	Len Hampston	81 15 3	Junction Stadium, Manchester	W	PTS
			vacant BBBofC Northern Area Bantamweight Title		
1936-07-13	Johnny Cusick	32 5 1	Junction Stadium, Manchester	W	PTS
1936-05-18	Johnny Cusick	31 5 1	King's Hall, Belle Vue, Manchester	L	PTS
1936-04-23	Ted Green	6 10 2	Earls Court Empress Hall, Kensington	W	KO
1936-03-27	Tucker Winch	28 17 4	Tower Circus, Blackpool	W	KO
1936-03-06	Fred Nipper Morris	24 15 2	King's Hall, Belle Vue, Manchester	W	KO
1936-02-28	Jacky Ryan	25 14 3	Tower Circus, Blackpool	W	KO
1936-02-07	Nicolas Petit-Biquet	55 29 16	King's Hall, Belle Vue, Manchester	W	KO
1935-12-22	Ellis Ashurst	34 11 2	Brunswick Stadium, Leeds	W	KO
1935-11-22	Johnny King	128 25 12	King's Hall, Belle Vue, Manchester	L	RTD
1935-11-04	Tommy Pardoe	10 5 1	Embassy Rink, Sparbrook	W	KO
1935-10-14	Bert Kirby	117 52 14	Embassy Rink, Sparbrook	W	TKO
1935-09-09	Benny Lynch	70 9 16	King's Hall, Belle Vue, Manchester	L	TKO
			BBBofC British Flyweight Title		
			National Boxing Association World Flyweight Title		
1935-08-15	Eric Jones	63 21 10	Darnall Greyhound Track, Sheffield	W	KO
1935-07-29	Jackie Quinn	28 31 7	King's Hall, Belle Vue, Manchester	W	TKO
1935-07-29	Syd Rose	16 9 2	King's Hall, Belle Vue, Manchester	W	TKO
1935-06-24	Ernst Weiss	12 3 2	King's Hall, Belle Vue, Manchester	W	PTS

1935-05-30	George Marsden	87 48 21	The Stadium, Liverpool	W	KO
1935-03-25	Maurice Filhol	31 25 21	Embassy Rink, Birmingham	W	PTS
1935-03-11	Kid Francis	103 12 13	King's Hall, Belle Vue, Manchester	D	PTS
1935-03-04	Benny Lynch	68 9 15	Kelvin Hall, Glasgow	D	PTS
1935-02-22	Henri Barras	27 33 16	Tower Circus, Blackpool	W	PTS
1935-02-11	Orlando Magliozzi	25 27 7	King's Hall, Belle Vue, Manchester	W	KO
1934-06-18	Valentin Angelmann	56 10 4	Belle Vue Speedway Stadium, Manchester	D	PTS
			International Boxing Union World (1913 - 1946) Flyweight Title		
			National Boxing Association World Flyweight Title		
1934-04-16	Aurel Toma	6 2 5	King's Hall, Belle Vue, Manchester	W	PTS
1933-12-11	Ginger Foran	28 1 1	King's Hall, Belle Vue, Manchester	W	PTS
			BBBofC British Flyweight Title		
			Commonwealth (British Empire) Flyweight Title		
			International Boxing Union World (1913 - 1946) Flyweight Title		
			National Boxing Association World Flyweight Title		
1933-10-30	Midget Wolgast	129 11 7	Royal Albert Hall, Kensington	L	PTS
1933-09-26	Jimmy Young Knowles	13 2 2	Music Hall, Edinburgh	W	PTS
1933-09-11	Valentin Angelmann	49 8 2	King's Hall, Belle Vue, Manchester	W	PTS
1933-07-24	Mickey McGuire	42 4 6	King's Hall, Belle Vue, Manchester	L	DQ
1933-07-03	Young Perez	64 9 11	King's Hall, Belle Vue, Manchester	W	PTS
1933-06-12	Valentin Angelmann	48 7 2	Olympia, Kensington	W	PTS
			International Boxing Union World (1913 - 1946) Flyweight Title		
			National Boxing Association World Flyweight Title		
1933-05-07	Billy Bryon	75 14 3	The Ring, Blackfriars Road, Southwark	W	TKO
1933-05-01	Dave Crowley	55 8 5	King's Hall, Belle Vue, Manchester	L	DQ
1933-02-15	Etienne Mura	16 13 13	Palais de la Mutualité, Paris	L	PTS
1932-12-02	Emile Degand	20 11 7	Charleroi	W	SD
1932-10-31	Young Perez	57 6 10	King's Hall, Belle Vue, Manchester	W	RTD
			International Boxing Union World (1913 - 1946) Flyweight Title		
			National Boxing Association World Flyweight Title		
1932-09-19	Jim Maharg	15 3 0	King's Hall, Belle Vue, Manchester	W	DQ
			BBBofC British Flyweight Title		
			EBU European Flyweight Title		
1932-08-13	Tucker Winch	9 6 4	Hyde Park, Sheffield	L	DQ
1932-08-01	Bob (Young) Fielding	30 4 5	Blackpool Football Ground, Blackpool	W	RTD
1932-07-06	Johnny Regan	10 12 5	Winter Gardens, Morecambe	W	TKO
1932-06-09	George Marsden	16 21 13	Palace Coliseum, Douglas	W	TKO
1932-04-18	Len Beynon	38 7 4	King's Hall, Belle Vue, Manchester	W	PTS
1932-03-07	Emile Degand	20 9 7	King's Hall, Belle Vue, Manchester	W	PTS
1932-02-22	Mickey McGuire	31 1 6	New St James Hall, Newcastle	L	PTS
1932-02-15	Benny Thackray	64 21 6	Town Hall, Leeds	W	TKO
1932-02-01	Jean Cuart	20 12 4	King's Hall, Belle Vue, Manchester	W	TKO
1931-12-02	Percy (Young) Dexter	36 24 6	Winter Gardens, Morecambe	W	PTS
1931-11-13	George Aziz	15 20 10	Tower Circus, Blackpool	W	PTS
1931-11-08	Benny Thackray	59 18 6	Royton NSB, Royton	W	RTD
1931-10-12	Ottavio Gori	0 11 4	King's Hall, Belle Vue, Manchester	W	DQ
1931-08-24	Jim Maharg	10 1 0	King's Hall, Belle Vue, Manchester	W	PTS
1931-07-20	Desire Collignon	5 3 2	Sportman's Group Gardens, Sheffield	W	PTS
1931-07-06	Vincenzo Savo	11 3 3	King's Hall, Belle Vue, Manchester	W	PTS
			EBU European Flyweight Title		
1931-06-15	Emile Degand	18 5 5	Olympia, Kensington	W	PTS
			EBU European Flyweight Title		
1931-05-04	Lucian Popescu	20 1 3	King's Hall, Belle Vue, Manchester	W	PTS
			EBU European Flyweight Title		
1931-02-02	Bert Kirby	79 14 7	King's Hall, Belle Vue, Manchester	W	PTS
			BBBofC British Flyweight Title		
1930-09-22	Billy Kid Hughes	17 10 4	King's Hall, Belle Vue, Manchester	W	TKO
1930-07-20	Billy James	53 17 9	Palais de Danse, West Bromwich	L	PTS
1930-06-23	Rene Chalange	33 18 11	King's Hall, Belle Vue, Manchester	W	PTS
1930-05-18	Percy (Young) Dexter	25 13 4	Ice Rink, West Bromwich	W	KO
1930-04-21	Emile Degand	17 2 3	King's Hall, Belle Vue, Manchester	W	PTS
1930-03-03	Bert Kirby	65 11 6	National Sporting Club (Holborn Stadium), Holborn	L	KO
			BBBofC British Flyweight Title		
1929-12-22	Harry Hill	47 36 16	Palais de Danse, West Bromwich	W	TKO
1929-11-13	Phineas John	37 15 13	Holborn Stadium Club, Holborn	W	PTS
1929-10-13	Bert Kirby	55 10 6	Palais de Danse, West Bromwich	W	KO
			vacant BBBofC British Flyweight Title		
1929-06-18	Jim Campbell	4 3 1	King's Hall, Belle Vue, Manchester	W	TKO
1929-04-22	Phineas John	35 13 11	National Sporting Club, Covent Garden	W	PTS
1929-03-19	Tony Roberti	debut	Free Trade Hall, Manchester	W	RTD
1929-03-05	Walter Lemmon	2 1 0	Free Trade Hall, Manchester	W	RTD
1929-02-12	George Greaves	8 13 0	Free Trade Hall, Manchester	W	PTS
			vacant BBBofC Northern Area Flyweight Title		
1929-01-06	Arthur Boy Edge	15 3 4	National Sporting Club, Leeds	W	KO
1928-12-26	Cuthbert Taylor	1 0 0	Snow's Pavilion, Merthyr	D	PTS

1928-12-15	Billy Kid Hughes	13 8 3	Pavilion, Bridgend	W	PTS
1928-12-09	Dickie Inkles	36 13 6	National Sporting Club, Leeds	W	PTS
1928-12-04	Tommy Brown	33 6 6	Free Trade Hall, Manchester	W	PTS
1928-11-24	Phineas John	23 11 11	Gess Pavillion, Pontypool	L	PTS
1928-11-03	Jerry O'Neil	2 2 2	Gess Pavillon, Pontypridd	W	PTS
1928-10-20	Dickie Inkles	31 13 6	Palais de Danse, Ashton under Lyne	L	PTS
1928-10-13	Freddy Morgan	7 5 7	Baths, Ogmore Vale	D	PTS
1928-09-21	Harry Yates	22 12 6	Palais de Danse, Ashton under Lyne	W	PTS
1928-08-11	Dickie Inkles	29 13 6	Hyde Park, Sheffield	L	PTS
1928-08-02	Jim Crawford	11 3 2	Liverpool Stadium, Pudsey Street, Liverpool	W	PTS
1928-07-09	Jean Locatelli	2 2 0	Winter Gardens, Morecambe	W	PTS
1928-07-05	Ernie Barker	3 22 1	Osborne Theatre, Manchester	W	PTS
1928-07-03	Siki Coulton	23 11 6	Palais de Danse, Ashton under Lyne	W	RTD
1928-06-27	Arthur Young Evitt	3 2 2	Winter Gardens, Morecambe	W	PTS
1928-06-14	Jack Glover	20 8 8	Liverpool Stadium, Pudsey Street, Liverpool	D	PTS
1928-05-26	Joe Fleming	2 4 0	Palais de Danse, Ashton under Lyne	W	PTS
1928-05-23	Freddy Webb	4 6 2	Winter Gardens, Morecambe	W	PTS
1928-05-20	Freddy Webb	4 5 2	Adelphi Club, Salford	W	PTS
1928-04-30	Martin Gallagher	2 4 0	Co-op Hall, Leigh	W	PTS
1928-04-21	Freddy Morgan	5 3 5	Gess Pavillon, Pontypridd	W	PTS
1928-04-02	Jim Crawford	6 2 2	Adelphi Club, Salford	W	PTS
1928-03-16	Ernie Barker	3 21 1	Royal Pavilion, Blackpool	W	PTS
1928-02-14	Young Fitz	2 4 1	Free Trade Hall, Manchester	W	PTS
1928-01-13	Jack Glover	17 7 7	Tower Circus, Blackpool	D	PTS
1927-12-29	Jim Crawford	2 1 2	Liverpool Stadium, Pudsey Street, Liverpool	W	TKO
1927-12-11	Jack Glover	15 7 7	Adelphi Club, Salford	L	PTS
1927-11-24	Young Siki	15 6 11	Liverpool Stadium, Pudsey Street, Liverpool	W	PTS
1927-11-18	Jack Cantwell	6 3 1	Drill Hall, Mountain Ash	W	PTS
1927-11-04	Freddy Webb	3 3 2	Ashbury Hall, Openshaw	W	PTS
1927-10-07	Harry Yates	14 6 2	Ashbury Hall, Openshaw	W	PTS
1927-09-27	Joe Fleming	2 3 0	Free Trade Hall, Manchester	W	PTS
1927-07-26	Ben Doyle	2 0 1	Liverpool Stadium, Pudsey Street, Liverpool	W	TKO
1927-07-07	Young Fargill	debut	Liverpool Stadium, Pudsey Street, Liverpool	W	DQ
1927-05-15	Ernie Hendricks	1 3 0	Adelphi Club, Salford	D	PTS
1927-03-15	Freddy Webb	0 0 1	Free Trade Hall, Manchester	L	TKO
1927-03-08	Billy Cahill	3 10 0	Free Trade Hall, Manchester	W	KO
1927-03-06	Tommy Brown	14 1 3	Sussex Street Club, Salford	L	PTS
1926-03-23	Dick Manning	0 1 0	Free Trade Hall, Manchester	W	PTS
1925-05-18	Harry Gainey	debut	Arena, Collyhurst	W	PTS

Jock McAvoy

132 (88) - 14 (2) - 1

1945-09-10	Tommy Davies	38 15 4	Vetch Field, Swansea	W	PTS
1945-08-07	Johnny Clements	42 37 2	Connaught Drill Hall, Portsmouth	W	KO
1945-07-17	George Howard	17 6 0	White Hart Lane (Tottenham FC), Tottenham	W	KO
1942-02-23	Freddie Mills	60 11 6	Royal Albert Hall, Kensington	L	RTD
1941-12-08	Jim Berry	68 27 13	Royal Albert Hall, Kensington	W	KO
1941-10-20	Jack Hyams	103 45 13	Seymour Hall, Marylebone	W	PTS
1940-10-28	Eddie Maguire	48 38 12	Ice Rink, Nottingham	L	PTS
1940-08-26	Charlie Parkin	110 72 13	Ice Rink, Nottingham	W	TKO
1940-08-08	Freddie Mills	49 9 6	The Stadium, Liverpool	L	PTS
1940-04-29	Jim Berry	63 25 13	King's Hall, Belle Vue, Manchester	W	RTD
1939-11-20	Jack Hyams	93 42 13	King's Hall, Belle Vue, Manchester	W	PTS
1939-07-10	Len Harvey	121 13 10	White City Stadium, White City	L	PTS
		BBBofC British Light Heavyweight Title			
		vacant Commonwealth (British Empire) Light Heavyweight Title			
1939-05-22	Arthur (Ginger) Sadd	128 15 12	King's Hall, Belle Vue, Manchester	W	PTS
		BBBofC British Middleweight Title			
		Commonwealth (British Empire) Middleweight Title			
1939-03-09	Tino Rolando	70 33 7	The Stadium, Liverpool	W	TKO
1939-02-27	Emile Lebrize	63 33 15	King's Hall, Belle Vue, Manchester	W	KO
1938-12-06	Jack Robinson	40 29 6	Granby Halls, Leicester	W	TKO
1938-11-28	Frank Hough	93 31 4	King's Hall, Belle Vue, Manchester	W	KO
1938-11-21	Joe Quigley	8 17 4	King's Hall, Derby	W	PTS
1938-11-02	Jack Strongbow	38 45 6	Victoria Road Baths, Birmingham	W	RTD
1938-05-06	Marcel Lauriot	30 27 5	Theatre Royal, Dublin	W	KO
1938-04-07	Len Harvey	118 13 10	Harringay Arena, Harringay	L	PTS
		BBBofC British Light Heavyweight Title			
1938-02-28	Jack Strongbow	38 43 6	King's Hall, Belle Vue, Manchester	W	TKO
1938-01-24	Bill Hardy	76 27 5	Granby Halls, Leicester	W	KO

Date	Opponent	Record	Venue	Result	Method
1937-12-06	Vasile Serbanescu	14 8 5	King's Hall, Belle Vue, Manchester	W	TKO
1937-11-23	Alban Mulrooney	25 12 5	Victoria Hall, Hanley	W	TKO
1937-10-25	Jack Hyams	83 36 13	King's Hall, Belle Vue, Manchester	W	TKO
		BBBofC British Middleweight Title			
		Commonwealth (British Empire) Middleweight Title			
1937-05-03	Dai Jones	29 12 3	Colston Hall, Bristol	W	PTS
1937-04-27	Eddie Phillips	19 4 3	Empire Pool, Wembley	W	KO
		BBBofC British Light Heavyweight Title			
1937-03-08	Cheo Morejon	46 22 10	King's Hall, Belle Vue, Manchester	W	PTS
1936-12-01	Rienus De Boer	39 17 16	Drill Hall, Sheffield	W	PTS
1936-10-26	Bill Wainwright	16 10 0	King's Hall, Belle Vue, Manchester	W	KO
1936-09-14	Albert Barjolin	77 15 12	King's Hall, Belle Vue, Manchester	W	RTD
1936-08-03	Bob (Young) Simpkins	17 7 4	Blackpool Football Ground, Blackpool	W	KO
1936-04-23	Jack Petersen	34 3 0	Earls Court Empress Hall, Kensington	L	PTS
		BBBofC British Heavyweight Title			
		Commonwealth (British Empire) Heavyweight Title			
1936-03-13	John Henry Lewis	56 8 4	Madison Square Garden, New York	L	UD
1936-02-24	Anson Green	26 32 2	Arena, Philadelphia	W	PTS
1936-02-17	Jimmy Smith	58 13 4	St. Nicholas Arena, New York	W	KO
1935-12-20	Babe Risko	59 11 10	Madison Square Garden, New York	W	KO
1935-11-29	Al McCoy	94 18 17	Madison Square Garden, New York	W	UD
1935-10-07	Marcel Lauriot	24 19 5	King's Hall, Belle Vue, Manchester	W	PTS
1935-06-24	Al Bourke	51 17 4	King's Hall, Belle Vue, Manchester	W	PTS
		BBBofC British Middleweight Title			
		Commonwealth (British Empire) Middleweight Title			
1935-04-08	Francisco Garcia Lluch	27 28 8	King's Hall, Belle Vue, Manchester	W	PTS
1935-01-14	Marcel Thil	98 20 10	Palais des Sports, Paris	L	UD
		EBU European Light Heavyweight Title			
1934-12-03	Kid Tunero	31 5 3	King's Hall, Belle Vue, Manchester	W	TKO
1934-10-08	Jack Etienne	106 37 9	King's Hall, Belle Vue, Manchester	W	KO
1934-08-13	Charlie Parkin	43 18 3	King's Hall, Belle Vue, Manchester	W	KO
1934-06-18	Teddy Phillips	5 2 1	Belle Vue Speedway Stadium, Manchester	W	KO
1934-04-30	Ernie Simmons	8 3 2	King's Hall, Belle Vue, Manchester	W	PTS
1934-03-19	Eddie Maguire	15 10 3	King's Hall, Belle Vue, Manchester	W	KO
1934-02-28	Al Bourke	35 15 2	Royal Albert Hall, Kensington	W	KO
1934-01-29	Eddie Peirce	11 1 3	King's Hall, Belle Vue, Manchester	W	PTS
1933-11-12	Jack Forster	4 6 0	Royton NSB, Royton	W	PTS
1933-10-09	Archie Sexton	137 19 19	King's Hall, Belle Vue, Manchester	W	KO
		BBBofC British Middleweight Title			
		Commonwealth (British Empire) Middleweight Title			
1933-08-21	George Brown	10 17 4	King's Hall, Belle Vue, Manchester	W	PTS
1933-06-12	Oddone Piazza	17 6 1	Olympia, Kensington	W	PTS
1933-05-14	Jack Hyams	54 25 11	The Ring, Blackfriars Road, Southwark	W	PTS
1933-04-10	Len Harvey	110 9 9	King's Hall, Belle Vue, Manchester	W	PTS
		BBBofC British Middleweight Title			
		Commonwealth (British Empire) Middleweight Title			
1933-02-27	Leonard Steyaert	6 4 6	King's Hall, Belle Vue, Manchester	W	KO
1933-02-20	Ernie Red Pullen	7 19 7	Queen's Hall, Blackburn	W	KO
1933-02-12	Les Ward	25 19 8	Royton NSB, Royton	W	KO
1933-01-30	Glen Moody	17 15 3	King's Hall, Belle Vue, Manchester	W	TKO
1932-12-07	Hans Seifried	24 14 14	Royal Albert Hall, Kensington	W	PTS
1932-11-25	Mihai Fulea	12 10 10	King's Hall, Belle Vue, Manchester	W	TKO
1932-11-07	Ted Coveney	11 35 7	Blackburn	W	TKO
1932-10-12	Tommy Moore	10 2 0	Winter Gardens, Morecambe	W	KO
1932-09-30	Phil Green	65 35 19	Palace Theatre, Rawtenstall	W	TKO
1932-09-11	Billy Roberts	9 4 4	Royton NSB, Royton	W	TKO
1932-08-31	George Brown	7 12 2	Winter Gardens, Morecambe	W	PTS
1932-08-01	Tom Benjamin	4 2 2	Blackpool Football Ground, Blackpool	W	TKO
1932-07-18	Jack (Kid) Casey	114 40 14	King's Hall, Belle Vue, Manchester	L	DQ
		BBBofC Northern Area Middleweight Title			
1932-07-04	Carmelo Candel	52 10 7	White City Stadium, White City	W	PTS
1932-06-28	Billy Thomas	16 18 9	Tower Circus, Blackpool	W	TKO
1932-06-19	Sandy McKenzie	22 11 2	Royton NSB, Royton	W	KO
1932-05-29	Bill Hood	48 53 12	Royton NSB, Royton	W	KO
1932-05-09	Edwin John	6 4 1	King's Hall, Belle Vue, Manchester	W	TKO
1932-03-21	Len Harvey	104 8 8	King's Hall, Belle Vue, Manchester	L	PTS
		BBBofC British Middleweight Title			
		Commonwealth (British Empire) Middleweight Title			
1932-03-01	Jack Etienne	94 29 9	King's Hall, Belle Vue, Manchester	W	PTS
1932-02-02	Seaman Albert Harvey	13 3 3	King's Hall, Belle Vue, Manchester	W	PTS
1932-01-17	Jack Marshall	6 15 1	Royton NSB, Royton	W	KO
1931-12-20	Ernie Red Pullen	5 10 2	Royton NSB, Royton	W	KO
1931-11-22	Sonny Doke	5 17 3	Royton NSB, Royton	W	TKO
1931-11-16	Billy Adair	16 22 6	King's Hall, Belle Vue, Manchester	W	KO
1931-11-06	Paul McGuire	39 10 1	Tower Circus, Blackpool	W	TKO
1931-10-12	Alfred Pegazzano	67 23 16	King's Hall, Belle Vue, Manchester	W	TKO

Date	Opponent	Record	Venue	Result	Method
1931-09-07	Jerry Daley	7 8 2	King's Hall, Belle Vue, Manchester	W	KO
1931-08-30	Jack Hyams	48 20 8	Brunswick Stadium, Leeds	W	TKO
1931-08-10	Joe (Young) Lowther	30 14 5	King's Hall, Belle Vue, Manchester	W	RTD

BBBofC Northern Area Middleweight Title

Date	Opponent	Record	Venue	Result	Method
1931-07-19	Jack O'Brien	1 3 0	Tolka Park, Dublin	W	TKO
1931-07-11	Jack Bottomley	1 5 0	Rochdale Hornets Rugby League Ground, Rochdale	W	KO
1931-06-21	Con van Leeuwen	0 1 0	Royton Stadium, Royton	W	TKO
1931-05-24	Sonny Doke	4 12 1	Royton Stadium, Royton	W	PTS
1931-05-11	Fred Shaw	11 12 1	King's Hall, Belle Vue, Manchester	W	PTS
1931-04-19	Johnny Seamarks	4 7 2	Royton Stadium, Royton	W	KO
1931-04-15	Sonny Doke	4 10 1	Winter Gardens, Morecambe	W	PTS
1931-04-03	Seaman Jim Cox	25 21 7	Bolton	W	PTS
1931-03-30	Paul McGuire	35 9 1	King's Hall, Belle Vue, Manchester	L	DQ
1931-03-08	Charlie Keeling	9 6 0	Royton NSB, Royton	W	KO
1931-02-16	Dick Red Burt	21 17 14	King's Hall, Belle Vue, Manchester	W	TKO
1931-01-22	Charlie McDonald	38 11 3	Liverpool Stadium, Pudsey Street, Liverpool	W	PTS
1931-01-11	Bill Shocker Bowman	0 1 0	Royton Stadium, Royton	W	PTS
1930-12-14	Jim Johnson	2 4 1	Royton NSB, Royton	W	KO
1930-11-04	Tate Evans	debut	Free Trade Hall, Manchester	W	TKO
1930-11-02	Seaman Jim Cox	25 19 7	Royton Stadium, Royton	W	PTS
1930-10-22	Joe (Young) Lowther	28 10 4	Winter Gardens, Morecambe	W	PTS
1930-10-14	Joe Rostron	46 4 4	Free Trade Hall, Manchester	W	PTS
1930-10-03	Patsy Flynn	7 2 2	Majestic Rink, Preston	W	KO
1930-09-30	Billy Delahay	0 4 0	Free Trade Hall, Manchester	W	PTS
1930-09-14	Jim Pearson	11 11 2	Royton NSB, Royton	W	PTS
1930-08-27	Seaman Jim Cox	25 18 7	Winter Gardens, Morecambe	W	PTS
1930-08-12	Farmer George Jackson	21 10 2	Royton Stadium, Royton	W	PTS
1930-07-30	George Porter	7 6 2	Winter Gardens, Morecambe	W	PTS
1930-07-26	Eddie Strawer	1 1 0	Royton Stadium, Royton	W	KO
1930-06-11	Billy Green	7 19 4	Winter Gardens, Morecambe	W	TKO
1930-05-25	Eddie Strawer	debut	Royton Stadium, Royton	W	KO
1930-04-25	Joe Rostron	36 3 4	Majestic Theatre, Preston	L	PTS
1930-04-14	Dai Beynon	0 1 0	King Street Barracks, Blackburn	W	KO
1930-04-13	Teddy Lewis	4 3 0	Royton Stadium, Royton	W	KO
1930-03-28	Jim Pearson	10 8 2	Majestic Theatre, Preston	L	PTS
1930-03-21	Fred Oldfield	9 11 1	Drill Hall, Haslingden	W	TKO
1930-03-16	Jack Wilkinson	debut	Royton Stadium, Royton	W	KO
1930-03-10	Fred Blything	0 1 0	Stourbridge	W	PTS
1930-03-07	Bill Shocker Bowman	debut	Market Hall, Penrith	W	KO
1930-02-27	Bill Lee	4 3 1	Town Hall, Rhyl	W	KO
1930-02-14	Frank Oldfield	debut	Majestic Theatre, Preston	W	PTS
1930-02-09	Andy Ross	debut	Royton Stadium, Royton	W	KO
1930-02-07	Jack Ogden	0 4 0	Public Hall, Haslingden	W	KO
1930-01-24	Sid Young Aldridge	11 1 2	Majestic Theatre, Preston	W	KO
1930-01-12	Marine Davies	0 0 1	Royton Stadium, Royton	W	KO
1929-12-27	Griff Williams	0 1 0	Rhyl	D	PTS
1929-12-20	Billy Horner	2 1 0	Majestic Rink, Preston	W	TKO
1929-12-15	Lud Gresvig	debut	Royton Stadium, Royton	W	TKO
1929-12-06	Ted Abbot	5 4 3	King Street Barracks, Blackburn	W	TKO
1929-12-05	Soldier Jones	21 32 2	Rhyl	W	TKO
1929-12-02	Jack Harrison	debut	Hanley	W	TKO
1929-09-30	Jack Ogden	0 2 0	Fleetwood	W	PTS
1929-09-29	Billy Chew	1 1 0	Royton Stadium, Royton	W	PTS
1929-09-25	Seaman Douglas	debut	Winter Gardens, Morecambe	W	RTD
1929-09-17	Bob Tiger Ennis	debut	New Market Stadium, Burnley	W	KO
1929-08-28	Jack Jukes	0 1 0	Winter Gardens, Morecambe	W	TKO
1929-08-14	Eric Basher Bargh	debut	Winter Gardens, Morecambe	W	TKO
1929-08-06	Billy Chew	1 0 0	New Market Hotel, Burnley	W	PTS
1929-07-14	Jack Ogden	0 1 0	Royton Stadium, Royton	W	KO
1929-07-04	Frank Ormerod	1 3 0	New Market Stadium, Burnley	W	KO
1928-03-19	Teddy Cox	debut	Drill Hall, Todmorden	W	KO
1928-01-27	Billy Chew	debut	Public Hall, Haslingden	L	RTD
1927-11-27	Bert Hilditch	0 4 0	Royton Stadium, Royton	W	TKO
1927-11-06	Billy Longworth	debut	Royton Stadium, Royton	W	KO

Johnny King

162 (74) - 50 (8) - 15

Date	Opponent	Record	Venue	Result	Method
1947-02-10	Jackie Paterson	55 14 3	King's Hall, Belle Vue, Manchester	L	KO
			BBBofC British Bantamweight Title		
1947-01-14	Teddy O'Neill	40 26 7	Seymour Hall Baths, Marylebone	L	PTS
1946-11-08	Frank Kenny	43 19 8	King George's Hall, Blackburn	L	PTS
1945-09-08	Eddie Miller	62 13 0	Sydney Stadium, Sydney	L	KO
1944-08-07	Nel Tarleton	117 21 8	City Ground, Nottingham	L	PTS
1944-03-24	Nel Tarleton	116 20 8	King's Hall, Belle Vue, Manchester	W	DQ
1943-12-15	Syd Worgan	56 33 8	Queensberry Club, Soho	W	PTS
1943-11-19	Ben Duffy	20 6 1	King's Hall, Belle Vue, Manchester	D	PTS
1942-06-23	Fred Barry	debut	Colombo	D	PTS
1940-03-18	Jackie Rankin	27 15 7	Empress Hall, Earl's Court	L	PTS
1939-11-20	Billy Charlton	39 16 4	King's Hall, Belle Vue, Manchester	L	PTS
1939-10-14	George Marsden	188 93 38	Sportsdrome, Southampton	W	TKO
1939-10-09	Frank Kenny	29 13 8	King's Hall, Belle Vue, Manchester	L	PTS
1939-09-30	Johnny McManus	16 12 4	Cartyne Greyhound Track, Glasgow	W	TKO
1939-07-03	Phineas John	131 64 28	Corn Exchange, Stroud	W	PTS
1939-04-10	Frank Parkes	39 5 3	Brook Street Baths, Sutton-in-Ashfield	L	PTS
1939-03-13	Len Beynon	143 28 10	Mannesmann Hall, Swansea	L	RTD
1939-02-06	Jackie Hurst	31 18 6	Millbay Rinkeries, Plymouth	W	TKO
1939-01-16	Tom Smith	58 8 2	New St James Hall, Newcastle	L	PTS
1938-12-08	Frank Kenny	25 7 6	The Stadium, Liverpool	W	PTS
1938-11-25	Harry Edwards	58 45 9	Batley Carr Rink, Dewsbury	W	PTS
1938-11-21	Rafael Valdez	25 20 1	Public Baths, Gloucester	W	KO
1938-10-31	Johnny Cusick	54 10 2	King's Hall, Belle Vue, Manchester	L	PTS
1938-10-19	Harry Edwards	58 42 9	Tower Ballroom, Edgbaston, Birmingham	W	DQ
1938-10-10	Gustavo Ansini	22 17 11	Earls Court Empress Hall, Kensington	L	PTS
1938-09-30	Johnny McManus	13 9 3	Theatre Royal, Dublin	W	RTD
1938-09-01	Freddie Miller	206 22 7	The Stadium, Liverpool	L	PTS
1938-08-15	Hal Bagwell	30 0 3	Kingsholm Rugby Ground, Gloucester	W	KO
1938-06-22	Len Hampston	93 21 3	Headingley Rugby Ground, Leeds	W	DQ
			BBBofC British Bantamweight Title		
1938-04-28	Paul Dogniaux	50 7 5	Salle Wagram, Paris	L	PTS
1938-03-03	Dan McAllister	14 2 0	The Stadium, Liverpool	L	PTS
1938-02-09	Johnny McGrory	53 8 3	Kelvin Hall, Glasgow	L	PTS
1938-01-27	Billy Pleace	17 21 4	Drill Hall, Exeter	W	PTS
1938-01-10	George Williams	28 27 10	Colston Hall, Bristol	L	PTS
1937-12-20	Benny Sharkey	117 45 16	New St James Hall, Newcastle	W	PTS
1937-11-30	Joe Green	34 8 2	Victoria Hall, Hanley	W	PTS
1937-11-02	Tommy Burns	28 17 5	Drill Hall, Oldham	W	TKO
1937-10-11	Young Chocolate	11 9 1	Colston Hall, Bristol	W	KO
1937-10-04	Johnny Ryan	20 12 7	Arena, Coventry	W	KO
1937-09-13	Spike Robinson	23 23 2	King's Hall, Belle Vue, Manchester	W	TKO
1937-08-14	George Marsden	131 74 31	Poole Sports Arena, Poole	L	PTS
1937-08-02	Alex Alston	13 19 2	Tower Circus, Blackpool	W	PTS
1937-05-31	Jackie Brown	93 17 8	King's Hall, Belle Vue, Manchester	W	KO
			BBBofC British Bantamweight Title		
1937-04-23	Alex Alston	13 17 2	Tower Circus, Blackpool	W	DQ
1937-04-19	Gustavo Ansini	21 12 10	Waverley Market, Edinburgh	W	PTS
1937-03-17	George Marsden	124 69 30	Corn Exchange, York	W	TKO
1937-03-08	Alex Alston	12 16 2	King's Hall, Belle Vue, Manchester	L	PTS
1937-01-04	George Marsden	119 66 28	Granby Halls, Leicester	D	PTS
1936-12-10	Jimmy Lester	35 6 2	Holborn Stadium Club, Holborn	W	PTS
1936-11-19	Ginger Foran	45 8 2	The Stadium, Liverpool	L	PTS
1936-10-12	Johnny Cusick	34 6 2	King's Hall, Belle Vue, Manchester	L	PTS
1936-09-28	Benny Sharkey	114 44 16	New St James Hall, Newcastle	L	PTS
1936-08-03	Boyo Burns	28 5 1	Blackpool Football Ground, Blackpool	W	PTS
1936-07-23	Tommy Steele	86 23 12	Hyde Park, Sheffield	W	TKO
1936-06-30	KO Morgan	92 12 1	Cathkin Park, Glasgow	L	PTS
1936-06-14	Karel Vercammen	1 5 1	Stadium, Rotherham	W	KO
1936-05-06	Nel Tarleton	96 14 8	Anfield Football Ground, Liverpool	L	PTS
			BBBofC British Featherweight Title		
1936-02-21	Gilbert Johnstone	17 8 0	King's Hall, Belle Vue, Manchester	W	PTS
1936-02-18	Spike Robinson	16 13 2	Ulster Hall, Belfast	W	TKO

1936-01-19	Fred Todkill	19 3 2	Junction Stadium, Manchester	W	TKO
1935-12-16	Joseph Parisis	33 25 17	King's Hall, Belle Vue, Manchester	W	PTS
1935-11-22	Jackie Brown	79 15 8	King's Hall, Belle Vue, Manchester	W	RTD
1935-10-21	Simon Chavez	34 8 4	King's Hall, Belle Vue, Manchester	W	PTS
1935-10-10	Nel Tarleton	91 14 7	The Stadium, Liverpool	D	PTS
1935-09-09	Giovanni Sili	23 17 14	King's Hall, Belle Vue, Manchester	W	KO
1935-08-29	Frank Barron	11 10 4	Hyde Park, Sheffield	W	TKO
1935-07-08	Len Beynon	90 17 7	Vetch Field, Swansea	W	RTD
1935-05-27	Len Hampston	64 13 3	King's Hall, Belle Vue, Manchester	W	PTS

vacant BBBofC British Bantamweight Title

1935-04-29	George Williams	14 20 8	King's Hall, Belle Vue, Manchester	W	PTS
1935-04-06	George Williams	13 20 8	Labour Stadium, Merthyr Tydfil	L	PTS
1935-03-25	Nel Tarleton	91 12 7	King's Hall, Belle Vue, Manchester	W	PTS
1935-03-01	Karel Vercammen	1 3 1	Tower Circus, Blackpool	W	PTS
1935-02-25	Domenico Bernasconi	44 20 5	King's Hall, Belle Vue, Manchester	W	PTS
1935-02-08	Michel Escargeuil	24 11 15	Town Hall, Blackpool	W	TKO
1935-01-27	Joe Horridge	15 14 2	Royton NSB, Royton	W	TKO
1934-12-28	Johnny Holt	9 2 2	Tower Circus, Blackpool	D	PTS
1934-12-16	Joe Horridge	15 12 2	Royton NSB, Royton	W	PTS
1934-11-19	Phineas John	95 40 20	King's Hall, Belle Vue, Manchester	W	RTD
1934-10-22	Dick Corbett	83 19 11	King's Hall, Belle Vue, Manchester	D	PTS
1934-10-01	George Marsden	71 43 20	King's Hall, Belle Vue, Manchester	W	PTS
1934-09-24	George Marsden	70 42 20	King's Hall, Belle Vue, Manchester	L	PTS
1934-08-27	Ellis Ashurst	28 4 2	King's Hall, Belle Vue, Manchester	W	RTD
1934-08-20	Dick Corbett	83 19 10	Clapton Greyhound Track, Clapton	D	PTS

BBBofC British Bantamweight Title
Commonwealth (British Empire) Bantamweight Title

1934-07-19	Mog Mason	10 2 1	The Stadium, Liverpool	W	KO
1934-06-18	Len Beynon	77 11 6	Belle Vue Speedway Stadium, Manchester	W	PTS
1934-06-03	Stan Jehu	13 19 5	Stadium, Rotherham	W	PTS
1934-05-19	Albert Lindley	11 9 3	Drill Hall, Sheffield	W	TKO
1934-05-14	Len Beynon	75 11 6	King's Hall, Belle Vue, Manchester	L	PTS
1934-04-30	Marcel Sartos	9 4 4	King's Hall, Belle Vue, Manchester	W	RTD
1934-04-15	Stan Davies	16 15 5	Stadium, Rotherham	W	TKO
1934-04-02	Len Beynon	71 11 6	Drill Hall, Swansea	L	PTS
1934-03-11	Dave Crowley	60 13 5	The Ring, Blackfriars Road, Southwark	L	KO
1934-02-12	Dick Corbett	79 18 10	King's Hall, Belle Vue, Manchester	L	PTS

BBBofC British Bantamweight Title
Commonwealth (British Empire) Bantamweight Title

1934-01-26	Benny Thackray	96 35 7	Tower Circus, Blackpool	L	DQ
1933-12-24	Jackie Quinn	18 23 6	Ulster Hall, Belfast	W	PTS
1933-12-11	Teddy Higgins	4 2 0	King's Hall, Belle Vue, Manchester	W	KO
1933-11-24	Johnny Peters	36 21 9	King's Hall, Belle Vue, Manchester	W	RTD
1933-11-16	Benny Thackray	91 34 7	Imperial Ballroom, Nelson	W	KO
1933-11-06	Frans Machtens	37 42 8	King's Hall, Belle Vue, Manchester	L	PTS
1933-10-29	Teddy Higgins	10 18 3	Royton NSB, Royton	W	TKO
1933-10-22	Johnny Barrett	15 5 3	Brunswick Stadium, Leeds	W	KO
1933-10-01	Syd Rose	8 7 0	Royton NSB, Royton	W	KO
1933-07-03	Panama Al Brown	106 12 11	King's Hall, Belle Vue, Manchester	L	PTS

International Boxing Union World (1913 - 1946) Bantamweight Title

1933-06-12	Bobby Leitham	27 11 8	Olympia, Kensington	W	PTS

Commonwealth (British Empire) Bantamweight Title

1933-05-21	Tucker Winch	15 9 4	The Ring, Blackfriars Road, Southwark	W	RTD
1933-05-15	Domenico Bernasconi	42 18 5	King's Hall, Belle Vue, Manchester	L	KO
1933-04-23	Benny Thackray	87 29 7	Brunswick Stadium, Leeds	W	KO
1933-04-10	Pat Boy Gorman	19 12 1	New St James Hall, Newcastle	W	KO
1933-03-27	Henri Poutrain	33 17 6	King's Hall, Belle Vue, Manchester	W	RTD
1933-03-06	Dave Crowley	55 6 5	King's Hall, Belle Vue, Manchester	W	PTS
1933-02-28	Jimmy O'Neil	16 8 3	Music Hall, Edinburgh	W	RTD
1933-02-20	Stan Davies	9 7 2	King's Hall, Belle Vue, Manchester	W	PTS
1933-01-09	Jean Locatelli	4 21 0	Music Hall, Shrewsbury	W	KO
1932-12-19	Stan Davies	7 4 1	Town Hall, Stockport	W	PTS
1932-12-09	Tommy Kirk	32 25 10	Tower Circus, Blackpool	W	TKO
1932-11-25	Dave Crowley	55 5 5	King's Hall, Belle Vue, Manchester	W	PTS
1932-10-10	Dick Corbett	66 13 9	King's Hall, Belle Vue, Manchester	W	PTS

BBBofC British Bantamweight Title
Commonwealth (British Empire) Bantamweight Title

1932-09-25	Harold Kid Lewis	8 4 1	Royton NSB, Royton	W	KO
1932-09-05	Alfredo Magnolfi	15 9 13	King's Hall, Belle Vue, Manchester	W	PTS
1932-08-24	Harold Kid Lewis	8 3 1	Winter Gardens, Morecambe	W	PTS
1932-08-01	Joe Myers	15 22 7	Blackpool Football Ground, Blackpool	W	KO
1932-07-18	Terence Tancy Morgan	100 38 29	King's Hall, Belle Vue, Manchester	W	TKO
1932-05-30	Johnny Peters	30 9 7	King's Hall, Belle Vue, Manchester	W	DQ
1932-03-13	Joe Myers	14 20 7	Royton NSB, Royton	W	PTS
1932-02-23	Arley Hollingsworth	42 38 5	Edmund Rd Drill Hall, Sheffield	W	RTD

COLLYHURST & MOSTON BOXING CLUB - 100 YEARS

1932-02-15	Dick Burke	35 4 3	King's Hall, Belle Vue, Manchester	W	PTS
			BBBofC Northern Area Bantamweight Title		
1932-01-24	Stan Jehu	7 12 4	Brunswick Stadium, Leeds	W	PTS
1931-12-21	Dick Corbett	63 13 8	King's Hall, Belle Vue, Manchester	L	PTS
			vacant BBBofC British Bantamweight Title		
			Commonwealth (British Empire) Bantamweight Title		
1931-11-23	Raymond Martinet	17 20 5	King's Hall, Belle Vue, Manchester	W	TKO
1931-11-09	Frank Markey	17 7 4	King's Hall, Belle Vue, Manchester	W	TKO
1931-10-25	Lew Sullivan	23 17 0	Royton NSB, Royton	W	DQ
1931-10-05	Nicolas Petit-Biquet	40 17 8	King's Hall, Belle Vue, Manchester	W	PTS
1931-09-07	Nicolas Petit-Biquet	40 16 7	King's Hall, Belle Vue, Manchester	W	PTS
1931-08-10	Pat Boy Gorman	13 8 0	King's Hall, Belle Vue, Manchester	W	RTD
			vacant BBBofC Northern Area Bantamweight Title		
1931-07-26	Benny Thackray	53 17 6	Royton NSB, Royton	W	KO
1931-07-06	Al Miller	12 5 0	King's Hall, Belle Vue, Manchester	W	KO
1931-06-14	Alf Grisdale	8 9 0	Royton NSB, Royton	W	TKO
1931-05-30	Arley Hollingsworth	34 30 3	Hyde Park, Sheffield	W	TKO
1931-04-27	Benny Thackray	44 15 6	King's Hall, Belle Vue, Manchester	L	PTS
1931-03-20	Benny Thackray	44 14 5	Tower Circus, Blackpool	D	PTS
1931-03-15	Jackie Kirk	3 4 1	Royton NSB, Royton	W	TKO
1931-02-23	Bert Kirby	79 16 7	King's Hall, Belle Vue, Manchester	W	KO
1931-02-13	Billy Shinfield	2 2 1	Tower Circus, Blackpool	W	KO
1931-02-09	Johnny Gibson	18 10 1	King's Hall, Belle Vue, Manchester	W	KO
1931-01-23	Tommy Barber	29 11 4	Tower Circus, Blackpool	W	PTS
1931-01-09	Joe Hagen	3 6 1	Hippodrome, Harpurhey	W	PTS
1930-12-28	Harry (Little) Minor	14 4 4	Royton NSB, Royton	W	PTS
1930-11-30	Spike Bradley	7 10 1	Royton NSB, Royton	W	PTS
1930-11-21	Tommy Brown	64 17 10	King's Hall, Belle Vue, Manchester	W	KO
1930-11-03	Young Perez	30 3 5	King's Hall, Belle Vue, Manchester	D	PTS
1930-10-29	Fred Bebbington	22 20 5	Drill Hall, Llandudno	W	PTS
1930-10-13	Jackie Quinn	5 4 1	King's Hall, Belle Vue, Manchester	W	KO
1930-10-05	Ted Griffin	1 2 0	Royton Stadium, Royton	W	TKO
1930-09-22	George Greaves	13 18 2	King's Hall, Belle Vue, Manchester	W	TKO
1930-08-24	Ted Griffin	0 2 0	Royton Stadium, Royton	N	NC
1930-08-03	Fred Bebbington	21 17 5	Royton NSB, Royton	W	KO
1930-07-13	Billy James	52 17 9	Palais de Danse, West Bromwich	L	PTS
1930-06-23	Tommy Brown	61 16 10	King's Hall, Belle Vue, Manchester	L	PTS
1930-05-25	Young Siki	36 38 22	Ice Rink, West Bromwich	W	RTD
1930-05-18	Arthur Boy Edge	45 10 7	Ice Rink, West Bromwich	W	KO
1930-05-04	Martin Gallagher	4 9 1	NSC, Royton	W	RTD
1930-05-02	Ted Perry	2 2 0	Collyhurst, Manchester	W	KO
1930-04-30	Tommy McLeish	0 3 0	Alexander Stadium, Colne	W	RTD
1930-04-06	Teddy Talbot	0 1 0	Princess Club, Salford	W	RTD
1930-03-15	Billy James	47 16 8	King's Hall, Belle Vue, Manchester	D	PTS
1930-02-26	Arthur Boy Tomlinson	4 3 3	Drill Hall, Llandudno	W	PTS
1930-02-16	Freddy Berresford	debut	Pendleton	W	KO
1930-02-11	Alec Farris	debut	Music Hall, Edinburgh	W	PTS
1930-01-01	Arthur Boy Edge	33 9 6	Holborn Stadium Club, Holborn	W	PTS
1929-12-10	Freddy Morgan	13 8 10	Holborn Stadium Club, Holborn	W	PTS
1929-12-10	Moe Mizler	25 6 5	Holborn Stadium Club, Holborn	W	PTS
1929-12-10	Bert Kirby	60 11 6	Holborn Stadium Club, Holborn	L	PTS
1929-12-03	Reg Hall	1 3 0	Holborn Stadium Club, Holborn	W	PTS
1929-11-25	Teddy Talbot	debut	Wargrave Social Club, Earlestown	W	PTS
1929-10-26	Billy Yates	24 8 2	Free Trade Hall, Manchester	L	RTD
1929-09-08	Jack Keelars	debut	Adelphi Club, Salford	W	PTS
1929-08-07	Jimmy Gould	debut	Winter Gardens, Morecambe	W	KO
1929-07-04	Alf Young Shaw	1 0 0	Liverpool Stadium, Pudsey Street, Liverpool	W	TKO
1929-06-28	Johnny Hyde	0 0 1	Ashbury Hall, Openshaw	D	PTS
1929-06-03	Joe Berstein	debut	Fenton Street Drill Hall, Leeds	W	PTS
1929-05-30	Paddy Dowling	2 8 3	Liverpool Stadium, Pudsey Street, Liverpool	W	PTS
1929-05-09	Paddy Dowling	1 8 3	Liverpool Stadium, Pudsey Street, Liverpool	L	PTS
1929-04-22	Bill Hagen	debut	Adelphi Club, Salford	W	PTS
1929-04-08	Eddie Sherry	1 2 0	Drill Hall, Northwich	W	PTS
1929-03-19	Eddie Sherry	1 1 0	Free Trade Hall, Manchester	W	PTS
1929-02-22	Harold Henthorne	3 3 0	Ashbury Hall, Openshaw	D	PTS
1929-02-15	Young Dick Lawton	5 0 0	Drill Hall, Burnley	L	PTS
1929-02-12	Dot Boxall	debut	Free Trade Hall, Manchester	W	PTS
1929-02-03	Jimmy Coupe	0 1 0	Adelphi Club, Salford	W	KO
1929-01-29	Frank Cooley	debut	Free Trade Hall, Manchester	W	PTS
1929-01-18	Eddie Sherry	1 0 0	Tower Circus, Blackpool	W	PTS
1929-01-06	Eddie Conway	debut	Adelphi Club, Salford	W	KO
1929-01-02	Harold Henthorne	3 2 0	Winter Gardens, Morecambe	W	PTS
1928-12-14	Harold Henthorne	2 2 0	Drill Hall, Oswaldtwistle	L	TKO
1928-11-27	Dom Randolph	debut	Co-op Hall, Leigh	W	PTS
1928-11-27	John Melia	0 3 0	Co-op Hall, Leigh	W	PTS

292

1928-11-23	Asa Hilditch	0 2 1	Public Hall, Haslingden	W	TKO
1928-11-16	Joe Coupe	debut	Hippodrome, Harpurhey	W	KO
1928-10-03	Jimmy Speight	0 2 0	Winter Gardens, Morecambe	W	KO
1928-09-01	Boy Knowles	debut	Palais de Danse, Ashton under Lyne	W	PTS
1928-08-19	Jimmy Coupe	debut	Adelphi Club, Salford	W	KO
1928-08-19	Willie Walsh	0 1 1	Royton Stadium, Royton	D	PTS
1928-07-28	John Melia	0 2 0	Palais de Danse, Ashton under Lyne	W	PTS
1928-04-15	Harold Henthorne	1 2 0	Royton Stadium, Royton	L	PTS
1928-02-05	Asa Hilditch	0 1 1	Royton Stadium, Royton	W	PTS
1928-01-24	Tich Cain	0 1 0	Grand Theatre, Douglas	W	PTS
1928-01-01	John Melia	0 1 0	Royton Stadium, Royton	W	PTS
1927-11-09	Tommy McLeish	0 2 0	Pier Kinema, Llandudno	W	PTS
1927-11-04	Young Leach	debut	Stakis Hotel, Blackpool	W	PTS
1927-10-25	Tommy Ross	debut	British Legion Club, Huddersfield	W	PTS
1927-10-04	Tommy McLeish	0 1 0	Free Trade Hall, Manchester	W	PTS
1927-09-25	Tommy McLeish	debut	Adelphi Club, Salford	W	PTS
1927-09-11	Young Fenn	0 1 0	Adelphi Club, Salford	W	PTS
1927-07-31	John Melia	debut	Boxing Club, Royton	W	PTS
1927-07-03	Harry Stafford	1 1 0	Boxing Club, Royton	L	PTS
1927-06-05	Willie Walsh	0 0 1	Boxing Club, Royton	W	PTS
1927-05-29	Jim Costello	1 1 1	Boxing Club, Royton	W	PTS
1927-05-15	Sid Longworth	5 1 0	Boxing Club, Royton	W	PTS
1927-03-27	Wilf Duckworth	debut	Boxing Club, Royton	D	PTS
1927-02-27	Sid Longworth	4 1 0	Boxing Club, Royton	L	PTS
1927-01-16	Young Sutton	1 0 0	Boxing Club, Royton	W	PTS
1926-11-21	Sid Longworth	3 1 0	Boxing Club, Royton	L	PTS
1926-08-29	Sid Longworth	1 1 0	Boxing Club, Royton	L	TKO
1926-07-25	Joe Murray	debut	Boxing Club, Royton	W	PTS
1926-06-27	Jim Costello	0 1 0	Boxing Club, Royton	D	PTS
1926-05-23	Sid Longworth	1 0 0	Boxing Club, Royton	W	PTS
1926-05-16	Sid Longworth	debut	Royton Stadium, Royton	L	PTS
1926-04-25	Jim Costello	debut	Boxing Club, Royton	W	PTS

Lance Lewis

TONY DORE 7(3) - 3(0) - 0

1989-12-13	Nigel Wenton	15 1 0	Sports Centre, Kirkby	L	PTS
1989-12-06	Peter Konyegwachie	12 0 0	Wembley Arena, Wembley	L	PTS
1989-11-20	Jim Moffat	14 6 0	St Andrews SC, Albany Hotel, Glasgow	W	TKO
1989-06-16	Museta Binguina	28 2 4	Milan	D	PTS
1989-05-26	Paziente Adobati	12 3 2	Bergamo	D	PTS
1989-05-08	Gary Maxwell	15 8 4	Grand Hotel, Leicester	W	PTS
1989-04-27	Alan McKay	5 0 0	Elephant & Castle Centre, Southwark	L	PTS
1989-04-06	Martin Reilly	1 0 1	Leisure Centre, Stevenage	W	TKO
1989-02-17	Joe Duffy	6 5 1	Volunteer Rooms, Irvine	D	PTS
1989-01-30	Harry Escott	11 2 0	St Andrews SC, Albany Hotel, Glasgow	D	PTS
1988-12-19	Kid Sumaila	4 23 1	Mayfair	W	PTS
1988-12-13	Steve Pike	3 1 0	Edmiston Club, Glasgow	W	TKO
1988-10-10	Neil Leggett	1 3 2	Edmiston Club, Glasgow	W	PTS
1988-09-05	Neil Leggett	1 2 1	Edmiston Club, Glasgow	W	PTS

LANCE WILLIAMS 19(8) - 6 (1) - 0

1982-05-05	Glyn Rhodes	13 9 3	Midlands Sporting Club, Solihull	W	TKO
1982-03-15	Paul Chance	26 3 0	Civic Hall, Wolverhampton	W	PTS
1981-11-24	Ken Buchanan	61 6 0	Wembley Arena, Wembley	W	PTS
1981-10-26	Glyn Rhodes	13 8 2	Anglo-American Sporting Club, Mayfair	D	PTS
1981-09-25	Ken Bowden	2 2 0	Perth	L	KO
1981-04-28	Paul Chance	23 2 0	Royal Albert Hall, Kensington	W	KO
1981-03-09	Walter Clayton	11 0 1	Anglo-American Sporting Club, Mayfair	W	TKO
1981-02-24	Paul Keers	11 8 2	Royal Albert Hall, Kensington	W	KO
1980-10-27	Jimmy Brown	13 2 0	Anglo-American Sporting Club, Mayfair	W	TKO
1980-09-24	Duncan Hamilton	5 2 0	Midlands Sporting Club, Solihull	W	TKO
1980-04-29	George McGurk	33 25 3	Poco-a-Poco Club, Stockport	W	PTS
1980-02-18	Ceri Collins	10 7 2	Poco-a-Poco Club, Stockport	L	PTS
1980-01-16	Robbie Robinson	9 4 1	Adelphi Hotel, Liverpool	L	PTS
1979-12-10	George McGurk	33 22 3	Arden Sporting Club, Birmingham	W	RTD
1979-11-19	Barry Price	20 18 8	Poco-a-Poco Club, Stockport	W	PTS
1979-10-29	Najib Daho	14 10 1	Arden Sporting Club, Birmingham	W	PTS

1979-10-11	Barry Price	20 17 8	Anglo-American SC, Liverpool		W	PTS
1979-06-26	Chris Sanigar	7 2 1	Empire Pool, Wembley		L	PTS
1979-05-21	Terry Welsh	5 5 0	Anglo American Sporting Club, Manchester		W	PTS
1979-04-24	Barry Price	17 14 7	20th Century Sporting Club, Southend		W	PTS
1979-03-27	Charlie Brown	6 0 0	20th Century Sporting Club, Southend		W	PTS
1979-02-28	George Schofield	3 0 0	Executive Sporting Club, Burslem		W	PTS
1979-01-17	Vernon Penprase	3 2 0	Stoke on Trent Executive SC, Stoke-on-Trent		L	PTS
1978-11-27	Terry McKeown	5 0 0	Govan Town Hall, Glasgow		L	PTS
1978-11-15	Selvin Bell	6 11 0	Midlands Sporting Club, Solihull		W	TKO
1978-11-08	Eric Wood	13 18 1	North Staffs Sporting Club, Stoke-on-Trent		D	PTS
1978-09-27	Shaun Durkin	1 4 0	Herringthorpe Leisure Centre, Rotherham		W	PTS
1978-09-19	John Cooper	4 1 0	20th Century SC, Cliffs Pavilion, Southend		D	PTS

Pat Barrett

37(28) - 4(0) - 1

1994-12-25	Marino Monteyne	16 24 4	Izegem		W	PTS
1994-03-11	Donnie Parker	11 41 1	Sharon		W	TKO
1993-11-01	Patrick Vungbo	28 6 0	Izegem		L	SD
			vacant World Boxing Federation World Super Welterweight Title			
1993-09-22	Del Bryan	27 11 1	York Hall, Bethnal Green		L	PTS
			vacant BBBofC British Welterweight Title			
1993-02-13	Juan Carlos Gonzalez Borquez	13 2 0	Free Trade Hall, Manchester		W	PTS
1992-12-19	Sam Gervins	20 43 0	Palazzetto dello Sport, San Severo		W	TKO
1992-11-20	Tomas Quinones	0 9 0	Cassino		W	TKO
1992-07-25	Manning Galloway	49 11 1	G-Mex Centre, Manchester		L	UD
			World Boxing Organisation World Welterweight Title			
1991-12-19	Mike Johnson	23 4 2	Sports Centre, Lord Street, Oldham		W	TKO
1991-10-09	Racheed Lawal	19 2 0	G-Mex Centre, Manchester		W	TKO
			EBU European Super Lightweight Title			
1991-04-17	Mark McCreath	9 1 0	Royal Albert Hall, Kensington		W	TKO
			EBU European Super Lightweight Title			
1991-02-13	Salvatore Nardino	20 2 2	Grand Hall, Wembley		W	KO
			EBU European Super Lightweight Title			
1991-01-16	Jimmy Harrison	18 3 0	Royal Albert Hall, Kensington		W	RTD
1990-11-15	Eduardo Jacques	2 2 0	Sports Centre, Lord Street, Oldham		W	TKO
1990-10-04	Dwayne Swift	26 8 1	York Hall, Bethnal Green		W	PTS
1990-08-24	Efrem Calamati	27 0 0	Salerno		W	KO
			EBU European Super Lightweight Title			
1990-06-02	Juan Carlos Nunez	0 4 0	G-Mex Centre, Manchester		W	TKO
1989-11-21	Joey Ferrell	8 9 2	Kelvin Hall, Glasgow		W	TKO
1989-10-24	Robert Harkin	13 4 1	Civic Hall, Wolverhampton		W	PTS
			BBBofC British Super Lightweight Title			
1989-09-19	Dana Roston	15 9 2	London Arena, Millwall		W	TKO
1989-06-27	Robert Trevino	5 3 1	Bellahouston Leisure Centre, Glasgow		W	KO
1989-06-07	John Rafuse	18 9 0	Wembley Arena, Wembley		W	KO
1989-05-09	Tony Willis	25 3 0	City Hall, St Albans		W	KO
			vacant BBBofC British Super Lightweight Title			
1989-04-11	Sugar Gibiliru	6 22 6	Sports Centre, Lord Street, Oldham		W	KO
			BBBofC Central Area Super Lightweight Title			
1989-03-28	Marc Delfosse	7 3 3	Kelvin Hall, Glasgow		W	KO
1989-03-06	Dean Bramhald	18 54 10	Edmiston Club, Glasgow		W	TKO
1988-11-29	Kevin Plant	9 15 8	Bowlers Exhibition Centre, Manchester		W	PTS
			vacant BBBofC Central Area Super Lightweight Title			
1988-11-01	Jeff Connors	11 17 4	Kelvin Hall, Glasgow		W	TKO
1988-10-10	Dave Haggerty	16 10 1	Edmiston Club, Glasgow		W	TKO
1988-06-08	Dave McCabe	30 7 0	Edmiston Club, Glasgow		W	TKO
1988-05-04	Lenny Gloster	13 23 1	Midlands Sporting Club, Solihull		W	PTS
1988-04-12	Stanley Jones	7 4 4	National Sports Centre, Cardiff		W	TKO
1988-03-22	Donnie Parker	6 17 1	Teamsters Local 557 Hall, Baltimore		W	PTS
1988-03-01	Sugar Gibiliru	6 17 3	Midland Hotel, Manchester		D	PTS
1988-02-08	Oliver Henry	9 7 1	Anglo American Sporting Club, Hotel Piccadilly, Manchester		W	TKO
1987-10-20	Michael Howell	1 0 0	European SC, Kings Hall, Stoke-on-Trent		W	PTS
1987-08-03	Mike Russell	5 6 0	European SC, Kings Hall, Stoke-on-Trent		W	PTS
1987-07-01	Iskender Savas	3 1 0	Interlaken		W	TKO
1987-06-13	Eamon Payne	5 8 0	Hippodrome, Great Yarmouth		W	TKO
1987-06-01	Paul Burke	4 1 0	Yorkshire Executive SC, Norfolk Gardens Hotel, Bradford		L	PTS
1987-05-18	Jim Moffat	5 1 0	Hospitality Inn, Glasgow		W	RTD
1987-05-01	Gary Barron	1 0 0	Wirrina Stadium, Peterborough		W	TKO

Craig Dermody

13(6) - 1(0) - 0

1993-03-31	Karl Taylor	6 16 1	Broadway Theatre, Barking	L	PTS
1993-02-13	Karl Taylor	6 15 1	Free Trade Hall, Manchester	W	TKO
1992-10-13	Russell Davison	11 16 1	Castle Leisure Centre, Bury	W	PTS
			BBBofC Central Area Featherweight Title		
1992-07-02	Alan Smith	2 4 0	Middleton	W	TKO
1992-02-27	Miguel Matthews	6 33 8	Everton Park Sports Centre, Liverpool	W	PTS
1991-12-19	Peter Buckley	17 13 4	Sports Centre, Lord Street, Oldham	W	PTS
1991-11-28	Peter Buckley	17 12 4	Central Hall, Liverpool	W	PTS
1991-11-21	Miguel Matthews	5 29 7	Meadowside Leisure Centre, Burton-on-Trent	W	PTS
1991-08-01	James Hunter	6 10 2	Leisure Centre, Dewsbury	W	TKO
1991-06-20	Gary Hickman	4 6 1	Everton Park Sports Centre, Liverpool	W	TKO
1991-05-16	Andrew Robinson	6 11 2	Everton Park Sports Centre, Liverpool	W	PTS
1991-04-16	Miguel Matthews	5 20 5	Victoria Leisure Centre, Nottingham	W	PTS
1991-03-14	Kelton McKenzie	1 1 2	Civic Theatre, Middleton	W	TKO
1991-01-31	Karl Morling	2 0 0	Quaffers Club, Bredbury	W	TKO

Robin Reid

42(29) - 8(3) - 1

2012-10-20	Kenny Anderson	17 1 0	Sheffield Arena, Sheffield	L	TKO
			vacant BBBofC British Super Middleweight Title		
2012-01-28	Daniel Cadman	14 6 1	York Hall, Bethnal Green	W	TKO
2011-06-25	Wayne Reed	6 2 0	Hillsborough Leisure Centre, Sheffield	W	TKO
2011-03-23	Tobias Webb	4 0 1	Olympia, Liverpool	L	UD
2011-02-26	Jamie Ambler	9 45 2	De Vere Whites Hotel, Bolton	W	PTS
2007-11-09	Carl Froch	21 0 0	Nottingham Arena, Nottingham	L	RTD
			BBBofC British Super Middleweight Title		
2007-03-30	Jesse Brinkley	26 4 0	Metro Radio Arena, Newcastle	W	UD
2005-08-06	Jeff Lacy	19 0 0	St. Pete Times Forum, Tampa	L	RTD
			International Boxing Federation World Super Middleweight Title		
			International Boxing Organization World Super Middleweight Title		
2005-02-13	Ramdane Serdjane	17 16 2	Brentwood Centre, Brentwood	W	PTS
2004-06-26	Brian Magee	22 0 0	Kings Hall, Belfast	W	UD
			International Boxing Organization World Super Middleweight Title		
2003-12-13	Sven Ottke	32 0 0	Nuernberg Arena, Nuremberg (Nürnberg)	L	UD
			International Boxing Federation World Super Middleweight Title		
			World Boxing Association Super World Super Middleweight Title		
2003-10-24	Dmitry Adamovich	9 6 0	York Hall, Bethnal Green	W	KO
2003-10-04	Willard Lewis	17 8 2	Stadthalle, Zwickau	W	TKO
2003-04-05	Enrique Campos	11 5 0	Leipziger Arena, Leipzig	W	TKO
2002-11-29	Mondli Mbonambi	17 9 1	Olympia, Liverpool	W	TKO
2002-07-10	Francisco Antonio Mora	34 5 0	Conference Centre, Wembley	W	UD
			World Boxing Federation World Super Middleweight Title		
2001-12-19	Julio Cesar Vasquez	63 3 0	Skydome, Coventry	W	UD
			World Boxing Federation World Super Middleweight Title		
2001-10-20	Jorge Andres Sclarandi	26 16 1	Kelvin Hall, Glasgow	W	KO
			World Boxing Federation World Super Middleweight Title		
2001-07-14	Soon Botes	21 7 0	Olympia, Liverpool	W	TKO
			World Boxing Federation World Super Middleweight Title		
2001-05-19	Roman Babaev	19 15 1	Wembley Arena, Wembley	W	TKO
			World Boxing Federation World Super Middleweight Title		
2000-12-08	Mike Gormley	11 2 0	National Sports Centre, Crystal Palace	W	TKO
			vacant World Boxing Federation World Super Middleweight Title		
2000-06-24	Silvio Branco	39 4 2	Hampden Park, Glasgow	L	UD
			World Boxing Union (1995-2004) Super Middleweight Title		
1999-02-13	Joe Calzaghe	25 0 0	Telewest Arena, Newcastle	L	SD
			World Boxing Organisation World Super Middleweight Title		
1998-04-18	Graham Townsend	8 3 0	Nynex Arena, Manchester	W	TKO
1997-12-19	Thulani Malinga	41 10 0	London Arena, Millwall	L	UD
			World Boxing Council World Super Middleweight Title		
1997-09-11	Hacine Cherifi	24 2 1	Kingsway Leisure Centre, Widnes	W	SD
			World Boxing Council World Super Middleweight Title		

1997-05-03	Henry Wharton	25 2 1	Nynex Arena, Manchester	W	MD
			World Boxing Council World Super Middleweight Title		
1997-02-08	Giovanni Pretorius	22 0 1	London Arena, Millwall	W	KO
			World Boxing Council World Super Middleweight Title		
1996-10-12	Vincenzo Nardiello	30 5 0	Forum di Assago, Milan	W	TKO
			World Boxing Council World Super Middleweight Title		
1996-08-31	Donnie Penelton	5 41 0	The Point, Dublin	W	RTD
1996-06-08	Mark Lee Dawson	11 26 0	Telewest Arena, Newcastle	W	KO
1996-04-26	Hunter Clay	38 17 1	Welsh Institute of Sport, Cardiff	W	TKO
1996-03-16	Andy Flute	18 6 1	Scottish Exhibition Centre, Glasgow	W	TKO
1996-01-26	Paul Mason	8 16 4	Metropole Hotel, Brighton	W	KO
1995-11-10	Danny Juma	2 3 1	Moorways Leisure Centre, Derby	W	PTS
1995-09-15	Trevor Ambrose	10 17 0	Mansfield Leisure Centre, Mansfield	W	KO
1995-07-22	John Duckworth	10 9 4	London Arena, Millwall	W	PTS
1995-06-10	Martin Jolley	10 17 1	G-Mex Centre, Manchester	W	KO
1995-05-06	Steve Goodwin	5 8 0	Bath & West Country Showground, Shepton Mallet	W	KO
1995-03-04	Marvin O'Brien	2 23 2	Forum, Livingston	W	TKO
1995-02-04	Bruno Wuestenberghs	16 9 1	National Ice Rink, Cardiff	W	TKO
1994-11-19	Chris Richards	9 27 1	National Ice Rink, Cardiff	W	TKO
1994-08-17	Andrew Jervis	6 3 1	Hillsborough Leisure Centre, Sheffield	W	TKO
1994-06-04	Andrew Furlong	18 12 5	National Ice Rink, Cardiff	W	KO
1994-04-09	Kesem Clayton	12 15 2	Mansfield Leisure Centre, Mansfield	W	TKO
1993-12-18	Danny Juma	0 1 0	Wythenshawe Forum, Manchester	D	PTS
1993-10-09	Ernie Loveridge	18 12 3	Old Trafford Stadium, Manchester	W	PTS
1993-09-10	Jose Angel Garcia	0 5 0	Alamodome, San Antonio	W	PTS
1993-04-10	Andrew Furlong	17 11 5	Dillwyn Llewellyn Centre, Swansea	W	PTS
1993-03-06	Julian Eavis	13 46 4	Scottish Exhibition Centre, Glasgow	W	TKO
1993-02-27	Mark Lee Dawson	5 2 0	Goresbrook Leisure Centre, Dagenham	W	TKO

Michael Gomez

38(25) - 10(7) - 0

2009-03-27	Ricky Burns	25 2 0	Bellahouston Leisure Centre, Glasgow	L	TKO
			Commonwealth (British Empire) Super Featherweight Title		
2008-12-21	Chris Long	9 21 3	Dalziel Park Hotel & Conference Centre, Motherwell	W	PTS
2008-10-10	Baz Carey	11 37 4	Dalziel Park Hotel & Conference Centre, Motherwell	W	PTS
2008-09-28	Chris Brophy	3 22 2	Municipal Hall, Colne	W	TKO
2008-06-21	Amir Khan	17 0 0	National Indoor Arena, Birmingham	L	TKO
			Commonwealth (British Empire) Lightweight Title		
2008-03-29	Baz Carey	11 28 4	Scottish Exhibition Centre, Glasgow	W	PTS
2007-10-19	Carl Johanneson	26 3 0	Doncaster Dome, Doncaster	L	TKO
			BBBofC British Super Featherweight Title		
2007-06-24	Youssef Al Hamidi	2 3 1	Robin Park Centre, Wigan	W	TKO
2007-05-06	Daniel Thorpe	21 60 3	Leisure Centre, Altrincham	W	TKO
2006-01-28	Peter McDonagh	7 11 0	National Stadium, Dublin	L	TKO
			vacant BUI Ireland National Lightweight Title		
2005-02-11	Javier Osvaldo Alvarez	31 4 1	M.E.N. Arena, Manchester	L	TKO
			World Boxing Union (1995-2004) Super Featherweight Title		
2004-10-01	Levan Kirakosyan	14 3 0	M.E.N. Arena, Manchester	W	TKO
			World Boxing Union (1995-2004) Super Featherweight Title		
2004-05-22	Justin Juuko	39 7 1	Kingsway Leisure Centre, Widnes	W	TKO
			World Boxing Union (1995-2004) Super Featherweight Title		
2004-04-03	Ben Odamattey	10 2 2	M.E.N. Arena, Manchester	W	TKO
			vacant World Boxing Union (1995-2004) Super Featherweight Title		
2003-10-25	Alex Arthur	16 0 0	Meadowbank Sports Centre, Edinburgh	W	TKO
			BBBofC British Super Featherweight Title		
			World Boxing Association Inter-Continental Super Featherweight Title		
2003-04-05	Wladimir Borov	15 15 1	M.E.N. Arena, Manchester	W	TKO
2003-01-18	Rakhim Mingaleyev	25 31 0	Guild Hall, Preston	W	RTD
2002-09-28	Jimmy Beech	8 4 0	M.E.N. Arena, Manchester	W	TKO
2002-06-01	Kevin Lear	12 0 0	M.E.N. Arena, Manchester	L	RTD
			vacant World Boxing Union (1995-2004) Super Featherweight Title		
2001-10-27	Craig Docherty	12 0 1	M.E.N. Arena, Manchester	W	TKO
			BBBofC British Super Featherweight Title		
2001-07-07	Laszlo Bognar	26 3 2	Velodrome, Manchester	W	TKO
			World Boxing Organisation Inter-Continental Super Featherweight Title		
2001-02-10	Laszlo Bognar	25 3 2	Kingsway Leisure Centre, Widnes	L	TKO
			World Boxing Organisation Inter-Continental Super Featherweight Title		
2000-12-11	Ian McLeod	11 1 1	Kingsway Leisure Centre, Widnes	W	PTS
			BBBofC British Super Featherweight Title		

2000-10-19	Awel Abdulai	8 11 1	Zembo Shrine, Harrisburg	W	UD
2000-07-08	Carl Greaves	20 4 0	Kingsway Leisure Centre, Widnes	W	KO
			BBBofC British Super Featherweight Title		
2000-06-24	Carl Allen	13 22 2	Hampden Park, Glasgow	W	KO
2000-02-29	Dean Pithie	19 2 1	Kingsway Leisure Centre, Widnes	W	PTS
			BBBofC British Super Featherweight Title		
2000-01-29	Chris Jickells	13 29 0	M.E.N. Arena, Manchester	W	TKO
1999-12-11	Oscar Galindo	11 6 1	Everton Park Sports Centre, Liverpool	W	TKO
			World Boxing Organisation Inter-Continental Super Featherweight Title		
1999-11-06	Jose Manjarrez	13 20 4	Kingsway Leisure Centre, Widnes	W	UD
			World Boxing Organisation Inter-Continental Super Featherweight Title		
1999-09-04	Gary Thornhill	16 1 1	York Hall, Bethnal Green	W	TKO
			vacant BBBofC British Super Featherweight Title		
1999-08-07	William Alverzo	15 4 0	Taj Majal Hotel & Casino, Atlantic City	W	PTS
1999-05-29	Nigel Leake	5 4 0	North Bridge Leisure Centre, Halifax	W	TKO
			International Boxing Federation Inter-Continental Featherweight Title		
1999-02-27	Chris Jickells	11 22 0	Sports Centre, Lord Street, Oldham	W	TKO
			vacant BBBofC Central Area Featherweight Title		
1999-02-13	Dave Hinds	4 12 0	Telewest Arena, Newcastle	W	PTS
1998-12-19	Kevin Sheil	1 10 2	Everton Park Sports Centre, Liverpool	W	TKO
1998-11-14	David Jeffrey	3 8 0	Grundy Park Leisure Centre, Cheshunt	W	TKO
1998-09-05	Peter Buckley	25 88 6	Ice Rink, Telford	W	PTS
1998-05-16	Craig Spacie	2 0 0	York Hall, Bethnal Green	W	TKO
1998-04-18	Benny Jones	4 12 0	Nynex Arena, Manchester	W	PTS
1997-09-11	Wayne Jones	6 21 2	Kingsway Leisure Centre, Widnes	W	TKO
1997-05-03	Chris Williams	0 1 0	Nynex Arena, Manchester	L	PTS
1997-03-22	John Farrell	debut	Wythenshawe Forum, Manchester	W	TKO
1996-11-09	David Morris	2 0 0	Nynex Arena, Manchester	W	PTS
1996-09-19	Martin Evans	3 12 0	Bowlers Exhibition Centre, Manchester	W	TKO
1995-11-24	Danny Ruegg	2 8 0	Bowlers Exhibition Centre, Manchester	L	PTS
1995-09-15	Greg Upton	7 6 1	Mansfield Leisure Centre, Mansfield	L	PTS
1995-06-10	Danny Ruegg	2 6 0	G-Mex Centre, Manchester	W	PTS

Anthony Farnell

33(22) - 4(2) - 0

2004-06-12	Eugenio Monteiro	12 7 0	M.E.N. Arena, Manchester	L	TKO
			World Boxing Union (1995-2004) Middleweight Title		
2004-03-06	Lawrence Murphy	13 0 1	Braehead Arena, Glasgow	W	TKO
			World Boxing Union (1995-2004) Middleweight Title		
2003-12-13	Tomas Da Silva	4 11 2	M.E.N. Arena, Manchester	W	PTS
2003-04-05	Wayne Elcock	10 0 0	M.E.N. Arena, Manchester	L	UD
			World Boxing Union (1995-2004) Middleweight Title		
2003-01-18	Nikolay Talalakin	22 2 1	Guild Hall, Preston	W	RTD
			World Boxing Union (1995-2004) Middleweight Title		
2002-09-28	Ruben Groenewald	18 2 3	M.E.N. Arena, Manchester	W	SD
			World Boxing Union (1995-2004) Middleweight Title		
2002-06-01	Ruben Groenewald	17 2 3	M.E.N. Arena, Manchester	L	UD
			vacant World Boxing Union (1995-2004) Middleweight Title		
2002-02-09	Matt Galer	5 3 0	M.E.N. Arena, Manchester	W	TKO
2001-10-27	Pavel Melnikov	11 1 0	M.E.N. Arena, Manchester	W	TKO
			World Boxing Organisation Inter-Continental Super Welterweight Title		
2001-09-15	Lee Blundell	13 2 2	M.E.N. Arena, Manchester	W	KO
			World Boxing Organisation Inter-Continental Super Welterweight Title		
2001-07-07	Mehrdud Takaloo	16 2 0	Velodrome, Manchester	L	TKO
			vacant World Boxing Union (1995-2004) Super Welterweight Title		
2001-03-17	Shakir Ashanti	13 3 0	Wythenshawe Forum, Manchester	W	TKO
			World Boxing Organisation Inter-Continental Super Welterweight Title		
2001-01-15	Sergio Ernesto Acuna	24 3 0	Wythenshawe Forum, Manchester	W	UD
			World Boxing Organisation Inter-Continental Super Welterweight Title		
2000-11-25	Scott Dixon	22 3 2	Wythenshawe Forum, Manchester	W	KO
			World Boxing Organisation Inter-Continental Super Welterweight Title		
2000-09-04	Juan Carlos Sanchez	20 13 2	Wythenshawe Forum, Manchester	W	UD
			World Boxing Organisation Inter-Continental Super Welterweight Title		
2000-05-29	Howard Clarke	26 12 2	Wythenshawe Forum, Manchester	W	UD
			World Boxing Organisation Inter-Continental Super Welterweight Title		
2000-04-08	Ojay Abrahams	14 23 3	York Hall, Bethnal Green	W	PTS
2000-01-29	Ian Toby	4 14 1	M.E.N. Arena, Manchester	W	TKO
1999-11-27	Marino Monteyne	23 49 6	Hansehalle, Luebeck	W	KO
1999-10-09	Javier Santibanez	14 10 1	Bowlers Exhibition Centre, Manchester	W	KO
			World Boxing Organisation Inter-Continental Super Welterweight Title		

1999-08-07	Israel Ponce	11 9 0	Taj Majal Hotel & Casino, Atlantic City		W	TKO
1999-05-29	John Long	12 3 1	North Bridge Leisure Centre, Halifax		W	TKO
	vacant World Boxing Organisation Inter-Continental Super Welterweight Title					
1999-05-01	Alan Gilbert	5 2 0	National Sports Centre, Crystal Palace		W	TKO
1999-02-27	Koba Kulu	2 5 0	Sports Centre, Lord Street, Oldham		W	TKO
1998-12-19	Koba Kulu	2 4 0	Everton Park Sports Centre, Liverpool		W	RTD
1998-11-28	George Richards	14 5 0	Hillsborough Leisure Centre, Sheffield		W	TKO
1998-10-31	Mark Richardson	7 8 2	Convention Center, Atlantic City		W	UD
1998-09-05	Darren Williams	4 1 0	Ice Rink, Telford		W	RTD
1998-07-18	Lee Molyneux	3 5 4	Sheffield Arena, Sheffield		W	KO
1998-05-09	David Thompson	8 24 3	Hillsborough Leisure Centre, Sheffield		W	KO
1998-04-18	Harry Butler	1 10 0	Nynex Arena, Manchester		W	PTS
1998-03-21	Hugh Davey	17 14 1	York Hall, Bethnal Green		W	PTS
1998-01-24	Steve Brumant	1 0 0	International Arena, Cardiff		W	PTS
1997-19-13	Paul Scott	3 7 0	Ponds Forge Arena, Sheffield		W	TKO
1997-09-20	Dominique Vandersteene	4 10 1	Tivoli Eissporthalle, Aachen		W	KO
1997-08-02	Martin Renaghan	2 0 0	Metrodome, Barnsley		W	TKO
1997-05-03	Lee Molyneux	1 2 0	Nynex Arena, Manchester		W	PTS

Michael Jennings

36(17) - 3(2) - 0

2010-09-18	Kell Brook	21 0 0	LG Arena, Birmingham		L	TKO
	BBBofC British Welterweight Title					
	World Boxing Organisation Inter-Continental Welterweight Title					
2009-10-30	Laszlo Komjathi	35 26 2	Echo Arena, Liverpool		W	PTS
2009-05-15	Willie Thompson	6 0 1	Odyssey Arena, Belfast		W	TKO
2009-02-21	Miguel Cotto	32 1 0	Madison Square Garden, New York		L	TKO
	vacant World Boxing Organisation World Welterweight Title					
2008-11-14	Jason Rushton	18 6 0	Kelvin Hall, Glasgow		W	PTS
2008-04-05	Giorgi Ungiadze	12 5 0	Bolton Arena, Bolton		W	TKO
2008-02-02	Ross Minter	17 2 1	ExCel Arena, Dockland		W	TKO
	World Boxing Union (1995-2004) Welterweight Title					
2007-09-28	Volodymyr Khodak-ovskyy	15 15 2	Guild Hall, Preston		W	PTS
2007-04-07	Mehrdud Takaloo	25 5 0	Millennium Stadium, Cardiff		W	UD
	World Boxing Union (1995-2004) Welterweight Title					
2006-09-02	Rastislav Kovac	18 8 1	Bolton Arena, Bolton		W	KO
2006-01-28	Young Mutley	19 1 0	Nottingham Arena, Nottingham		L	SD
	BBBofC British Welterweight Title					
2005-10-25	Bradley Pryce	20 5 0	Guild Hall, Preston		W	UD
	BBBofC British Welterweight Title					
2005-07-16	Jimmy Vincent	21 18 2	Bolton Arena, Bolton		W	KO
	vacant BBBofC British Welterweight Title					
2005-06-03	Gavin Down	29 5 0	M.E.N. Arena, Manchester		W	TKO
	BBBofC English Welterweight Title					
2005-02-11	Vasile Dragomir	11 2 1	M.E.N. Arena, Manchester		W	KO
2004-10-01	Chris Saunders	22 21 1	M.E.N. Arena, Manchester		W	RTD
	BBBofC English Welterweight Title					
2004-05-22	Rafal Jackiewicz	12 4 0	Kingsway Leisure Centre, Widnes		W	PTS
2004-04-01	Brett James	14 1 2	York Hall, Bethnal Green		W	RTD
2003-12-13	Peter Dunn	9 23 3	M.E.N. Arena, Manchester		W	PTS
2003-09-27	Sammy Smith	10 5 0	M.E.N. Arena, Manchester		W	TKO
2003-05-08	Jimmy Gould	9 2 0	Kingsway Leisure Centre, Widnes		W	RTD
2003-01-18	Leeroy Williamson	10 30 2	Guild Hall, Preston		W	RTD
2002-11-01	Richard Inquieti	7 31 2	Guild Hall, Preston		W	TKO
2002-09-28	Karl Taylor	15 58 6	M.E.N. Arena, Manchester		W	TKO
2002-06-01	Leeroy Williamson	9 26 2	M.E.N. Arena, Manchester		W	PTS
2002-02-09	James Paisley	1 3 0	M.E.N. Arena, Manchester		W	TKO
2001-09-15	Gary Harrison	3 3 0	M.E.N. Arena, Manchester		W	PTS
2001-07-07	David Kirk	9 33 2	Velodrome, Manchester		W	PTS
2001-02-10	Mark Haslam	9 5 1	Kingsway Leisure Centre, Widnes		W	TKO
2000-12-11	Paul Denton	7 19 2	Kingsway Leisure Centre, Widnes		W	PTS
2000-11-25	Ernie Smith	6 23 1	Wythenshawe Forum, Manchester		W	PTS
2000-09-04	Mark Ramsey	15 29 6	Wythenshawe Forum, Manchester		W	PTS
2000-07-08	Paul Denton	7 14 2	Kingsway Leisure Centre, Widnes		W	PTS
2000-05-29	William Webster	1 11 0	Wythenshawe Forum, Manchester		W	PTS
2000-05-16	Brian Coleman	21 85 7	Spectrum Arena, Warrington		W	PTS
2000-03-25	Brian Coleman	21 84 7	Olympia, Liverpool		W	PTS
2000-02-29	Lee Molyneux	3 18 4	Kingsway Leisure Centre, Widnes		W	PTS
1999-12-11	Lee Molyneux	3 16 4	Everton Park Sports Centre, Liverpool		W	PTS
1999-05-15	Tony Smith	2 12 1	Winter Gardens, Blackpool		W	TKO

Matthew Hall

26(16) -7(3) - 0

2015-04-18	Dan Blackwell	6 43 0	Sports Centre, Lord Street, Oldham	W	PTS
2013-03-21	Billy Joe Saunders*	16 0 0	York Hall, Bethnal Green	L	UD
			BBBofC British Middleweight Title		
			Commonwealth (British Empire) Middleweight Title		
2012-11-30	Lee Noble	15 23 3	Manchester Arena (formerly M.E.N Arena), Manchester	W	PTS
2012-07-14	Gary O'Sullivan*	14 0 0	Upton Park, West Ham	L	UD
			vacant World Boxing Organisation International Middleweight Title		
2012-04-28	Sam Webb	17 2 0	Royal Albert Hall, Kensington	L	SD
2011-11-25	Kris Carslaw	14 0 0	Ravenscraig Sports Centre, Motherwell	W	UD
2011-10-28	Alexey Ribchev	11 3 1	Bowlers Exhibition Centre, Manchester	L	PTS
2010-09-18	Lukas Konecny	44 3 0	LG Arena, Birmingham	L	TKO
			vacant EBU European Super Welterweight Title		
2010-05-15	Tony Randell	11 20 2	Upton Park, West Ham	W	TKO
2009-07-18	Anthony Small	21 1 0	M.E.N. Arena, Manchester	L	TKO
			vacant BBBofC British Super Welterweight Title		
			Commonwealth (British Empire) Super Welterweight Title		
2009-03-14	Bradley Pryce	27 6 0	M.E.N. Arena, Manchester	W	TKO
			Commonwealth (British Empire) Super Welterweight Title		
2008-12-12	Jason Rushton	18 7 0	Kingsway Leisure Centre, Widnes	W	TKO
2008-10-10	Ciaran Healy	8 8 1	Everton Park Sports Centre, Liverpool	W	TKO
2008-09-06	Taz Jones	11 4 3	M.E.N. Arena, Manchester	W	TKO
2008-03-22	Kerry Hope	11 0 0	International Arena, Cardiff	W	TKO
2007-12-03	Tyan Booth	9 3 0	Piccadilly Hotel, Manchester	W	PTS
2007-07-14	Martin Concepcion	11 4 0	O2 Arena (Millenium Dome), Greenwich	L	TKO
2006-07-08	Kevin Phelan	10 7 0	Millennium Stadium, Cardiff	W	TKO
2006-03-11	Rob Burton	11 13 3	Newport Centre, Newport	W	KO
2006-01-28	Jon Foster	6 7 1	Nottingham Arena, Nottingham	W	TKO
2005-06-04	Matt Scriven	12 22 0	M.E.N. Arena, Manchester	W	TKO
2005-02-11	Sylvestre Marianini	8 14 2	M.E.N. Arena, Manchester	W	TKO
2005-01-21	Leigh Wicks	17 64 4	Bridgend Leisure Centre, Bridgend	W	PTS
2004-12-03	Jason Collins	15 31 6	Meadowbank Sports Centre, Edinburgh	W	PTS
2004-11-12	Ojay Abrahams	20 58 4	North Bridge Leisure Centre, Halifax	W	KO
2004-10-01	Howard Clarke	27 48 2	M.E.N. Arena, Manchester	W	TKO
2004-06-12	Isidro Gonzalez	0 2 0	M.E.N. Arena, Manchester	W	TKO
2004-05-06	Craig Lynch	4 10 1	Metrodome, Barnsley	W	PTS
2003-05-08	Patrick Cito	6 9 1	Kingsway Leisure Centre, Widnes	W	PTS
2003-04-05	Brian Coleman	22 112 7	M.E.N. Arena, Manchester	W	TKO
2003-01-18	Clive Johnson	4 6 0	Guild Hall, Preston	W	PTS
2002-12-14	Pedro Thompson	5 17 2	Telewest Arena, Newcastle	W	PTS
2002-09-28	Pedro Thompson	5 16 2	M.E.N. Arena, Manchester	W	TKO

Scott Quigg

34(25) -2(0) - 2

Date	Opponent	Record	Venue	Result	Method
2018-03-10	Oscar Valdez	23 0 0	StubHub Center, Carson	L	UD
		World Boxing Organisation World Featherweight Title			
2017-11-04	Oleg Yefimovych	29 2 1	Casino de Monte Carlo Salle Medecin, Monte Carlo	W	TKO
		World Boxing Association Continental Featherweight Title			
2017-04-29	Viorel Simion	21 1 0	Wembley Stadium, Wembley	W	UD
2016-12-10	Jose Cayetano	20 4 0	Manchester Arena (formerly M.E.N Arena), Manchester	W	TKO
		vacant World Boxing Association International Featherweight Title			
2016-02-27	Carl Frampton	21 0 0	Manchester Arena (formerly M.E.N Arena), Manchester	L	SD
		International Boxing Federation World Super Bantamweight Title			
		World Boxing Association Super World Super Bantamweight Title			
2015-07-18	Kiko Martinez*	32 5 0	Manchester Arena (formerly M.E.N Arena), Manchester	W	TKO
		World Boxing Association World Super Bantamweight Title			
2014-11-22	Hidenori Otake	22 1 3	Echo Arena, Liverpool	W	UD
		World Boxing Association World Super Bantamweight Title			
2014-09-13	Stephane Jamoye	26 5 0	Phones 4u Arena (formerly M.E.N Arena), Manchester	W	TKO
		World Boxing Association World Super Bantamweight Title			
2014-04-19	Tshifhiwa Munyai	24 2 1	Phones 4u Arena (formerly M.E.N Arena), Manchester	W	TKO
		World Boxing Association World Super Bantamweight Title			
2013-11-23	Diego Oscar Silva	29 2 4	Phones 4u Arena (formerly M.E.N Arena), Manchester	W	TKO
		World Boxing Association World Super Bantamweight Title			
2013-10-05	Yoandris Salinas	20 0 1	O2 Arena (Millenium Dome), Greenwich	D	MD
		World Boxing Association World Super Bantamweight Title			
2013-06-29	William Prado	21 3 1	Bolton Arena, Bolton	W	KO
2012-11-24	Rendall Munroe	24 2 1	Manchester Arena (formerly M.E.N Arena), Manchester	W	TKO
		interim World Boxing Association World Super Bantamweight Title			
2012-06-16	Rendall Munroe	24 2 0	Velodrome, Manchester	D	TD
		interim World Boxing Association World Super Bantamweight Title			
2012-02-04	Jamie Arthur	18 5 0	De Vere Whites Hotel, Bolton	W	TKO
		BBBofC British Super Bantamweight Title			
2011-10-22	Jason Booth	36 7 0	De Vere Whites Hotel, Bolton	W	RTD
		BBBofC British Super Bantamweight Title			
2011-07-23	Franklin Varela	19 5 0	Castle Leisure Centre, Bury	W	TKO
		World Boxing Association Inter-Continental Super Bantamweight Title			
2010-11-26	Daniel Kodjo Sassou	29 14 4	De Vere Whites Hotel, Bolton	W	UD
		World Boxing Association Inter-Continental Super Bantamweight Title			
2010-09-25	Santiago Allione	16 6 1	Castle Leisure Centre, Bury	W	KO
		vacant World Boxing Association Inter-Continental Super Bantamweight Title			
2010-07-16	Gavin Reid	6 6 1	Bolton Arena, Bolton	W	TKO
2010-05-29	Andrey Kostin	20 14 0	Castle Leisure Centre, Bury	W	TKO
2010-02-19	Nikita Lukin	10 17 2	Fenton Manor Sports Complex, Stoke-on-Trent	W	KO
2009-11-27	Yuriy Voronin	27 9 2	Robin Park Centre, Wigan	W	TKO
2009-09-25	Nico Schroeder	4 7 1	Velodrome, Manchester	W	TKO
2009-07-11	Ricardo Tanase	11 0	Leisure Centre, Altrincham	W	KO
2009-03-28	Faycal Messaoudene	3 9 1	Leisure Centre, Altrincham	W	TKO
2009-01-24	Carl Allen	18 73 7	Tower Circus, Blackpool	W	PTS
2008-12-06	Gheorghe Ghiompirica	8 42 0	Robin Park Centre, Wigan	W	PTS
2008-11-07	Sumaila Badu	4 12 0	Robin Park Centre, Wigan	W	TKO
2008-07-19	Peter Allen	5 31 2	Olympia, Liverpool	W	TKO
2008-07-04	Angelo Villani	4 1 1	Everton Park Sports Centre, Liverpool	W	TKO
2008-06-07	Sid Razak	3 7 0	Robin Park Centre, Wigan	W	RTD
2008-03-14	Gheorghe Ghiompirica	8 35 0	George Carnall Leisure Centre, Davyhulme, Manchester	W	PTS
2007-12-03	Delroy Spencer	10 59 3	Piccadilly Hotel, Manchester	W	PTS
2007-09-28	Sandy Bartlett	4 6 0	Guild Hall, Preston	W	TKO
2007-08-11	Shaun Walton	3 21 3	Olympia, Liverpool	W	PTS
2007-06-30	Shaun Walton	3 20 3	George Carnall Leisure Centre, Davyhulme, Manchester	W	TKO
2007-04-21	Gary Sheil	0 4 0	Jarvis Hotel, Manchester	W	PTS

Thomas McDonagh

34(7) -3(0) - 3

2009-11-27	Anthony Small	22 1 0	Robin Park Centre, Wigan	L	UD
			BBBofC British Super Welterweight Title		
			Commonwealth (British Empire) Super Welterweight Title		
2009-05-02	Sam Webb	13 1 0	Crowtree Leisure Centre, Sunderland	L	PTS
2009-03-28	Max Maxwell	9 5 1	Leisure Centre, Altrincham	W	TKO
2008-11-07	Michael Monaghan	17 23 0	Robin Park Centre, Wigan	W	PTS
2008-10-12	Jason Rushton	18 5 0	Leigh Sports Village, Leigh	W	PTS
2008-05-24	Andrew Facey	19 5 1	City of Manchester Stadium, Manchester	D	PTS
			BBBofC English Super Welterweight Title		
2008-03-30	Yassine El Maachi	4 3 0	Municipal Hall, Colne	W	PTS
2007-06-30	Oleksandr Matviychuk	7 18 3	George Carnall Leisure Centre, Davyhulme, Man-chester	W	PTS
2007-04-21	Volodymyr Borovskyy	20 23 1	Jarvis Hotel, Manchester	W	PTS
2006-10-14	Martin Concepcion	11 2 0	M.E.N. Arena, Manchester	W	PTS
2006-03-04	Wayne Alexander	23 3 0	M.E.N. Arena, Manchester	L	SD
			World Boxing Union (1995-2004) Super Welterweight Title		
2005-10-25	Dean Walker	11 6 1	Guild Hall, Preston	W	PTS
2005-06-03	Barrie Lee	9 0 1	M.E.N. Arena, Manchester	W	TKO
2004-11-12	Darren Rhodes	16 7 3	North Bridge Leisure Centre, Halifax	W	PTS
2004-05-06	Bradley Pryce	18 3 0	Metrodome, Barnsley	W	UD
2004-04-03	Craig Lynch	4 9 1	M.E.N. Arena, Manchester	W	PTS
2004-02-26	Bobby Banghar	11 3 1	Kingsway Leisure Centre, Widnes	W	KO
2003-09-27	Eugenio Monteiro	10 5 0	M.E.N. Arena, Manchester	W	UD
2003-05-08	Marcus Portman	8 3 1	Kingsway Leisure Centre, Widnes	W	PTS
2003-04-05	Paul Wesley	16 47 5	M.E.N. Arena, Manchester	W	PTS
2003-01-18	Tomas Da Silva	4 6 1	Guild Hall, Preston	W	PTS
2002-09-28	Brian Coleman	22 108 7	M.E.N. Arena, Manchester	W	TKO
2002-06-01	Delroy Mellis	9 16 1	M.E.N. Arena, Manchester	W	PTS
2002-02-09	Tomas Da Silva	3 2 0	M.E.N. Arena, Manchester	D	PTS
2001-10-27	Mark Richards	6 2 1	M.E.N. Arena, Manchester	D	PTS
2001-09-15	Howard Clarke	26 22 2	M.E.N. Arena, Manchester	W	PTS
2001-07-07	Paul Denton	7 26 2	Velodrome, Manchester	W	PTS
2001-03-17	David Baptiste	6 21 0	Wythenshawe Forum, Manchester	W	PTS
2001-02-10	Harry Butler	5 35 0	Kingsway Leisure Centre, Widnes	W	PTS
2001-01-15	Michael Halls	3 2 0	Wythenshawe Forum, Manchester	W	TKO
2000-12-11	Richie Murray	2 1 0	Kingsway Leisure Centre, Widnes	W	PTS
2000-09-04	Colin Vidler	1 6 1	Wythenshawe Forum, Manchester	W	PTS
2000-05-29	David Baptiste	5 15 0	Wythenshawe Forum, Manchester	W	PTS
2000-05-16	Richie Murray	1 0 0	Spectrum Arena, Warrington	W	PTS
2000-03-25	Lee Molyneux	3 19 4	Olympia, Liverpool	W	PTS
2000-02-29	William Webster	0 8 0	Kingsway Leisure Centre, Widnes	W	RTD
2000-01-29	Emmanuel Marcos	0 1 0	M.E.N. Arena, Manchester	W	PTS
1999-12-11	Arv Mittoo	6 29 3	Everton Park Sports Centre, Liverpool	W	TKO
1999-11-06	Lee Molyneux	3 14 4	Kingsway Leisure Centre, Widnes	W	PTS
1999-10-09	Lee Molyneux	3 12 4	Bowlers Exhibition Centre, Manchester	W	PTS

All statistics courtesy of BoxRec

Index